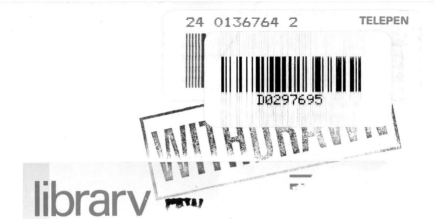

TRANSNATIONAL COMMERCIAL LAW

Transnational Commercial Law

by

EUGEN LANGEN

Dr. jur., Member of the Bar of Coblence, one-time
Lecturer in the University of Cologne

A.W. SIJTHOFF LEIDEN 1973

Translated from the German manuscript by Bernard Noble

ISBN 90 286 0322 0 √

Library of Congress Catalog Card Number: 72-89475

© A.W. Sijthoff International Publishing Company, N.V. 1973

Printed in the Netherlands

TABLE OF CONTENTS

"At present, nationalism—at its beginning a great inspiration, widening and deepening the understanding of man, the feeling of solidarity, the autonomous dignity of the masses—seems unable to cope, politically and emotionally, with the new situation. Once it increased individual liberty and happiness; now it undermines them and subjects them to the exigencies of its continued existence, which seems no longer justified. Once it was a great force of life, spurring on the evolution of mankind; now it may become a dead weight upon the march of humanity."

HANS KOHN, *The Idea of Nationalism,*
The Macmillan Company, New York
1945, page 22.

FOREWORD

This work is based on a new conception of international commercial law:

A private international case can never, on the one hand, be decided in complete disregard of any system of municipal law; nor, on the other hand, would it be correct to overlook the fact that such a case is not, strictly speaking, domestic in character but occurs between two or more areas of jurisdiction. For that reason, no convincing solution will be forthcoming either from classical private international law, which consigns the case as a whole to one municipal system, or from modern efforts to create a *lex mercatoria* independent of any municipal law and decide the case by its lights. Today, the *via media* leading to a satisfying solution can only be found by working out the transnational legal principles underlying both of the domestic systems involved. This is more difficult than the procedures hitherto adopted, but the results are more convincing. The aim of this book is to stimulate use of the new method and to demonstrate that it does not ask the impossible of judges.

It is indeed to practising men of law and judges that this work is addressed, and for that reason the accent has been placed on case-law rather than doctrine. In the international field, law-making desicions will always enjoy more authority than ratiocination. Moreover, the theoretician is notoriously more prone to excessive generalization than the judge, whose only concern is to arrive at a just decision of the specific case before him and give convincing reasons for it.

I have endeavoured to investigate as many decisions as possible. Those I have examined—more than 400 in all—are listed chronoligically in the Appendix irrespective of their country of origin. Nationality, in fact, is largely irrelevant when the aim is to inspect a case of international character with an eye, first and foremost, to extracting whatever transnational legal elements it may have to offer. The level of the court in question is likewise secondary for the purpose, though not, of course, wholly immaterial. Not all the decisions examined have received a mention in the text, but even those merely listed in the Appendix may offer valuable materials for further study. Wherever criticism of decisions was called for, I have endeavoured as far as possible to confine myself to pronouncements of German courts.

There is one other important reason for the preferential treatment given to judicial decisions in this work. The quest for transnational rules of law can only be undertaken and succeed in conditions of utter detachment from all systematic constructions. So long as there does not—happily, I am inclined to say—exist any fixed system of transnational law, every furtive glance at familiar domestic or even foreign systems brings a risk of backsliding into the old mental grooves.

The need to keep the work within reasonable bounds imposed a certain selectivity which was not easy to exercise. The final choice, of four main topics, was made in the light of the following considerations:

The *licensing agreement* is a legal institution of fairly recent date which has developed concurrently and in similar circumstances in every country. The practical requirements, having been everywhere the same, have, logically enough, led to legal results which are similar, even if they are still dressed in more or less national costume. At all events there are but few other types of contract—apart from reinsurance, air-transport and the like—which are so little burdened with petrified doctrine and national peculiarities.

In contrast, the *contract of sale* is an age-old institution thickly encrusted with dubious generalizations, petrified doctrines and laggard conventions of international law. Yet the international contract of sale is not merely practicable but, in turnover terms, probably stands at the head of all commercial contracts in the world. If we have chosen it for study, it is precisely because the ease with which a legal institution can be reduced to simple basic rules is inversely proportional to its degree of evolution. In this connection the Hague Sales Rules of 1964 and the Uniform Commercial Code of 1962 are treated as being of equal status, in view of the "model effect" which these texts are acknowledged to possess.

By way of further contrast, the chapter on *limitation* deals with an institution in regard to which the individual results can all be more or less reduced to one general principle. Hence it may afford some idea of what could be achieved in respect of such analogous concepts as unjust enrichment and tort.

Our fourth topic is the *practice of transnational adjudication*. The most difficult question to decide in this connection was whether it was preferable to distil transnational commercial law from individual legal cases and in this way to arrive at general principles, or, on the contrary, to postulate the general principles presumed to exist and then to demonstrate their presence in individual cases. A hundred years ago, when there were virtually no concrete results to ascertain, there can be no doubt that a purely deductive course would have been correct. Nowadays, however, we are in the midst of a development which has already reached an advanced stage. Certain conclusions have become essential instruments of progress all along the line. We must be bold enough to anticipate and posit them as general principles; and be prepared on that account to swallow the accusation of wishful thinking.

X

For "What is possible, what is to be expected, is an important constituent of our reality, and one which may not simply be forgotten alongside given fact" (Albert Einstein, quoted in Werner Heisenberg, *Der Teil und das Ganze*, Munich 1969, p. 95).

The author is especially indebted for valuable encouragement and suggestions to Professor Helmuth Coing of Frankfurt am Main, Professor Günther Beitzke of Bonn, Judge Philip C. Jessup and Professor Martin Domke in New York, Professors Clive Schmitthoff and George Schwarzenberger of London and Otto Riese, Lausanne. For financial support his gratitude is due above all to his friends Friedrich Silcher of Leverkusen and Erich Selbach, Krefeld, and to his brother Victor.

In concluding this preface it gives the author particular pleasure to place on record his warm appreciation of the work of Mr Bernard Noble, who translated in The Hague the German manuscript of this work.

Oberwinter am Rhein   *Eugen Langen*
November 1972

Part One

INTRODUCTION

The years from 1820 to 1913 witnessed a thirtyfold growth in the volume of international commerce. This powerful expansion, though disrupted up to 1945 by periods of worldwide conflict, has continued to the present day. Yet legal scholars have paid little heed to this phenomenon. To their minds, this immensely swollen volume of trade still pursues its course in accordance with rules of "private international law" which were propounded in the first half of the last century by the works of Joseph Story (1834) and Friedrich Karl von Savigny (1849) and stand in a direct line of descent from the views of North Italian, French and Netherlands jurists whose premises and preoccupations were those of the fifteenth century—an age when America had yet to be discovered and no world trade as such existed. The goods and services of those days were quite different from those of the present, the means of transport were horsedrawn vehicles and sailing vessels, news was brought by runner or courier. Our only contact with all this today is that of the museum.

We will here refrain from theorizing on the general problem of whether it is actually possible in such circumstances to retain the same legal outlook and approach as before—whether, that is to say, changes in the material background must needs condition the intellectual sphere. It will of course not be possible to avoid this theme in touching upon the question of whether, and to what extent, a community of transnational law can be said to exist between the legal systems of the West and those of the socialist States. For present purposes, however, it will be adequate to take it as a working-hypothesis that, even should legal methodology remain unchanged, the transformation of the raw material is in itself sufficient to make novel demands on it. That much can scarcely be denied.[1]

We will begin by considering the ways in which legal scholars have hitherto endeavoured to come to terms with the altered circumstances of international trade, and the role played herein by the fact that international commercial law has so far been unable to rise to the occasion and take independent shape

---

1. On the importance of the factual background for historical jurisprudence, see in particular Arthur Nussbaum, *Die Rechtstatsachenforschung*, Tübingen 1914 and Berlin 1968; Hedeman, *Die Fortschritte des Zivilrechts*, Berlin 1930/1935.

within the framework of general private international law. Next we will lend an ear to those who would do away with the "classical" method entirely and replace it by one more suitable. Finally we will see whether a transnational commercial law can be conjured out of the thesis of classical private international law and its antithesis, a supranational *lex mercatoria*.

I. *The classical doctrine*

The classical private international law of all countries proceeds on the assumption that:

> "Any contract which is not a contract between States in their capacity as subjects of international law is based on the municipal law of some country."[2]

On this premise, the judge, before he can say anything about a contract, must link it to some municipal system or other, establish the "proper law of the contract". He must make up his mind and state which set of municipal laws he intends to apply to the contract. This can be a matter of some embarrassment, as is revealed by the frequent recourse to a figure of speech in referring to this problem: the "the seat of the obligation". According to Savigny it is a matter of "ascertaining for every legal relation that legal territory to which, in its proper nature, it belongs or is subject (in which it has its seat)".[3] Again, in 1891 Franz Kahn, writing on conflicts of laws in *Jherings Jahrbücher*, Vol. 30, said:

> "We apply the law of a foreign country because it is in accordance with our legal notions that a given legal relationship has its 'seat' in, or appertains to that territory."[4]

As against this, Gutzwiller said in 1923 that although the word "seat" was certainly a succinct and striking image, it was nothing more, because "legal relationships cannot be localized".[5]

Laws on the treatment of enemy property refer to the *situs* of a claim, while the word they use in German, *belegen*, even likens a claim to a boat that is tied up to a given shore. Still stranger is another metaphor which is gaining ground in private international law, that of the "centre of gravity" of a contractual relationship. This is borrowed from physics, where it helps to

---

2. *P.C.I.J. Serbian Loans, Judgment, 1929, Series A, Nos. 20/21*, p. 41; cf. criticism in Jessup, *Transnational Law*, p. 95

3. *System des heutigen Römischen Rechts*, Vol. 8, Berlin 1849, pp. 28 and 108; trans. W. Guthrie as *The Conflict of Laws*, Edinburgh 1880, pp. 70 and 133. Except in this instance, quotations from Savigny have for the sake of modernity been retranslated.

4. Reprinted in *Abhandlungen zum internationalen Privatrecht*, Vol. 1, Munich and Leipzig 1928, p. 111.

5. *Der Einfluss Savignys*, 1923. p. 45.

predicate the position of an object in repose or coming to rest. But none of these figures of speech can be regarded as really correct. The ancient Romans knew better: *obligatio est juris vinculum*. Indeed, as etymology suggests, it is only to a bond linking debtor and creditor that *obligatio* can be compared, unless it be also with a bridge crossing from bank to bank over a river: *scilicet*, frontier. Now it is scarcely compatible with the nature of a bridge to judge the whole structure on the strength of the ramp at one end or to bisect it and allocate half to one bank, half to the other. Similarly, until the nature of the international contract is properly grasped, just decisions will not be reached, except perhaps by chance or through tortuous détours. Not surprisingly, therefore, the picture revealed by even a cursory glance at classical writings and decided cases in this domain is something of a patchwork.

Neither is there any uniformity in the rules for allocation to a particular municipal system. There is no private international law—no uniform body of rules—for the treatment of the conflict of laws; instead, each State develops its own norms in this respect. Aside from the few existing international treaties on the subject, the extent to which one State is willing to recognize the conflicts law of another, or its legal system in general, still depends, as of old, on reciprocity and neighbourly regard, the *comitas gentium*.[6]

It is on this basis of comity that, as a departure from the earliest doctrine of compulsory *lex fori*, whereby a case could only be decided in accordance with the local law of the court, foreign law came in certain instances to be recognized.[7] But then the question arose as to what precise circumstances warranted the recognition by a domestic court of a foreign legal system. Another age-old doctrine which continued to bear fruit until recently renders

6. In this connection Joseph Story, citing the Dutch jurists Voet and Ulrich Huber, says (p. 7): "It is plain, that the laws of one country can have no intrinsic force, *proprio vigore*, except within the territorial limits and jurisdiction of that country. They can bind only its own subjects, and others who are within its jurisdictional limits; and the latter only while they remain there. No other nation, or its subjects, are bound to yield the slightest obedience to these laws. Whatever extra-territorial force they are to have is the result, not of any original power to extend them abroad, but of that respect which from motives of public policy other nations are disposed to yield to them, giving them effect, as the phrase is, *sub mutuae vicissitudinis obtentu*, with a wise and liberal regard to common convenience and mutual necessities." As recently as 16 October 1952 the *British Nylon Spinners* decision spoke of the "comity which subsists between civilized nations" in dealing with the possible recognition by the English courts of an American decision. Cf. in particular H. Yntema, "The Comity Doctrine", *Festschrift Dölle* II, 1963, p. 65.

7. On the resuscitation of the *lex fori* doctrine by the three American jurists Currie, Cavers and Ehrenzweig, see Schmitthoff, *Zeitschrift für Rechtsvergleichung* 1970, p. 12; Kegel, RdC 1964-II, p. 91; Heini, *Zeitschrift für schweizerisches Recht* 1967, p. 265; Lando, 15 AJCL, 1966-67, p. 230; also our remarks towards the end of this Introduction.

the law of the place of conclusion applicable to a contract.[8] However, given the changed factual background of today, it is obvious that this rule can no longer exert the same influence, for in modern conditions of air-travel the place of conclusion has become a purely fortuitous detail, open to easy manipulation.

From ancient times to the present, courts have also, under certain circumstances, given priority to the law of the domicile or of the nationality of a party. In this they have given due weight to the point that the party having to supply goods or services is sure to have more legal rules to observe than the other, whose duty is merely to pay. It has also been held material that a party may have a particular interest in the application of his own domestic law if it is part of his business to conclude many contracts of the same kind with people from widely differing lands.[9] As a matter of national principle, however, French court decisions in this field have tended to favour the French debtor.[10] Whether nationality is held of account in determining the applicable law will in fact depend on the circumstances of each case.[11]

The same considerations as those we have noted with regard to the significance of domicile for allocation to a given municipal system are relied on to the present day in, for example, German jurisprudence as grounds for regarding the law of the place of performance of the contract as authoritative. It may obviously be the case, however, that each party has to honour his commitment in a different place, so that this criterion offers no solution. More-

---

8. Kegel points out that this rule prevailed for centuries until put aside by the Swiss Federal Tribunal in 1952 and the New York Court of Appeals in 1954 (*Grundriss des internationalen Privatrechts*, Munich 1964, p. 55). Cf. Part Three below on the Conclusion of Contracts of Sale.

9. See Lichtenstein, "Ausland-Lizenzen", NJW 1964, p. 1350.

10. On the case-law, see the standard commentaries (e.g. Kegel, *op. cit.*, p. 230), Part Three below on the Conclusion of Contracts, and the references under "homing instinct" in the Subject-Index. See also the award given by the Czecho-German Mixed Arbitral Tribunal on 24 May 1923, re the payment of a purchase-price in sterling or devalued marks, holding it scarcely tenable, given the particular nature of the transaction, that one party would have concluded the contract without tacitly reserving the advantages of his domestic law, and that so obvious a condition did not cross the other's mind.

11. In French jurisprudence, when both parties have the same (i.e. French) nationality, French law applies irrespective of the other circumstances of the contract (cf. Bordeaux, 1 March 1889, and unprinted judgements mentioned in Stoufflet, *Juris-Classeur*, droit international, 565/109). Cf. Berne court of appeal, 25 September 1963: three Swiss nationals, all domiciled abroad, were sued by two Swiss residents for the return of a sum paid for a painting sold in Switzerland, and Swiss law had been applied as the one having the closest connection with the case; however, what was at issue was only the amenability of the decision to appeal and not the substantive legal position. Cf. also the decision of the German *Reichsarbeitsgericht* discussed by Kegel (*op. cit.*, p. 231), on a contract between two German nationals concerning a labour-relationship to be given effect in the United States (*Seuff. Arch.*, Vol. 89, p. 321).

over, the identity of the place of performance is in itself a preliminary question which can scarcely be settled without deciding which law is applicable. Hence, although there have been numerous judgments in favour of the place of performance and these represent an increasingly important practice, this too offers anything but a reliable or predictable solution.[12]

Some progress can no doubt be achieved, when more than one domicile or place of performance is involved, by sizing up the relative importance of each. This is what is done by the doctrine which seeks out the "centre of gravity" of the contract and regards it as conclusive in determining the applicable law.[13] As in physics, however, situations arise in law where there are two centres or one fluctuating centre of gravity. In any case, one should be able to demonstrate that the mass of the contract is overwhelmingly concentrated round the centre of gravity before venturing to transpose the whole legal relationship into one municipal system, to the disadvantage of one of the parties. Thus it is not this doctrine, either, that will provide an overall solution of the problem.

In this quandary many courts have resorted to a veritable judgment of Solomon and split the contract in two, declaring one system of law applicable to one part, and another system to the other.[14] This theory of "bisection" has been condemned, or viewed with dubiety, by legal scholars in Germany and elsewhere, [15] but it should be stressed that we are only concerned with its rejection in relation to commercial contracts, for it may possibly have useful applications in other areas.

12. On this problem in French law, see Colmar, 27 July 1931. The comparative aspect is dealt with by Rabel in *Conflict of Laws* II, 1947, pp. 462 ff.

13. The centre of gravity test is prevalent in German courts and is also winning ground in the USA; cf. the very thoroughgoing decision given by the Supreme Court of Washington on 13 June 1967 in *Baffin Corp.*, in particular the dictum on p. 620, n. 1, to the effect that the expression "most significant relationship" used in the *Restatement* was synonymous with "center of gravity". Use was also made of this doctrine in the Swiss decision of 4 July 1953, dealing with the case of a stateless seller of no fixed abode.

14. Cf. the German decisions of 16 June 1903, 28 April 1920, 18 March 1958 and 4 August 1961, and the case-law of the *Bundesgerichtshof* relative to contracts of sale in decisions of 10 January, 14 February and 18 September 1958, together with further illustrations in Raape, *Internationales Privatrecht*, p. 518. See also the decision of the Düsseldorf *Oberlandesgericht* on 4 August 1961 and (rejecting the doctrine) that given on 2 November 1954 by the arbitration tribunal of the Prague Chamber of Commerce.

15. See especially the thoroughgoing decision given on 12 February 1952 by the Swiss Federal Tribunal in *Chevaley* v. *Genimportex*; Cheshire (p. 214, with further references); Langen, *Studien*, p. 12; Nussbaum, p. 269 ("intolerable artificialities"); von Caemmerer, JZ 1959, p. 361; Batiffol, on *Aramco* award, p. 659; Rabel, *Conflict of Laws* II, p. 537. English practice is to presume that the parties do not desire bisection, which is therefore allowed only by way of exception: cf. decisions of 22 July 1924, 20 October 1949 and 8 December 1958.

The various difficulties we have so far described are magnified when the system of laws which the judge decides to apply refers him on, or back, to the law of the opposite party or a third law. This is the institution of *renvoi*, which is familiar in all private international law and is everywhere regarded as controversial. The notion of *comitas gentium* here gives rise to a situation comparable to that of two excessively courteous gentlemen who are unable to pass through a doorway because each insists on yielding precedence to the other. Ernst Rabel has also likened it to a catoptric box.[16] Some of the trouble over *renvoi* experienced by the Mixed Arbitral Tribunals set up under the Treaty of Versailles was succinctly reported by Lewald in 1926.[17] The more meticulous judges are in such instances, the more the case is protracted.[18]

It is understandable, in view of the foregoing, that municipal judges should have particular difficulties in the domain of private international law. This is detrimental to the economic interests concerned in three respects. Firstly, cases take a disproportionate length of time.[19] Secondly, the result of a case involving private international law is often somewhat speculative, because the judge lacks specialist knowledge and those charged with the legal research do not always show the requisite thoroughness.[20] Thirdly, the difficulty itself tempts the judge to apply his own domestic law if at all possible. This "homing instinct" of judges, remarks Kegel (*Grundriss*, p. 40) in commenting on Nussbaum,[21] is "understandable, though scarcely laudable". In practice, therefore, a party unable to secure the specification in the contract itself of a

16. *Conflict of Laws* I, 1945, p. 77.

17. JW 1926, p. 2815. The MAT decision of 26 November 1926 dealt with an English claim for payment from a German in respect of a transaction in securities dating back to 1905(!). This was refused, and rightly so. However, in its reasoning, the court first noted the difference between the English (procedural) and German (substantive) approaches to limitation and then fell back on *renvoi* to German law. This carried little conviction and drew sharp criticism (Niboyet, 40 RdC, 1932, p. 229; Lipstein, 27 *Trans. Grotius Society*, 1942, p. 155).

18. E.g., the case dealt with by the Swiss Federal Tribunal on 5 March 1923 seven years after the expiry of a sales-contract and the subsequent period allowed for notice of defect: even this belated decision consisted merely in the rescission of the lower court's judgment and the return of the case to it.

19. There are numerous examples in addition to the Swiss case decided on 5 March 1923. In another Swiss case (*Chevaley* v. *Genimportex*) goods delivered in 1948 had at the time of the decision, 12 February 1952, still not been paid for despite the fact that evidence substantiating the claim had been presented long before, and even this decision did not close the proceedings. Seven years were required for the English *NV Kwik Hoo* decision of 23 May 1927, even though the facts of the case were utterly simple, concerning as they did the most blatant forgery of shipping-papers.

20. Cf. the *Bundesgerichtshof* decision of 30 January 1970 and my criticism in NJW 1970, p. 998.

21. *Deutsches internationales Privatrecht*, 1932, p. 43.

6

jurisdiction favouring his interest will endeavour to make sure that the case goes to a court whose local law would work to his advantage. Thus a tug-of-war may arise over the designation of the competent court, a situation vividly described by Ernst Cohn (ICLQ 1957, p. 389). It has been acknowledged in decided cases that an advantage lies from the outset in the choice of the right court, and still more in that of the domestic law.[22] It very frequently happens that in settling the preliminary issue of the applicable law the substance of the case is also decided, without stopping to ask whether the special features of an international affair are being given the consideration they deserve.

As no less an authority than the Swiss Federal Tribunal has pointed out (in its decision of 31 August 1953), it is a matter of general experience that in concluding a contract parties usually give no thought whatever to the question of the applicable law, a problem which tends not to occur to them until difficulties arise in the course of implementing the bargain. For this reason, the free choice of law allowed the parties by doctrine and jurisprudence in most countries, with a view to providing at least one possible escape-route out of the above-described difficulties, often misfires, despite the liberal use made of it. Indeed it is precisely this indulgence which has caused international arbitration tribunals to flourish, which is of course by no means to deny their essential contributions to both substantive and procedural law.

But even with free choice of law the parties to a contract are not on absolutely firm ground. The sort of problems that arise may be illustrated by one example: it is still a subject of controversy whether the parties must make their choice of law before the case opens or may also do so during the proceedings.[23]

Thus while the *Serbian Loans* dictum of the Permanent Court of International Justice with which we opened this brief survey may be right, it is not borne out in practice. This, however, has not prevented doctrine and jurisprudence from clinging to it with a certain obstinacy. Over twenty years after, in 1950, the French Court of Cassation repeated it word for word, but for the addition of a *"nécessairement"* which is surely a sign that the French

---

22. In the MAT decision of 24 May 1923 (*Goldschmiedt v. Fremery*) it was assumed that a businessman will not renounce the benefit of his own domestic law without a special reason (cf. also MAT 27 April 1923, para. 9). On 16 May 1965 the German *Bundesgerichtshof* spoke of the "Natural interest which each has in seeing his case decided by a court of his own country".

23. On 31 August 1953 the Swiss Federal Tribunal very carefully substantiated the possibility of the parties' making a choice of law even in the course of proceedings. Unfortunately the Prague Chamber of Commerce seemed unaware of this decision when on 2 November 1954, it ruled against the same possibility in the *Motokov* arbitration.

judges felt the need to banish a twinge of doubt.[24] It is probably no exaggeration to say that nowadays every legal scholar of note admits the defectiveness of the classical doctrine. As Batiffol recently said: *"On 'rigidifie' la séparation au lieu d'organiser la collaboration"* (RdC 1967-I, p. 173).

II. *The "law merchant" doctrine—lex mercatoria*

It is not surprising that cases soon emerged in which the courts had considerable difficulty in following the model of *Serbian Loans*. In France and Germany matters came to a head in a virtual revolt of the trial courts, which the supreme courts and theoreticians combined to suppress.[25] For, once cases occurred which could be more easily related to existing and adequately developed "supranational" law than to any given municipal system, or cases in which it might seem inequitable to follow one such system exclusively, as classical doctrine would demand, the courts which by their nature had the greater contact with reality were very strongly tempted to base their decisions wholly on available "supranational" law. As early as 1933 the first great controversy of this kind had arisen. The dispute, between a charterer domiciled in Germany and a Norwegian shipping company, concerned the interpretation of the "usual Leningrad ice-clause" in respect of a Hamburg-Leningrad voyage under the Norwegian flag. The parties' first point of dispute lay in the question of whether German, English or Russian law should be applied. The Hanseatic court of appeal (*Oberlandesgericht*) in Hamburg, which had a distinguished record in such cases, decided in the following terms:

> "This point of dispute requires no decision, because the case concerns a clause which has become firmly established over the years in international traffic on the Baltic and consequently does not admit of differing interpretation in different countries, and because the representative of the plaintiff company declared in answer to a question of the court

24. Judgment in *Messageries Maritimes* (21 June 1950: critique in my *Kommentar zum Aussenwirtschaftsgesetz* § 6, 23). No less an authority than Ernst Rabel takes this classical doctrine less for granted, when in *Conflict of Laws* II (1947, p. 482), he writes: "But, roughly speaking, we need a developed system of conflict rules on contracts, rather than just one or two rules, and we have to build it not on rules so vague as to abandon the judge regularly to his worry or fancy, nor on specifications so tight as to omit important kinds of agreements. This program requires comparative research in the municpal laws and in commercial practice with respect to each single type of contract, a work so far only partially started."

25. For references to German decisions, see Kegel, *Einführungsgesetz, vor Artikel 7*, n. 86.

that he was unable to cite any provision of the foreign systems of law he had named which diverged from German law for the purposes of interpreting the clause."

The court went on to construe the clause as it stood, with the backing of Norwegian, English and Dutch decisions.

The German Supreme Court, the *Reichsgericht*, rescinded this judgment on the ground that the court of appeal ought first to have scrutinized the case and determined what law was applicable; it then opted for the applicability of English law and returned the case to the *Oberlandesgericht* for final decision.[26] Thus the *Reichsgericht*, in effect, refused to consider the "usual Leningrad ice-clause" except as a component part of the German legal order, an attitude which even at that date scarcely fitted the facts. For the *Oberlandesgericht* had been able to rely on the fact that this clause was of tried international validity and to point, in particular, to a long line of case-law concerning it, more particularly in England. Moreover, as the decisions showed, there was not the slightest difficulty in taking the clause as it stood and interpreting it without reference to any particular municipal law.

In the case of the *Messageries Maritimes* the *Tribunal de la Seine* found itself in a far more precarious position. Before the first World War this great company had floated a Canadian dollar loan with a gold clause, the interest and redemption being payable at the creditor's option in Canada or Holland on the agreed gold-basis. Nothing was specified as to the applicable law. At length there came an official devaluation of the Canadian dollar. The Amsterdam Stock Exchange Committee sued the ocean navigation company in France for payment on the basis of the former gold value of the Canadian dollar. The claim was fought as far as the Court of Cassation but upheld at all three levels, albeit on different grounds. The defendant company had submitted that the contract must necessarily be based on the laws of some particular country and that the parties had in fact, explicitly or tacitly, accepted the authority of Canadian law. This argument was rejected by the courts of first instance and appeal on the ground that, in the case of an international contract of this kind, the agreed arrangements regarding payment in gold form the law of the parties. The Court of Cassation confirmed the decisions of the lower courts in substance, but altered the reasoning in one decisive point. As we have indicated above, it repeated the *Serbian Loans* dictum almost literally.[27] It is noteworthy in itself that the legal struggle in this case lasted twelve long years. Subsequently the supreme court of France, and that of Germany also, suppressed all opposition and made a decisive

26. Hamburg *Oberlandesgericht*, 10 March 1933; *Reichsgericht*, 4 November 1933; Hamburg *Oberlandesgericht*, 5 May 1934.

27. *Tribunal de la Seine*, 16 November 1938; Paris Court of Appeal, 24 April 1940; Court of Cassation, 21 June 1950.

contribution to the maintenance of the 1929 doctrine as the prevailing view. It is no less predominant in England and America. The celebrated American judge, Learned Hand, in his judgment of 13 March 1931, made use of an imaginative popular expression which has been much quoted ever since.[28] No less outright, if less witty, was the rejection of any independent supranational law by Mr. Justice Megaw in a more recent English decision, that in the *Orion* case (31 October 1962). Here a *compromis* had contained an express instruction to the arbitrator to the effect that he should ignore all legalistic formalities and strict rules of law and decide the case rather *ex aequo et bono* than on the basis of any strict system of law. The parties were two insurance companies, one Belgian, one Spanish. Judge Megaw refused to recognize this clause, saying that if it must be recognized no contract would exist, because the parties would not have intended to conclude an agreement with legal effect; and if a question of law was present, then it must remain a question of law in every respect and for every purpose, and could not be transformed by the parties into anything else, whether by an arbitration clause or in any other way.[29]

A thorough search might well reveal a number of decisions in favour of a "supranational" law. There have at all events been very many judicial decisions in arriving at which the question of the applicable law was either not raised at all or was settled out of hand without pausing to consider the possible interaction between the determination of this preliminary issue and the case as such. The significance of the fact that there have been at least two major leading cases on this theme in France and Germany is underlined by our having to record that after the concordant reasoning of the supreme courts in either country, order was restored among the regular judiciary and calm has continued to reign, so far as the direct recognition of "supranational" law is concerned.

This is not the case in the fields of economics, arbitration or—to a considerable extent—legal scholarship. In view of the spontaneous and rapid growth of economic law, the business world could scarcely let the matter rest as the courts have done. The more it organized itself in large industrial or regional associations, the more it was inclined to take into its own hands the ordering of the legal questions which most closely concerned it—a tendency which explains the flourishing state of international arbitration. As early as 1933 the

28. "People cannot by agreement substitute the law of another place; they may of course incorporate any provisions they wish into their agreements—a statute like anything else—and when they do, courts will try to make sense out of the rule, so far as they can. But an agreement is not a contract, except as the law says it shall be, and to try to make it one is to pull on one's bootstraps. Some law must impose obligation, and the parties have nothing whatever to do with that; no more than with whether their acts are torts or crimes." (48 F. 2d., pp. 115 ff., at p. 117.)

29. *Orion*, 31 October 1962, p. 264.

German professor Grossmann-Doerth, who later fell in the war, had given the title of "Self-made economic law and State law" ("*Selbstgeschaffenes Recht der Wirtschaft und staatliches Recht*") to an inaugural lecture which attracted much notice. Though this title could at first have been taken to refer to a self-made law produced within and complementary to national systems, the law in question pursued a sponaneous path of rapid growth and two decades later, after the second World War, had overrun State law to such effect that a young Swiss author of the Gutzwiller school could write:

"The situation is now no longer that the autonomous law of economics augments national laws in a number of special fields, but that national and supranational law come to the aid of the self-made legal system where it still evinces lacunae and deficiences." [30]

Scholarship had here caught up with the Paris and Hamburg courts of appeal at the point where, a quarter of a century earlier, their supreme courts had pulled them up short. The brakes could not, however, be similarly applied to free research, and it ventured farther afield, with deepening understanding. The new doctrine of *lex mercatoria* was connected up with the mediaeval "law merchant" of England and to the praetorian law of Rome.[31] Scholars everywhere have produced such a variety of opinions on this subject that it would be as well to begin by distinguishing certain main groups. The division roughly corresponds to the age of the theorist, for it would seem that the older the scholar is, the less radical his opinions become. Schmitthoff [32] mentions among supporters of the doctrine certain older names which one would tend rather to rank with the second group of cautious well-wishers. The radical group quite certainly includes Fouchard, Fragistas and Klein. [33] The more or less radical Philippe Kahn, P.A. Lalive and Copelmanas can also be counted in this group.[34]

30. Wolfgang Luithlen, *Einheitliches Kaufrecht und autonomes Handelsrecht* (Fribourg University, Legal Seminar, monograph 15), 1956, p. 57; cited by Schmitthoff, *RabelsZ* 1964, p. 71.

31. Cf. Schmitthoff, "Das neue Recht des Welthandels", *RabelsZ* 1964, pp. 47 ff.; Langen, "From Private International Law to Transnational Commercial Law", *Comparative and International Law Journal of Southern Africa* 1969, p. 313.

32. "The unification or harmonization of law by means of standard contracts and general conditions", ICLQ 1968, p. 563.

33. Philippe Fouchard, *L'Arbitrage commercial international*, 1965; Fragistas, "Arbitrage étranger et arbitrage international en droit privé", *Revue critique* 1960, p. 1; Klein, *Annuaire suisse de droit international* 1963, p. 41. Their theses have been attacked by F.A. Mann in *International Arbitration, Liber amicorum for Martin Domke*, 1967, p. 157 (German version in *Zeitschrift für das gesamte Handelsrecht* 1968, p. 89).

34. Philippe Kahn, *La Vente commerciale internationale*, Paris 1961; P.A. Lalive, "L'Arbitrage international privé", 120 RdC, 1967-I, p. 649; Copelmanas in Schmitthoff (ed.), *The Sources of the Law of International Trade*, London 1964, p. 126.

A larger group comprises those authors whose views can be described as cautiously welcoming or as critical even if they do not wholly reject the theory.[35] The group of those who do utterly reject it includes F.A. Mann and, more recently G. van Hecke and Frank Vischer, who shares Batiffol's apprehension that such freedom could rapidly lead to anarchy.[36]

Thus we have seen that the courts are solidly opposed to *lex mercatoria*, while the scholars are divided. What is the position in international arbitration?

Unfortunately this important question can scarcely be answered with certainty for so long as the great majority of arbitral awards remain unpublished. Going by what has been published, commentaries upon it and the opinions of individual experts in the matter, it can however be presumed that a considerable proportion of these awards dispense with the allocation of the case to any particular municipal system. The Mixed Arbitral Tribunals set up after the Versailles Treaty form a special category, to which we shall presently turn. The practice of arbitration tribunals may moreover be to some extent inferred not only from their popularity in the business world and the non-publication of awards but also from the openness with which they are urged by many writers to apply a law deriving—now or in the future—from the agreement of the parties, custom, comparative law and the general principles of civilized nations.[37] Though Lord Asquith's famous *Abu-Dhabi* award of 28 August 1951 cannot be adduced in this context without qualification, because in the last analysis it was based on English law, the *Lena Goldfields* and *Sapphire* awards, of 3 September 1930 and 15 March 1963 respectively, offer suitable examples.[38]

---

35. Kegel, "The Crisis of Conflict of Laws", 112 RdC, 1964-II, pp. 95 ff., at p. 257; Riese, "Ueber die Methoden der internationalen Vereinheitlichung des Privatrechts", 86 *Zeitschrift für schweizerisches Recht*, 1967, pp. 11 ff.; Von Caemmerer, *RabelsZ* 1966, p. 362, and in Schmitthoff (ed.) *Sources...*, pp. 88 and 99, and in Honnold (ed.) *Unification ...*, pp. 313 and 410, and in the *Hallstein Festschrift* 1966, p. 64; Tallon, in *Sources...*, pp. 157 f.; Goldstajn, in *Sources...*, p. 117; Berthold Goldman, p. viii of preface to P. Kahn, *La Vente commerciale internationales*, Paris 1961; see also discussion on pp. 257 ff. of Schmitthoff (ed.), *Sources....*

36. F.A. Mann, *loc. cit.* and ZHR 1968, p. 97; G. van Hecke, 126 RdC, 1969-I, pp. 465 and 474; F. Vischer, *Internationales Vertragsrecht*, Berne 1962, pp. 14 ff.

37. René David, 1962, cited by Riese, 86 Z. *für schweizerisches Recht*, 1967, p. 11, n. 19. Cf. Fouchard, Fragistas and Klein, *op. cit.*, and the attack upon them by Mann, *loc. cit.*

38. *Lena Goldfields*: see 42 *Cornell Law Quarterly*, 1950. The Swiss arbitrator Cavin says on p. 1013 of *Sapphire*: "It is therefore perfectly legitimate to find in such a clause evidence of the intention of the party not to apply the strict rules of a particular system but rather to rely upon the rules of law, based upon reason, which are common to civilized nations." The award was welcomed by J.F. Lalive and characterized expressly as "transnational law" (ICLQ 1964, p. 1011); it was also well received by P.A. Lalive in "L'Arbitrage international privé", 120 RdC, 1967-I, pp. 634 ff.

Even to the present day, there has been no softening in the rigid adherence of the regular courts to the principle enunciated in *Serbian Loans* and the decision of the French supreme court in *Messageries Maritimes*. That tenet is still, as we have indicated, supported by a considerable proportion of the leading jurists, though attacked by other scholars and to a large extent, it may be presumed, no longer followed in arbitral practice. The *Messageries* decision was a few years ago sharply attacked by an authoritative scholar, who described it as narrow-minded and outdated.[39] Thus the harsh antinomy, between reference to national law and to self-made "supranational" economic law, persists. Yet voices have begun to be raised which point out the necessity of reconciliation and progress. Batiffol has written:

"It is reasonable to believe that it is not the business of law to set up a static system which is rigid in certain matters against a liberty which could easily turn to anarchy in others. What is needed is a synthesis and continuity."[40]

In this admonition from a Frenchman one seems to catch an echo of warnings which were heard in Germany over a century ago, and which a generation ago were literally repeated:

"Moreover, if a definite emphasis on nationality is one of the predominant tendencies of modern times, this of all tendencies may not prevail in a field of teaching which, of its very nature, must set out to resolve national antitheses in an acknowledged community of the various nations." [41]

About sixty years ago it looked for a time as if a way might have been found of striking a balance between the claims of competing municipal systems instead of forcibly thrusting an international case into the arms of one or the other. At that time the German *Reichsgericht* had before it a dispute about freight charges arising out of a charter-party agreement concluded in London between a German and an English shipowner with respect to a vessel which was to carry ore from Spain to Dunkirk but, following a storm, sank in another French harbour (Granville) before the cargo could be fully discharged.[42] The decision hinged on whether the law to be applied was that of the specified port of destination or the domestic law of one of the parties. The Hamburg Hanseatic *Oberlandesgericht*, which was highly expert in such matters, had proceeded on the assumption that there was no reason why the

39. Schlesinger-Gündisch, 28 *RabelsZ*, 1964, p. 13.
40. 120 RdC, 1967-I, p. 188.
41. Savigny, *System des heutigen Römischen Rechts*, Vol. 8, 1849, p. VI; reiterated by Rabel, *RabelsZ* 1935, p. 6.
42. *Reichsgericht*, 4 April 1908, RGZ 1968, p. 203 ("*Cassia*").

parties should have wished to base their transaction on the law, foreign to both, of the French port of destination. Furthermore, as each party had presumably been willing to commit himself only to such obligations as would be incumbent upon him under his own domestic law, only the defendant's domestic law, in this instance German law, could be taken into consideration. This was contradicted by the *Reichsgericht*. As a rule, it said, parties did in fact intend that their contract should be based on one particular system of law. But:

> "Only in exceptional cases will they be aware of the possibility that the contractual relationship could be governed by two different systems and that there might not correspond, to the obligations on the one side, such obligations on the other as might be presumed from the system of laws determining the former. It follows that when one is nevertheless forced to infer, in the case of contracting parties of different national status, that no agreement took place on any one law whereby to judge the contractual relationship, it will often be impossible to avoid the disturbing conclusion that the obligations of one party are different from those on which the other, in accordance with the legal system he had in mind, believed that he was making the acceptance of reciprocal obligations dependent. Moreover, the result itself will not infrequently be unfair, because every individual system of law may surely be presumed, in regulating contractual relationships, to aim at striking an equitable balance by making sure that the faculties and responsibilities attributed to the one side are approximately matched on the other. But if two different legal systems are involved and a difference should emerge affecting the legal relationship at issue, then there is absolutely no presumption that any such equitable balance can be struck. The fact that such an outcome may not infrequently contradict the presumable suppositions of the contracting parties regarding the consequences of the contract is exemplified in the instant case: the English shipowner may be supposed to have assumed, from the viewpoint of his own domestic law, that he could not charge freightage in proportion to the distance the goods were actually carried, but only claim the whole sum if he duly delivered them in Dunkirk. It is also on this basis that he must have set about fixing the level of the figures for carriage and insurance. It follows that if he subsequently demands payment for the partial transport as far as Granville, he may be supposed to enter into contradiction with his own assumptions on signing the contract."

Notice that the international case is here already recognized, and rightly so, as a process lying within the spheres of influence of two different systems of law. It is also correctly seen that, although every system in its own sphere endeavours to strike an equitable balance between conflicting legal claims, when two systems clash "there is absolutely no presumption" that any such balance can be struck. Finally there is even an indication of how the equitable balance could be struck in the instant case, for that is implicit in the observation that if the English shipowner were to charge freightage he would be demanding more than would be his due according to his expectation on the basis of his own domestic law. This brings into play an important transnational argument which would have been quite capable of sustaining the decision and lending it a greater power of conviction than the actual decision of the *Reichsgericht*, which relied exclusively on the application of German law. At that time, there was certainly no "presumption" of determining the equitable balance between two systems of law, but the trouble could very well have been taken to look for it in each successive case.

But by then Savigny was already a half-forgotten figure. Otherwise it would have been possible to take a lead from his authority. For he had said:

"It follows from these considerations that in any given case the rule of law to be applied is determined and delimited first and foremost by the subjection of the person concerned to a particular jurisdiction, while at the same time the most manifold and important modifications may be introduced through the relationship obtaining between particular things or, it may be, particular acts or background circumstances, and other jurisdictions" (p. 13).

There is also one other eminent scholar whose work could have made an important contribution to legal development, but whose significance for private international law has not been recognized: Friedrich Lent.[43] He realized for example that:

"The variety and multiplicity of legal systems does not create any presumption as to the actual state of affairs. Difference of laws does not preclude identity of actual situations" (p. 90).

And the conflict, or rather competition, of statutes (*Gesetzeskonkurrenz*) he defined as follows: "one concrete state of affairs, two or more laws which fit it" (p. 9). Unfortunately even Lent himself did not connect up his studies—which were moreover built on the groundwork of other scholars in the fields of criminal and of civil procedural law—with private international law.[44] Neither was he aware of the 1908 decision of the *Reichsgericht* in the "*Cassia*" case—or if he was, he did not find it worthy of mention. Yet in the light of that judgment it is clear that the aphorisms just quoted provided Lent with an excellent starting-point for a far-reaching development of the kind which, in fact, we find resurfacing half a century later in Germany, in the work of Steindorff, who rediscovered and explored the "international case"

43. F. Lent, *Die Gesetzeskonkurrenz im bürgerlichen Recht und Zivilprozess*, Vol. 1, Leipzig 1912.
44. The subject of private international law is not mentioned in the summary of related topics on p. 92 of Lent's work.

qua process in the context of competing legal systems.

The idea of competing legal systems and the necessity of striking a just balance between them evidently hung in the air at that time. This is shown with special clarity by the *Reichsgericht's* decision of 19 December 1922. In this case a Swiss litigant who had procured a so-called *Verlustschein* ("certificate of loss") in Switzerland had relied on the fact that under Swiss law the claim attested by such a certificate is imprescriptible. The Karlsruhe *Oberlandesgericht* ruled that such imprescriptibility was incompatible with German *ordre public* and consequently decided in accordance with German law. When the case came before it on application for revision, the *Reichsgericht* demurred in the following terms:

> "Only on being satisfied that the gaps could not be filled from Swiss law should the appeal court have applied German law, and even then it was under obligation to ascertain which particular provision of the latter came closest to the way of thinking of the foreign law."

These dicta could have acquired the greatest jurisprudential significance and set the trend for posterity.[45] They actually indicated the judge's duty to explore transnational law before venturing to assign the case wholly to one particular system of law. They could have provided the jurisprudence of the post-Versailles Mixed Arbitral Tribunals that began work about this time with the basis for which they were groping. At that juncture, however, German influence was largely discounted and, even shorn of historical considerations, had waned since the link with Savigny had grown tenuous. Be that as it may, the oft-cited *Negreanu* decision of 16 June 1925 observed (pp. 210 ff.) that, with few exceptions, the Mixed Arbitral Tribunals had desisted from determining the applicable law, inasmuch as they set out from the assumption that the two competing systems would produce the same result; this easy way out was frankly risky, for in many cases a more thorough analysis of both laws would reveal differences not apparent at first sight; at all events the tribunal considered that it was desirable in principle for such difficulties to be confronted and resolved, for that was how the Mixed Arbitral Tribunals could make their special contribution to the creation of international law. It is the hand of Froelich, the German rapporteur in this case and a later member of the *Reichsgericht*, that one thinks to detect herein. However, these propositions remained a mere programme and cannot be said to characterize the

---

45. The *Verlustschein* decision was not mentioned in the German *Bundesgerichtshof's* judgment of 28 October 1965 in a case concerning lawyer's fees (NJW 1966, p. 296), when the court expressed the opinion that the invocation of *ordre public* was an exceptional state of affairs which as such should be interpreted liberally, so that the foreigner would receive the benefit of any concession it was still possible to make. This is cited with approval in Soergel/Kegel, 10th ed., *ad* Art. 30, n. 23, and Doelle, *Der ordre public im internationalen Privatrecht*, 1950, p. 409.

jurisprudence of the Mixed Arbitral Tribunals, which were later alleged to have failed in this very task.[46]

For some decades this insight into the subject of competing legal systems disappeared from jurisprudence and the writings of publicists. Only in a few documents, of markedly special character, were traces of it visible. One of the best-known examples is to be seen in the articles of association of the Saarlor AG, which provide in terms that the applicable law, in addition to the relevant Franco-German treaty and the charter of the company, shall include the common principles of German and French law, and that in the absence of such principles a decision should be taken in accordance with the spirit of co-operation which presided over the formation of the company.

It might also be interesting if one could sift through all those numerous decisions to be found in all countries—notably in the United States—in which, despite the plainly international character of the case, the question of the applicable law was not even raised, or the local law of the court was applied in all simplicity without more ado. Examples, to mention preferably but some of more recent times, are to be found in the decisions of 17 November 1937, 27 July 1943, 13 February 1946 and 9 December 1960 in the United States, of 28 April 1953 in France, of 10 December 1957 in England, and of 11 February 1933 and 5 August 1965 in Czechoslovakia (Prague Chamber of Commerce).

In a large proportion of such decisions it would probably transpire, if only the circumstances of the case had been more fully reported, that the judge had reached an understanding with the parties not to raise the question of the applicable law because the case could be decided on the basis of concordant material rules or, at all events, in accordance with the 1922 reasoning of the *Reichsgericht* regarding a just balance between two differing systems of law.

After the failure of the Mixed Arbitral Tribunals, the endeavour to strike a just balance between competing systems was again ousted by the old antinomy whereby cases were more or less arbitrarily allocated to one of the domestic laws concerned, or a third, supranational law was looked for. Only Gutzwiller held aloof from these preconceptions. In 1931 he wrote that the Mixed Arbitral Tribunals had unfortunately not been so free—

"... that they would have been allowed to slight 'international justice' with its ingrained traditions and the claims of its temper and spirit ... It is precisely among the States participating in the Mixed Arbitral

---

46. H. Isay, *Die privaten rechte und Interessen im Friedensvertrag*, Berlin 1923; Gutzwiller, *Nussbaums internationales Jahrbuch für Schiedsgerichtswesen* III, 1931, pp. 123 ff.; Rudolf Blühdorn, 41 RdC, 1931-III, pp. 141 ff.; the entire jurisprudence of the MAT is thoroughly analysed by Lipstein in the *Transactions of the Grotius Society*, Vol. 27, 1942, pp. 142 ff.; see also Rabel, "Rechtsvergleichung vor den Gemischten Schiedsgerichtshöfen", 1934 (*Gesammelte Abhandlungen*, 1965, Vol. II, p. 1), and Lewald, JW 1926, p. 2815 (*ut supra*).

Tribunals that, because of a common historical evolution, a series of such special transnational norms has come into being. Generally speaking, as stressed in particular by Ernst Rabel, one will first and foremost have to collate both of the national laws involved in the case. Should they not concord, the cumulation principle proposed by K. Neumeyer (JW 1922, pp. 753 and 1556) may prove useful in particularly ripe exceptional cases."

Above all:

"... anyone wishing to take the lofty supranational view must think the case out supranationally from beginning to end".[47]

It was surely in the above passage that the term "transnational" was used for the first time in modern legal history, not in an English textbook of 1934.[48] However, the appearance of the term did not in itself connote any progress, so long as it merely signified a kind of programme for the future. It was much rather the emergence of comparative law as a new academic discipline which constituted the decisive step forward. What could have been expected of the Mixed Arbitral Tribunals and their practice at a time when comparative law was scarcely more than embryonic, and quite unable to provide a judge, however progressive, with the tools he needed? The very fact that they threw in their hand may indeed have stimulated the rise and development of this new branch of legal scholarship, more particularly in Germany, where this abandonment was felt with particular keenness. Viewed in this light, it does not appear fortuitous that Ernst Rabel's programme on the task and necessity of comparitive law was drawn up in 1925, that the International Institute for the Unification of Private Law was founded in Rome in 1926 and that Schlegelberger's great *Handwörterbuch* of comparative law began to appear in 1929. Around 1950, the important periodicals devoted to comparitive law began to appear all over the world, and today the value of comparative law as an indispensable adjunct to private international law has received full recognition.[49]

We will deal more closely with the beneficent influence of comparative law

47. Gutzwiller, as in preceding note, pp. 128 and 150.

48. In "Specific Principles of Private Transnational Law" (124 RdC, 1968-II, p. 255) Ehrenzweig assumes that Gustav Walker first used the word in his *International Private Law* of 1934. It was however only through Philip C. Jessup's *Transnational Law* (YUP) of 1956 that the term really became known, and it was from Jessup that J.F. Lalive (ICLQ 1964, p. 1008) took it over. Recently, in "Contemporary Conflicts Law" (131 RdC, 1970-III), Cavers has unfortunately used the word "transnational", in an entirely general sense, speaking of "transnational business", "transnational transactions" etc. On the different senses of "transnational", cf. also Sicher, *RabelsZ* 1970, p. 600, n. 72, with further references.

49. See David/Grasmann, *Einführung in die grossen Rechtssysteme der Gegenwart*, Munich 1966, and the article *"Rechtsvergleichung"* by Konrad Zweigert in *Handwörter-*

18

on the development of private international law, and with the transnational commercial law born in this interpenetration, in Part Five of this work below.

Before proceeding, we must briefly glance at the further development of the classical doctrine and of *lex mercatoria* up to the present day. The state of deadlock reached by these opposite points of view is particularly well illustrated in their respective answers to the question of the law to be applied in deciding disputes between States and private persons. One school of thought leans toward the classical doctrine, according to which a particular municipal system of laws must be applied, and the choice could naturally not fall on any other than the legal system of the State party to the dispute, for the simple reason that in the absence of any express declaration a State could scarcely be expected to submit itself to the private law of another State. [50] The opposing school of thought takes its stand more on the doctrine of *lex mercatoria*, contending for example that an agreement for the constitution of a mixed arbitral tribunal creates a presumption that it was the will of the parties to conclude the contract outside the ambit of all municipal legal systems, if the contract was made between a State and a private party. [51] However, there have also been some noteworthy pronouncements in favour of a middle-of-the-road approach. According to such views, although a contract may be based on one particular system of law (Islamic, in the cited case) [52] from which it derives its validity and binding force, it need not have to be interpreted solely and exclusively in terms of that system.

In regard to the "general principles of civilized nations" total confusion still reigns. Over against the purely positivist view represented by Joseph Story, [53] whereby there are no general principles capable of directly creating obligations for every citizen but merely the tacit mutual tolerance by States of foreign legal principles, only one step forward—albeit a cardinally essential one—has been achieved.

Nowadays—and not least after the decisions of the Nuremberg Military

---

buch des Völkerrechts, 2nd ed., Berlin 1962, with further references. There is no need here to go into the doubts cast on the utility of comparative law in Dicey/Morris, *The Conflict of Laws*, 8th ed., London 1967, pp. 25 and 28.

50. Cf. F.A. Mann, "State Contracts and State Responsibilities", 54 AJIL, 1960, p. 572; *Liber Amicorum Domke* 1967, p. 157 (=130 ZHR, 1968, p. 97); "State Contracts and International Arbitration", BYBIL 1967, p. 1. See also the advisory opinion of the Max Planck Institut, Hamburg, 4 November 1965, on development-aid and limitation of claims.

51. Zweigert, *Berichte der deutschen Gesellschaft für Völkerrecht* 1964, p. 208; J.F. Lalive, "Contracts between a State and a Foreign Company", ICLQ 1964, p. 487.

52. *Aramco* award of 23 August 1958 by Sauser-Hall; cf. A. Broches, "Choice-of-law Problems in Contracts with Governments" in Reese (ed.), *International Contracts*, New York 1962.

53. *Commentaries on the Conflict of Laws*, Edinburgh 1835, p. 29.

Tribunal—there can no longer be any doubt that it would mean a relapse into barbarism for a judge to deny the direct obligatory effect of certain supreme principles of civilized nations.[54] It may also now be regarded as the predominant opinion that common basic ethical concepts must underlie these general principles.[55] This is a view which commands ready assent. Nevertheless, the question immediately arises as to whether it is really possible to discover, all over the world, an adequately developed ethical consensus.[56] In jurisprudence—notably in arbitral case-law—very frequent reference is made to general principles, but as a rule these allusions are fairly vague and hardly pass the tests by which grounds of decision in the field of economic law are customarily appraised. We shall have more to say on this subject in Part Five.

In reality the term "general principles" acts as a blanket for two quite distinct notions. Along with the vague but nonetheless effective rules of law sometimes termed "the ethical denominator" there are rules of a more technical nature stemming from the practical experience of centuries, rules which are virtually the same or very similar in all countries, many taking the form of commercial customs, and many expressed in legal tags, as often as not in Latin (when they are also known as *paroemiae*). But the objectively binding force of legal maxims and customs is also a matter of continuing controversy. Joseph Esser has pleaded their cause with persuasive eloquence.[57]

54. Cf. George Schwarzenberger, "The Fundamental Principles of International Law", 87 RdC, 1955, p. 372; Wolfgang Friedmann, "The Usage of General Principles in the Development of International Law", 57 AJIL, 1963, p. 279; Bin Cheng, *The General Principles of Civilized Nations*, London 1953; Langen, "From Private International Law to Transnational Commercial Law", *Comparative and International Law Journal of Southern Africa* 1969, p. 320; I. Seidl-Hohenveldern, "General Principles of Law as applied by the Conciliation Commissions established under the Peace Treaty with Italy of 1947", 53 AJIL, 1959, p. 853.

55. According to Schwarzenberger, *The Frontiers of International Law*, London 1962, p. 42, the right of reciprocity does not necessarily require "constitutional homogeneity but an indispensable minimum of an ethical common denominator"; assented to by Langen in *Studien zum internationalen Wirtschaftsrecht*, Munich 1963, p. 20, with whom F.A. Mann concurs in turn (ICLQ 1964, p. 720). Seidl-Hohenveldern, however, remains skeptical, in AWD 1964, p. 32.

56. R.B. Schlesinger gives an affirmative answer in "Research on the General Principles of Law recognized by Civilized Nations", AJIL 1957, p. 747. I myself express some doubts in my *Studien . . .* (p. 521) and see rather a dichotomy between States with market-economies and States with other economic systems, referring in particular to Carl Schmitt, *Der Nomos der Erde*, Cologne 1950.

57. J. Esser, *Grundsatz und Norm in der richterlichen Fortbildung des Privatrechts*, 2nd unaltered ed. Tübingen 1964, p. 319: "Maxims possess an enduring value as the starting-points of new developments, freed from dogmatic wrappings, in which a 'legal idea' like that of § 817 (2) of our Civil Code breaks out of its systematic framework and

In 1963 I myself endeavoured, in my *Studien zum internationalen Wirtschaftsrecht* (pp. 24 ff.), to extract the rules and customs valid only for commercial law from out the sphere of general principles, which as such was far too vast, and to explain them as possessing an objective character *qua* legal system of an international kind, if treated as "rules of the game" for a particular realm of legal facts, namely that of international commerce. [58] Eisemann, who through his position in the International Chamber of Commerce has acquired special experience, is clearly sympathetic to this proposal. [59]

At that time I imagined that such "rules of the game" could build up into an objective and supranational legal system. O. Riese demurred at this, and rightly so, though he probably went too far in doubting "whether there were in fact any internationally uniform trade usages". [60] Another critic who strongly doubted whether such universal rules of the game really existed or could be developed as a supranational legal system was the Japanese Michido. He was probably right in his conclusion that, while there may have been one unified market for all articles of world trade in mediaeval times, there are nowadays only very different markets, different both in type of merchandise and in geographical location: we should therefore have refrained from over-hasty generalization and accorded separate treatment to at least the following markets: those for natural and agricultural produce, those for industrial products (plant and machinery) and those for durable consumer goods. [61]

---

in its old formulation of '*in pari turpitudine melior est causa possidentis*' renders visible the universal affinities with such structurally different institutions as *abus de droit*, estoppel or the clean-hands doctrine. The *paroemia* may be regarded as the very prototype of the formulation of universal principles of law. Even such specifically national coinages as '*possession vaut titre*' reveal with a little reflection the ubiquity of the underlying principle".

58. See also my report in the *Yearbook* of the Washington Conference of World Peace through Law, Minneapolis/St. Paul 1967, p. 315.

59. Frédéric Eisemann, *Die Incoterms im internationalen Warenkaufrecht,* Stuttgart 1967, p. 66: " . . . by applying the description 'rules of play of international economic law' to the 'general principle' of good faith, this author has surely found the most apposite characterization of the way in which, by virtue of the freedom of contract as thus understood, the legal order of modern States operates beyond its frontiers and decisively, even if indirectly, works towards the formation of a uniform international economic law".

60. "Die Methoden der internationalen Vereinheitlichung des Privatrechts", 86 *Z.f. schw. Recht*, 1967, p. 12. However, Riese here quotes a sentence from a manuscript of mine which was never printed. The report on the Geneva Conference of World Peace through Law appeared only later, in Vol. III of the series of writings by the German section of the *Association des Auditeurs de l'Académie de La Haye:* I. Seidl-Hohenveldern and H. Nagel (eds.), *Beiträge aus Völkerrecht und Rechtsvergleichung*, Baden-Baden 1967, pp. 31 ff.

61. Michido, in Honnold (ed.), *Unification . . .,* Paris 1966, p. 264.

21

Thus, on closer inspection, this endeavour too comes virtually to nothing.

This notwithstanding, before despairing of all progress in this direction it is worth considering the many vigorous attempts that have been made—without seeking universal rules of play—to bring markets for particular goods, or particular kinds of transaction or figures of law, under some kind of regulation. Here one must begin by making a distinction between public international treaties and conventions of private law. There is no need here to enumerate all the successful or unsuccessful attempts of this kind. They are well known, and range from the draft treaties of the European Economic Commission which form the underlying material of Philippe Kahn's book to the Hague Convention on the Law of Sale. However necessary it doubtless is that such efforts be pursued, all these treaty-made systems have one unsatisfactory feature in common: the time it takes them to come into being: the vigorous development of case-law can be expected to produce better effects more rapidly.[62] The various codifications may possibly aggravate the splitting of the world's trade-law into two distinct regions, which would obviously run counter to Batiffol's exhortation to unify,[63] and they also have this most serious drawback: that, even where they are confined to regulating for only one region, it remains extremely difficult to bring them into harmony with the underlying national legal systems. Hence we find, for example, that the great codifications of the law of sale are still quite unattuned to each other,[64]

---

62. Arthur Nussbaum, "Conflict theories of contracts: cases *versus* restatement", *Yale Law Review* 1942, p. 893; Kurt H. Nadelmann, "Uniform legislation *versus* international conventions revisited", 16 *American Journal of Comparative Law*, 1968, p. 28.

63. Cf. among others Szazy, "The proper law of the contract in trade between Eastern Europe and the West: the position of East European socialist States", ICLQ 1969, p. 103, with further references.

64. Here are a few points culled from the copious and widely divergent literature on the subject: The admission of English as a working-language alongside French was not decided until the 10th Hague Conference on Private International Law, on 27 October 1964 (Ficker, *RabelsZ* 1966, p. 609). As long ago as the London Colloquium of 1962 (Schmitthoff, ed., *Sources . . .*) it was correctly pointed out that the legal regulation of international trade is similar in nature in all States even though the basic conceptions of the State legal systems may differ, influenced as they are by the politico-economic structures as well as historical considerations including inherited legal tradition (Kalensky, "Die Grundzüge des Gesetzes über den internationalen Handel", *RabelsZ* 1966, p. 296). The Uniform Commercial Code is based on the belief that business circles have a better grasp of their needs than governments and should therefore enjoy the greatest possible freedom; it cannot simply be written off but should be looked to as a model and point of reference wherever a competitive economy obtains (Sonya Mentschikoff, "The Uniform Commercial Code", *RabelsZ* 1966, p. 403). The Conventions do not show sufficient concordance (Honnold, in Schmitthoff, ed., *Sources . . .*). Further literature mentioned in Dölle, "Einheitliches Kaufrecht und internationales Privatrecht", *RabelsZ*, 1968, p. 447, n. 22.

and the skepticism they thus provoke receives further fuel from the idealistic outlook with which the subject is approached in the United Nations context:

"International trade law should in principle be declared by an international organization and not by States; the role of the latter is merely to say whether and to what extent they agree to apply the rules of such law, and by thus expressing reservations, to give directions to its development." [65]

All honour to such zeal: but the practical success of any further harmonization depends on whether the Hague Sales Rules and the Uniform Commercial Code can be brought into line with each other. [66] The Sales Law Convention of 1964 is a code predominantly based on continental European thinking. [67] Its background of collective enterprise and co-operation correspond rather to the conditions of internal or intra-European trade than to those of overseas commerce. [68] The use of two languages in itself demands threefold the expenditure of time; there are linguistic difficulties even between England and the United States. [69]

If the developments of the 45 years since 1925—the approximate birthdate of comparative law—are viewed as a whole, a negative comment is justified, but there is also something positive to be said. Negatively, it must be put on record that the exhortations of prominent legal scholars in 1945, and again from 1954 to the present, have so far made little difference to the fragmentation of private international law. In 1945 Ernst Rabel wrote in the foreword to his *Conflict of Laws*: "The conditions of the law of conflicts are deplorable" (p. xxi). Ten years later Yntema still had to say:

"In the prolific literature devoted to these problems, many fruitful lines have been revealed, as the preceding account of the evolution of the basic ideas in the subject matter may perhaps suggest. And prospectively, it is even more important that the evolution for the time being has reached an inherently untenable position. How can the formal doctrine postulated by the modern theories, that the local law is supreme, explain the phenomenon of conflicts law, the precise purpose of which is to define the necessary exceptions to be made in the substantive rules

65. Uncitral/III/CRP/3 of 6 April 1970, p. 8: Draft Basic Convention, submitted by the French delegation, Cf. Carey, "Uncitral, its origins and prospects", 15 *American Journal of Comparative Law*, 1967, p. 626.

66. Hellner, in Ziegel/Foster, *Aspects of Comparative Commercial Law*, Montreal 1969, pp. 97 and 106.

67. Riese, *RabelsZ* 1965, p. 100.

68. Berman, *Law and Contemporary Problems: the Unification of Law*, Duke University 1965, p. 368.

69. Tunc, *Revue internationale de droit comparé* 1964, p. 551; Farnsworth, Nadelmann and Daw, "Some problems raised by the draft uniform law on the international sale of goods", 1965 Proceedings of Am. Foreign Law Assoc., *Am. J. Comp. Law* 1965, pp. 226 ff.

23

of this very local law? Obviously, the reasons for these exceptions, and not the formal doctrine, present the real issues. The fact that the historic logic has aborted in a sterile truism makes it possible and even imperative to begin anew. The monumental research in comparative law of the outstanding jurist to whom this volume is dedicated has been of fundamental importance in these efforts to reconstruct the law of conflicts."[70]

Yntema refers in his last sentence to the role played by comparitive law in the reconstruction of the law of conflicts. It was to take more than one decade before the initial results of this influence of comparative law on private international law bore fruit in the field of practice.

To see these results in clearer perspective it will first be necessary to differentiate three stages of progress, though they were not in reality sharply contrasted. At the first stage, greater attention was paid to the substantive aspect in considering matters of private international law, and that aspect gained in importance relative to the preoccupation with conflicts of law by which it had formerly been outweighed. It was more fully recognized that an international case is something different from one which lies exclusively in the national domain. At the second stage, once the—often unthinking—"nationalization" of an international case had become a thing of the past, more attention was paid to the question of what the special and appropriate objective rules for an international case might be. At the third and last stage it was progressively realized that appropriate objective norms for international cases cannot simply be imported from the national systems that are ready to hand, but that there must first ensue a special process of law-comparison wherein the national norms are fused together in the framework of the freedom of contract. It is in this that transnational commercial law comes into being.

So far as the first stage is concerned, certain events in the fields of jurisprudence and legal doctrine were of salient importance. The Dutch jurist Jitta was one of the first scholars in more recent times to accord special attention to the international case.[71] Less important than his conclusions is the fact that he was one of the first to recognize the international case as something *sui generis* rather than to nationalize it out of hand. In fact national systems of law are never of more than limited use in the international field, because they are created in response to other postulates, i.e., a circumscribed territory, specific historical relationships and specific national ways of thought

70. H.E. Yntema, in *Festschrift für Ernst Rabel* I, 1954, p. 537, revision of "The historic bases of private international law", *Am. J. Comp. Law* II, 1953, pp. 297 ff., at p. 317.
71. Josephus Jitta, *La Méthode du droit international privé*, 1890, p. 200; *idem, La Substance des obligations dans le droit international privé* I, 1906, p. 20, and II, 1907, p. 493.

expressed in one specific language. These postulates either do not exist in the international field or, if they do, are not present in the same way or do not stand in the same interrelation. At a time when the influence of Story and Savigny reigned supreme, however, this simple truth still needed rediscovering. The difficulties which stood in the way can be discerned in the mistrust evinced by the municipal courts in, for example, France vis-à-vis arbitration clauses having the effect of removing the dispute from their jurisdiction, and possibly from the purview of French law altogether. Even as late as 1966 the *Cour de Cassation* had to be called in to establish in terms the admissibility of an arbitration clause in an international case.[72] In Germany it was above all Wengler who set about uncovering the peculiar nature of international cases and treating them accordingly.[73] Steindorff not only demanded special solutions for international cases (p. 261) but also advanced the opinion (p. 282) that even foreign norms must be treated as formal constituents of national law.

It was only when the international case as such had come to the fore as the object of special attention that it was possible to give due consideration to the problem of the interrelation and relative importance of substantive norms, on the one hand, and conflict norms on the other. Efforts in this direction constitute the second phase in the development of transnational commercial law. It is again a lofty maxim of Savigny's that offers a point of departure here: "Questions about conflicts of law ... are by their very nature derivative or subordinate questions" (p. 3). This subordination of conflict-norms to substantive norms is a far more fruitful approach than the reverse, which is advocated by classical doctrine, according to which, however—and

72. The Greek vessel "*Aspasia*" was chartered in 1940 by the French Government. When a dispute arose, a London arbitration tribunal was seised in accordance with the arbitration clause. The State refused to comply with an award of 12 October 1953 on the ground that the clause was invalid under Articles 83 and 1004 of the Civil Procedure Code read with Article 3 of the Civil Code. The award was therefore negated in first instance, but it was reinstated in appeal and on application for revision, when the Court of Cassation had this to say: "All that the Court of Appeal had to pass upon was the question whether the statutes mentioned, which were enacted for domestic contracts, must be applied in the same way to international contracts, which have been concluded for the purpose and in accordance with the observances of maritime trade; the attacked decision rightly found that the above-mentioned prohibition was not applicable to a contract of that kind and had accordingly declared the arbitration clause valid" (Cass. 2 May 1966). Regarding the uncertainty subsisting in France, see also, for example, the Colmar decision of 27 March 1957 and the extensive comments thereon of Francescakis.

73. Wilhelm Wengler, "Die Belegenheit von Rechten", *Festschrift der Berliner Juristenfakultät zum 41. Deutschen Juristentag*, 1955, pp. 350 ff.; *idem*, 158 *Archiv für die zivilistische Praxis*, 1959-60, pp. 543 ff., in the discussion of Steindorff's book; Ernst Steindorff, *Sachnormen im internationalen Privatrecht*, Frankfurt-am-Main 1958, esp. pp. 9, 23 ff. and 261 ff.; Steindorff's work has been criticised by Kegel, 112 RdC, 1964-II, pp. 244 and 252, and by the Belgian van Hecke, 126 RdC, 1969-I, p. 474.

not surprisingly—"the line between conflict-law reference and substantive reference is often hard to draw.[74] Melchior, in 1932, resorted to a metaphor in offering his solution of the problem: the foreign substantive norm, he said, must be fitted into the pigeon-holes of the domestic law.[75] Sandrock suggested allowing complementary interpretation in the case of atypical contracts, but this was justly criticized because it was not clear on what basis a judge could tell, in the individual case, whether the clause before him was atypical or not.[76] Wengler, in his review of Steindorff, sounded a note of pessimism:

> "But what law does the judge find in place of the national legal order ...? This is a point which, it seems to me, Steindorff has left somewhat obscure." [77]

The skepticism and pessimism exhibited by representatives of the classical school derive from the fact that their outlook on transnational law is still distorted by the supposition that if national law *tout court* is not applied, then an independent overriding law of some special kind must be discovered. We have already described certain efforts to establish a *lex mercatoria*. They failed because they ask too much of the judge. They require of him a constructive initiative (*einen Gestaltungsakt*) far in excess of his powers, and place upon him a weight of responsibility for the stability of the law which his shoulders are not broad enough to bear. It is Wilhelm Wengler who has expressed this in the clearest way.[78]

---

74. Kegel, *Grundriss . . .*, p. 228.

75. *Grundlage des internationalen Privatrechts*, 1932, p. 83; reproduced by Batiffol in his critique of Cass. 4 June 1941.

76. Otto Sandrock, *Zur ergänzenden Vertragsauslegung im materiellen und internationalen Schuldvertragsrecht*, Cologne and Opladen 1966, p. 262: see comments of F.A. Mann, JZ 1968, p. 112. Of course the difficulty subsists only in respect of mandatory rules of law. In this connexion Soergel/Kegel (*Art.* 30, n. 23) says: "That, in a given case, law should be applied which is otherwise not valid (either abroad or in Germany) is not objectionable, since we are dealing with exceptional cases. It is a matter of developing new substantive law in private international law." Dölle had already expressed the same idea in *Der ordre public im internationalen Privatrecht*, 1950, p. 409, with reference to Wengler, JR 1949, p. 72.

77. 158 *Archiv für die zivilistische Praxis*, 1959-60, p. 547.

78. "Die Funktion der richterlichen Entscheidung über internationale Rechtsverhältnisse", 16 *RabelsZ* 1951, p. 10: "If all these violations of the schema of private international law are being passively accepted, this shows in my opinion that private international law is already won over to the idea that judicial decision is here very largely capable of becoming something more than the inquest-like ascertainment of the observance or non-observance of standards of conduct. However, if it is not such ascertainment, it takes on, whether one likes it or not, the character of a constructive qualification *ad hoc* of the concrete legal relationship (*den Charakter einer konkreten Gestaltung des konkreten Rechtsverhältnisses*). The decision of an international case in the situations we have just described becomes a constructive initiative (*Gestaltungsakt*) not because it aims to be one, but because it is no longer a mere act of determination."

However, no such great leap forward was in fact necessary. No constructive initiative is called for on the part of the judge. Instead, a series of pioneer decisions have shown us the way: all the decisions of municipal courts which recognize arbitration clauses having reference to the supranational fora set up for particular sectors or trades. In all these cases it was no difficult problem to uncover and define the supranational substantive norm, because the arbitration tribunals concerned and the organizations behind them were held in high esteem. So much so that the exceptional cases when such an arbitration clause is denied effect have become a matter for raised eyebrows. [79]

By now, however, all courts—as a rule—recognize to a certain extent the prevailing force of the substantive norm, even in cases where the operative norm has not been determined with all the authority wielded by the specialized arbitration tribunals. For an example of a borderline case one may refer to the Hamburg decision of 4 March 1930, in which part of the English law governing bills of lading was recognized, though with the express comment in the grounds of judgment that German law did not exclude agreement by the parties to be guided, as to the content of their obligations, by foreign provisions which would be applicable in that context not as laws, but as terms of the contract.

That is the same opinion as is found in the English *Kwik Hoo* judgment of 23 May 1927, where Lord Dunedin, having found that English law must apply, continues:

And: "If there has recently been talk of the possibility of private international law developing from a system of referral to one of decision (*Verweisungsrecht* and *Entscheidungsrecht* in the terminology of Dölle, DRZ, 5th ed., Tübingen, 1948, p. 5; with reference to Neuhaus, DRZ, 1948, p. 87), this seems to me to be not so much a development of positive law as a development in outlook and methodology. The above observations are therefore intended not to reveal any new discoveries in positive law but to make a contribution to the way private international law is or should be regarded."

79. From French jurisprudence, with indication of source of arbitration: Lyons, 30 July 1913 (sugar-trade); Marseilles, 20 December 1922 (Liverpool United General Produce Assoc. Ltd.); Rouen, 24 December 1924 (London coffee-arbitration—refused, however); Cass. 8 January 1924 (Strasbourg Bourse); Cass. 3 March 1924 (London Rice Brokers); Cass. 19 February 1930: "Whereas, in view of the fact that these agreements thus place the interests of international trade at stake, and in view of the nullity of the arbitration clause under Art. 1006 (Civil Procedure) as incompatible with *ordre public* in France, the parties . . . have invalidly . . ."; Cass. 27 January 1931 (London Corn Trade Assoc.). On 1 March 1954 the arbitration tribunal of the Prague Chamber of Commerce rejected an arbitration clause bestowing competence on it simultaneously with an English tribunal dealing specifically with jute-deliveries, which was regarded as self-contradictory. For recognition of the competence and law of the arbitral body of the London Corn Exchange, see the English decision of 10 May 1894 (*Hamlyn*) and the unvarying line of ensuing case-law.

"That does not mean that everything that would have to be decided would necessarily be decided by English law. It means that the underlying law was the law of England, but if by appropriate, that is to say relevant, averment, it was alleged that any incident of the contract fell to be be determined by a foreign law, then the English tribunal would proceed to inquire into that law as a question of fact and give judgment accordingly."

Certainly, one has to reckon with the fact that any synthesis of rules from different systems of law will give rise to a problem similar to that known in medicine when organs are transplanted: not only must the transplantation be technically successful, but the graft must "take". The Hamburg appeal-court decision of 29 October 1958 in the *Braugerste* case is thought-provoking here. We have already alluded to objections on these lines. They can certainly be overcome. An international case does not merely demand the striking of a balance between disparate domestic and foreign legal rules, for at times the balance in itself does not yield the solution, which calls for considerably more. An illustration of one such situation, and of its solubility, is provided by the grafting into continental law of the English institution of the trustee. In France as in Austria this process has already been carried as far as the highest competent tribunals. [80]

The direction in which thought and practice have been moving should now be clear. The mere realization that the merits of a case are peculiarly international is now sufficient to bestow priority on the solution of the substantive problem and to minimize the importance of a consistent choice of applicable law. This automatically enhances the prospect of seeing that problem solved not, as before, speculatively, by seeking some overriding third rule, but scientifically, through the consonance or by the attunement of the legal orders engaged.

European jurists are wondering whether the three great reformers in the United States—Currie, Cavers and Ehrenzweig—are on the right path. Misgivings prevail, even though the Americans are applauded for their energy in seeking solutions. [81] Kegel's criticisms, however, go much too far, for he insists from the outset on seeing the movement at work in America as a crisis, hence as something to be overcome, whereas one would do better to speak,

80. French cases: Cass. 3 March 1924 (*London Rice Brokers*), 4 June 1941 (approvingly annotated by Batiffol); Austria: *Oberst-Gerichtshof* 3 March 1967, recognizing a trust-agreement concerning a sleeping-partner's share registered in Czechoslovakia and concluded between two nationals of that State in 1922; Germany: *Bundesgerichtshof* 19 October 1960 (replacement delivery in French law), and (limited recognition) 11 February 1953 (contract of insurance in Switzerland).

81. For the misgivings, see the references given in Kegel, 112 RdC, 1964-II, pp. 95, 251 and 263, and Siehr, pp. 595 ff. Heini (p. 275) gives a favourable account, and so does Schmitthoff in "Der Einfluss ausserrechtlicher Elemente", p. 93.

like the Americans themselves, in terms of evolution or progress. Moreover it is still too early for a foreign observer to pass any final judgment on this development, concerning which an especially respected and experienced American observer has said: "Choice of law in the United States is in the midst of a revolution." [82] One should also reserve judgment for the simple reason that the significant American practice has developed first and foremost in cases concerning traffic-accidents, hence not involving commercial law, and also because this specialized branch belongs in that country to American inter-State law, rather than to international law.

In passing, be it remarked that German scholars are singularly handicapped in coming to grips with developments in America by the relative poverty in this domain of the law libraries on which they must rely, not to mention the formidable problems of translation, which are multiplied by the idiosyncratic terminology of an Ehrenzweig, for example. [83]

The Americans probably have the assent of the great majority of English and continental jurists in rejecting the notion of a super-law. Their theories would give ground for apprehension, however, if the *lex loci* approach were overstressed, and still more if the courts were to make a habit of wielding it as a convenient tool. [84] For it is to be hoped that American judges will view the signposts set up by the professors, pointing to "forum policies", "governmental interests" and "result-selective approach", with the greatest circumspection and with a proper understanding for what will produce a reasonable and legally convincing outcome. [85] An imaginative slogan like "stay at home" can be dangerous precisely because of the connotations of the image: a judge might be tempted to believe he could remain in his own house and barely do more than glance out of the window. But the cogency of his decision would be sure to suffer. Suppose a judge on the international plane were to presume from the outset the applicability of his own domestic law? Doubtless he will not be denied the use of that law as a starting-point, but only on the pre-

82. Willis M. Reese, "Recent developments in torts", *Columbia Journal of Transnational Law* 1969, p. 181.

83. I gave some statistics illustrating the inadequacy of our law-libraries in NJW 1969, p. 2232. On translation problems, cf. the vivid description given by Arnold Brecht of the toil and trouble it cost him to translate his own book on *Political Theory* back from the American in which it originally appeared (in 1959) into his native German, on p. xv of the foreword to the German version, *Politische Theorie*, Tübingen, 1961. As an illustration of the way linguistic difficulties act as a clog on the spread of understanding, one might point to the fact that the important work of Cavers, which appeared in 1965, has at the time of writing this footnote (1971) still not been reviewed in the columns of *Rabels Zeitschrift*.

84. Cf. Siehr's criticism (pp. 613 ff.) of Ehrenzweig, and the sharp criticism of the *Chaparral* decision by Lawrence Collins, ICLQ 1971, pp. 550 ff.

85. Cf. Reese, *op. cit,*, p. 187; Kegel, 112 RdC, 1964-II, p. 207; Siehr, pp. 595, 609 and 613.

supposition that he is capable of handling its individual rules flexibly, and not with inept rigidity.

Cavers's "result-selective approach" might show the way here. Cavers himself recently wrote:

> "The court's principal objective is to reach a result that is compatible with the reasonable expectations of the parties, actual or fairly imputed. The purposes and policies of the states' laws are, *ex hypothesi*, subordinate to that end."[86]

Cavers is one of the targets of the complaints of vagueness made by several of the above-mentioned critics, and doubtless not without reason. Yet he himself, as Heini has pointed out (pp. 277 and 280), has already taken steps to profit from advances in the field of comparative law. In a country in so commanding a position as the United States, with only 4% of the national product going into exports, as opposed to 40% in many European lands, there is understandably less incentive to get to grips with comparative law than on the other side of the North Atlantic. Nevertheless, the more a country and its legal science occupy a leading position in the world, the more, in the long run, it will have to realize that the recognition accorded internationally to the views of its publicists, and to the reasoning and decisions of its courts, depends on their persuasiveness. In consequence I venture to suggest that the Americans would do well to adopt the auxiliary technique of comparative law which we have commended, so as to remove the burden of uncertainty still weighing upon recent endeavours, and thereby promote the universally desired unification of international law, more particularly in the field of commerce.

The question of the desirable harmonization of judicial decisions in cases of international scope brings us to the third stage of the advance towards transnational commercial law. In view of the immense and intractable variety of legal situations which might arise in the course of international trade, there can of course be no question of achieving this goal through pure excogitation. Theoretical considerations cannot be ignored, however, if we are to view these situations from a consistent modern standpoint, and for that reason alone we have certain general observations to make on this third stage in the formation of transnational commercial law. But the time has not yet come to deal with the fundamental question of whether such law really exists. For that we shall first have to consider the practice, which is dealt with in Part Five of this work. At the moment we must regard transnational commercial law as little more than an inscription on a signpost: a signpost erected by the many decisions from various countries which have relegated the applicable-law question to second place, despite the priority accorded it by classical methodology, inasmuch as they have accepted the competence of arbitral

86. *Contemporary Conflicts Law*, p. 224.

bodies set up *ratione materiae* or by particular exchanges, and thus at the same time admitted the international trade-law practised in such fora.

One is tempted to say that twenty years are needed to progress from one stage to another. Around the year 1922 the Mixed Arbitral Tribunals came to grief over the task of developing a transnational commercial law; but 20 years later Lipstein, after a thorough inspection of the seven volumes of their decisions, demonstrated the presence in this case-law of two different trends, one firmly bent on the application of national law, the other in favour of a comparative approach.[87] A good 20 years further on it was recognized and plainly acknowledged that intensified law-comparison had led not only to the unification of various national substantive norms which had originally differed but also to the relegation of conflict-norms.[88]

Comparative law has now developed to the point where it can progress from a purely analytical comparison of laws, typified in the 1929 *Handwörterbuch,* to a synthetic kind which is not content to observe and analyse but handles national laws as the raw material from which, by a technique analogous to fusion, refining or distillation, the shared quintessence of both municipal systems is extracted, and is recognized and applied as something common. Comparative law has nowadays to be functional.[89]

87. Lipstein, "Conflict of laws before international tribunals", 27 *Transactions of the Grotius Society*, 1942, pp. 142 ff., at p. 151.

88. Zweigert/Drobnig, "Einheitliches Kaufgesetz und internationales Privatrecht", 29 *RabelsZ*, 1965, p. 148: "In principle, unified substantive norms supplant conflict-norms (whether unified or not)". This follows "from the material superiority of the unified substantive norm over every conflict-norm, even a unified one; this solution avoids a senseless periphrasis in conflicts-law and (in the case of non-unified conflict-norms) national differences in private international law". Cf. also Beitzke, "Betrachtungen zur Methodik im internationalen Privatrecht", *Festschrift Smend*, p. 22: "It is a peculiar paradox that the goal of a unified private international law can only be reached by means of a closer rapprochement to substantive laws, i.e., by means which render private international law partly redundant."

89. As plainly demanded by the American Wolfgang Friedmann, *Legal Theory*, 4th ed., London 1960, p. 23: "Only where there is an understanding on fundamentals can legal relations develop between nations ... But a comparison of codes, statutes, decisions may give a misleading impression of either affinity or diversity unless it is checked by a functional comparison. Legal systems may greatly differ in theory, and a particular legal institution of one system may be unknown to another. Thus English law does not recognise a general notion of unjust enrichment like all Continental systems; but it leads to largely similar results, through the application of equitable principles." The "normological" theory of the Spaniard Werner Goldschmidt tends in the same direction and has encountered the approval of the Frenchman Ernst Mezger (Goldschmiedt, "Die philosophischen Grundlagen des internationalen Privatrechts", *Festschrift für Martin Wolff*, Tübingen, 1952, pp. 203 ff., at p. 212; Mezger, review of Goldschmiedt's *Sistema y filosofía del derecho internacional privada*, Barcelona 1948, in 37 *Revue critique*, 1948, pp. 382 ff., at p. 384). In Germany the talk is of "adaptation"

The new task of comparative-law studies has barely been broached. But it must be made clear from the start that transnational commercial law denotes much rather a working-method than a new legal order, indeed it can be said here and now that it does not constitute a system of law, as continental jurists would prefer. As always happens, the new law accretes in the first place from the individual case: it is a case-law. Ernst Rabel, in his *Conflict of Laws* (2nd ed., I, p. 45) once used the expression "crystallization of law", and this is an apt image to describe the process that takes place in our third stage. Just as crystals form in a dish of sodium-solution, or frost-crystals on a windowpane, first in isolation then spreading together, so transnational commercial law will take shape with the help of the new method of work. As long ago as 1928 Franz Kahn foresaw this development when he wrote:

> "Generally speaking, we shall be able to regard our goal, the harmony of positive laws, as something attainable when the competing substantive norms stand in closer affinity." [90]

Before concluding this introduction, I would just like to mention two decisions as examples of the way it is no longer admissible to do things. First, the judgment of 3 April 1933 by the Supreme Judicial Court of Massachusetts, in a case concerning the enforcement of a hire-purchase agreement. The relevant laws of sale of Massachusetts and Pennsylvania differed in that one provided for an automatic lapse of days of grace whereas the other required explicit notices to be given. Instead of thoroughly examining the sense of both laws and coming to a joint decision, the judges were unable to agree on the applicable law, and the outcome was a judgment with dissenting opinion. It need hardly be said that such a judgment carries little conviction.

As our second example, let us take the judgment delivered by the French Court of Cassation on 15 May 1935. The question was whether the plaintiff, a Strasbourg pharmacist, could charge arrears of interest on a debt for goods

---

(*Anpassung*) or of "assimilation" (*Angleichung*) in the sense of likening or analogization (cf. the references in Kegel, 112 RdC, 1964-II, pp. 106 ff., and Soergel/Kegel, 10th ed., *vor Art.* 7, n. 71 ff.; also, for terminology, Jochen Schröder, *Die Anpassung von Kollisions- und Sachnormen*, Cologne 1961, p. 37; cf., further, Max Rheinstein, address to the annual general meeting of the German Society for Comparative Law, Regensburg, 24 September 1969).

90. Franz Kahn, "Über Inhalt, Natur und Methode des internationalen Privatrechts", *Abhandlungen* I, p. 316; cf. also, especially, Ernst Rabel, "Deutsches und amerikanisches Recht", *RabelsZ* 1951, pp. 341 and 358 ff.; W. Friedmann, *op. cit.*, p. 23; Walter Hallstein, "Rechtsangleichung in der EWG", *RabelsZ* 1964, p. 230; and more particularly Schlesinger/Gündisch, "Allgemeine Rechtsgrundsätze im Schiedsverfahren", 28 *RabelsZ*, 1964, p. 46: "The law must therefore be actualized and at the same time developed further by the practice of the courts and above all of the arbitral tribunals. Scholarship can and must help in this. New methods of law-comparison, which have been worked out in recent years, make it possible to explore, formulate and systematize the common elements existing in the contract-law of the leading industrial nations".

supplied some time before the outbreak of war in 1914. The legal position in France was different from that in Germany. The court gave judgment for the plaintiff, but in so tortuous a way that Niboyet, in a critical note on the judgment, described it as "somewhat sibylline". Here again the court, by going back to the common substratum of the French and German rules of limitation, could easily have found a simpler and more convincing basis for its judgment.

Nevertheless, it is our intention not to dwell upon the flaws in decisions of an earlier age, but to gather together, from selected realms of law, such decisions as are significant for the development of transnational commercial law. This we shall do in the remainder of this book.

To summarize, by transnational commercial law we mean the aggregation of all those rules which hold good in the same or a very similar way for a given concrete legal situation in two or more spheres of national jurisdiction. If the parties have explicitly or implicitly chosen transnational commercial law, or if it appears *prima facie* that transnational commercial law can apply, then the following, according to the new method, should be the sequence of judicial assessment:

First, the judge may take his own domestic law as the point of departure. At the same time, however, he must test the decision he would give under that law for compatibility with the foreign law. If it is so compatible, he applies his domestic law, but in so doing refers to its compatibility in order that his judgment may carry due conviction. Should the domestic law not appear compatible with the foreign law, the judge must endeavour to pinpoint the difference and to strike a balance, so long as it is possible to do so within the ambit of the non-mandatory rules of both laws concerned. A decision of this kind is not a decision in pursuance of the foreign law but remains a decision in pursuance of the domestic law, because it stays within the domain of the domestic non-mandatory rules. Only in certain cases, comparatively rare in commercial law, where considerations of domestic or foreign *ordre public* preclude a decision in accordance with transnational commercial law, is the judge compelled to make a choice of national law and to proceed accordingly.[91]

---

91. On the foregoing cf. p. 116, n. VII 2, of my *Kommentar zum Aussenwirtschafts-gesetz* and my article, "Some Thoughts about Transnational Commercial Law, for the use of judges and arbitrators", in Vol. III of the writings of the German section of the *Association des Auditeurs de l'Académie de La Haye*, ed. I. Seidl-Hohenveldern and H. Nagel, Baden-Baden, 1969, p. 31.

Part Two

THE LICENSING AGREEMENT

I. *The underlying concept*

The licensing agreement[1] affords a model illustration of the formation process of transnational commercial law. Although it plays an important role in all major industrialized societies, it has not been shaped by statutory regulation in any of them, but is the creation of practice, assisted by doctrine and jurisprudence. If, therefore, one were to adopt a classical approach and attach an international licensing agreement to a given national system of law, it would prove impossible to discover within that system any statutorily regulated type of contract to which the agreement could be assimilated in the usual convenient way; one would have to rely for help entirely on the findings of the local courts and publicists, and since these findings are equally determined in all countries by common facts of economics, the outcome must be the same or very similar in all countries. In the domain of economics, there is only ever one just way of dealing with a given legal situation, in whatever territory that situation materializes, or, to put it more cautiously, the area in which the just solution may be found is always extremely circumscribed. That this is so can be demonstrated with particular clarity in the case of licensing agreements, for judicial decisions from the most widely different countries are, in this field, practically interchangeable. Even when a court is unable to reach its decision by the sole construction of the agreement and is compelled to fall back on the general principles of its national law, these principles, almost without exception, are so universal as to be common to all national systems. It is thus exceptional for an international licensing agreement to embody rules of distinctly national, e.g. mandatory law. Normally,

1. *Bibliography*:
Aeberhard, *Rechtsnatur und Ausgestaltung der Patentlizenz im deutschen, französischen und schweizerischen Recht*, Berne 1952.
Von Beringe, "Lizenzverträge mit dem Ausland", *Der Betrieb,* Beilage 8/1957.
Brumbaugh, "Choice-of-law provisions in licensing contracts", in Reese (ed.), *International Contracts, Choice of Law and Language*, New York 1962.
Chavanne, "Brevet d'invention", *Répertoire Dalloz de droit commercial*, Paris 1956.
Corpus Juris Secundum (CJS), Vol. 69, pp. 763-835, Brooklyn N.J. 1951.

nowadays, it will feature a preponderance of rules which are already part of transnational commercial law. What this means will be clarified below.

First evidence of the transnational character of licensing agreements is to be seen in the fact that the term used to denote this type of contract preserves the same root in all the major trading languages—a remarkable fact considering how seldom this is so in the case of other types. Etymologically this uniform term derives from the Latin *licere*, to allow or to permit, which renders in a nutshell the essential characteristic of licensing agreements. This characteristic leads a transnational existence.

It is not, however, in itself sufficient to enable a judge to rule: this contract is a licensing agreement. Far from it, for even in the most recent German and French decisions stress has been laid on the fact that in this particular field it is the agreement itself which forms the law of the parties.

Nevertheless, *falsa demonstratio non nocet* is a valid maxim of transnational commercial law even for international licensing agreements. Accordingly a French decision in respect of a contract signed in Turin between French and Italian parties accepted it as a licensing agreement despite certain formal defects.[2]

Though it is not at present possible to define the strict limits of "the licensing agreement" as a type of contract, it has one constant feature which is evident from the start: it is a contract concerning use and never a contract for the assignment of the subject-matter. In the case of non-international agreements this distinction may for various reasons be very important—e.g., in patent-infringement suits instituted by the licensee in countries not granting

---

Demein, *Le Contrat de know-how*, Brussels 1968.

Durand, "Le 'know-how' ", *Jurisclasseur Périodique* 1967, No. 2078.

Ellis, *Patent Licenses*, New York 1958.

Langen, *Internationale Lizenzverträge*, 2nd edn, Weinheim 1958.

Lichtenstein, *Die Patentlizenz nach amerikanischem Recht*, Tübingen 1965.

Lüdecke/Fischer, *Lizenzverträge*, Weinheim 1957.

Mathély/Plaisant, "Brevets d'invention – La licence des brevets", *Jurisclasseur commercial*, fasc. XXIV, Paris 1957.

Meinhardt, "Conflict-avoidance in the law of patents and trademarks", 21 *Law and Contemporary Problems*, 1965, pp. 563 ff.

Plaisant, "Les inventions non brevetées", *Jurisclasseur commercial*, fasc. III bis, 1966.

Pollzien/Bronfen, *International Licensing Agreements*, Indianapolis/New York 1965 (2nd edn, Pollzien/Langen, printing).

Stumpf, *Der Lizenzvertrag*, 4th edn, Frankfurt am Main 1968.

Timberg, "International patent-licensing and national anti-trust law", 43 *Journal Pat. Off. Soc.*, 1961, pp. 171 ff.

Troller, *Das internationale Privat- und Zivilprozessrecht im gewerblichen Rechtsschutz und Urheberrecht*, Basle 1952.

Troller, "Internationale Lizenzverträge", GRUR *Ausland*, 1952, pp. 108 ff.

2. *Tribunal civil de la Seine*, 18 June 1955, (*S. à r.l. Usines Calox* v. *S.A. Mécanoplastiques*), *Ann. propr. ind.* 1956, p. 7.

mere licensees such an action.[3] The same question can arise in other connections, for example in relation to tax-assessment.[4] In the case of international licensing agreements, however, the problem, as we will show, may not be so serious, as far as the licensee's right of legal action is concerned.

As the licensee provides a consideration in return for his right of use, the right of use must possess for him a commensurate economic value. In the case of non-international agreements, the bounds of this value are obviously set by the national law valid for either party, including the accepted legal doctrine of the land. But in the case of international contracts there is no such boundary. This means that a balance has somehow to be struck between the so-called "waiver" doctrine of some countries (USA, France) and the "splinter" (*Abspaltung*) doctrine developed in others (e.g., Germany and Switzerland). This can be done if it be kept in mind that in every case of an international agreement the licensor has an obligation, in transnational law, and even if the waiver doctrine obtains in his own country, to afford the licensee every assistance in the exercise of the right of use he has sold him, at least to the extent that the assistance does not cost him anything. To decide otherwise would be to offend against one of the supreme principles of transnational commercial law, namely that the decision may not be unreasonable.

Thus it is only at the level of comparative law that an irreducible antinomy exists between the two doctrines, either of which any given national system is free to espouse. This choice is irrelevant for international contractual practice and transnational commercial law. For them, the premises of the national laws concerned, however contrasted they may be, are overshadowed by the agreement itself. It is a rule of transnational commercial law that if the licensor's waiver has no economic value, or none commensurate with his fee, he has also to provide something positive, the extent and details of which result from the interpretation of the contract and, in particular, the nature of the performance undertaken in return. The purely doctrinal considerations of national legal orders must yield in transnational commercial law to the principle that decisions may not be unreasonable.

This rule, without being stated so explicitly, has already acted as *ratio decidendi* in a number of important cases. The courts have constantly interpreted international licensing agreements, as also national agreements, in such a way that the signatories received their appropriate share of benefits regardless of any conceptual constructions. Thus for example an English judge, affording an English licensee protection vis-à-vis American claims, explained:

---

3. Cf. in USA the leading decision of 2 February 1891 in *Waterman* v. *Mackenzie*, US 138, p. 252, and more recently *Western Electric* v. *Pa-Cent Reproducer*, 42 F. 2d., p. 116; for France, see the detailed presentation of Mathély/Plaisant in *Juris-Classeur commercial*, Ann. "Brevets d'invention", Fasc. XXIV, No. 43, with copious case-references.
4. Cf. *Conseil d'Etat*, 14 April 1956 (req. 1544); J.C.P. 56, ed. C.I. No. 58204.

"Now an English patent is a species of English property of the nature of a chose in action and peculiar in character. By English law it confers certain monopoly rights, exercisable in England, upon its proprietor. A person who has an enforceable right to a licence under an English patent appears therefore to me to have at least some kind of proprietary interest which it is the duty of our courts to protect."[5]

Much earlier, a court had even applied the law governing the sale of goods in order to reach an equitable decision in a licensing case.[6] Another, far more recent German decision spoke of the *"quasi-dinglich"* nature of a licence right.[7] Decisions of this kind show that in the international field doctrinal considerations must give way before the necessity of avoiding an unreasonable decision at all costs. We shall return to certain detailed aspects of such cases in other connections below.

It should further be considered a transnational rule that international licensing agreements are synallagmatic, i.e. mutually binding. The existence of this principle in the practice of German courts needs no special demonstration. French practice also is characterized by a forthright *a priori* assumption that the relationship of the parties is synallagmatic.[8] In the USA, where the term synallagmatic is less frequently employed than on the continent of Europe, the judge does, it is true, test each case to see whether reciprocity is present according to the meaning of the contract or by explicit agreement; however, in most instances he ends by assuming that it is, and in this the rule of reasonableness plays no small part.[9] To tread warily, as it beseems, let us put the position of American case-law no higher than this: that in regard to international licensing agreements a presumption of reciprocity of obligations exists.

Reciprocity, however, does not necessarily mean that the obligations must also be in equilibrium. That much must be conceded Lichtenstein (p. 94). There is no immediate correlation between a finding that obligations are mutual and a finding that they are evenly balanced. Viewed entirely in the limited context of the special American doctrine of consideration, there is nothing to object to in Lichtenstein's relying on an American decision in the following terms (p. 747):

5. *British Nylon Spinners* v. *I.C.I.,* 13 August 1952, Reports of Patent, Design and Trade Mark Cases, Vol. 69, p. 294.

6. *A.G. für Cartonnagenindustrie* v. *Temler,* 10 November 1900, Reports of Patent Cases, 1901, p. 14.

7. Düsseldorf *Oberlandesgericht,* 4 August 1961, AWD 1961, p. 295.

8. Chavanne, No. 279; Mathély/Plaisant No. 1; Fernand-Jacq in notes to *Ann. propr. ind.* 1926, p. 356, and 1934, p. 37 (with case-law).

9. *Rosenthal Paper* v. *National Folding Box,* 20 May 1919, 123 N.E. Reporter, pp. 766 ff., at p. 768.

"It is not for the courts to control the amount of consideration in contracts. The parties must agree upon that."[10]

If one confines oneself to the comparison of national legal orders, the notion of evenly-balanced obligations at first appears unsuitable for transnational commercial law. Lüderitz has expounded the antithesis of German and American thinking hereon with particular lucidity.[11]

In practice, however, as we here observe for a second time, antitheses of national laws lose their raison d'être on the supranational plane. Even at the national level in American law, the balance of obligations is by no means an insignificant factor, only it is not with the aid of the obsolescent doctrine of consideration that it is brought into play, but with the aid of a principle which is actually a cardinal feature of transnational law too, namely the principle of reasonableness or also of good faith. One decision, in particular, may be cited in this respect.[12]

According to another, it would be unreasonable to assume that the licensee intended to pay the fee for an exclusive licence for the agreed five years if he did not have the licence throughout that period.[13] In yet another decision the court pronounced in favour of the tacit acceptance of a duty to exploit, inasmuch as the licence fee was payable exclusively out of the proceeds from the patent licensed. This was founded on the principle of good faith, with reference to copious case-law.[14]

It can therefore be regarded as a transnational rule for licensing agreements that, though a court does not have to ensure an absolute equilibrium of obligations, there must not be any gross imbalance. Not to admit even so cautious a formulation would be to abandon international dealings in licences to lawlessness and uncertainty.

II. *The subject-matter of the agreement*

It is common ground to all national systems of law that the subject-matter of the right of use conferred by a licensing agreement can never be something tangible, but can be an industrial patent, or an invention in respect of which a patent has been applied for; it can also be an invention which it is not

10. *Cook Pottery*, 9 December 1921; 89 W Va, p. 7; 109 SE, p. 747.

11. *Auslegung von Rechtsgeschäften*, Karlsruhe 1966, pp. 83 ff.

12. *Frost Ry. Supply Co. v. T.H. Symington and Son*, 11 July 1938, 24 F. Supp., pp. 20 ff., at p. 27.

13. *Rosenthal Paper*, 20 May 1919, 123 NE, p. 768.

14. *Mechanical Ice-Tray Corp. v. General Motors Corp.*, 26 August 1944, 144 F. 2d., pp. 720 ff., at p. 725.

intended to register or publicize—indeed it may be a mere trade-secret which does not even rank as an invention.[15]

In practice, moreover, certain vague imponderables are sometimes treated as licensable assets. It would however not be feasible to allow such latitude in the transnational field. "Know-how", for example, may be regarded as licensable—at least, for so long as it is exclusive. [16]

It is the sense and purpose of a "know-how" licence which here provide the crucial test. This explains why, in certain circumstances, an export-prohibition can be inferred from the agreement.[17] In any case, the applicability of the law of patent-licences to such contracts[18] has been challenged even at national level, on the ground that their subject-matter is essentially different.[19] On the transnational plane that challenge must surely be upheld.

Neither is it possible, for purposes of transnational law, to relate licence-law to the law of leasehold, if only because the latter is by nature very closely connected with the specific national law of land-tenure. Even in countries where the association of licence and lease law has been a recurrent theme, there is now an increasing tendency to regard the licensing agreement as a contract *sui generis*.[20] More particularly, the outdated notion of the licensee as comparable to a lessee has been responsible in no small measure for the difficulties arising in infringement suits. On the transnational plane, there can be no doubt that the proper course is to treat the licensing agreement as a type of contract in its own right.

The rules to which applications for patents must be subject in transnational law are not hard to determine, for in this respect the major national laws agree. They all begin by seeking to ascertain the intention of the parties: was it merely to license the invention regardless of whether a patent was granted or not; or was the acquisition of a patent by the invention a *conditio sine qua non*; or was the subject-matter to comprise, in addition to an awaited patent, certain inventions or technical knowledge not yet ready for patenting or inten-

15. Cf. Paul Demein, *Le Contrat de Know-how*, Brussels 1968, with further references.

16. On this point in general, see the American decisions of 23 January 1929 (*Monsanto*), p. 191; 16 November 1959 (*Warner-Lambert*); 8 January 1963 (Opinion of Comptroller General); 14 June 1960 (*Invengineering*); 22 June 1959 (*Henry J. Kaiser*); 20 June 1963 (*Great Lakes Carbon*); 12 March 1958 (*Hyde*) and 4 June 1958 (*Hyde*); also Cass. 13 July 1966 (*Société Almes*); *Reichsgericht* 12 April 1913.

17. Cf. the American decision of 12 July 1957 concerning the export of Bofors guns by the US Government.

18. *Sic* Mathély/de Guardia; see Langen, p. 154.

19. Extensively treated in Langen, *Kommentar zum Kartellgesetz*, § 21.

20. Cf. German *Reichsgericht* 29 April 1931, *Markenschutz und Wettbewerb* 1931, p. 441, with further references; French decision in *Virgilio* v. *Mohr, Ann. propr. ind.* 1926, p. 353, with annotation by Fernand-Jacq.

tionally not patented? Under German, American and French law the agreement remains valid in the first event, no matter what becomes of the patent-application; in the second, it loses the basis of its validity if no grant of patent results from the application; in the third case it only remains valid if, in the event of the expected patent not being granted, the residue of the subject-matter would be sufficiently substantial to stand by itself.[21]

Though the remaining area of agreements not linked with any patent includes numerous and significant contracts of an international kind, the whole of it will for the time being have to be regarded as barren ground for developing transnational law, as the national conditions in this area are insufficiently comparable. Quite apart from these national differences and, at present, very great uncertainties, recent developments in international agreements on undivulged inventions, know-how and industrial research have been a sitting target for criticism from the viewpoint of anti-trust legislation and the establishment of norms of private law outside State jurisdiction.[22] The distinguished expositions of domestic law by Durand and Plaisant (France) or Blanco-White and Turner (England) shed no light for present purposes; neither do such supreme-court decisions as that of the German *Bundesgerichtshof*, GRUR 1960 (p. 44) or that delivered by the French Court of Cassation on 13 July 1966 in a case concerning an Italo-French licensing agreement on plastic buttons.[23] All these serve rather to illustrate the uncertainty which prevails even within the national legal orders. The same must be said of the American decisions cited by Lichtenstein (p. 115). A certain tendency to exercise caution over agreements concerning inventions—e.g., to confine them within as narrow bounds as possible—has long been a noticeable feature of American tribunals.[24]

21. Cf. Germany: *Bundesgerichtshof* 26 November 1954, GRUR 1955, p. 338, older case-law in Lüdecke/Fischer, C 64, n. 367; USA: *Burton* v. *Burton Stock-Car Co.*, 22 June 1898, 50 NE, p. 1029; France: Cass. 26 January 1955 (*Cheffrais*), *Ann. propr. ind.* 1956, p. 1.

22 Cf. in particular Kronstein, *Das Recht der internationalen Kartelle*, with further references; and my *Kommentar zum Kartellgesetz*, 4th ed, *ad* § 21.

23. *Société Almes* v. *Société Dita Bottonificio Fossanese, Juris-Classeur périodique, La Semaine juridique* 1967, 15131.

24. Cf. esp. *Monsanto Chemical Works* v. *Jaeger*, 23 January 1929, 31 F. 2d., pp. 188 ff., quoting on p. 191 the famous words of older decisions: "A naked assignment, or agreement to assign, in gross, a man's future labors as an author or inventor—in other words, a mortgage on a man's brain, to bind all his future products—does not address itself favorably to our consideration" and "The law does not look with special favor on such covenants." In the *Krell* v. *Bovaird Supply Co.* decision of 20 April 1936, 83 F. 2d., p. 414, the limits of the inventor's obligation of further development were narrowly circumscribed in his favour, on the basis of the text of the licensing agreement. A similar delineation was effected in the licensee's favour in *Krantz* v. *van Dette* on 5 September 1958, 165 F. 2d., p. 776.

The question as to what constitutes the subject-matter of agreements concerning an invention for which a patent is later sought has been answered by Lord Denning in a way which may also be significant for the purposes of transnational law. It had been decided in two lower courts that the scope of the invention covered by the licence was determined by the content of the applications for patent, notwithstanding the undisputed fact that these applications went beyond the scope of the actual invention disclosed. But these had been unknown to the licensee at the time of conclusion of the agreement. This gave Lord Denning the ground of his judgment, according to which it was the scope of the invention disclosed which was decisive, and not the wider scope of the applications:

> "The licensees must pay royalties on that which was disclosed to them. It would be absurd to hold that the licensees were to be bound by applications to the Patent Office which they never saw and which they had no right to see, which were far wider than this invention which was disclosed. It seems to me that Fluflon Ltd. by their conduct set the limits to the invention themselves. If these applications do form part of the processes and apparatus covered by the licence, they ought to have disclosed them and they did not. By their own conduct they have shown what is the ambit of the invention. It is not the patent application but the invention which they have disclosed."[25]

In the great majority of cases it is not just one patent but several which are the subject-matter of the agreement, not infrequently in combination with the licensing of secrets.[26] The most essential question arising here is that of the ending of the contract; this will be dealt with later. If a patent is licensed simultaneously for several countries, it is evidently advisable to assume that the agreement is governed by a uniform law.[27]

As all patent laws are unanimous herein, it is undoubtedly a rule of transnational law that, in the absence of any evidence to the contrary, a patent-licence encompasses the whole of the patent, i.e., that it covers the rights of production, use and marketing. For the same reason it is a transnational rule that the licence may embody restrictions, whether by withholding from the licensee one or other of the three rights mentioned or by imposing on all three, in the same or in differing degree, limitations of time, place, application or whatever. Hence it may even make price-stipulations or forbid the licensee to export.

25. *Fluflon Ltd.* v. *William Frost & Sons Ltd.* 11 May 1965, Reports of Patent Cases 1965, pp. 562 ff., at p. 579.

26. Cf. Troller, GRUR *Ausl.* 1952, p. 17, and Terrell/Shelly, 9th ed., p. 257.

27. Munich *Oberlandesgericht*, 29 January 1959 (*Le Mans motor-racing*); Düsseldorf *Landgericht*, 18 March 1958.

However, the most recent legal developments in the leading countries in the field have shown how the freedom of contract in the domain of licensing agreements is open to abuse, notably where the aim of placing restrictions on the licensee or on the exchange of licences is rather to regulate the market than to protect inventors' rights. Thus in most countries agreements covering patents are subject to certain anti-trust prohibitions or to legislation against restrictive practices. The United States, as it happens, has gone farther than Germany towards a doctrine of misuse of patent.[28] Territorial restrictions, especially prohibitions to export, may also be ruled invalid as against the public interest.[29] Here the formation of transnational law comes up against peremptory norms of national or supranational law.

There are really no special rules for the interpretation of licensing agreements, apart from the undoubtedly transnational principle that a court may presume the validity of a patent within the ambit of its claims.[30] The general law of contracts thus holds good for this interpretation. In England it has been said of licensing agreements in particular that tacit understandings should not be presumed without subjecting the substance of the contract to a reasonable and businesslike appraisal.[31] This certainly accords with the conception prevalent elsewhere. In one case the *Kammergericht*, in order to verify its interpretation of an agreement, went back to an older contract existing between the parties, because the more recent instrument was fully comprehensible only when read with it.[32]

Also taken into account in transnational law is slackness in defence of one's rights. In German law this may incur forfeiture, and the analogous doctrine of laches was applied in an American decision which found against the plaintiff on the ground that he only raised his objections when the licensing agreement had run for ten years.[33]

III. The form of licensing agreements

There can be no doubt that, to satisfy transnational law, international licensing agreements must take written form. In view of the facts it is scarcely

28. Cf. D. Maier, "Patentmissbrauch durch Lizenzgebühren nach Ablauf des Patents", GRUR *Ausl.* 1965, p. 406.

29. Cf. esp. Finger, NJW 1968, p. 2178, with further references on the law of the European Economic Community.

30. *Eastern States Petroleum*, 14 May 1938, 2 Atlantic 2d, p. 138; *Ball-and-Socket Fastener*, 27 October 1893, 58 F., p. 818.

31. Terrell/Shelly, 10th ed., pp. 230-232, with case-law.

32. 8 May 1935, GRUR 1935, p. 892.

33. *Violet Virginia Kohagen Boris* v. *Hamilton Manufacturing Co.*, 27 March 1958, 253 F. 2d., p. 526.

necessary to justify this rule. The very fact that two different languages are as often as not involved in such agreements is enough to preclude viewing any suggestion of an unwritten contract as anything but frivolous. Some allusion to this point was made in a French decision already cited.[34] In the international business world the enshrining of licensing agreements in written documents is a universal practice, and one on which transnational law may safely rely. In comparison with this universality, it is irrelevant that the great majority of national systems allow in principle a free choice of form for licensing agreements. They do not prescribe but merely guarantee such freedom of choice, and permit parties to opt for stricter arrangements. Hence it is on the common accord of parties that the written form for international licensing agreements rests. It is that common accord which makes the norm.

The normal written form is that of a contract with the signatures of both parties apposed to the same document. Under transnational law, a mere exchange of letters, though not an infrequent phenomenon, cannot be regarded as equivalent. The opposite opinion occasionally encountered in judicial decisions is always founded on special circumstances, and more especially on precedents for the solemn character of such exchanges in the previous relations of the parties.[35]

As the normal written form is in national, and *a fortiori* in transnational law a matter of common accord and not of legal prescription, the onus of proving that in a given case both parties knowingly departed from the usual practice lies on the party wishing to rely on that point. Conversely, evidence to this effect must be entertained. There is no statutory presumption, and to that extent the position in transnational law is the same as that laid down in 150 of the German Civil Code.

In considering any understandings reached prior to the conclusion of the agreement, the general rules of transnational law apply: If the text of the agreement is clear and unambiguous, it must be presumed that the agreement itself contains absolutely everything agreed. Any party urging the contrary

34. *Usines Calox* v. *Mécano-plastiques*, 18 June 1955, *Ann. propr. ind.* 1956, p. 8; concerning a licensing agreement concluded in Turin between French and Italian parties but couched only in an exchange of letters; although the court noted certain irregularities of form, the agreement was recognized—as a cession—after it had already been registered.

35. Cf. *Usines Calox (ut supra)* and *British Nylon Spinners* v. *I.C.I.*, 16 October 1952, Patent Reports 69, pp. 288 ff., at p. 292. In the latter case the licensor had imparted certain modifications by a letter of 5 March 1947 which expressly alluded to the speedy conclusion of an agreement; instead, however, the parties had developed their business-relationship on the basis of the letter itself. In the American decision of 25 June 1928 in *Horvath* v. *McCord Radiator*, 27 F. 2d., p. 148, the court very properly observed that the significance of tentative understandings prior to the conclusion of an agreement depends on each individual case. That is universally valid.

must prove it.[36] If, however, the text is not clear and unambiguous, alleged sub-agreements may play a part in the interpretation of the agreement which then becomes requisite. A party invoking a sub-agreement must prove its existence, and evidence to that effect may only be refused if the contract states that no sub-agreements were concluded.

With regard to the modification of agreements, most systems of law allow a free choice of form even when the agreement itself has been concluded in written form. The parties' joint choice of written form is deemed to extend no further than the conclusion of the agreement. This rule, however, subsists only on the national plane. In the internaional field the same is valid for modifications of or additions to agreements as for the conclusion of agreements in general: the written form is the norm. Evidence to the contrary can likewise be entertained in respect of modifications or additions, provided however that the parties have not decided together—which they do as a rule—that such modifications or additions must be clothed in written form.

IV.   Duties of the licensor

At the beginning of this Part we pointed out that the antitheses between the national doctrines of waiver, on the one hand, and "splinter" theories, on the other, are necessarily resolved in the international field, thanks to the preeminent transnational principle of good faith. Quite special reliance is constantly placed on this principle by the English courts, in regard to both international and national agreements, and to the obligations of the licensor no less than of the licensee. [37] The principle of good faith certainly implies that the licensor should be held under obligation to deliver to the licensee what the latter pays for. Only in very exceptional cases, which have moreover been challenged on grounds of public policy ("blocking" patents), is the subject-matter of a licensing agreement a mere patent in isolation from a related invention. Only in such rare cases are the parties solely concerned with the protective effect of the patent, remaining indifferent to the invention. As a rule the situation is different. The economic value of the licence lies in the invention, the patent being a welcome extra whereby the invention is more closely defined, and assured, within that definition, of statutory protection. From the relationship of the rule and the exception the following tenet of transnational law emerges: An onus of proof lies on anyone who maintains that the scope of a given patent-licence is limited to the waiver of the right of

36. *RCA* v. *Cabel Radio*, 29 August 1933, 266 F. 2d., p. 778, with further references.

37. Instances of application with regard to the licensor, e.g.: *British Nylon Spinners* (*ut supra*); *Patchett* v. *Sterling Engineering*, 22 October 1953, Patent Reports 70, p. 269.

restraint implicit in the patent; in the absence of proof to that effect, it is to be presumed that in addition to the above waiver the parties intended from the outset to agree upon something more, e.g. the attribution of positive duties to the licensor.

The connection between patents and inventions has been emphasized by the French courts, more especially in cases concerning the liquidation of matters arising between licensor and licensee on account of the nullity of the patent.[38] The strict waiver-doctrine professed in the United States and underlined in comparative research is a merely platonic obstacle to the view here put forward, because there has so far not been one American decision on an international case featuring facts of this kind. In international cases, therefore, before presupposing, by reference to this doctrine, that the range of the licensor's obligations is very small, one should pay heed to the above tenet of transnational law and give close attention to the merits of the case.

Not a few licensing agreements comprise special obligations for the licensor over and above his general duty to place the licensee in the promised position.[39] As a rule such obligations must be expressly agreed and may not be assumed as implicitly incorporated in the contract. On the other hand, in the case of international agreements the transnational principle of good faith must be viewed as considerably more effective than when both parties to the contract which is to be appraised are together in a single country where the waiver doctrine is traditional. The converse is also true. When a party from a country where the "splinter" doctrine prevails (Germany, for example) is dealing with another party from a waiver background, he must considerably lower his expectations as to the range of the licensor's obligations.

What, in any case, does the licensor have to warrant, under what conditions and to what extent? These questions, in accordance with our premises, can be answered in terms of transnational law without harking back to national law,[40] and (just as in contracts for the sale of goods—see Part Three below) are entirely separate from any question of *culpa in contrahendo*.

It is expedient to divide the warranty requirements into three degrees: those appertaining to the licensing of an invention only, those appropriate when an application for patent is also included in the subject-matter, and those to do with the licensing of patents. The fact that the licensor must

38. Cass. 6 November 1957, *Exhenry* v. *Sté Fridor, Ann. prop. ind.* 1958, p. 169; Paris 29 January 1963, *Audibert* v. *Machines Havas,Ann. prop. ind.* 1963, pp. 361 ff., at p. 371; *Tribunal civil de la Seine*, 30 June 1953, *Gazette du Palais* 1953, *Sommaire* No. 15.

39. For example the obligation to deliver a prototype, as in the above-mentioned *Audibert* case, or very far-reaching obligations to deliver plans or train staff or even to fit out a complete factory, as in the *Mouriaque* case, Paris, 19 December 1929, *Ann. prop. ind.* 1930, p. 143.

40. Cf. *Bundesgerichtshof*, 1 December 1964, NJW 1965, p. 759, GRUR 1965, p. 298, with further references.

warrant the novelty of the licensed invention forms the very basis of the transaction and is, therefore, a matter of course.

In what condition does a licensor warrant a new invention to be? This question bulks large in the jurisprudence of all countries. There is general agreement among courts that the invention must be technically feasible, but not necessarily an immediate economic proposition. The applicable standards of technical serviceability will of course be more stringent in the case, say, of a costly mechanism designed to improve traffic-safety than in that of a pocket umbrella.[41] Here French is at one with German case-law,[42] and the same rule holds good in English and American law.[43] The economic viability of the invention is normally not guaranteed.[44]

These rules applicable to all licensing of inventions are unaffected by the consideration whether an application for a patent also forms part of the subject-matter of the agreement.[45] The proviso indicated with reference to American law by Lichtenstein (p. 121), to the effect that a sufficiently clear description of the invention is a prerequisite of a licensing agreement concerning an invention for which a patent has been sought, will, in accordance with general principles, also apply in all other laws.

When a patent forms the subject-matter of the licence, it is generally agreed that the licensor must, in the first place, stand surety for his own title to dispose of it.[46]

It is tempting to assume, in the case of such a licence, that, as a rule, the licensor guarantees the legal soundness of the patent. However, if we examine judicial practice in all the major countries concerned, we shall see that this would be an overhasty conclusion. From the 1886 American *Pope* judgment down to the *Isolatoren* decision of the *Reichsgericht* in 1936 there runs an

41. *Reichsgericht* 1 March 1911 (uncoupling apparatus), 75 RGZ, p. 400, and 13 April 1918 (pocket umbrella), LZ 1918, col. 1216. German case-law has remained consistent: cf. e.g. *Reichsgericht* 29 April 1931 (cast iron), *Markenschutz und Wettbewerb* 1931, p. 441, and *Bundesgerichtshof*, 1 December 1964 (reaction-meter), NJW 1965, p. 759.

42. Cf. Cass. 29 June 1933; *Tribunal civil de la Seine*, 30 June 1953.

43. Cf. the American decision of 10 October 1918 (*Bird's Eye*), 259 F., p. 266.

44. Cf., for French law: Paris 16 March 1963, and *Tribunal civil Ribérac* 19 March 1936; for German law: *Bundesgerichtshof* 26 November 1954 (spectacle-lenses), GRUR 1955, p. 340.

45. Cf. in Germany the above-mentioned "spectacle-lens" decision, and in the USA *Burton* v. *Burton Stock-Car*, 22 June 1898, 50 NE, p. 1029.

46. Cf., in USA, 65 NY Eq., p. 138; 55 Atlantic, pp. 401 ff., at p. 407; also headnote 4 of *Krantz* v. *van Dette*, 5 September 1958, 165 F. Sup., p. 778: "Where licensor did not disclose to licensees, when he licensed nine applications for patents on storm windows, that he had sold prior applications for patents relating to storm windows to licensees' competitor or that he had assigned to competitor all improvements which he might make on windows, licensor was not entitled to collect royalty from licensees on any of disclosures contained in patents which were later issued on prior applications."

unbroken chain of cases in which what mattered to the parties was whether a patent actually existed, while it was not absolutely necessary for it to be good in law. The crucial point was its bare existence, for that mere fact had a certain effect—and one useful to the licensee.[47] The situation in another case, decided in England, underlines the need for caution. The court remarked:

> "It is one thing for both parties to agree to perform the Agreement forthwith on the understanding or assumption that the Patent is sound; it is quite another that one party should guarantee that it is."[48]

To these examples we would add a French decision in which it was doubtful what had been stated with reference to a guarantee.[49] In view of this state of affairs in judicial practice, it can scarcely be made a rule of transnational law that the licensor guarantees the legal soundness of the licensed patent. Instead, each case will have to be considered on its own merits. However, Lichtenstein (p. 139) rightly draws attention to the fact, fraught with practical consequences, that American law presumes the soundness of a patent and places the onus of proof of the contrary on the challenger.

If it is not a rule of transnational law that the licensor necessarily guarantees the legal soundness of the licensed patent, how much less can he be expected to guarantee the continuance of its legal validity. This point has been consistently made in American case-law.[50] In Germany it is maintained that the licensor must even guarantee the licensee against seeing his rights of exploitation wholly or partly negated by the rights of third parties.[51] It follows that one can only speak of a transnational rule in this matter when the same conception prevails in both of the laws to which a given licensing agreement could be related.

In a French decision we find something similar to the German position. The key-sentence runs:

> "The guarantee to be afforded the licensee by the patent-holder covers no more than the possibility of exploitation and the undisturbed enjoyment of the licence granted."[52]

---

47. *Pope Manufacturing Co.* v. *Owsley*, 1886, 27 F., p. 100; *Reichsgericht* 15 February 1936 (insulators—*Isolatoren*): "Even a patent covering a useless and impracticable invention can, for so long as it exists and is recognized, bring business advantages to the proprietor or licensee." Stumpf (p. 137, n. 321) does not find this decision convincing.

48. *Suhr* v. *Crofts*, 20 April 1932, Patent Reports 49, p. 366.

49. Paris 16 March 1963 (*Consorts Outhier*).

50. Cf. *Pope Manufacturing* (*ut supra*) and another American decision, 27 July 1943 (*ENO*).

51. Stumpf, p. 148; the decision cited by Stumpf in this connection, Hamburg *Oberlandesgericht* 17 June 1913, OLGE 34, 32, refers however not to a licensing agreement but to the hire of a telephone installation.

52. Cass. 16 July 1957.

However, it is not certain that this dictum was intended as a generalization. For the rest, the reader is referred to the section on the upkeep and defence of the patent, below.

With regard to the licensor's right himself to continue using what is licensed, or even to produce and market goods in his own country on the basis thereof, there is no definite transnational rule except in the case of a non-exclusive licence, by which term, or its equivalent in all countries, is meant an agreement the sense of which is not to disentitle the licensor. Opinions are however divided in relation to exclusive licences, so that one can at most say that transnational law obtains when the two national laws concerned are at one on the matter. Even so, the preponderance of opinion leans to the conclusion that when an exclusive licence is granted, the licensor must refrain from further use of what is licensed. [53]

With regard to the transferability of claims arising out of licensing agreements, a distinction must be made according to whether it is the licensor or the licensee who wishes to assign his rights. *A priori*, transnational law will more readily admit the transferability of the licensor's claims than a change of licensee, for the former concerns a money transaction, whereas the latter involves essentially more delicate relationships. A change of licensor does not unduly disturb the licensee in favourable circumstances: i.e., if it is for him a matter of indifference to whom he pays royalty and if his position is otherwise wholly or essentially unaffected by the change. It is highly doubtful, however, whether such a situation can be regarded as the norm. As a rule, considerations of a technical nature, or to do with marketing policy, are also material where licensing agreements are concerned. It follows that the transnational rule must be to the effect that, in the event of the assignment of the licence, the licensee has a right of protest and that it is the licensor who has the onus of proving the protest unfounded. [54] In every country, cases where

53. *Sic*, in USA, the decisions of 5 January 1905, 136 F., p. 600, and 28 June 1901, 110 F., p. 26. For France and Germany, see Stumpf, p. 340; for the less plainly expressed English view, see *Martin Baker Aircraft* v. *Canadian Flight Equipment*, 10 June 1955, Patent Reports 72, pp. 236 ff., at p. 246.

54. *Sic* the *American Rosenthal Paper* v. *National Folding Box* decision of 20 May 1919, 23 NE, p. 766, which hinges on whether the agreement is not of a special personal kind; the English decision of 7 July 1936 in *National Carbonising* v. *British Coal Distillation* disallowed assignment by the liquidator of the licensor. The decision given by the German Patent Office on 15 March 1954 (GRUR 1954, p. 286) dealt with an interesting special case: In July 1939 the parent American IBM Corporation, having regard to the German currency laws, transferred to its German subsidiary, which had been its licensee since 1910, the corresponding German patents. After the war the subsidiary company, reying on Law No.8 of the Board of Control, applied for an extension of the patents, which had meantime expired. This was refused, on account of the transfer effected in 1939. The decision said: "It is not possible to concur with the Applicant's argument that, despite a transfer of title, it has a claim under Article 5 of Law No. 8, because the

a licensed patent is assigned to a third party without mention of the licensing agreement give rise to great difficulties. The legal position here is simple, and the applicability of transnational law may be assumed when the national laws involved treat the process, in like fashion, as an assignment merely of claims *inter partes*. To the assignment of claims, transnational law applies the Roman maxim: *nemo plus iuris transferre potest quam ipse habet*. It follows that even when the acquirer of a patent has no knowledge of the licensing agreement, he cannot obtain anything more than the assignor himself possessed, i.e. a patent which is inseparably encumbered with a licensing agreement. In this respect there is no difference between an exclusive and a non-exclusive licence.

If the national laws in question agree in treating the assigned patent as somewhat in the nature of a thing or chattel (*quasi-dinglich*), the case can be treated as one for bilateral transnational law and the possibility is opened of a *bona fide* acquisition of the patent unencumbered by the licensing agreement. [55] On the basis of the English *Cartonnage* decision (1900) the special rule of transnational law applicable to such cases is as follows: It is possible for patents, like other absolute rights, to be acquired in good faith, with the result of lifting any restrictions placed on the absolute right by the rights of third parties. The *bona fide* acquirer may for his part further assign the right thus discumbered without restriction.

American company owns nearly 100% of the shares in the company at Hänen so that the Applicant is to be regarded as a foreign company within the meaning of Law No. 8 or the patents viewed as, economically speaking, the property of the American company. In this respect also, one may not disregard the fact, which we have already invoked, that Law No. 8 lays down precise formal requirements for entitlement to bring a claim which are not fulfilled in the instant case. According to Article 14 b (i) only a legal entity instituted under the law of a foreign State may be considered foreign. The Applicant, to which patent had already been transferred in 1939, does not answer this description. Moreover the *Senat* has already found, in its decision of 18 June 1953 (*Bl.f.PMZ* 1953, p. 348), that a German limited company (*GmbH*) whose share-capital is wholly owned by a foreign person may not claim prolongation of patent-protection under Article 5 of Law No. 8, for even a one-man company does not, according to German and foreign (English, French or American) law lose its autonomy as a legal entity, so that there is still, as between the property of the company on the one hand and that of the sole member of the company on the other, a separation which is to be observed, the more so in view of the precise definition laid down in the aforesaid Article 14 b (i). Reference should here be made to the detailed grounds on which the *Senat* relied in this decision. They apply with even greater force to the present case, because here the American company does not own all the shares and it would become practically impossible to determine the legitimate claimants with any degree of clarity if one were to seek a criterion in the greater or lesser participation of a foreign company in the capital of a domestic company."

55. *AG für Cartonnagenindustrie* v. *Temler*, 10 November 1900, Patent Reports 1901, pp. 6 ff.

If the national laws involved do not agree in regarding the patent ceded as an absolute right, no transnational law is *a priori* discernible. Only where the possibility of registering licence-agreements exists in both countries can the problem be viewed transnationally. For example, Article 34 (3) of the Swiss Patents Act of 25 June 1954 provides that licences not entered in the patents register cannot be relied upon vis-à-vis a *bona fide* acquirer of rights in the patent, and § 23 (2) of the Austrian Patents Act of 1950 enunciates a similar rule. It might be thought possible, on equitable grounds, to view any high degree of concordance in such rules of registration as a basis for a bilateral transnational solution in appropriate cases, but that, for the moment, is a point we must leave undecided.

V. *Duties of the licensee*

Where the duties of the licensee are concerned, it is helpful to follow the American example and to distinguish between claims against the licensee resulting from the international licensing agreement as such, and claims which arise out of the patent in cases of its infringement by the licensee. Claims of the latter kind are invariably based on municipal law, whereas those of the former may to a very large extent be matters of transnational law.

Generally speaking, the conduct of the licensee is governed no less than that of the licensor by the principle of good faith. That is undoubtedly transnational law, and is evinced by the jurisprudence of every country. It is a principle on which reliance has been placed in the interpretation of licensing agreements in various leading cases, e.g., in support of the assumption that where the payment of the licence fees is entirely contingent on earnings from exploitation the licensee is under obligation to make use of the licence.[56] In other significant instances it determines the conduct open to the licensee; for example, it estops him, in the event of notice of termination, from relying on a state of affairs he himself has created.[57] Indeed, when extraordinary notice for cause is given, the principle of good faith affords a most sensitive test.[58]

56. *Krantz*, 5 September 1958, p. 779; *Mechanical Ice-Tray*, 26 Augustus 1944, p. 725; *Devos*, Paris, 1 March 1963.
57. *Sbicca* v. *Milius Shoe*, 18 November 1944, 145 F. 2d., pp. 389 ff., at p. 400.
58. *Bundesgerichtshof* 26 November 1954 (spectacle-lenses), GRUR 1955, p. 338: The Plaintiff was a sub-licensee of the Defendant's in regard to a secret process (patent applied for) for the production of non-mist coatings on glass, more particularly in the restricted field of spectacle-lenses. The licensor had terminated the licensing agreement for serious cause, but the termination had been declared invalid by the *Oberlandsgericht*. The *Bundesgerichtshof* rescinded this judgment and returned the case for reconsideration. The court, it said, must consider even more carefully whether the following facts, alleged by the licensor, did not constitute grave infringements by the licensee of its duty

Sometimes, however, the good-faith principle may justify exonerating the licensee from continuing with the agreement. But the circumstances must in this case be extremely unusual.[59] In considering the relevant German decisions the factors peculiar to German legal history, including economic collapse twice over in this century, must of course be taken into account. Nevertheless, the principle of good faith, however differently applied, remains a constant of transnational law.[60] Certain cases of the applicability of the good-faith principle are discussed below, in connection with the duty not to attack the patent, the obligations to provide warning and assistance and the further consequences of a licensing agreement.

The foremost obligation of the licensee is to pay the licence-fee or royalties. Unless otherwise agreed, this payment covers all modes of use throughout the territory of the State granting the patent and for so long as the patent remains valid.[61] A secret, unless otherwise agreed, is licensed for the whole world.[62] The definition that "royalties are the rents payable for the right to

---

to the licensor and did not therefore give the latter sufficient cause for notice of termination: premature press advertising and cheapjack publicity, fixing of exorbitant prices, offering the process to third parties without the knowledge or consent of the licensor, attempts to ferret out the secret.

59. For example, *Kammergericht* 8 May 1935, GRUR 1935, p. 892 ("agricultural machines"): the setting of this case was the German economic depression of October 1932. The judgment had this to say with regard to the licensee's duty to exploit the patent: "However, the duty of exploitation declines or disappears if so required by good faith or the purposes of the agreement. One may reckon among such circumstances all cases of diminished economic viability in the object concerned, including the relegation of an obsolescent invention by technical progress. For just as the licensor, if he himself puts the invention to use, has to reckon with such causes of reduced or vanished profitability, so he must make due allowance for the effect of such causes on his licensee, inasmuch as the licence has as its purpose the making of profits and in no way partakes of the character of a life-annuity ... According to the nature and object of the licensing agreement as a synallagmatic contract which also lays obligations on the licensor, and for general considerations of good faith and fair dealing, the licensee cannot be expected to continue an activity which has lost its profitability simply to keep up a flow of royalties to the licensor ... In such a case it is open to the licensor, for his part, to turn the patent in question to account, without hindrance, in some other direction. Such a view appears the more justified when one considers that it is quite inconceivable that the Defendant would have bound himself to the payment of recurrent licence fees irrespective of continued exploitation, had the Plaintiff demanded that of him at the time of the formation of the contract."

60. Cf. in particular the remarks of Chavanne (293) on the good-faith principle in the implementation of licensing agreements, with references to the decision of Bourges, 7 July 1942, *Ann. propr. ind.* 1940-1948, p. 95; cf. also the American "fashion-clothes" decision of 17 April 1909, according to which the licensee company had done its utmost for the licensed object in vain.

61. Cf. the American decision of 14 November 1939.

62. Cf. the American decision of 19 January 1962.

use the invention"[63] has implications which all find their place in transnational law. The most important is that the licensee, though barred from attacking the patent, is nevertheless not precluded from contending that he makes no use of it. He is, in other words, under no obligation to refrain from challenging the scope of the protection afforded by the patent.[64] The notion of the balance of obligations (or equivalent performance) to which we have already had occasion to refer may sometimes justify a reduction or even total abolition of the royalties.[65] Conversely, it is axiomatic among businessmen that nothing is transacted without a consideration. This is no less applicable to licensing agreements, so that in cases of doubt a commensurate fee must be assumed to have been agreed.[66]

In certain special circumstances, the same notion of balanced obligations may justify the payment of royalties after the expiry of the patent, and even after the secret has become general knowledge. Something of the kind is certainly possible in the case of agreements to do with patent applications where the main interest lies not in the application but in the invention; in these circumstances, although the secret is revealed by the application, continuance of royalty-payments on a certain scale may be justified for so long as the secret is still of economic value to the licensee.[67] In the case of agreements to do with granted patents, on the other hand, no transnational law can be said to exist regarding the continuance of royalty-payments after expiry of the patent or even as to the validity of any agreement to that effect; in the United States, in particular, these possibilities are still contested. What does, however, qualify as transnational law is that the obligation to pay royalties does not, unless otherwise provided, cease until the nullity of the patent is finally established.[68] In fact, the contractual prolongation of the monopoly position bestowed by patent laws could be permitted only in highly exceptional circumstances, though it would appear that this consideration did not carry conclusive weight with an English judge, who thus decided:

63. North Carolina Supreme Court, 1 February 1957; 112 PQ, p. 405, cited Lichtenstein, p. 1.

64. Cf. the American decisions of 8 December 1924 and 18 November 1944.

65. Thus in one English decision a renunciation of unforeseeable excess licence-fees occasioned by wartime mass-production was regarded as legally effective despite lack of consideration: *Tool Metal Mfg.* v. *Tungsten Electric*, 16 June 1955, Patent Reports 1955, p. 209.

66. Cf. the American *Dysart* decision of 11 July 1941; also *Burton* v. *Burton Stock-Car*, 22 June 1898, 50 N E, p. 1029; also German decisions on the extension of patent validity under Control-Board Law No. 8 after the Second World-War: German Patent Office—2 November 1954, GRUR 1954, p. 587; 17 January 1955, GRUR 1955, p. 294 (IPRP 1960, p. 421); 21 February 1955. GRUR 1955, p. 297.

67. Cf. the American decision of 22 December 1920.

68. Cf. *Bundesgerichtshof*, 17 October 1968.

"If a patent has lapsed both in the United Kingdom and in all the export countries, then according to this agreement no royalties will be payable in respect of the sale anywhere of products made by the use of the invention covered by the lapsed patent. If, on the other hand, the patent has lapsed in the United Kingdom but subsists in one or more of the export countries, no royalties will be payable in respect of the sale of products made by use of the invention covered by the patent in question elsewhere than in the particular country in which it is still subsisting. It certainly does not seem very reasonable that one particular person should be obliged to pay for the use of an invention after the monopoly granted to the inventor has expired and the rest of the world can use it free of charge. There is, however, nothing to prevent people entering into an agreement to this effect, if they choose to do so."[69]

In a French decision the clause that "royalties are payable throughout the period of use of the subject of the patent" was construed to mean, not that royalties must be paid even after expiry of the patent, but only that the payment of royalties could be discontinued even during the period of validity of the patent, if the licensee ceased using what was licensed.[70]

With regard to the level of licence-fees and royalties, the method of calculating them and the mode of payment, there is complete freedom of contractual choice, so that it is not possible to discern much in the way of basic transnational ideas. One, for example, could be expressed in the rule that, wherever royalties are to be calculated as a percentage of net profits, the term "net profit" should in case of doubt be taken to mean what remains after deduction of all expenses.[71] In an unclear case it can also be assumed as a rule of transnational law that the claim to fee or royalty arises as soon as the licensee exercises the right conferred upon him by the agreement. Thus if the licensee has been empowered to produce, use and sell, the claim arises from the moment of production, even if the product is not sold at all.[72] Royalties contractually dependent on the fact of sale do not—particularly in view of exchange-control experiences in many countries—fall due as soon as the contract of sale is concluded, but only when the licensee has received the pro-

69. *Bristol Repetition Ltd.* v. *Fomento*, 24 February 1961, Patent Reports 1961, pp. 222 ff., at p. 226.

70. *Audibert* v. *SA des machines Havas*, 29 Januari 1963, *Ann. propr. ind.* 1963, p. 363; cf. esp. Troller, GRUR *Ausl.* 1952, p. 117, and G. Mayer, GRUR *Ausl.* 1956, p. 406.

71. *Bates Machines* v. *Cookson*, 24 April 1903, 66 N E, p. 1093 (not accessible to author).

72. Cf. the American decision of 24 June 1940.

ceeds.[73] If the level of the royalties is undefined or doubtful, some appropriate return—normally a figure between 3% and 10%—must be taken as agreed. The decisions of the German Patent Office, cited above, provide a distinct indication as to the principle of transnational law applicable here: that a mid-way solution may be assumed correct.[74] If minimum royalties have been agreed, this does not bestow on the licensee a legal option to upset the agreement by not paying this amount.[75] If the licensor covenants with the licensee that all other licensees, without exception, must pay the same royalties ("most-favoured" clause), the onus of proof of any preferential treatment lies on the licensee invoking this covenant.[76]

Under most municipal systems, if only as a matter of general law, the licensor enjoys some right of inspection, and it would seem reasonable to regard this as transnational law. The inspection, however, must be confined to the checking of books and writings, and in Germany it has been termed standard practice to agree to entrust this to a neutral auditor.[77] There is no right to search or make determinations beyond this, especially in regard to technical matters or patent-law. One English decision appears to have admitted a more extensive right of inspection, but can perhaps be explained by the peculiar status of auditors in English law: at all events, it offers no valid precedent for transnational law.[78] The actual nature and extent of inspections are largely at the mercy of good faith. As a rule, therefore, the licensee is under no obligation to reveal information if to do so would be disproportionately unfavourable to his interests.

---

73. American decision of 1 February 1961, 69 CJS Patent § 261, p. 801. That Lichtenstein (p. 171) should mention this in connection with a commensurate time-limit is scarcely comprehensible, because, generally speaking, quite specific time-limits apply both to the receipt of payments and obligations to pay.

74. Cf. the *Bates* decision, *ut supra*.

75. *Banolas* v. *Société La Soudure*, 31 October 1955, *Ann. propr. ind.* 1957, p. 427.

76. *Sbicca* v. *Milius Shoe*, 18 November 1944, 145 F. 2d., p. 389.

77. Moser von Filseck in note on *Bundesgerichtshof*, 17 March 1961, which denied such a right of inspection, in cases of doubt with regard to book-entries.

78. *Fomento* v. *Selsdon Fountain-Pen,* House of Lords, 4 December 1957, Patent Reports 1958, p. 8; for French law, cf. Paris 30 April 1913, *Ann. propr. ind.* 1913, 2, p. 70, cited in Chavanne, 293; in the USA the problem is solved by the provision of § 724 Rev. Stat.: "In the trial of actions at law, the courts of the United States may, on motion and due notice thereof, require the parties to produce books or writings in their possession or power, which contain evidence pertinent to the issue, in cases and under circumstances where they might be compelled to produce the same by the ordinary rules of proceeding in chancery. If a plaintiff fails to comply with such order, the court may, on motion, give the like judgment for the defendant as in cases of non-suit; and if a defendant fails to comply with such order, the court may, on motion, give judgment against him by default." German jurisprudence, relying on § 666 of the Civil Code, likewise submits the licensee to certain appropriate controls: *Reichsgericht,* 12 February 1930, RGZ 127, p. 243.

It is not possible to give an unhesitant answer to the question whether any transnational law exists in respect to the licensee's obligation to exercise, use or exploit the privileges bestowed on him by the licensor. The reason is that it is not always sufficiently evident from the published French decisions whether the licences concerned are exclusive or non-exclusive. Nevertheless, in view of the difference between these two types of licence and the clear jurisprudence of other countries, one may venture to say that in the case of the non-exclusive licence transnational law does not as a rule recognize any such duty, the existence of which has therefore to be proved by the party invoking it. If it can be supposed that, where this duty was a factor in the French decisions noted below,[79] the licences concerned were exclusive, one may conclude that there is general agreement in all countries to the effect that such a duty exists as a rule in the case of exclusive licences, the burden of proof thus resting on whoever maintains the reverse.[80] Not only the conclusion of these decisions from many countries, but also the reasoning underlying them is the same: namely, that by granting an exclusive licence the licensor places in the licensee's hands a powerful capital asset and source of profit, so that the licensee must in good faith do with it what the licensor or any other possessor of this asset would normally do, i.e., put it to work. This can be deduced from the principle of good faith no less than from the specific tenor of a licensing agreement.

The obligation was, in one French decision,[81] regarded as sufficiently discharged if the licensee had himself passed on the licence in some appropriate way. The question also arises as to what is meant by a "best endeavours" clause. One English judgment gave the answer that the phrase meant what it said, i.e., not "second-best endeavours"; it all depended on what was reasonable in the circumstances.[82] An American decision, moreover, found that the duty to use was not dissolved by the mere appearance on the scene of a rival patented process: even in the altered situation the licensee company could be held to its obligation "to use its best efforts to manu-

79. Cf. the cases mentioned in Chavanne (291): Tribunal de la Seine, 28 June 1933, *Ann. Propr. ind.* 1934, p. 38; Paris 31 May 1906, D.P. 1908, 5, p. 1 (in two further decisions, *Marbot* v. *Helleux*, 19 March 1936, *Ann. Propr. ind.* 1939, p. 185, and *Filippi* v. *Lévy*, 9 February 1963, *Ann. propr. ind.* 1964, p. 179, the facts are not altogether clear); Paris 8 April 1964 (JCP 1964-II, No. 13876, annotated R. Plaisant) is unambiguous.

80. In addition to the French decisions mentioned, cf., for Germany, *Kammergericht* 3 September 1938, p. 66, but also *Reichsgericht* 14 May 1935, GRUR 1935, p. 590; for USA, *Krantz* v. *van Dette*, 5 September 1958, 165 Sup., p. 776, and *Rogers* v. *Engelhard*, 11 May 1960, 183 F. Sup., p. 573; for England, *Terrell* v. *Mable Todd*, 31 July 1952, Patent Reports 69, p. 234.

81. *Verrerie* v. *Hollandsche Glas- en Metaalbank*, 11 May 1932, *Ann. propr. ind.* 1932, pp. 259 ff., at p. 268.

82. *Terrell, ut supra* (*re* fountain-pens).

facture and sell devices produced under the mentioned patents. However," the court continued:

"whether such efforts would be feasible and profitable is another question, upon which would depend the amount of damages, if any, the plaintiff may have suffered."[83]

The licensee may not attack the licensed patent and must not himself reveal the licensed trade-secret for so long as the licensing agreement remains in force. This would seem to be transnational law. It corresponds to the principle of good faith, for it is inadmissible that the licensee should in the business world rely on the patent for his own protection, exploit it and derive advantage from it, while at the same time, in his private relationship with the patentee, relying on its alleged invalidity.[84] But where the requirement of good faith does not stand in the way of an attack on the patent—where, for example, the licensee at the same time waives his rights under the licence—, such an attack must be viewed as admissible in transnational law. It is questionable, moreover, whether this may be obviated by a clause prohibiting attacks on the patent, as appears to be accepted practice. Of recent years such clauses have been regarded with deepening suspicion from the public-interest viewpoint embodied in anti-trust legislation, whereby, however valid in themselves, they remain subject to the particular scrutiny of the courts and, in some countries, of a trust-supervisory organ.[85]

The licensee may be under obligation to mark the manufactured goods in accordance with the wishes of the licensor.[86] Such cases involve special

---

83. *Rogers, ut supra*, at p. 577.

84. Cf. with regard to American law, the *Westinghouse* case of 8 December 1924, also *Universal Rim* v. *Scott*, 16 March 1922, 21 F. 2d., p. 346, and *Sbicca* v. *Milius Shoe*, 18 November 1944, 145 F. 2d., p. 389; for English law: *Fuel Economy* v. *Murray*, 30 April 1930, Patent Reports 47, p. 346, and *Suhr* v. *Crofts*, 29 April 1932, Patent Reports 49, p. 359; for Germany and Switzerland, the cases cited in Stumpf, p. 192, where emphasis is laid, in part incomprehensibly, on the singularity of each particular case. Closer inspection reveals that the decisions based on Article 34 of the Law of 1844, which are adduced by Chavanne (289), are not in conflict with this transnational principle. Article 34 provides that anyone with an interest in it may bring an action for nullity of the patent. But this is also possible in transnational law, provided that the licensee, at the same time as he brings the action, renounces his claims arising out of the licensing agreement. Cf. also the following French decisions: *Virgilio* v. *Mohr*, 26 July 1917, *Ann. propr. ind.* 1926, p. 353, and *SA Dognin* v. *SA Gaine Scandale*, 17 December 1964, *Ann. propr. ind.* 1965, p. 172.

85. Cf. § 20 of the German Act of 1957 against of competition, and see more especially Mertens, "Ausländisches Kartellrecht im deutschen internationalen Privatrecht", *RabelsZ* 1967, p. 385. Cf. also the French decisions adduced by Chavanne (290), likewise considering non-attack clauses as valid in themselves, and the American case-law in Lichtenstein, p. 182 and, especially, p. 185. Cf. further Deringer, "International licence agreements and anti-trust law", 11th Conference of the International Bar Association, The Hague 1966, pp. 112 ff., and *idem*, GRUR *Ausl.* 1968, p. 179.

86. Cf. *Patchett* v. *Sterling*, 22 October 1953, Patent Reports 71, p. 269.

questions of licensing trademarks which it would be out of place to discuss here.[87]

Is the licensee entitled to assign his rights derived from the licensing agreement to a third party, or at least to grant him a sublicence? In a doubtful case, transnational law must refuse this right, on account of the personal character of both non-exclusive and exclusive licences, and here it can make little difference whether one follows the doctrine of waiver or the "splinter" theory. On the assignment of rights, the position of transnational law is more forthright than in the matter of sublicensing. For in no country is free assignability admitted in case of doubt, where the agreement is silent on the point.[88] A sublicence, on the contrary, may prove admissible in transnational law, because in this case—at least, in the German view—the principal licensee remains under obligation toward the licensor. This construction, however, does not hold good in all other countries. In most of them, the above-mentioned personal character of the licence conferred by the original agreement is held to militate against the admissibility of a sublicence. Hence in any doubtful case a sublicence must be ruled inadmissible.[89] The prevalence in Germany of the contrary view is attributable to what is by now a very old line of case-law in favour of free assignability and of freedom to sublicence, at least in the case of exclusive licences.[90] The doubtful quality of this jurisprudence is evident, in particular, from the commentary of Lüdecke/Fischer. If the decisions in question were subjected to critical scrutiny, the resultant elucidation might well lead to harmonization with transnational law.

There do not so far appear to have been, for our purposes, sufficient decisions in regard to the question whether a change in the ownership of a licensee company, or of the principal interest therein, can really be without effect on the continued subsistence of the licensing agreement. If it can, that is hardly consonant with the personal character of an exclusive licence. Publicists differ hereon.[91] With regard to the occasionally encountered dividing of a licence and partial transfer, there have likewise been few decisions, and they scarcely enable any transnational rule to be deduced.[92]

87. Cf. Beier, Deutsch and Fikentscher, *Die Warenzeichenlizenz: rechtsvergleichende Untersuchungen*, *Festschrift Ulmer*, Munich 1963.

88. For the American case-law, see the references in Walker, § 388, p. 1500; for Germany, Stumpf, p. 118 (according to Stumpf, the views are "not uniform"). Cf. also Lüdecke/Fisher, A36, p. 85;

89. Cf. for American law the decisions mentioned in Lichtenstein, p. 88; for English law, *Terrell*, p. 258; for French law, Mathély/Plaisant, *Juris-Classeur*, pp. 71 ff.

90. Cf. decisions in Lüdecke/Fischer, *loc. cit.*, more recently confirmed by the *Bundesgerichtshof* in the "spectacle-lens" decision of 26 November 1954, GRUR 1955, p. 338.

91. Cf. the American decision of 2 December 1914.

92. Cf. the American decision of 6 October 1892, and, for French law, see Mathély/Plaisant, 72.

On the other hand, it is possible to adopt, as a maxim of transnational law, the ruling of a French court to the effect that discontinuance of the patent licence renders all sublicences *ipso facto* null and void.[93]

VI. *Upkeep and defence of the patent*

In ascertaining transnational law it is advisable to begin by marshalling the pertinent questions which tend to be dealt with at various points in national law. There are broadly three which emerge in the present context: Who is responsible for the upkeep of the patent—i.e., essentially, for the payment of renewal fees? Whose duty is it to defend the patent against attacks by third parties? Who must assert the rights of the patent in the event of third-party infringements? In reality these questions amount to six, for the answers to be given must often vary according to whether the licence concerned is an exclusive or a non-exclusive one. This makes discernment of transnational law somewhat difficult, yet it is not only possible but also a practical proposition to arrive at a synthesis of this whole complex of questions, for the crux of the matter is always the preservation of the capital asset forming the basis and subject-matter of the licensing agreement. It makes, perhaps, some difference of degree, but certainly no fundamental difference, whether the licensor is considered bound to a mere waiver of rights or (under the "splinter" theory) to the assignment of a value for use. For the fact of waiver itself, *qua* subject-matter of the agreement, becomes worthless once the licensor no longer possesses anything the waiver of which might represent an economic return for the payment of a licence-fee. This simple point will not only permit us to encompass all the questions listed above in one and the same perspective, but may stand as the first rule of transnational law in this particular field.

On the other hand, it is certainly insufficient to create any presumption that the licensor has in every case to maintain in force and defend the patent. Here differences of degree are important, and it is necessary to envisage individual cases illustrative of the whole range of licensing agreements. The minimum obligation of the licensor is undoubtedly that of preserving the monopoly of patent rights for the exercise of which he gets paid by the licensee. If this were not the meaning and minimum content of each and every licensing agreement, there would be absolutely no sense in concluding such agreements. It is also self-evident from the fact of the licensing-agreement that throughout the period of its validity the licensor is under obligation to pay the fees required to keep any licensed patent in force. Here no appeal even to good faith is necessary. This obligation can be presumed even in the silence of the contract, and if the licensor would contend the reverse he

93. *Héritiers Demolder* v. *Eveno*, 23 June 1933, *Ann. propr. ind.* 1934, p. 35.

has the onus of proof. The French courts offer a basic decision for trans-national law on this point.[94]

It is a considerable step from this duty to pay patent fees to the next obligation we have to discuss, that of defending the patent against attacks, and the related question of whether the licensee has a right to exercise such protection in case the licensor has no duty of defence. It will furthermore be necessary to answer this same dual question in the highly important context of the necessity that may arise of suing third parties for infringement in order to preserve the value of the patent.

It is true that, so far as the first question is concerned, namely that of the existence or otherwise of a duty to defend the patent against attacks by third parties, we have already shown above that there is no transnational law according to which the licensor can be presumed to have warranted the legal validity of his patent. However, this negative rule scarcely entitles the licensor to remain inactive in the fact of attacks on the patent, so long as some action is open to him which does not involve him in excessive expense or otherwise disadvantage him. If, therefore, he seeks to rely on his lack of obligation to warrant validity, he must at least alert the licensee in good time to attacks on the patent, and thus enable him to bring a suit at his own expense. This may be regarded as transnational law, and as proceeding from the contract without any need to invoke the principle of good faith.

In the event that, by the terms of the licensing agreement, both parties could be regarded as entitled to take measures of protection, and that either of them could bring an action in the country where the protection is to be afforded, it cannot be assumed that either of them owes the other a duty of protection.[95] This is deducible from the rules of the general law of obliga-tions, let alone the principle of good faith, and it is therefore transnational law.

More important than attacks against the patent and its defence are its maintenance and assertion in the face of infringement. Is it possible to say that under transnational law the licensor has a duty of defence in such cases? Certainly it is not, with reference to the grantor of a non-exclusive licence; for if in this case the licensee could not even prevent the acquisition by third parties of licences in the same protected domain, how much less could he require that same domain to be defended against intru-sion?[96] Exceptional circumstances are however conceivable in which the licensee must accept the grant of further licences but does not have to stomach infringements of the licensed patent. That is a question of inter-pretation.

94. *Fridor* v. *Exhenry*, 3 March 1953, *Ann. propr. ind.* 1953, p. 1.
95. Lüdecke/Fischer, p. 294.
96. Boulogne 2 October 1923, *Ann. propr. ind.* 1924, pp. 1 ff., at p. 32.

In the case of exclusive licences, the difference between them and assignments of patents must first be stressed. Only assignment really places the acquirer in the shoes of the other. The grantor of an exclusive licence, on the other hand, keeps something, however great or small, for himself. In view of the very wide range of relationships which are possible between the parties to exclusive licensing agreements, it cannot be assumed that the licensor as such will *ipso facto* have incurred any obligation to protect the licensee against infringers of the patent. In the United States the waiver doctrine finds expression in unanimous and adamant agreement on this point, and does not even permit the licensee, unless so provided in the agreement, to join the licensor in a suit for infringement, arguing that it was in the former's power to have what he wanted written into the agreement at the time of its conclusion.[97] The prevalent opinion in Germany likewise denies that the licensor has a duty to take steps against infringers of the patent.

This, then, is the normal legal position, and it may as such be of importance from the viewpoint of transnational law. Occasional exceptions do however arise. Only recently, for example, the German *Bundesgerichtshof* decided that, as a rule, the grantor of a non-exclusive patent-licence who is bound by a "most-favoured treatment" clause is, even in the absence of express provision to that effect in the agreement, under an obligation to proceed against continual infringement by third parties. If he fails to take action, his claim to the further payment of royalties may be held an unreasonable expectation on the test of good faith.[98]

Wherever the licensor cannot be viewed as obliged to defend the patent, it would be contrary to the transnational principles of good faith and reasonable decisions to deny the licensee a right to exercise protection in the event of the licensor's declining to act. It is indeed a tempting idea to predicate the licensee's *a priori* right to defend the patent against infringement whenever such defence is not a duty of the licensor. That would however be going too far and would venture outside the confines of transnational law, except in cases where such a conclusion can be shown to represent bilateral transnational law. For in this particular field the development of legal norms has plainly not advanced to the stage of multilateral transnational law. Not only in France, but also in the United States, and in England up to the Act of 16 December 1949, the holder of an exclusive licence is not empowered to sue for infringement of patent-rights.[99] Owing to the "splinter" theory, however,

97. *Martin* v. *New Trinidad*, 2 January 1919, 255 F., p. 93; *Western Electric* v. *Pa-Cent Reproducer*, 5 May 1930, 42 F. 2d., pp. 116 ff., at p. 118.
98. *Bundesgerichtshof* 23 September 1965, NJW 1965, p. 1861; approved by Stumpf, p. 258.
99. So far as France is concerned, this derives from the Law of 1844, which has been strictly applied by the courts but severely criticized by jurists as obsolescent and unpractical; cf. Chavanne (271), Mathély/Plaisant, *Juris-Classeur*, pp. 43 and 48, both with

he does enjoy a right of action where this doctrine holds sway, i.e., in Germany, Switzerland, Italy and Austria. In these countries that view is virtually uncontested, and is constant jurisprudence. [100]

A certain progress towards the construction of multilateral transnational law on the subject is however already discernible in various developments and pronouncements on the national plane. In the first place we may point to the Patents Act of the Netherlands, Article 43 (5), and the English Patents Act of 16 December 1949, Section 35 (3), the terms of which are fairly similar. The English law confers on the licensee, unless otherwise provided in the agreement, the right to call upon the licensor to take such measures as may be necessary to prevent infringements of the patent. Should the licensor not have complied within the space of two months, the licensee may institute proceedings in his own name, as if he himself were the patentee. The same time-limit is stipulated in the Dutch law. In regard to the development of French law herein, the pronouncements mentioned above may be recalled. In Germany, the above-cited decision of 1956 placed strong emphasis on the aspect of good faith, which is a special touchstone where international agreements are concerned. The observations of Lüdecke/Fischer (p. 58) are also highly relevant to the construction of transnational law in individual cases. Everything hinges, in their view, on the question as to which party to the agreement stands the closer to the patent. The patentee status of the licensor may have become a purely formal title, while in reality, and from the economic standpoint, the licensee alone "possesses" the patent, so that the licensor is the patentee only in name, having in fact turned into a mere receiver of royalties. Moreover Lüdecke/Fischer repeatedly make the point that a legal obligation becomes objectless if it cannot be implemented through legal proceedings. This reasoning merits special attention from the viewpoint of transnational law, and under certain circumstances may even be held applicable not only to cases of procedural impotence but also to any case where, for no matter what reason, the formally obligated party would incur an essentially heavier burden in taking the action required, or where the measures he might take would meet with appreciably less success than those of the other party to the agreement if he, for his part, were to act. By following out this line of thought, however, one would very soon arrive at the borderline beyond which a licensing agreement might turn into a contract of association. Of this, we shall have more to say below.

---

case-law references; also the more recent decision of 23 April 1956 in *Malsert* v. *S. à r.l. Reliac, Ann. propr. ind.* 1961, p. 260. In the USA, on account of the "waiver" doctrine, the licensee does not have a right of action for infringement in any case. Nevertheless, the owner of the patent is regarded as under an obligation to authorize his exclusive licensee to bring an action for infringement on his behalf (Lichtenstein, p. 154, without substantiation).

100. Cf. corroborative references, where Germany is concerned, in Stumpf, p. 389.

The transnational solution for all such cases surely lies in the *Western Electric* decision of 5 May 1930. [101] In this, the American court held in the case of an exclusive licence that, whether a patent were licensed or assigned, in either case the patentee conferred full powers upon the other party to institute proceedings for infringement, not only in his own behalf but also in behalf of the patentee, to the extent that the latter declined to join in the suit. Even the French courts, which, feeling bound by the law of 1844, have been the most conservative in this field, are being urged by the writings of French jurists to take the same road and already appear, in one or two decisions, to have set foot upon it, going so far as to contemplate the possibility in certain cases of reading into the licensing agreement an irrevocable faculty for the licensee to institute infringement proceedings. [102]

The importance of the duty of defence as an element in the licensing agreement itself—and hence the question whether any dereliction of that duty gives rise to a claim for damages and/or avoidance of the contract—is not a matter on which generalization is easily possible: it all depends on the individual case. That, and that alone, can explain certain contradictions in the various decisions that have been given on this point. [103]

VII. *Improvement of the invention; new patents; association*

A licensing agreement may be restricted to the precise state of the invention or patent at the time of signature, and thus preclude *a priori* any modification of the subject-matter. An agreement of this kind may be termed static. The opposite is a dynamic agreement, meaning one more or less extensively covering future modifications or improvements. Both types are encountered in practice, together with a wide range of intermediate forms. Dynamic licens-

101. 42 F. 2d., p. 119: showing how this decision relies in turn on *Waterman* v. *Mackenzie*, 138 US, p. 256.

102. Cf. on all these points the observations, with case-law references, of Chavanne (286) and Mathély/Plaisant, pp. 43 and 58, also the footnote on the *Montalbetti* decision of 20 July 1953 in the *Recueil Dalloz* 1953, p. 704, wholly rejecting, so far as can be seen from what is reported, the *Malsert* decision of 23 April 1956, *Ann. propr. ind.* 1961, p. 260.

103. The Paris decision of 14 March 1901, *Ann. propr. ind.* 1901, p. 349 (cited *Juris-Classeur*, p. 46) ruled in favour of the voidability of the contract. On the other hand, the English *Kolynos* decision of 28 November 1929 (Patent Reports 47, p. 403) found that even where the licensor had an agreed duty of defence, that did not go to the root of the contract, so that dereliction of that duty did not render it voidable. The American *Frost Ry.* decision of 11 July 1938 (24 F. Sup., pp. 20 ff., at p. 27) confirms our view that it all depends on the particular case, inasmuch as the court declared that the licensing agreement would be voidable if there remained no protection against infringements of monopoly.

ing agreements give rise to problems, chief among which are the following: How far-reaching is the dynamic effect, i.e., within what ambit are improvements governed by the agreement? To what extent are any obligations to make creative efforts in the future to be recognized from the legal viewpoint? In case of doubt, can obligations of that kind be presumed to exist, or not?

It would appear highly improbable that any transnational law exists with regard to the question as to what may be held to constitute "improvements" within the meaning of a licensing agreement. This being a matter on which there are no hard and fast rules even within municipal jurisdictions, there is *a fortiori* little chance of their existing in the intercourse of nations, and still less when the plurality of languages is taken into account. For the problem is basically one of terminology and interpretation. And for the purposes of the latter, the standpoint of anti-trust law is a major restrictive factor. It accounts for the tendency to construe agreements narrowly rather than broadly and hence, for example, to disallow the freedom of the contracting parties to bring anything beyond the discovery of improvements in the strict sense, or new uses and applications, within the scope of their agreement. Thus parallel inventions would definitely be excluded. [104]

However, certain restrictions on the freedom of contract qualify as transnational law to the extent that they can be explained, so far as European laws are concerned, in terms of public policy:

"A naked assignment or agreement to assign, in gross, a man's future labors as an author or inventor—in other words, a mortgage on a man's brain, to bind all his future products—does not address itself favorably to our consideration." (*Aspinwall*, 32 F., p. 697 [105])

---

104. Cf. my *Kommentar zum Kartellgesetz,* § 20, pp. 70-72; also the English decision of 15 June 1965 in *National Broach* v. *Churchill Gear Machines*, Patent Reports 1965, p. 516; the American decision of 5 September 1958 (*Krantz*), 165 F., pp. 776 ff., at p. 781; the French decision of 1 March 1963 (*Devos* v. *Erop*), *Ann. propr. ind.* 1963, p. 28.

105. Cited is *Monsanto Chemical Works* v. *Jaeger*, 31 F. 2d., p. 191, with further references. The French decision of 2 February 1961 (*Recueil Dalloz* 1961, p. 652, with extensive notice by Vasseur) probably concerns quite a different situation, for we find in the headnote: "As the parties are entitled, in accordance with Article 1627 of the Civil Code, to increase or diminish the effects of the legal obligation of guarantee laid upon them, covenants whereby the grantor of a licence pledges the grantee a share in the benefit of new inventions exceeding the scope of mere improvements are valid"; this particular case concerned the investment of capital in a company and a corresponding guarantee. A pointer may be found in the German *Reichsgericht* decision of 19 June 1935 (GRUR 1936, p. 57), in which it was at first only a question of establishing what the words "place at the disposal" meant in a licensing agreement; it was decided that the granting of a licence was sufficient and that there was no obligation to assign any new patent.

Covenants of a sweeping nature are all the more open to objection when the future improvements referred to in an international licensing agreement are subject to different treatment from country to country, as is not seldom the case in practice. [106]

There is virtually unanimous agreement that in case of doubt the licensor is under no obligation to make improvements available to the licensee. [107] This may accordingly be regarded as a rule of transnational law.

Transnationally speaking, the licensee is in a similar position, for he is *a priori* under no obligation to make improvements available to the licensor. Only in exceptional cases may it be his duty to do so, for example if it had been mutually understood that the licensed invention needed perfecting and that the licensee had a duty of exploitation. [108] The legal situation is uncertain as to whether a licensee is *a priori* entitled to modify the licensed object and produce what he would claim to be improvements. Whether they really are improvements is something which, strictly speaking, may only be determined in common accord with the licensor, for if they are not, the latter's business could in certain circumstances be adversely affected by the appearance on the market of a variant article. This militates against predicating any right of improvement in favour of the licensee. [109] If it should be conceded that the licensee has in fact improved the licensed object, he has a *prima facie* claim to modification of royalties. [110]

As was briefly mentioned in the preceding chapter on the defence of the patent, a licensing agreement not infrequently contains elements of a contract of association. This becomes even more evident when the agreement under consideration is one of the dynamic variety, and the further development and improvement of the licensed object are thus factors of no small importance. In recent times the anti-monopoly trend has provided a stimulus in this direction, inasmuch as it tends to make the legal validity of improvement obligations dependent on their being assumed on a basis of reciprocity and in like degree by both licensor and licensee. The time is not yet ripe for the development of transnational law in this connection, apart from certain rules

106. References in Stumpf, p. 160.

107. For USA see decision of 30 July 1959, 176 F. Sup., pp. 104 ff., at p. 127. France – Mathély/Plaisant, 33; Chavanne (281); decision of 2 February 1961 (*ut supra*); Cass. 16 July 1957 (*Charvet* v. *Martin*), *Ann. propr. ind.* 1959, p. 219. England– *National Carbonising* v. *British Coal Distillation*, Patent Reports 54, p. 41.

108. *Reichsgericht* 14 July 1934, *Mitteilungen des Verbandes deutscher Patentanwälte* 1934, p. 236 (cited in Stumpf, p. 97); for England cf. *National Broach, ut supra*; for USA, *Krantz, ut supra*; for France, Mathély/Plaisant, 35 (without case-law references).

109. Cf. the English decision of 11 July 1958 in *Advance Industries* v. *Paul Frankfurther*, Patent Reports 1958, p. 392; see also Stumpf, p. 156 (without substantiation).

110. Cf. *Advance Industries* (*ut supra*), Stumpf, p. 157, and the above-mentioned *Reichsgericht* decision of 14 July 1934.

of interpretation. These rules would include the following: where a licensing agreement expressly binds the parties to mutual disclosure of improvements, that is not enough to justify treating the contract as *ipso facto* an instrument of association; [111] the period of validity of a licensing agreement is essentially unaffected by covenants on the subject of improvements; [112] in special cases, a relationship of association, or quasi-association, may result from a secret agreement touching an undisclosed invention still in need of development; [113] in certain circumstances, when the associative quality of a licensing agreement is particularly evident, it may justifiably be inferred that licensor and licensee are under a mutual obligation to collaborate in the development of the licensed object. [114]

The more the character of a licensing agreement approximates to that of a contract of association and forsakes that of a bilateral instrument, the more it is drawn into the orbit of anti-trust law. An extensive treatment of this aspect would not, however, be in place here. [115]

We again find little upon which transnational law can be founded in the present state of the question whether clauses prohibiting competition are valid in licensing agreements. [116]

VIII. *Termination of the licensing agreement*

According to the principle of liberty of contract, the parties are free to fix the duration of a licensing agreement by common accord. In this connection there are essentially two questions to be answered. First, can the agreement be unilaterally terminated before the expiry of the period fixed? Secondly, if the agreement does not specify the duration, can it be terminated other than

111. *Reichsgericht* 29 April 1931, *Markenschutz und Wettbewerb* 1931, p. 441 (*Rütteleisen*).

112. *Devos*, 1 March 1963, *Ann. propr. ind.* 1963, p. 28.

113. *Bundesgerichtshof* 26 November 1954, GRUR 1955, p. 338 (spectacle-lenses - *Brillengläser*). This decision concerned at the same time the relationship with a delivery-contract; cf. the *Schweissbolzen* ("rivets") decision of 25 October 1966 (BGHZ 46, p. 365).

114. *Sic* Chavanne (282), citing Roubier, Vol. 2, p. 278.

115. Cf. Mathély/Plaisant, pp. 98 ff., and more recently Kronstein, *Das Recht der internationalen Kartelle*, Berlin 1967, pp. 172 ff. and 399 ff.

116. For France, cf. headnote of *B. . .* v. *Thermosac*, 2 February 1961, *Recueil Dalloz* 1961, p. 652 ("The no-competition clause is valid when limited as to time, area and products concerned"), and the note by Vasseur, p. 659, with further material. A prohibition of competition cannot go without saying: Paris 8 April 1964, with note by Plaisant. It may however be implicit in the special circumstances of a "confidential relationship": cf. the American decisions of 13 March 1944, 4 June 1958, 24 December 1963 and 15 May 1964.

by mutual consent? It has been put forward that the silence of the agreement precludes unilateral termination, since *pacta servanda sunt*. On the other hand, it is common knowledge that parties often refrain from settling a question in terms, because they wish to leave it to the future to extract the answer from the sense of the contract and the workings of circumstance. One English decision went very thoroughly into the implications of this fact and came up with the surely correct conclusion that the judge must in every case ascertain the will of the parties, and must thus entertain the notion that unilateral termination can be shown admissible even where the agreement is silent.[117] In a later English decision, which arrived at the same conclusion, reliance was further placed on the express terms of the 1949 Patents Act, Section 58 of which provides for the termination of licensing agreements on service of three months' written notice to the other party.[118] American case-law follows essentially the same line.[119] So far as France is concerned, attention may be drawn to a decision which, in the silence of the agreement, allowed that it might be construed as having been concluded for the duration of the underlying patent.[120] German authorities are in harmony with this French decision, inasmuch as they are unwilling *a priori* to regard patent-licences as terminable before the expiry of the licensed patent, while they hold § 595 of the German Civil Code (termination on six months' notice) applicable to licences of which an invention forms the subject-matter.[121]

The foregoing reveals that the only variation affecting the formation of transnational law lies in the period of notice required: three months in England, six in Germany and a "reasonable" length of time in the USA. This discrepancy can however be overcome by falling back on the basic notion that the notice may never, in any case, be anything other than reasonable.

The doctrinal antitheses between the waiver and "splinter" theories, or the contract of exchange and the contract of association, disappear more or less completely in transnational law, because both are overshadowed by the principle of good faith. Thus no decision is to be found which refused a right of unilateral termination on the ground that the relationship of licensor and licensee was simply that of parties in an interchange. What, rather, the courts have in all cases sought to ascertain is whether a party had serious reason for termination, i.e. whether the circumstances relied on were such that he could not reasonably be expected to continue with the agreement. This is a fairly severe test for the other party. Accordingly, American courts are apt to

117. *Martin-Baker Aircraft*, 10 June 1955, Patent Reports 73, p. 236.
118. *Advance Industries*, 11 July 1958, Patent Reports 1958, p. 392.
119. Cf. *Ruby* v. *Ebsary Gypsum*, 20 September 1929, 36 F. 2d., p. 244, and *American Type Founders* v. *Lanston Monotype Machines*, 4 August 1943, 137 F. 2d., p. 728.
120. *Devos* v. *SA Erop*, 1 March 1963, *Ann. propr. ind.* 1963, p. 28.
121. Stumpf, 477 and 483; Lüdecke/Fischer, pp. 576 ff.

inquire with great care whether the obligation the breach of which is alleged to justify determination is, in fact, one with which the agreement stands or falls, or perhaps some quite independent obligation—in which case the breach of it may not found termination. [122] They have further established that any non-receipt of royalties, if due merely to casual delay or inefficiency, does not in itself afford the licensor sufficient cause to determine the agreement. [123] However, if more than one payment remains overdue despite warning, the licensor is entitled to give notice of termination. [124] A similar decision has been given in France. [125] The English and German courts also decide according to whether the contractual relationship can still reasonably be relied on. [126] It is not so far possible to discern any transnational law governing the special case of a licence granted outright for a lump-sum. [127]

Sometimes the licensee's failure to make sufficient use of the licensed object is alleged to constitute a breach of obligation serious enough to warrant termination. In such cases, however, the particular circumstances are all-important, and courts everywhere apply stringent tests before accepting this contention. [128]

It is also, generally speaking, a corollary of the good-faith principle that the licensee must have a right of termination if the conditions of competition— irrespective of whether any patent subsists—have developed to a point where he no longer has any prospect of entering or remaining in the market. [129] A situation justifying notice of termination may also arise out of circumstances which at first glance have only a remote connection with the agreement, e.g. when the exploitation of the licence produces prejudicial side-effects. [130]

122. *Krell* v. *Bovaird Supply Co.*, 20 April 1936, 83 F. 2d., p. 414.

123. *Foster Hose Supporter Co.* v. *Taylor*, 9 January 1911, 184 F. 2d., p. 71.

124. *Ruby*, 36 F. 2d., p. 244.

125. *SA Pulsa* v. *Dutrieux*, 19 June 1962, *Ann. propr. ind.* 1962, p. 168.

126. Cf., for Germany, the illustrations given by Stumpf, 485, and especially *Reichsgericht*, 12 June 1942 (aluminium foil). In England the problem hardly arises, because of the basic voidability of contracts.

127. Cf. two decisions which are at variance hereon: *Bundesgerichtshof* 5 July 1960 (BB 1960, p. 998), and Munich *Landgericht* 18 November 1954(GRUR 1956, p. 413), both cited by Stumpf (492); also the English *Gujot* decision, Patent Reports 11, p. 552, cited by Terrell, p. 256.

128. Cf. the French *Devos* decision, *Ann. propr. ind.* 1963, p. 28, and the decision of the German *Reichsgericht* of 14 January 1938, GRUR 1939, p. 380 (reported by Stumpf, 150), for the unusual event of a licensee catching up on his duty to exploit after a period of neglect.

129. *Sic*, very plainly, the American decisions *Critcher* v. *Linker*, 17 April 1909 (169 F., p. 653) and *Frost Ry* v. *Symington & Son*, 11 July 1938 (24 F. Sup., p. 20).

130. Düsseldorf *Oberlandesgericht*, 1 May 1929, JW 1929, p. 3093 (cited Stumpf, 72), enlisting the typically German legal concept of positive breach of contract - cf. Zweigert, "Some comparative aspects of the law relating to sale of goods", ICLQ, Sup. 9, 1964, p. 3.

How far may be gone in recognizing unusual circumstances may only be gauged from the facts of each case, but in every instance the notion of reasonable expectations will lead to a solution of some kind. One English decision concerned the unusual case of wartime conditions resulting in an unforeseen over-exploitation of the licence, which led the licensor to renounce the swollen royalties of his own accord. The House of Lords held the renunciation to be valid in the circumstances, though the requisite feature of consideration was absent. [131]

The termination of the agreement is in transnational law also circumscribed by further considerations of a general kind. Thus for example, according to general principles of law, a party may not, for the purpose of avoiding a contract, rely on circumstances which he himself has brought about (*venire contra factum proprium*). [132] There is another general consideration, to be found in one French and many German decisions, which can probably be shown to form transnational law. It concerns the notion that contracts must if at all possible be maintained in force and that formal termination is therefore only admissible when all other means have been exhausted. The party notified must therefore be given an opportunity of averting termination in some way, or in certain circumstances the parties should even amend the agreement to suit their altered relationship. [133]

When licensed patents lapse in whole or in part, it makes a difference of principle in the various municipal systems of law, and at the same time an important practical difference, whether a corresponding and, in given circumstances, a retroactive lapse of the licensing agreement is to be presumed, or whether such occurrences should have no retroactive effect on the agree-

131. *Tool Metal Mfg. Co.* v. *Tungsten Electric Co.*, 16 June 1955, Patent Reports 72, p. 209. Cf. also *Reichsgericht* 12 June 1942.

132. This covers in particular the case of a party giving notice of termination in reliance on the lapse of the patent who has nevertheless persisted in the contractual relationship for quite some time since that lapse. Cf. *American Type Founders*, 4 August 1943 (137 F. 2d., p. 729), and the similar *Krell* case decided on 20 April 1936 (83 F. 2d., p. 414), also *Rowland* v. *Biesecker*, 14 February 1911 (185 F. 2d., p. 515). In the English *Patchett* v. *Sterling Engineering* decision of 22 October 1953 (Patent Reports 70, p. 269) the party seeking termination was held to be under an obligation, when notifying the same, not to shorten the periods of notice which had been customary between the parties. In a case which concerned not a licensing agreement, but a contract of association of the potash syndicate, the German *Bundesgerichtshof* framed the matter in a somewhat different, and most interesting, manner: "A party may not base notice of termination on circumstances originating in its own area of risk".

133. Cf. the more cursory dictum in the French decision, *Marbot* v. *Helleux*, 19 March 1936, *Ann. propr. ind.* 1939, p. 187, and the constant German jurisprudence to the effect that the possibility of adjusting the contract to meet the changed situation must be tested before proceeding to the definitive termination of the contractual relationships of an association (*Bundesgerichtshof* 15 June 1951, NJW 1951, p. 386, concerning the potash syndicate - *Kali-Syndikat*).

ment and in the event, for example, of its continuance can even remain unremarked for some time. Looking at the vast maze of decided cases, stretching back many years, one has first the impression that the extrication of any transnational law on this ramified issue is out of the question, for even on the national plane the state of the law is nowhere settled and unequivocal. In fact, however, a trend has set in during the last ten years or so which clearly represents progress on the road to transnational law. This progress has gone hand in hand with the increasing attention everywhere paid to economic aspects in legal analysis and theory; and nowhere is this attitude more prominent than in dealing with international cases.

The problem can best be approached by considering a fairly recent English decision, the subject of which was a licensing agreement covering patents in many countries and intended to last until 1998 and even beyond, so long as patents for improvements on the licensed invention were still in force. As a result of circumstances which cannot be gone into here, the question arose of whether this marathon agreement might not be brought to a premature end. The court found it to be material in this connection:

"that the contemplated variations in process and composition were to be of a sufficiently substantial character as to impart both novelty and inventive ingenuity". [134]

Nowadays the very frequently encountered clause to the effect that a licensing agreement should last until the expiry of every patent licensed thereunder is no longer treated formally in Germany either. Instead, weight is laid on the actual economic worth of any unexpired patent, with a view to ascertaining whether it can be regarded as a so-called basic patent (*Grundpatent*). [135] In German case-law, the transition from formal legal assessment to the economic approach is particularly easy to trace, for while the older judgments of the *Reichsgericht* primarily relate cases involving this question to Roman-law rules of obligation, discriminating therefore between original and subsequent impossibility, objective impossibility and subjective incapability, the more recent decisions of the *Bundesgerichtshof* show an evident leaning toward the economic viewpoint. [136] The American courts have been moving in the same direction. They acknowledge from the start as rule and principle that a licensing agreement is "in time and territory co-extensive" with the patent. [137] On the other hand, the economic viewpoint may occasionally produce the kind of result where a licensee is estopped from

134. *Advance Industries* 11 July 1958, Patent Reports 1958, p. 394.

135. *Bundeskartellamt* 20 June 1960, WuW/E B Kart A, pp. 254 ff., at p. 258; cf. my *Kommentar zum Kartellgesetz*, § 20, p. 33.

136. Cf. copious case-references in Stumpf (44 ff.), down to *Bundesgerichtshof* 12 April 1957 (GRUR *Ausl.* 1958, p. 136) and 24 September 1957 (NJW 1958, p. 222); also *Bundesgerichtshof* 17 October 1968.

137. American decision of 15 June 1939.

arguing the expiry of the agreement from the lapse of the patent if, knowing the patent expired, he went on working and paying royalties on the basis of it. [138]

French jurisprudence has followed similar lines. As long ago as 1917 it produced a finding to the effect that the lapse of the licensed patent left a factual situation which required appraisal. [139] In recent times, the ostensibly more rigorous, traditional conception enshrined in a 1957 decision of the Court of Cassation has been counterbalanced by a 1960 decision of the same court, which takes better account of the real situation, and an unambiguous decision in second instance. [140]

In sum, therefore, it may already be regarded as transnational law, in appropriate cases, not only that the lapse or shrinkage of patent-rights affords a test of the continuing validity of the licensing agreement, but that the decisive test may in fact be whether the licensee, despite the lapse of the patent, still found himself in a particularly advantageous position which he continued to exploit. [141]

As we have already seen, the recognition of a right to terminate the agreement for cause is made subject to strict conditions on the plane of national law. This is so not only in relation to the substantive grounds for termination but also as concerns the formal prerequisites and procedure. In ascertaining transnational law, one will, in line with this tendency, be more inclined to adopt the stricter requirements than the less onerous. It is the United States which imposes the strictest, requiring that explicit and unambiguous notice be served even when the agreement provides for automatic expiration. A much-cited judgment says in particular:

> "A licensor is entitled to assume that his licensee remains such until the latter, by a clear, definite and unequivocal notice emanating from lawful and competent authority, throws off the protection of the license and stands admittedly an infringer if the patent is valid. The licensor is not to be left in danger of being defeated in a suit for infringement by a plea of license never effectually or authoritatively renounced; or, if he sues for royalties, of being beaten because there was merely an infringement, if anything." [142]

In the special circumstances of one English case, the House of Lords treated

138. *American Type Founders*, 4 August 1943, 137 F. 2d., p. 729.
139. *Virgilio* v. *Mohr*, 26 July 1917, *Ann. propr. ind.* 1926, p. 353.
140. *Exhenry* v. *Fridor*, 6 November 1957, *Ann. propr. ind.* 1958, p. 169; *Forest* v. *Punski*, 5 April 1960, *Recueil Dalloz* 1960, p. 717; *Audibert* v. *SA des machines Havas*, 29 January 1963, *Ann. propr. ind.* 1963, p. 361.
141. Cf. especially *Reichsgericht* 12 June 1942.
142. Decision of 28 December 1893, 140 NY, p. 217; 35 N E, p. 491. Cf. also 6 June 1963, 138 PY, p. 411.

the submission of a counterclaim as sufficient formal notice.[143] In France, one decision has correctly ruled that the not infrequent case of both parties asserting serious grounds for termination is not to be confused with dissolution of the agreement by common consent.[144]

IX. *Licensing of trademarks and design*

It is in all countries regarded as permissible to conclude licensing agreements having registered trademarks or design as their subject-matter. Everywhere, moreover, such agreements are related to general contract law and to legal principles which have already been developed in the law of patent licences.[145] If an invention is protected both by a patent and by a trademark, and if the rights in both are licensed, the position of the trademark licence is *ex hypothesi* bound up with that of the patent licence.[146] Inseparable as they are from the notion of quality-protection, trademark licences are particularly susceptible to legislation in the public interest.[147] The development of the law is still in a state of flux, but is moving in a direction which has thus been described by Deutsch:

"Now that adjacent markets are tending to merge, foreign travel is commonplace, and subsidiary undertakings or licensees in many States are supplied from a single centre of manufacture, the territorial autonomy of the brands owned by a person or corporation can easily become a fiction. The territorial principle can in the long run be maintained as a basis of international trademark law only where territory and market coincide."[148]

143. *Tool Metal*, 16 June 1955, Patent Reports 72, p. 209.
144. *Pulsa* v. *Dutrieux*, 19 June 1962, *Ann. propr. ind.* 1962, p. 168.
145. Mathély/de Guardia, in Langen, p. 154; Kronstein, *Das Recht der internationalen Kartelle*, pp. 441, 445 ff. and 459; more especially Beier, Deutsch and Fikentscher, *Die Warenzeichenlizenz, Festschrift Ulmer*, Munich 1963.
146. Cf. a French decision on an employee's invention: Paris 10 November 1959 (*Comminches*).
147. Langen, *Kommentar zum Kartellgesetz*, 4th ed., 1964; Neuwied, 20, para. 16; Switzerland: Federal Tribunal, 26 February 1935 ("*Preolit*").
148. *Festschrift Ulmer*, p. 478. Cf. *inter alia* Hamburg *Oberlandesgericht*, 3 October 1952 ("*Le Rouge Baiser*"); Switzerland: Federal Tribunal, 4 October 1960 ("*Philips*"); Frankfurt *Oberlandesgericht*, 22 February 1962 ("*Maja*"). All concern bans on the export of proprietary brands.

Part Three

THE SALE OF GOODS

I. *Two great steps on the road to harmony*

The law governing the international sale of goods, if only because of its economic importance, is a subject without which no account of transnational commercial law, at the advanced stage of formation it has already reached, would be complete. It is moreover admirable how leading scholars from many countries have in this field combined their efforts with experienced practitioners to hammer out transnational principles from the rich diversity of national rules of law.[1] The decades-old dispute as to whether the desired unification of law could better be achieved via improved and standardized conflicts rules or through the harmonization of substantive rules has now, where sales law is concerned, been settled in favour of the latter course.[2]

It is true, though at the same time of minor importance compared with the

1. Notably in the Diplomatic Conference on the Unification of Law governing the International Sale of Goods, The Hague 1964: *Records* (Vol. I) and *Documents* (Vol. II) published in French and English by the Netherlands Ministry of Justice, 1966. The Conference adopted by Conventions of 1 July 1964 two Uniform Laws on the International Sale of Goods, the first so called (Vol. I, pp. 336 ff.) and the second entitled "Uniform Law on the Formation of Contracts for the International Sale of Goods" (*ibid.*, pp. 352 ff.); the official commentary by André Tunc (*ibid.*, pp. 357 ff.) applies to both. The English texts of these Uniform Laws are more conveniently presented in the *Register of Texts of Conventions and Other Instruments concerning International Trade Law*, Vol. I, UN New York, 1971, Sales No. E. 71. V. 3, pp. 39 ff. and 64 ff.

Nota bene: For the sake of simplicity, the two Uniform Laws are referred to in this book as the "Hague Sales Rules" and the "Contract Formation Rules" respectively, the latter being dealt with more especially in chapter II of this Part. References to the "Hague Rules" cover both.

For the literature, see especially Schmitthoff, Honnold, Graveson/Cohn, Riese and Von Caemmerer in the *Bibliography*.

2. On the observations of Zweigert/Drobnig already mentioned (29 *RabelsZ*, 1965, pp. 146 ff.) see especially Honnold (ed.) *Unification . . .*, p. 33, citing E. Eörsi and Von Caemmerer. The decisive question is, which course offers the better probability of greater and more rapid progress? Beside this issue it is a secondary consideration that, as Nadelmann not unjustly remarked (*Proceedings*, p. 239), the rules of conflicts law would still not be redundant even if the Sales Rules were adopted worldwide.

thrust towards unification, that the two most ambitious undertakings, the Uniform Commercial Code of 1962 and the Hague Rules of 1964, exhibit disparities which cannot be overlooked.[3] Such disparities must and can be reconciled through the test of practice and polemics. The essential task, according to what is probably the predominant view in every country, is to bring the American Code and the Hague Rules into harmony.[4] To do so, however, will take years. The transnational law of sale which will thereby come to light will retain a birthmark to which Professor Mentschikoff has drawn attention with reference to the Uniform Commercial Code,[5] namely that it will reflect an economy of overproduction rather than one of husbanded resources. The essential premise of its remedies is a free society. However desirable it may be to arrive as quickly as possible at transnational rules applicable to trade with socialist States, and however much the endeavours in that direction are to be welcomed,[6] the words of Professor Mentschikoff must give us pause. The wholly different economic system of the socialist States must necessarily result in a basically different approach to the law of sale, and there is a risk that overeagerness to achieve unification may give rise to confusion on either side. It would on the whole be better, at least for this aspect of the problems in question, to adopt for the time being the wary viewpoint of Nadelmann. This decision is not without practical impact, as will later become evident when, for example, we deal with the question of the contract of sale without a determinable price, or that of the avoidance of a contract of sale.

The "synchronization" of the Uniform Commercial Code and the Hague Rules can be left to the efforts of the individual judge and scholar. There would be little point in continuing the series of conferences on the law of sale which began half a century ago. Nadelmann has described the doubts aroused by such conferences, and by the pressure to reach conclusions under which they labour;[7] these misgivings are confirmed in many passages of Otto Riese's reports.[8] Indeed the phenomenon will be familiar to anyone with much experience of conferences. Thus no excessive hopes may be pinned on

3. The most important disparity probably lies in the fact that, according to American ideas, the Hague Rules favour the seller more than the UCC does (cf. Farnsworth, *Proceedings*, p. 235).

4. Hellner, in Ziegel/Foster, p. 106; Daw, *Proceedings*, p. 243.

5. Mentschikoff, 29 *RabelsZ*, 1965, p. 412.

6. Cf. the colloquia instituted by the International Association of Legal Science and the reports thereon of Schmitthoff, *The Sources of the Law of International Trade*, London 1964, and of Honnold, *Unification of the Law governing the International Sale of Goods*, Paris 1966; also Philippe Kanh, *La Vente commerciale internationale*, Paris 1961, with the elaboration of the ECE conditions.

7. 16 AJCL, 1968, pp. 28 ff.

8. 22 *RabelsZ*, 1957, pp. 1 ff., and 29 *RabelsZ*, 1965, pp. 1 ff.

the United Nations Commission on International Trade Law (Uncitral), despite the head-start given it by the appointment as its Secretary-General of a leading American expert in the field, Honnold. To reiterate: the progress already achieved is sufficient for the further elaboration of transnational principles to be left without qualm to jurists and, more especially, the courts.

Obviously, the narrower the field of endeavour, the easier it is to succeed. In this respect there is a noteworthy difference between our two models, the Uniform Commercial Code and the Hague Sales Rules, in that the former is limited to commercial transactions, whereas the latter, according to Article 7, may also apply to sales which are not commercial transactions. For that reason the Rules are in many respects more cumbersome than the Code. Their authors are inclined to attach at least equal importance to the purchase of non-fungibles as to the purchase of mass-produced articles or staple commodities. Yet through the rapidly increasing standardization of all goods and consumer articles, the sphere of sale by specification, especially in the domain of international commerce which alone concerns us here, has shrunk to a mere fraction of its size 30 years ago. The bespoke object of old—horse and carriage, boats, implements, clothes, furniture—has given way to the special jigs, machine-tools, whole factories and power plants of the modern "one-off" order. In standard practice this transformation appears in the well-known ECE conditions for the sale of capital goods. We shall have to consider this phenomenon when we come to deal with the problem of specific performance. However, for the purposes of transnational commercial law, the delimitation of the concept "goods", despite certain discrepancies between Article 5 of the Sales Rules and Section 2-105 of the Code, should not present any insuperable difficulties so long as one refrains from making difficulties oneself.[9] Whenever there is a difference of opinion as to whether the subject-matter of a contract falls under the category of "goods", it will in practice turn on questions of fact or, at most, of commercial policy—seldom, at all events, of law.

Neither will there be any difference of opinion as to whether a given contract is a contract of sale or one of another kind, except in the rare case where the subject-matter is not a thing but a right, such as a patent-right for example. For that reason we have already, in Part Two on licensing agreements, had to go into the difference between sale on the one hand and leasing or hire on the other. But where things are the subject-matter, practice shows that any disagreement concerns at most the question whether the thing was transferred as property or as collateral. On one occasion, in connection with an export transaction of a very peculiar kind, a distinction had to be drawn

9. Here I have in mind certain exaggerations of Philippe Kahn's (pp. 12 ff.) which Lorenz has rightly deplored (ZHR 1964, p. 150).

between a sales contract and a contract for service.[10] The parties do not always express themselves clearly. Consequently, only the circumstances of the particular case can decide. This, in view of the concordance of all national laws, may be regarded as a principle of transnational law. The different situation in each particular case accounts for the fact that in one case sale is assumed, and in another the transfer of collateral.[11] As the Sales Rules refrain from defining sale, the definition given in Section 2-106 (1) of the Uniform Commercial Code will have to suffice:

"A 'sale' consists in the passing of title from the seller to the buyer for a price."

This definition agrees with the practice in nearly every country and is to that extent transnational.

This does not mean, however, that this definition is readily applicable to special kinds of sales contract. There is still considerable uncertainty in this area, as is shown by the vacillating evolution of the Sales Rules in regard to the contract for work and materials: compare the earlier Article 10 with the present Article 6 and, for that matter, Section 2-704 of the Code. The future alone will show how far special kinds of sales contract will give rise to national rules from which transnational principles may emerge.

In the case of one kind of contract not unallied to sale, the unusual situation prevails that transnational law has come closer to grips with it than national systems or even our two model codifications. I refer to barter, sometimes known as exchange, offset trading or compensation business. Thousands of years more ancient than sale, it is distinguished from the latter in the fact that not money but something else—usually other goods—forms the consideration. Barter is always preferred to sale, and is often the only solution, when there is no money readily available or when the money that is available is for some reason mistrusted. This explains why the authors of national systems of law have always paid much less attention to barter trade than international businessmen have had to do. Naturally, even in the national context (more especially in German experience), barter has always assumed greater economic importance when currencies have collapsed and lost all purchasing-power. But in international trade there was an era lasting right up to the Middle Ages during which the commerce of the Levant, for example that between Venice and the Near and Far East, was conducted almost exclusively on the basis of barter—and on no small scale at that. This

10. MAT 24 May 1923 (*Goldschmidt*).
11. In the American decision of 20 July 1927, the Russian prince Yusupov submitted that he had handed over a Rembrandt against a credit of £ 100,000 only by way of security, as the painting had an uncontroverted value of £150,000, but he lost his case. On the other hand, in one (not international) case decided by the German *Reichsgericht* (RGZ 1947, p. 132) the transference of a *Bausparvertrag* (savings agreement for building purposes) was regarded not as an assignment but as a pledge.

basis is very different from that of the money-transaction, and Ernst Rabel (*Warenkauf* II, p. 3) was therefore quite right in seeing no point in attempting to subsume barter under sales law.Only by ignoring such facts of economic history is it possible to assert that:

> "The common-law distinction between sale and barter, based upon the definition of 'price' in terms of money, seems very archaic and unnecessary."[12]

In Germany the problem has been eluded in a different way, namely by laying down, in § 515 of the Civil Code, that the provisions governing sale shall be "correspondingly" applicable to barter, and the Hague-Sales Rules evade the difficulty by defining neither sale nor barter.[13]

The Uniform Commercial Code, in Section 2-304, unfortunately provides that each party shall be regarded as a seller where the price is payable wholly or partly in goods. It is as well, therefore, that the official comment on this provision recommends that it be interpreted with prudence. Actually there are often cases of spurious barter, in which two contracts of sale are interlinked in the way described in Section 2-304. In practice the decision as to whether the case is one of sale or barter is often difficult, and in the final analysis can only be properly reached if the economic circumstances alluded to above are given due weight. In case of doubt it may also be useful to study the foreign-exchange law, because where the transfer of payments and the transfer of goods are subject to different regulations, the question boils down to one of narrowly ascertaining whether the transaction falls into the payments category (sale) or is exclusively covered by the transfer of goods.[14] The correct pigeonholing of the contract is important not only for determining which national law controls it in the last resort, or for deciding whether two distinct transactions and two different laws might not be involved, but also for settling a host of questions concerning the time or place of delivery, matters of quality, etc. If it is a barter agreement, it may not in any circumstances be

---

12. Fridmann, in Ziegel/Foster, p. 32. One connotation of "barter", no longer very current, is that of a "corrupt transaction" (*Black's Law Dictionary* – citing the American *Troy* decision of 8 December 1920, concerning a seat on the Federal Supreme Court). And barter transactions will in fact be regarded charily, if only because they eliminate the possibility of checking by reference to the objective money-standard. Yet there is no justification for belittling the significance of barter in international trade.

13. In their annotation of Article 5, Graveson/Cohn point to conference document Conf./C.R./Com.6 as evidence that the Sales Rules are not suitable for application to pure barter-contracts.

14. Cf. especially Hartenstein, *Devisennotrecht*, Berlin 1935, *ad* "Private Verrechnungsgeschäfte" and "Kompensationsgeschäfte"; Langen, *Internationale Zahlungsabkommen*, Tübingen 1958, with instructive Swiss examples, p. 41, n. 3; Langen, *Kommentar zum Aussenwirtschaftsgesetz*, Munich 1958, *vor* § 8, n.11, with further references.

torn into two parts.[15] The overall conclusion for transnational law is that the distinction between sale and barter must be established with greater care than is the case in many national legal systems.

In seeking transnational rules for the international sale of goods, one should not lose sight of the fact that the forwarding of goods is the usual procedure in such transactions. National regulations, and even the Hague Sales Rules in Article 19 (2), proceed on the supposition that it is not the rule but the exception. The same reversal of rule and exception, though not quite to the same extent, obtains in regard to the subject-matter of the sales contract. Very many national systems, those of civil-law countries among them, start from the assumption that the subject-matter of a contract of sale will as a rule be a specific article, and then make special provision for cases where a *"Gattungssache"*, i.e. merchandise or commodities, is the subject of the contract. It will be advisable to treat this problem as belonging to the realm of facts, and not so much as a matter of law. Certain details arising in this connection will be dealt with later, when we come to examine the seller's obligation to deliver.

Parties often disagree as to whether a transaction is really international, or whether one particular national law ought not to be exclusively applied. Such cases arise for example when both parties are domiciled in the same country while the deal between them concerns goods located abroad. The most numerous cases of this kind are those in which the dealings in question are being conducted in accordance with the rules of certain exchanges, a specific trade code, or arbitral regulations, which generally apply to the commodity in question, as in the case of wheat, cotton, wool, metals etc. In classic private international law these questions are regarded as extremely important, because the point to be resolved is whether one legal system or another should be employed, to the exclusion of all others. Our two model codifications give different kinds of answer; the Hague Sales Rules in Article 1, by attempting a close delineation of the circumstances they cover, and the American UCC in Section 1-105 (1) with a blanket clause: "this Act applies to transactions bearing an appropriate relation to this State". The question therefore arises as to whether the right opened by Article 4 of the Hague Sales Rules, that of choosing them as the law of the contract, is not excluded

15. That is the dubious feature of the award given on 2 November 1954 by the Prague Chamber of Commerce, dealing with the exchange of Czech freight-cars against French goods unspecified. "Article 5 of the contract provided that payment must be effected by compensation, different goods to be supplied by the plaintiffs. The payment was not therefore to be made in money but in counterdelivery of goods, and this is shown also in Articles 3 and 7 of the contract, whereby deliveries of the two parties depended on each other" (p. 461). The arbitral tribunal explicitly established the points of difference between "sale" and "barter", but went on to base its decision on the place of conclusion of the contract and then subjected it wholly to Czechoslovak law.

by Section 1-105 of the Code.[16] Cases involving the question whether any other currency can be contractually imposed as between co-nationals in their own country than the national currency common to both, or whether it is even lawful for them to contract for settlement in another currency, are especially instructive in practice.[17]

A number of very important subjects can here be no more than indicated, as they do not specifically concern the sale of goods but are generally relevant to all kinds of contractual obligation. They will therefore be reverted to in a later Part of this book. Among them is the absolute preference to be accorded to commercial practices and usages as defined in Article 9 of the Hague Sales Rules which to that extent, being in harmony with all national laws, are also transnational law: cf. Section 2-103 of the Code—

> " 'Good faith' in the case of a merchant means honesty in fact and the observance of reasonable commercial standards of fair dealing in the trade."[18]

Another important question, that of the legal position of representatives, agents, branch offices and the like in international sales transactions, is very largely governed by mandatory national law, and the only hope of finding an overriding rule would appear to lie in application of the transnational principle of the protection of confidence (*Vertrauensschutz*)[19] Two American

16. This has already been asserted by an American writer. The decision would appear to depend upon whether the Hague Sales Rules are regarded by an American judge as equivalent to the legal order of another State, in the sense of Section 1-105. Strictly speaking, they cannot be. From the point of view of sense, however, one cannot help asking whether the law of the most microscopic State in the United Nations is to carry more weight than the International Convention on the Law of the Sale of Goods, especially as that Convention has after due ratification acquired force of law in several large States. So far as transnational law is concerned, the whole problem simply does not arise, because here the judge can in any case remain within the framework of the local law of one or the other party. An agreement between parties that the Sales Rules will apply has therefore the same significance as if they had agreed to be governed by the terms of a foreign standard contract, commodity exchange regulations or private-law convention. The validity of transnational rules may therefore be much more readily assumed than in the event of agreement on the applicability of a foreign legal system. However, the assumption of transnational rules, no less than that of a foreign legal system, may not cross the frontier of mandatory law.

17. Cf. especially the French decisions of 27 April 1964 and 4 May 1964; further, Rabel, *Warenkauf* I, p. 49 and, more particularly, p. 53, also "price" in the subject-index.

18. Cf. especially Farnsworth, 30 *University of Chicago Law Review*, 1963, pp. 666 ff., and, concurring, Eisemann, *Incoterms* ...., p. 60; also the English decisions of 17 May 1954, 3 February 1960 and 26 October 1967.

19. Rabel, *Conflict* III, p. 60, writes: "The problem of agency is not so simple." The Commission preparing the Sales Rules could not bring itself to propose an express formula covering liability for the acts of persons assisting in the performance of contractual obligations, but contented itself with acknowledging such liability in the

judgments, *Thrift Wholesale* (27 July 1943) and *State of Delaware* (17 March 1943), are especially relevant to the question of the sufficiency in law of statements made by "agents" or "salesmen".

II. *Formation of the contract*

A. *Preliminary and formal questions*

If the parties are in dispute as to whether a contract has actually been concluded, any attempt to relate the dispute to a specific national law will have two difficulties to overcome. The first lies in the fact that even a contract which has undoubtedly been concluded cannot, if the case is international, be allocated without a certain wrench to this or that municipal system. But at least the parties in this case will be in agreement about the existence of some transaction. What, then, if there is not even that much common ground? Here the second difficulty arises: to determine the proper national law, it will be necessary to resort to a double make-believe. One must imagine that a contract has come into existence, and then pretend either that the parties had made a choice of national law or that the contract, as supposititiously concluded, was more closely connected with a certain jurisdiction than with any other.

It follows that disputes over the actual existence of a contract are singularly ill-suited for determination in accordance with the rules of classical conflicts law. They must above all be decided as if any preferential link were out

---

deliberations. The general trend is probably typified by the recommendation of the 1952 Lucerne ILA Conference (Report of 45th Conf., pp. 309-314) that questions concerning the legal validity of powers of representation should be decided in accordance with the law of the place where the representative does his representing. Among decided cases one might draw attention here to the Paris decision of 27 January 1955, in which the Paris office of a Saar firm was treated as a simple mail-box; on the other hand, the German *Bundesgerichtshof* was probably right on 9 December 1964 when, relying on the principle of the protection of confidence, it treated the Frankfurt buying-office of a Bulgarian State-trading company as the latter's representative. On 5 March 1923, in respect of an Italo-Swiss sales-transaction, the Swiss Federal Tribunal treated the *gerente* of a Milanese firm in accordance with Swiss law, because he had appeared in his representative capacity in Switzerland; thus this decision is in harmony with the much later Lucerne recommendation. However, the time required to reach a legally enforceable decision in that case stretched from 10 July 1916 to 5 March 1923. On 27 April 1933 the *Reichsgericht* applied the German law on representation to the case of a hedgedeal in cotton concluded by an American firm's representative operating in Germany. Sir Arnold McNair said on 12 October 1951 in the *Bank Melli Iran* case: "It seems to me that a statement by some agent who purposes to be an authorized government official can properly be accepted as a statement by the government."

of the question, i.e. in such a way that any national rules touching the conclusion of contracts could be introduced only in so far as they obtained in the countries of both the parties, if not in more.

To view a private international dispute in this way is, in fact, to be confronted with the same problems as would *mutatis mutandis* subsist in relation to the conclusion of a treaty between States. And, indeed, public international law provides a number of valuable pointers for transnational law in regard to the conclusion of contracts. Thus, for example, it is of little importance for the law of nations whether an agreement between States is expressly described as a treaty. It could be labelled in any way whatever: the name is not the test. Considering the frequent bilingualism of private international instruments, the parallel is not unimportant.[20] Even so, the rule that the name is not decisive is really of but negative significance, inasmuch as it simply boils down to the observation that the contracts of public international law do not always bear the solemn name of "treaty".

A second negative observation is, however, more important. It is that there are no rules of public international law governing the form which treaties (*scil.* contracts) must be given. In practice, between a quarter and a third of all bilateral international agreements come into being through exchanges of Notes.[21] A French decision[22] treated an exchange of telegrams between the French and Soviet Governments over the details of the recognition of the USSR in 1924 as a treaty. Treaties can even be concluded orally: cf. the decision of the Mixed Arbitral Tribunals (MAT, Vol. 7, p. 147) cited by Dahm (p. 73) and, more particularly, the Permanent Court's Judgment of 1933 in the *Eastern Greenland* dispute between Denmark and Norway (*P.C.I.J., Series A/B, No. 53*, p. 71). However, the conclusion of treaties by tacit acceptance and constructive conduct does not seem to be generally recognized, though examples of such recognition are to be found in German and Swiss jurisprudence (cf. RGSt. 57, 61, and RGZ 111, 40 for Germany, and BGE 81 II 335 for Switzerland) and also in the *Caselli* case (United States v. Panama: UNRIAA VI, p. 378) which involved agreements to make certain payments. At bottom, in such decisions, it would appear to be a question not so much of textual interpretation as of applying the test of good faith.

The third important contribution of public international law concerns the initialling of instruments, a practice quite common in the context of private

20. In respect of public international law, see the Advisory Opinion of the Permanent Court of International Justice in the *Austro-German Customs Union* case, 1931: "From the standpoint of the obligatory character of international engagements it is well known that such engagements may be taken in the form of treaties, conventions, declarations, agreements, protocols, or exchanges of notes." (*Series A/B, No. 41*, p. 47.)

21. Lauterpacht, *The Law of Treaties*, UN doc. A/Cn.4/63 and 87.

22. Paris 24 March 1933 (Sirey 1933 II 201).

agreements also. In contrast to provisional signature, which establishes the point in time as from which the instrument takes effect if later confirmed or ratified, initialling does not normally produce any such retroactive effect: cf. the draft of the International Law Commission, UN Document A/CN. 4L. 83/Add. 2, Art. 10 (3). This draft, however, leaves open the question whether the mere fact of negotiations in progress can give rise to any obligations. Such a situation must be sharply distinguished from that of a preliminary agreement; it raises questions of good faith and lends itself much less to assessment by the lights of the *culpa in contrahendo* doctrine so much favoured in Germany.

There is another aid to finding one's way in the statuteless realm of international cases which has been used with marked success in the Hague Contract Formation Rules. It consists of an approach whereby, instead of following the usual trend of civil-law jurists and taking the end-term of a series of events, i.e. the conclusion of the contract, as the starting-point, one attentively traces out the events which, one by one and by their interaction, finally lead to that end-term. Offer and acceptance are thus the facts which are studied, for what they are in themselves and in their interaction, and which, properly evaluated, lead automatically to the end-result, namely the conclusion of the contract. In this process, offer and acceptance each appear as declarations sent forth on their way to the other party, all the risks by the wayside being borne as a rule by the declarer. These risks include not merely the consequences of arrival or non-arrival, but also the danger of reception in unintelligible or misunderstood form. It is moreover essential to this approach, and of particular importance in the international domain, that each step in this process should be outwardly discernible and should not, as continental doctrine would have it, consist of some barely discernible inner process such as the concordance of the will of the parties. This is not to say that judicial investigation of the concordant will of the parties (the *consensus* of Roman law) may not where wholly feasible be the more refined approach, the one productive of the more reliable result, whereas to confine oneself to the external facts is to accept a more rough and ready basis of work. When dealing, within the area of one national system, with people who more or less think alike, it will always be easier to establish an inward concordance of wills than can be the case in the international sphere. Thus we find that from time immemorial outward tokens of the conclusion of a contract have been more widely employed in foreign trade, where instantaneous and yet trustworthy understanding is requisite, than inward signs. One may recall the handshake seen as rendering a deal effective, or the "to-you/from-you" (*an Sie/von Ihnen*) formula in exchange business. All these facts and considerations explain a certain preference which transnational law will accord to externally recognizable signs of the conclusion of a contract. That has to be said at the outset if the Contract Formation Rules are to be properly understood and

81

evaluated. The offer is the first step. It brings the possibility of acceptance into being. By the acceptance the transaction enters into its second phase, that of the conclusion of the contract.

The party subsequently contesting the conclusion of the contract may be either the offeror or the acceptor; it will, at all events, be the party to whose advantage it would be for the contract not to exist. In the goods trade, therefore, at a time of rising prices it will as a rule be the seller who denies the conclusion of the contract, whereas when prices are falling it will be the buyer. Thus the price-trend will often give a clue as to whether the contestation is seriously motivated from the legal point of view.

The Hague Uniform Law on the Formation of Contracts of Sale [23] represents an important step forward in the development of transnational commercial law, because, under American influence, it resolutely averts its gaze from the internal, subjective process of contract-making and concentrates on the more unmistakable outward process of offer and acceptance. From the beginning the Convention enshrining it received more international recognition than the Sales Law Convention. Continental jurists, especially, having made considerable concessions to their American colleagues, are clearly prepared to acknowledge the model effect of the Contract Formation Rules. One finds such comments as the following:

> "On the whole it may be regretted that the Hague Conference did not see its way to adopting the clear and comprehensive German solution all along the line. In the practical event, however, the differences are probably microscopic. Admittedly this solution was only obtained at the cost of some highly complicated draftsmanship, as it was necessary to accept the outmoded revocability principle as the starting-point and then, through a string of special provisions in Article 5 (2) to (4), to whittle it away to insignificance. However, one ought not to strain at a certain lack of juristic elegance when what one gets in

23. *Bibliography.* French and English text of the Convention: *Records of the Diplomatic Conference on the Unification of Law governing the International Sale of Goods* (The Hague 1964), Netherlands Ministry of Justice 1966, esp. pp. 352-354 (and cf. commentary of André Tunc on both Conventions, pp. 358 ff.). English text: *Register of Texts of Conventions and other Instruments concerning International Trade Law*, United Nations 1971, pp. 64 ff. Commentary and elucidation: Gravesohn/Cohn, *The Uniform Laws on International Sales Act 1967*, London 1968, pp. 111-121; Folke Schmidt, "The International Contract Law in the Context of Some of its Sources", 14 AJCL, 1965, pp. 1-37; Von Caemmerer, "Haager Abkommen über den Vertragsabschluss", 29 *RabelsZ*, 1965, pp 101-145; Goldstajn, "The Formation of the Contract", and Lagergren, "Formation of Contract", in Honnold (ed.), *Unification of the Law governing International Sales of Goods*, Paris 1966, pp. 41 ff. and 55 ff. For comparative law: R.B. Schlesinger, *Formation of Contracts* I & II, New York and London 1968; Werner-Lorenz, *Vertragsabschluss und Parteiwahl im Obligationrecht Englands*, Heidelberg 1957.

return is, in practice, a high degree of legal unity in regard to the conclusion of international contracts of sale."[24]

or, with reference even to the Hague Rules as a whole:

"There is no comparison between applying the internal *lex fori* and the application, instead, of the Hague Rules, for in the latter case one judges in accordance with an international law elaborated by jurists of the most diverse countries, one tailored for international transactions, accessible in languages in worldwide use, one on which even a party in a non-signatory State can model his own contracts."[25]

Folke Schmidt (p. 37) has also expressly drawn attention to the model effect of the Contract Formation Rules.

Thus in all cases in which the parties have left the court some discretion with regard to the applicable norm and no compulsory rule of national law has to be observed, it is essential that judges should in future pay heed to the proposals of the Hague Convention on the Formation of Contracts of Sale, whether the parties are nationals of signatory States or not. This will be the easier insofar as the Hague Rules clearly pay more regard to the concepts of plain businessmen than to juristic doctrines.[26] From the same standpoint it will also be possible to find a solution where friction subsists with the material provisions in other conventions or in the standard contracts of trade associations.[27] Finally, the overwhelming majorities, if not the unanimity, with which the Hague resolutions were adopted, is particularly noteworthy.[28]

The report of the Commission gives understandable reasons why the questions of the time and place of the conclusion of a contract, or that of the validity of a contract once concluded, were not regulated by the Convention. Here reference should be made to the similar reservation expressed in Article 8 of the Sales Rules.

It is possible to do without a rule on the time of the conclusion of a contract if one rests content with the establishment of rules concerning offer and acceptance, from which the actual time contracting will then emerge. This is a novel idea for civil-law jurists, hence the Austrian, Belgian, Dutch and French delegates to the Hague conference proposed the retention of draft Article 12, which made provision for a rule on time of contract. The delegates of the United States, the Scandinavian countries and the International

24. Zweigert/Kötz, *Einführung in die vergleichende Rechtswissenschaft*, Vol. II: "Institutionen", Tübingen 1969, p. 41.

25. Von Caemmerer, "Rechtsvereinheitlichung und internationales Privatrecht", *Festschrift Hallstein*, Frankfurt am Main 1966, p. 83.

26. *Sic* Folke Schmidt, *loc.cit.*

27. The above-mentioned report by Goldstajn is directed above all to this end.

28. Cf. the indications given by Von Caemmerer, pp. 114, 121 and 125.

Chamber of Commerce, later joined by the German representatives, maintained on the contrary that it would be more practical to dispense with a rule on the point. The votes taken betray a significant inconsistency: first there were 10 votes to 8 in favour of having a rule, and then 9 to 5 against it. This very inconsistency is enough to show that there is no transnational law on the matter. In fact, it is not possible to set up a general regulation for the time of conclusion of contracts without recourse to "nasty conceptual jurisprudence".[29] The time of conclusion can be important from the most diverse standpoints, and these may not be left out of account:

"From the point of view of bankruptcy law, the question may be whether the liability was fully in being before the adjudication in bankruptcy. *Mutatis mutandis*, the same can be said of the transfer of title in those branches of law controlled by the principle of consent. Where knowledge of defects is in question, attention may perhaps centre on the point in time when the purchaser binds himself to pay the purchase-price. In other connections it may be the moment when the party concerned takes over the liability. In respect of exonerating circumstances, it may be a question of what the parties had to take into account by the terms of the contract. In all cases the judge must be left a free hand in the interpretation of the uniform sales law, to elicit from the purpose of the norm the meaning to be given to the time of conclusion of the contract."[30]

What has been said in regard to the time of conclusion applies with even greater force to the place of conclusion. It has repeatedly been observed that a contract *inter absentes* cannot be tied to a single place of conclusion without doing violence to sense, and that this difficulty is particularly apparent in the international sphere. Generalization on this question is therefore especially risky, and so is the view that when the time of conclusion is ascertained, the place of conclusion is thereby codetermined.[31] Just as in the case of the time, it may be necessary to establish the place of conclusion in accordance with the circumstances. It would however be wrong to set up general criteria of a transnational kind in regard to the place at which a contract is concluded. Courts rarely fail to exercise the requisite caution in this respect, and normally confine themselves to the circumstances of the

29. Von Caemmerer, p. 137.

30. Von Caemmerer, *loc. cit.* With regard to the time of conclusion when it is agreed that there will be a certificate of acceptance of delivery, see the Prague *Motokov* award of 2 November 1954.

31. *Sic* the decision given by the German *Bundesgerichtshof* on 24 February 1958, with a reference to the concurring view of writings on the subject and the following dictum: "The place of conclusion is the place at which the offeror receives the news of the acceptance of his offer."

particular case in determining the place of contract.[32] A very considerable proportion of disputes over the place of contract arises, moreover, out of situations quite beyond the purview of private law, for example in connection with the sequestration of enemy property, the application of currency regulations or international bankruptcy law.[33] Thus the time and place of the conclusion of a contract are frequently influenced by peremptory national rules, and there transnational commercial law reaches a borderline which it may not cross. There nevertheless remains a certain scope for the application of a transnational rule, for to the extent that the parties still have a choice of applicable law, no party, without misuse of law, may rely to his own advantage on the stricter formal requirements of the opponent's country: it should rather suffice for each party to have observed the form prescribed in his domestic law for the conclusion of contracts.[34] It is surely impermissible to supplant this test by the manipulation or doctrinaire treatment of the question of the place of contract.[35]

We shall not here deal with all the questions concerning the invalidity of a contract of sale—its voidability for error, fraud or duress, or its nullity as illegal, contrary to public policy or imperfectly agreed—, because in every country these form an essential part of general contract law.[36] It follows from this very fact that these general rules, however differently they may be couched in individual systems, all "work together for good".[37] The relative paucity of case-law on these subjects in relation to international sales contracts is perhaps also due to this fact.

An interesting, because recurrent case of unilateral mistake is dealt with the French decision of 6 December 1927 (Tourcoing). The Czech purchaser of combed wool from a Frenchman in Paris refused to take delivery or pay, on the grounds that under his own domestic law he would have the right to inspect the goods beforehand and that he had agreed to purchase only on that

32. E.g. the French decision Cass. 22 June 1956, ruling that in the case of a written offer of employment the place of conclusion of the contract is the place from which the declaration of acceptance is despatched.

33. On this last subject, cf. the decisions given in the opposite sense on the same case by the *Tribunal commercial de la Seine* on 6 September 1966 and by the *Tribunal civil* of Liège on 14 November 1907. In Lachau's note on the French judgment it is correctly pointed out that a distinction must be made between questions concerning the validity of a contract and questions of enforcement as in the case of bankruptcy. Cf. also the decision of the Colmar Court of Appeal given on 26 February and 27 March 1957, thoroughly annotated by Francescakis.

34. In the same sense, Zweigert, *Festschrift Rabel*, 1953, I, p. 631.

35. Cf. discussion of Article 3 of the Contract Formation Rules, below.

36. A comparison would here be in order between such blanket clauses as Section 2-302 UCC ("unconscionable contracts") and special rules of the kind found in § § 116 ff. of the German Civil Code.

37. Raape, *Internationales Privatrecht*, 5th ed. 1961, p. 492.

understanding. In the event that he did not have that right, he would contest the contract on grounds of unilateral mistake. The court correctly dismissed these arguments, not merely on account of a slight error in point of law but also because it was clear that the buyer had in reality made the purchase without any such precondition and wished to be released from the contract only on account of price-alterations.

The American *Ward Lumber* judgment of 2 January 1915 applies to a case of fraud the following statement of principle:

> "The seller may, on discovery that the contract was procured from him by fraud, rescind not only as against the original buyer, but as against a transfer with not a *bona fide* purchaser for value." [38]

Duress, or taking undue advantage of another person's difficulties, was the subject of the American *Yusupov* decision of 20 July 1927. In this famous case the Russian prince Yusupov had sold, in England, a Rembrandt located there to an American art-dealer for £100,000 and had later maintained that the painting had demonstrably been worth £150,000. One of the sentences in the headnote of the decision ran:

> "Where seller of pictures understood contract and there was no duress, contract held enforceable whether or not buyer obtained exceptional bargain when seller was financially embarrassed."

If not all, but only important parts of a contract have been concluded, or if part of a completed contract proves eventually to be null and void, national statutes which then provide for the nullity of the whole (such as § 139 and § 154 of the German Civil Code) cannot serve as models for transnational law. International practice looks with greater favour on texts which on the contrary provide for the transaction to be as far as possible enforced in conformity with its meaning even if the regulation of some particular aspect is lacking or invalid. A certain model effect may be ascribed to Section 2-305 of the Uniform Commercial Code, which admits the possibility of a contract of sale even where the price has not been settled (see "purchase price" below), likewise Section 2-302 (2) ("unconscionable clauses") and more especially Section 2-311.

Another subject which we will deal with only in the last part of this work is that of the nullity of a contract as contrary to law, *ordre public* or public policy. Such problems have nothing to do with the actual conclusion of a contract, but result only from its substance.

In the Hague Contract Formation Rules, the first clause of transnational significance is Article 2:

---

38. Cf. also the American decision of 26 February 1926 (*Obear-Nester Glass*).

"1. The provisions of the following Articles shall apply except to the extent that it appears from the preliminary negotiations, the offer, the reply, the practices which the parties have established between themselves or usage, that other rules apply.

2. However, a term of the offer stipulating that silence shall amount to acceptance is invalid."

This Article embodies three rules which together can without hesitation be regarded as transnational law. First, expression is given to the principle that in the international law of sale the will of the parties takes precedence not merely over the national statutes but even over the Hague Rules themselves. If therefore the parties desire their transaction to be handled in accordance with transnational law, that wish is to be respected. In fact the Article refrains from any general affirmation of the priority to be given to the parties' will, and instead enumerates the separate criteria from which this priority emerges. This corresponds to English drafting technique, but it would be wrong in practice to allow the difference between this and civil-law draftsmanship to make any difference. In any case, the Article merely confirms a view that was already generally held.[39] The advantage of the English technique in this text is moreover evident, in that any direct mention of the will of the parties would have constituted a reference to something essentially more nebulous and hard to construe than preliminary negotiations, offers, replies, established practices or commercial usage. The priority effectively given the will of the parties corresponds to Article 3 of the Sales Rules, which provides in terms that:

"The parties to a contract of sale shall be free to exclude the application thereto of the present Law either entirely or partially. Such exclusion may be express or implied."

The principle of the priority of the will of the parties has a negative and a positive side, which cannot very well be separated. The positive consequence of the possibility of excluding other rules of law than those wanted by the parties is that the parties can determine the rules that are to apply. We have already, in the Introduction, gone into the further requirement of private international law, that rules departing from the norm must be adequately defined or definable. It is particularly noteworthy that commercial practices and usage are enumerated among the elements which may take precedence over other rules. This expresses the Commission's deliberate decision[40] to allow trade practices priority even where they do not agree with the Contract

---

39. Cf. extensive observations on this theme by Philippe Kahn, p. 229. Cf. also Von Caemmerer's exegesis on Articles 2 & 3 (p. 112).

40. Cf. Von Caemmerer, pp. 113 and 139.

Formation Rules. On this point we shall have more to say when we consider the treatment of silence. [41]

So far as the transnational significance of paragraph 1 of Article 2 is concerned, it would be a mistake to cling to the literal meaning of each word: in a polyglot context that would in any case be senseless. What is important is certainly not the individual circumstances as separately enumerated, but all the background of the contract taken as a whole, including the conduct of the parties. In this respect there is an even better model for transnational law in Section 1-205 of the Uniform Commercial Code.

"Course of Dealing and Usage of Trade

(1) A course of dealing is a sequence of previous conduct between the parties to a particular transaction which is fairly to be regarded as establishing a common basis of understanding for interpreting their expressions and other conduct.

(2) A usage of trade is any practice or method of dealing having such regularity of observance in a place, vocation or trade as to justify an expectation that it will be observed with respect to the transaction in question. The existence and scope of such a usage are to be proved as facts. If it is established that such a usage is embodied in a written trade code or similar writing the interpretation of the writing is for the court.

(3) A course of dealing between parties and any usage of trade in the vocation of trade in which they are engaged or of which they are or should be aware give particular meaning to and supplement or qualify terms of an agreement.

(4) The express terms of an agreement and an applicable course of dealing or usage of trade shall be construed wherever reasonable as consistent with each other; but when such construction is unreasonable express terms control both course of dealing and usage of trade and course of dealing controls usage of trade.

(5) An applicable usage of trade in the place where any part of performance is to occur shall be used in interpreting the agreement as to that part of the performance.

(6) Evidence of a relevant usage of trade offered by one party is not admissible unless and until he has given the other party such notice as the court finds sufficient to prevent unfair surprise to the latter."

---

41. On the limits of the autonomy of the parties, cf. the articles of Ionesco and Nestor and Lagergren in Schmitthof (ed.), *Sources* ..., pp. 167 and 201. In Honnold (ed.), *Unification* ..., pp. 41 & 55, Goldstajn and Lagergren view contract-formation from the standpoint of comprarative law; the former mainly by comparing the General Conditions of Delivery of Goods, 1958, as applied by the Member Countries of the Council for Mutual Economic Assistance, the ECE Conditions, the Hague Contract Formation Rules and the UCC; see also what Honnold himself has to say, *op. cit.*, pp. 20 ff.

In the official comment on this text it is further explained that by virtue of Section 2-208 even conduct subsequent to the conclusion of a contract can be of importance.[42]

In transnational law the actual conduct of the parties is to be taken into account not only in the interpretation of the contract but in ascertaining whether any contract was in fact concluded. There is copious case-law on the subject, and one may cite in particular the *Negreanu* decision of the Mixed Arbitral Tribunals (16 June 1925), which held it incontestable that a course of dealing over many years could make the tacit acceptance of contracts possible, and, to a very great extent, Decision No. 543 of the arbitral tribunal of the International Chamber of Commerce (*L'Economie internationale*, December 1934, p.7). The German *Kammergericht*, in its judgment of 8 May 1935, even referred in interpreting a licensing agreement to a contract four years older. Statements on similar lines are to be found in the *Sapphire* award of 15 March 1963 and in the *Abu-Dhabi* award of 28 August 1951, where (on p. 251) Lord Asquith observes that the English maxim that preliminary negotiations should not be taken into account cannot be viewed as absolute in international cases. In the English *Kite* decision of 16 May 1933, previous practice was taken into account. Cohn (p. 112) finds it strange that preliminary negotiations should be allowed to influence the question of the conclusion of the contract. This doubt was met by Lord Asquith in the *Abu-Dhabi* award. Transnational law may accordingly be presumed, though with the caution that is always to be recommended.

In regard to the important question of how the conduct of the parties prior to the conclusion of the contract is to be evaluated, it would appear to be transnational law that preliminary negotiations and outlines of agreement from nothing more than an exchange of views without binding force. This is so in particular when agreement that a formal contract will be concluded is reached in the course of this exchange. In that case, it is only for the interpretation of the contract—or, as we have seen, for the question of whether it was truly concluded—that the different events preceding the appointed date of conclusion are significant, though they may then, indeed, be highly significant.

At first sight there appears to be a certain antithesis between the laws of continental Europe, which have more or less distinctly taken over the Roman-law notion of *culpa in contrahendo* (*Verschulden im Vertragsabschluss*: mutual liability of the prospective parties during the pre-conclusion period) and the laws of England and America, where this doctrine is regarded as too theoretical by half and is generally not recognized. [43] There is however

42. *Sic* the English decision of 22 May 1952 (*Plasticmoda*) and the American decision of 27 July 1943 (*Thrift Wholesale*).
43. Lagergren, on p. 73 of Honnold (ed.), *Unification* ... .

a common denominator in terms of which even this doctrine can be expressed, namely good faith.[44] This principle of transnational law is also capable of lending model effect to the particularly clear German jurisprudence concerning the duties of the parties to a so-called "hovering" contract, i.e., one which will only take effect after the fulfilment of a certain condition, typically the granting of official authorization.[45]

The definition of commercial usage is given in Article 13 of the Hague Contract Formation Rules:

> "Usage means any practice or method of dealing which reasonable persons in the same situation as the parties usually consider to be applicable to the formation of their contract."

As the Contracts Convention is even more in the nature of *lex specialis* than the Sales Law Convention, this provision takes precedence over the very similarly worded Article 9 of the latter, and *a fortiori* over all national laws. This can be said without hesitation, for:

> "The legal treatment of commercial usages in the major systems leads to practically unanimous results, apart from procedural questions which are here beside the point, as for example whether the judge is entitled to presume from his own knowledge that a commercial usage exists or whether an application for revision of an appeal judgment can be based on the alleged infringement of a commercial usage. Yet the different systems do not reach their results by the same path, and the overall picture is somewhat complicated."[46]

The fact that the word "practice" in Article 13 is not qualified with "established" is not significant. The passage of a certain period of time is already implicit in the word "usage" and is further indicated by the words "usually consider". But how "established" must a practice be, how longstanding must usage

---

44. Cf. Staudinger/Coing, 1st ed. 1957, *ad* § 145, nn. VII ff.; also Dieter Henrich, *Vorvertrag, Optionsvertrag, Vorrechtsvertrag*, Berlin 1965.

45. A leading decision for Germany was that given by the *Reichsgericht* on 23 June 1926 with regard to the liability of the seller of a property who, during the period of "hovering"–which lasted until the eventual refusal of official authorization–, got the buyer to make down-payments the value of which had been diminished by depreciation of the currency. The court said: "There seems to be no reason why claims of a more or less legal nature ought not to be brought in a case where there has been brought to completion–though legally and immediately conditional on the granting of official authorization–a process of contract-formation to which, however, only a limited binding force may be ascribed. If, during the period of this bond, one of the parties to the contract, in the manner here concerned, culpably causes prejudice to the other through inadequate regard for his interests, the first party is in principle under an obligation to make reparation." A similar ruling was given in the American decision of 29 July 1948 (*Atlas*). Cf. further my *Kommentar zum Aussenwirtschaftsgesetz*, § 31, n. 26, and my *Kommentar zum Devisengesetz*, C VII 12, with further illustrations.

46. Rabel, *Warenkauf* I, p. 58.

be, in order to satisfy the requirements of the text? This is something which can safely be left to the decision of the individual case. Certainly Section 1-205 of the Uniform Commercial Code goes to the farthest limit in this respect, if one considers point 5 of the official comment thereon:

"5. A usage of trade under subsection (2) must have the 'regularity of observance' specified. The ancient English tests for 'custom' are abandoned in this connection. Therefore, it is not required that a usage of trade be 'ancient or immemorial', 'universal' or the like. Under the requirement of subsection (2) full recognition is thus available for new usages and for usages currently observed by the great majority of decent dealers, even though dissidents ready to cut corners do not agree. There is room also for proper recognition of usage agreed upon by emergency in trade codes."

The German view of the formation of a commercial usage requires the passage of a certain period of time, the assent of the participants and evidence of regular practice. This does not, however, constitute an insuperable contrast if the relevant case-law be studied, notably the *Reichsgericht* decision of 28 September 1927 (RGZ 118, 140), which correctly denied the formation of a commercial usage aimed at constant-value payments in the most unsettled period of inflation.

Very interesting, and exemplary, is the reasoning whereby the Uniform Commercial Code solves the problem of the meaning of "reasonable person", the term used in Article 13. Point 6 of the official comment on Section 1-205 reads as follows:

"6. The policy of this Act controlling explicit unconscionable contracts and clauses (Sections 1-203, 2-302) applies to implicit clauses which rest on usage of trade and carries forward the policy underlying the ancient requirement that a custom or usage must be 'reasonable'. However, the emphasis is shifted. The very fact of commercial acceptance makes out a prima facie case that the usage is reasonable, and the burden is no longer on the usage to establish itself as being reasonable. But the anciently established policing of usage by the courts is continued to the extent necessary to cope with the situation arising if an unconscionable or dishonest practice should become standard."

This may be adopted as transnational law, especially as it does not conflict with any national law.

Thus it is not too difficult to accept the role of commercial usages or to define what is meant by them. The real problem arises when the usage in question is not international but obtains only in one of the countries, or when it ostensibly exists in both, but does so in fact with a substantial difference. Naturally the same principles as we apply in eliciting rules of transnational law also hold good for the formation of an international commercial usage. There is here too a limit to what is possible, but there are

91

several considerations which may be of assistance, first among them the rule that a party must concede the applicability against himself of a foreign commercial usage if he had knowledge of it.[47] It may be reasonable that a party should suffer the consequences of his negligent ignorance of a commercial usage, at least if he knew of its existence without bothering to ascertain its substance. Rabel *Warenkauf* (I, p. 63) cites English precedents for this, and the point is confirmed by Section 1-205 (3) of the Uniform Commercial Code:

> "A course of dealing between parties and any usage of trade in the vocation or trade in which they are engaged or of which they are or should be aware give particular meaning to and supplement or qualify terms of an agreement."

We have encountered a similar principle in connection with the protection of confidence. It is moreover accepted law in nearly all States, and may consequently be treated as transnational law, that the uses of the market or exchange are in every case valid for both parties.[48]

Finally, and significantly, our principle of model effect comes into play here, most radically in an Austrian *Oberst-Gerichtshof* decision of 20 February 1952 which on grounds of customary law went so far as to treat a statutory provision, according to which a specification of the price was essential to the conclusion of a valid contract of sale, as no longer effective. Another decision which deserves special attention is an American ruling of 12 September 1944. Here, in a dispute between a Brazilian party and a party from New York, the question was whether a missing item in an otherwise complete set of documents could be replaced by a bank guarantee, in accordance with the custom of New York banking circles. The court gave an affirmative answer, expressly stating that the custom could be viewed as tacitly incorporated in the contract, inasmuch as it was obviously reasonable and practical. Compare also the Swiss Federal Tribunal's judgment of 16 November 1965 concerning a partial alteration in a contract between a German and a Swiss; also a decision given by the Munich *Oberlandesgericht* on 31 March 1955 (BB 55,748) regarding duties of inspection in the importation of fruit from Italy. The idea of model effect is especially suitable for use when a decision calls for a development of transnational law which cannot wait upon the elaboration of standard forms of contract or intergovernmental conventions.

The prohibition contained in paragraph 2 of Article 2 of the Contract Formation Rules forbidding any clause stipulating that silence shall amount to acceptance, is peculiarly apposite, as it corresponds to what has been legal

47. *Sic* Rabel, *Warenkauf* I, p. 62.
48. Rabel, *loc. cit.*, cites in this connection the well-known tag used by the English judge Willes in *Lloyd Guibert*: "Who goes to Rome must do as those at Rome do" (65 LR 1 QB, pp. 115 ff., at p. 121).

practice in every land for the past hundred years,[49] and therefore goes to show how long transnational law has been in existence and how little it has to wait for national laws or conventions to bring it into being. The invalidity of such a clause will not normally bring about the invalidity of the offer, as that would run counter to the principle of good faith in international transactions.

It should be noted, however, that only a unilateral tacit-acceptance clause is forbidden; it is possible for both parties to agree—even tacitly—in the same sense. In practice, the great majority of disputes over tacit acceptance arise out of the question whether a tacit understanding can be presumed in the given case. In this context the old saw of *qui tacet consentire videtur* has exercised a most unfortunate influence, for the universal esteem in which this legal tag appears to be held is in this case based on a misunderstanding. It has moreover never been valid without qualification, but has always needed to be considered in conjunction with the great number and, in practice, overwhelming importance of the exceptions which have had to be made. The juristic method of setting up a rule and then making exceptions to it has here had a most insidious effect.[50] When faced with the necessity of deciding whether an offer has been tacitly accepted, a judge should therefore exercise the greatest caution.[51]

In transnational law, as elsewhere, disputes furnish the exceptions rather than the rule. The most important exceptions are the following:

(*a*)   There is tacit acceptance when the will to accept is in some way apparent from actual conduct. That is the sense of Article 6, paragraph 2, of the Hague Contract Formation Rules, and of countless decisions under municipal law. This exception may be analysed as a product of the good-faith test or, in English and American law, of the institution of estoppel. [52]

(*b*)   It follows from the same principles that the recipient of an offer may in certain circumstances be obligated by his own negligence. [53] This is especially important in international trade with countries where com-

49. Cf. the illustrations from Germany, England, Switzerland and France in Rabel, *Warenkauf* I, p. 99.

50. On this Latin tag see Dernburg, *Pandekten* I, 3rd ed., Berlin 1892, p. 229: "Silence in regard to an offer, the non-return of goods sent unasked for sight and purchase, are not acquiescence in themselves. But silence does count as acquiescence if honesty or common sense calls for the expression of dissent in the event of non-acceptance."; see also the further references to Roman law in notes 14 and 15 (*ibid.*). Cf., further, Broom, *Legal Maxims* 1938, p. 787.

51. Cf. the leading decision given by the House of Lords on 12 December 1940, A.C. 1941, pp. 108-156, in the *Luxor* case, concerning a broker's commission; it was here established as a rule of law that tacit agreements could only be taken into account in special circumstances; *sic* also the English *Bank Melli Iran* decision of 12 October 1951, p. 176; for Germany, see the references in the comments on § 133 of the Civil Code.

52. Cf. Rabel, *Warenkauf* I, p. 94, with further references.

53. Graveson/Cohn, p. 112.

mercial business tends to be dispatched with less than average care. International cases cannot be measured by the same yardstick as internal affairs. [54]

(c)   Silence may be construed as acceptance when that corresponds with the previous course of dealing between the parties. [55]

In transnational law, moreover, the presumption of tacit acceptance is reinforced if such acceptance would at the critical time have lain in the interest of the presumed acceptor. Here the qualified Latin maxim makes sense: *qui tacet consentire videtur ubi tractatur de eius commodo.* The principle of good faith entitles the seller to expect the prospective purchaser not unconscionably to hesitate only to refuse the offer at a moment, perhaps, when a good price can no longer be obtained. Such shilly-shallying is impermissible, especially when one considers the considerable price-fluctuations in the international sale of goods.

The Uniform Commercial Code also provides that the course of dealing between the parties may determine whether there is a tacit understanding (cf. official comment on Section 1-205, point 3).

Letters of confirmation are sources of dispute chiefly when they fail to reproduce exactly what was originally agreed or when confirmation and counter-confirmation conflict. For the former it would appear to be transnational law that one must first determine whether the letter signifies the conclusion of the contract or is to be regarded merely as documentary evidence.[56] Here it can make a considerable difference whether it was commercial goods or something else which formed the subject-matter of the contract of sale. Contracts for work and materials, in particular, are not properly concluded until the supplier confirms the terms of the order and thereby gives his client to understand that he has duly considered whether he can execute it and has made provision to do so.[57]

54. Cf. e.g. the French decision Cass. 2 May 1966.

55. Cf. MAT 16 June 1925 (*Negreanu*), and the *Sapphire* award of 15 March 1963. On p. 1014 of the latter, it is inferred from good faith that when a clause existed in earlier, similar contracts, its absence in a later contract is no proof that the clause was not desired in that instance. See also "longstanding business-relations" in the subject-index.

56. Cf. headnote to the *Bundesgerichtshof*'s decision of 18 March 1964: "If businessmen have orally negotiated a contract of sale, but at the same time agreed to exchange written confirmation of the result of their negotiations, it may have been the will of the parties that that exchange should only serve the purposes of evidence and thus not constitute a requirement on which the validity of the contract should depend. This may even be the case when a commercial usage is supposed to exist according to which, in the event of an agreement to confirm the result of negotiations, the contract is dependent on the exchange of concordant letters of confirmation." In the same sense: the English decision of 1 April 1953 (*Cie de Commerce*).

57. This is very clearly argued by Philippe Kahn, pp. 73 ff. Cf. the French decision Cass. 22 January 1958.

Caution in presuming the existence of relevant transnational rules is advisable when dealing with the question whether the recipient of a letter of confirmation may keep silence without prejudice. While in municipal law this might still create a presumption of tacit acknowledgment of the contents of the letter, [58] it is certain that no national norm in that sense may be applied to an international case without more ado. In a decision given on 21 March 1966 the German *Bundesgerichtshof* hit upon a distinction which could well be of importance for the development of transnational law. In a contract for the sale of a motorized cement-mixer, price DM 8,500, which the purchaser had had inspected, the seller inserted in his letter of confirmation an exclusion of all guarantee, a condition which had not been raised before. The purchaser did not challenge this in his own letter of confirmation. The court, however, held that a challenge had been necessary and stated:

> "Since the case concerns the purchase of a used motor vehicle which had, moreover, been inspected by an expert on behalf of the defendant, it was rather to be expected that the plaintiff should have inserted in his letter of confirmation a restriction of his liability for defects in the machine, even if the parties had not discussed this point in their telephone conversation; for in the used-motor trade the exclusion of guarantee is a dictate of commercial common sense ... Hence the plaintiff's letter of confirmation merely contained a supplementary condition of the contract of sale which is customary in the used-motor trade and whose inclusion in the letter could therefore not have surprised the defendant. It was much rather a condition that he should have expected and reckoned with. In this case we are not confronted with the typical case of crossing letters of confirmation wherein each party mentions conditions for the transaction concluded which cannot be reconciled ... The guarantee-exclusion clause in the plaintiff's letter simply represented a complementary reservation which could not have been unexpected by the defendant. If the defendant was not in agreement with this supplementary clause he should have contested it at once, for there is nothing in his own letter of confirmation to suggest that he would not be in agreement with it. The consequence of the fact that he raised no protest at the right time is that his silence counts as consent to the exclusion of guarantee."

The above ruling also contains an expression of the rule that in the case of crossing letters of confirmation which are contradictory, the contract has not been concluded if the discrepancy is not immaterial to it. This rule is further discussed below in connection with Article 7, paragraph 2, of the Hague Contract Formation Rules.

---

58. *Sic*, in Germany, the comments on § 346 of the Commercial Code; and for the Hague Contract Formation Rules see Von Caemmerer, pp. 114 and 127.

Transnational law calls for severity against sellers' attempts to insinuate clauses not contained in the contract by putting them on the invoice. Such proposed amendments do not belong in that document, the purposes of which are confined to stating the account and presenting a claim for payment in accordance with the contract. [59]

In regard to general terms of business or conditions of trade, which usually are referred to at the time of concluding the contract, the legal position may not be the same as in the case of letters of confirmation, which are mostly subsequent to conclusion. Here, what Rabel (*Warenkauf* I, p. 100) published in 1936 is by now scarcely suitable for use in transnational law. There has in many countries been a considerable development which has led to a more critical attitude towards such terms and conditions. There is no longer any clear consensus, not even within the separate municipal systems. [60] Though it may well be transnational law that the tacit acknowledgment of general terms and conditions of trade is subject to the test of good faith, [61] there are few decided cases indicating what requirements this test imposes in international trade. On one occasion it was correctly decided that an English purchaser could not have been under any obligation to have the German seller translate the finely printed German-language conditions of trade which the latter had annexed to the contract, which itself was in English.[62]

It is not the tacit conclusion of a contract but the lack of written form which is contemplated by paragraph 2 of Section 2-201 of the Uniform Commercial Code, whereby in certain cicumstances a letter of confirmation may do duty for this written form. The principle of freedom in the choice of form to be given to contracts for the international sale of goods is expressed in Article 3 of the Contract Formation Rules, which reads as follows:

"An offer or an acceptance need not be evidenced by writing and shall not be subject to any other requirements as to form. In particular, they may be proved by means of witnesses."

This rule corresponds exactly with Article 15 of the Sales Rules. In both cases there is not absolute congruence between the French and English texts, but the sense of the rule is clear. As there is no obligation to employ written form, it is also, in this connection, immaterial what is meant by "writing".

59. Duden, *Handelsgesetzbuch*, 15th ed., 1962, § 346, n. 4E, with reference to *Reichsgericht* 1965, p. 331; cf. for the comparative law Rabel, *Warenkauf* I, p. 97, with reference to French practice, at that time still uncertain. Further, see MAT 16 June 1925 (*Negreanu*), p. 213, in connection with longstanding business-relations.

60. Cf. Duden, *Handelsgesetzbuch*, 15th ed. 1962. Einführung U III, n. 3 C, for German law, and more particularly Wilhelm Weber, *Die allgemeinen Geschäftsbedingungen*, Berlin 1967.

61. *Sic*, at all events, for German law, *Bundesgerichtshof* 14 March 1963, NJW 1963, p. 1248.

62. Stuttgart *Oberlandesgericht*, 19 July 1962: MDR 1964, p. 412.

Correspondence is thus also included, but a document with just the signature of one party will not as a rule be sufficient. A paper of this kind was, as a consequence of provisions of Austrian law which were unequivocally opposed to it, treated as a mere receipt in the French decision of 18 December 1950, especially as the whole case smacked of currency fraud.[63]

The words "any other requirements as to form" make it clear that the rule is to be given the broadest interpretation. Graveson/Cohn (p. 113) even regard it as excluding the requirement of a "consideration". Requirements of legal competency or the obligation to obtain the approval of third parties, authorities etc., are outside the scope of the rule.

The explicit mention of proof by witnesses in the second sentence was the subject of lengthy debate in the Commission, as the addition was by some held superfluous. Von Caemmerer (p. 114) concludes therefrom that the rule expressed by Article 3 has procedural as well as substantive bearing. Coming as it does from a member of the Commission, this observation carries some weight. It agrees with other German positions.[64] Unfortunately the debate appears to be continuing, especially in America, where the point is of peculiar importance.[65] Meanwhile it is probably transnational law that proof by submission of a tape-recording or teleprinter message is admissible.[66]

Without prejudice to the free choice of form which in conformity with the Contract Formation Rules may be taken as the model for transnational commercial law, any particular form can of course be agreed between the parties, or be regarded as customary between them in accordance with Article 2. Written form may also be prescribed by municipal law.[67] Should one party allege that written form was agreed, evidence to the contrary may, as always in such cases, be entertained. On the other hand, agreed written form justifies a presumption that the written contract embodies all oral agreements in full. Thus any party wishing to rely on unwritten sub-agreements or modifications of contract has the onus of proof. It is often tempting to suppose that if the parties have elected to use a particular form at one stage of the transaction, they wish to employ it throughout. However, this presumption cannot be erected without qualification into transnational law: it is more advisable to take each case on its merits. In a given case the question may also arise as to

63. Cf. on the other hand the American decision of 9 December 1960 (*Pennsylvania Company*).

64. See Rabel, 9 *RabelsZ*, 1935, p. 55, and Zweigert/Kötz, p. 43, on the significance of this difference.

65. See Eörsi, Mentschikoff and Honnold in Honnold (ed.), *Unification* ..., p. 373.

66. On tape-recordings, cf. the French decision of 29 June 1955 (Dijon), concerning an acknowledgment of paternity; on teleprinters, see the English decision of 17 March 1955 (*Entores*) mentioned by Schmitthof (p. 51).

67. On prescribed form in the law of State-trading countries, cf. Schmitthoff (ed.), *Sources* ..., pp. 5, 10 and 14.

whether an exchange of letters was not, in the circumstances, sufficient, even though the parties had a formal contract in view.[68]

The admissibility of modifications of a contract[69] was a question which played a role in the discussion of Article 3 of the Contract Formation Rules, in relation to the form of contracts. It is dealt with by Section 2-209 of the Uniform Commercial Code in a manner which in many, though not all, respects is exemplary:

"(1) An agreement modifying a contract within this Article needs no consideration to be binding.

(2) A signed agreement which excludes modification or rescission except by a signed writing cannot be otherwise modified or rescinded, but except as between merchants such a requirement on a form supplied by the merchant must be separately signed by the other party.

(3) The requirements of the statute of frauds section of this Article (Section 2-201) must be satisfied if the contract as modified is within its provisions.

(4) Although an attempt at modification or rescission does not satisfy the requirements of subsection (2) or (3) it can operate as a waiver.

(5) A party who has made a waiver affecting an executory portion of the contract may retract the waiver by reasonable notification received by the other party that strict performance will be required of any term waived, unless the retraction would be unjust in view of a material change of position in reliance on the waiver."

The reference to "consideration" in paragraph 1 does no harm because no "consideration" is demanded. It is not too clear, on the other hand, what "waiver" means within the context of the Section. [70]

The model effect of Article 3 of the Contract Formation Rules is of course circumscribed by mandatory national law. Happily, however, the few municipal rules that conflict with it are not mandatory in character. [71] By virtue of Section 1-105 of the Uniform Commercial Code (applicable law), this also applies to the important rules on formal requirements laid down in Section 2-201 of that American Act, while as for French law, although Article 1341 of the Civil Code would not in itself be compatible, the area

68. American decision of 9 December 1960 (*Pennsylvania Company*), p. 732; Swiss Federal Tribunal 11 October 1918; English decision of 31 January 1952.

69. Cf. the American decision of 17 March 1943 (*Delaware*) and the English decision of 30 January 1952 (*Yello*).

70. *Sic* Hawkland, p. 62, with a vivid example. Nevertheless the provision may be ascribed model effect even in regard to "waiver", if "waiver", in accordance with *Black's Law Dictionary*, is taken to mean "the intentional or voluntary relinquishment of a known entitlement".

71. If one disregards the questions of procedural law already referred to.

covered by Article 109 of the French Commercial Code is exempted from its effects; consequently, there are at least two great jurisdictions in which no need should arise to oppose the rule's validity from the domestic point of view.[72]

The legal position vis-à-vis State-trading countries is at first sight more problematic.[73] It should not be regarded as contemporary jurisprudence to make the solution of cases involving them dependent, in the classical conflicts-law manner, on the place where the contract came into being.[74] One should further endeavour to avoid the use of reasoning based on close familiarity with business practices. Rabel (*Warenkauf* I, p. 112) reproduces an English law-report from which one gathers that a businessman in England would normally regard it as dishonourable and ruinous to his professional reputation to invoke the statute of frauds in reference to a formal defect. The passage is reproduced in Zweigert/Kötz (p. 59) with further illustrations. Yet one would "normally" concede a businessman a perfect right to take advantage of a formal defect and base a claim upon it, firstly because rules of form would otherwise lose their raison d'être and secondly because businessmen in a given milieu are eminently familiar with its formal requirements and may reasonably expect one another to comply with them.

The legal position, therefore, is not quite straightforward. It becomes somewhat simpler, however, if the "normal" case no longer obtains: e.g. if reliance on a formal defect as a basis of claim is lent an exceptional character by some circumstance peculiar to the case or if the transaction concerned two different milieux. By such tests, of course, an international transaction is likely to qualify as a special case. As it happens, there do not appear to have been any decided cases in which a ruling was given either way as to whether reliance on domestic formal requirements is *a priori* objectionable in international commerce. Yet it is obvious that much less familiarity with the other party's law can be expected in that sphere than in the case of dealings between fellow-countrymen. Against this background, attitudes of hurt reproach or individious comparisons of gentlemanlines can cut no ice. A decision whether formal defect is a sound basis of claim in international litigation can only be taken by reference to objective criteria.

72. As is done in Zweigert/Kötz, pp. 47 ff.
73. Cf. in particular the contributions of Goldstajn and Lagergren in Honnold (ed.), *Unification* ..., pp. 41 and 55, and the survey of Rubanov and Tschikvadse (*ibid.*, p. 349). It is Bulgaria, Romania and the USSR which prescribe written from, and it is clearly still a moot point whether this is a merely formal requirement or one which may affect questions of capacity or authority. If the latter, the mandatory character of the rule would be even more pronounced. See also the discussion on pp. 373 ff. of the same book, especially at p. 375.
74. The decision of this point could be avoided in the award given by the Prague Chamber of Industry and Commerce on 3 November 1965, because identity of law was noted as between the German Democratic Republic and Czechoslovakia.

The protection of confidence (*Vertrauensschutz*) is the only useful touchstone in arriving at that decision, and it is essential to make use of it. A contracting party is thus entitled to rely on a formal defect against the other party if the latter demonstrably knew or must have known of it, whereas even a proven formal defect is of no avail against a party entitled to benefit from the protection of confidence. Frequently such a party will be able to show that the other was bound in good faith to draw timely attention to the formal requirements subsequently invoked for personal advantage. Whether in fact the plea of debarment is justified by the test of good faith, protection of confidence or estoppel may be determined from case to case.[75]

A large majority of the scholars who have pronounced on this theme (Honnold, *Unification*, pp. 372 ff.), namely Mentschikoff, Schmitthoff, Tunc and Honnold, appear at all events to have taken this line. Once the significance of the protection of confidence for transnational law is more fully recognized, this principle will prove invaluable in overcoming the obstacle of mandatory formal requirements.

B. *The offer*

Article 4 of the Contract Formation Rules reads as follows:
> "1. The communication which one person addresses to one or more specific persons with the object of concluding a contract of sale shall not constitute an offer unless it is sufficiently definite to permit the conclusion of the contract by acceptance and indicates the intention of the offeror to be bound.
> 2. This communication may be interpreted by reference to and supplemented by the preliminary negotiations, any practices which the parties have established between themselves, usage and any applicable legal rules for contracts of sale."

The recommendations herein enshrined can unreservedly be treated as transnational commercial law. The first paragraph deals with the concept and criteria of a valid offer, while paragraph 2 provides certain rules of interpretation. The subject gave rise to only one sizeable conflict of views among the scholarly authors of the Convention, and the controversy continues. Yet it is so peripheral to the international sale of goods that it would be out of place to go into it here.[76] What "communication" means in the Convention is explained in Article 12.

The foremost elements of Article 4 are the two requirements to be satisfied for an offer to be valid. Of these, the first, namely that the offer must be

---

75. Cf. especially the German decision of 9 December 1964 (strawberry-pulp).

76. It is concerned with the treatment of offers which are addressed to persons unspecified, as in the case of newspaper advertisements, slot-machine sales and so on. No

"sufficiently definite to permit the conclusion of the contract by acceptance" is the more important. This is a blanket clause which outblankets the most general clauses existing even in national laws. At the same time it sweeps aside all non-mandatory national rules requiring offers to be more definite than Article 4 prescribes.[77]

I goes without saying that in making an offer the offeror must have the will to be bound. According to the wording of Article 4, the offer must also make this will manifest. In practice, this is everywhere assumed to be the case if the actual word "offer" or a synonym is employed, while in order to indicate that one does not wish to incur obligation, some expression to that effect must be added. In that event the message should be treated merely as an invitation to its recipient to make an offer himself. This rule must be kept separate from the question of the revocability of offers; all we are concerned with here is the problem of whether an offer within the meaning of Article 4 has been made: i.e., an offer sufficient in law for acceptance to establish a contract. A will to be bound may be held to exist even where the obligation would be conditional. [78]

The interpretation clause of paragraph 2 exists in two versions. The first, intended for non-signatories of the Sales-Law Convention, is printed above, whereas Annex II contains a version for signatories which differs in that a reference to "the provisions of the Uniform Law on the International Sale of Goods" replaces one to "any applicable legal rules for contracts of sale".

This latter is not however a mere referral to the rules of private international law, for it leaves open the possibility of recognizing the model effect of the Sales Rules for transnational law in particular cases. The rules of

---

consensus or predominant opinion has been reached on this controversial question: cf. Von Caemmerer, p. 118, and the contrary view of Folke Schmidt, pp. 6 ff. This dispute has in itself nothing to do with the treatment of public tenders, which for its part finds no place in the context of the sale of goods but forms an institution of law whose transnational content ought rather to be investigated in a special chapter.

77. In transnational law, therefore, even an offer without indication of price would be possible in certain circumstances. This was not assumed in the French decision of 18 December 1950, but inferred on the quite different ground of a presumed fiscal and currency fraud. Folke Schmidt (p. 9) hit upon an alternative formulation which merits recommendation, namely that it must be possible for the contract to be concluded without any further action on the part of its instigator. Lagergren (in Honnold (ed.), *Unification* ..., p. 57) points out that the rule allows the judge considerable latitude in certain circumstances to complete an incomplete offer in accordance with the meaning, and that in countries where State arbitration is possible he is also empowered if need be to declare a contract concluded even against the will of the parties.

78. In its award of 2 November 1954 the Prague Chamber of Industry and Commerce refused to entertain a conditional contract of sale. A conditional offer, i.e. one reserving a right of self-supply (liability only in accordance with the possibilities of a covering purchase), was dealt with by the German *Bundesgerichtshof* on 19 March 1957.

interpretation are moreover the same as already defined in Article 2 of the Contract Formation Rules. This leads to a peculiarity in cases where Article 3 of the 1958 Comecon Terms of Delivery applies, because this reads as follows:

> "After conclusion of the contract all previous correspondence and negotiations for the contract shall lose their force".[79]

The English *Rapalli* decision of 2 December 1958 offers a striking illustration of Article 4:

One party maintained that he had received a valid offer from the other, but the latter had merely used the word "interested"—in over ten instances—without a contract being formed. On a later occasion, a contract had ensued, but the judges all agreed that in the cases at issue there had been no valid offer: the expression "interested" was not sufficient and did not convey an offer susceptible of acceptance; if a contract later ensued, that was on the basis of new circumstances which could not be adduced with retroactive effect.

To establish any transnational commercial law with regard to the binding force of an offer would have been virtually impossible before the surprising compromise solution reached at the Hague Conference, which led to the formulation of Article 5 of the Contract Formation Rules. Up to then, there had been, essentially, three opposing groups on the subject among national systems. One major group, including German law, views the offer as in principle imposing an obligation on the offeror. English and American law, on the contrary, views it as in principle devoid of binding effect. A third group ascribes bindings force to offers at least for the duration of any period of validity to which the offeror himself has set the term.[80] The centre of gravity of Article 5 lies in paragraph 2:

> "After an offer has been communicated to the offeree it can be revoked unless the revocation is not made in good faith or in conformity with fair dealing or unless the offer states a fixed time for acceptance or otherwise indicates that it is firm or irrevocable."

Paragraph 1, which was without difficulty adopted unanimously in The Hague, is undoubtedly transnational law and requires no discussion here, inasmuch as all national laws are in agreement with its terms.

Irreconcilable antitheses first appear in regard to the question whether an offer, once it has been received, can be withdrawn. It is scarcely comprehensible from the German-law viewpoint how it can still be possible to take back an offer in such circumstances. In England and America, on the other

---

79. Lagergren (*Unification* ..., p. 57) refers in this connection to Berman's article on the "Unification of Contract Clauses in Trade between Member Countries of the Council for Mutual Economic Aid", ICLQ 1958, p. 659.

80. For more on comparative law see the standard work of Schlesinger *et al.*, *Formation of Contract, a Study of the Common Core of Legal Systems*, Vol. I, 1968; Rabel, *Warenkauf* I, pp. 69 ff.; Folke Schmidt, 14 AJCL, 1965, pp. 10 ff.

hand, it has been customary for three centuries to regard a unilateral offer as not binding, unless it has been matched by a "consideration". However, by the time of the Hague Conference, the doctrine of consideration had, in answer to the needs of practice, been extensively eroded or breached.[81]

Under the leadership of the American delegate, Professor Mentschikoff, the Hague Comission worked out a most felicitous compromise whereby revocability is stated as the premise, while irrevocability is nevertheless assumed for every case of significance for practice. This compromise was, in the end, adopted unanimously by the plenary, which is a fitting omen of its model effect for transnational law. The practical consequence of revocability being the premise is, however,—and this highly important—that any party alleging the exception, i.e., irrevocability, has the onus of proof. That proof could be grounded on any time-limit set for acceptance, or on some indication of irrevocability, whether explicit or to be inferred from the facts.

It is the express or implied indication of irrevocability which is likely to prove the more important ground in future, in view of the blanket coverage given by paragraph 3, which gives one to understand that all the circumstances must be taken into account, including preliminary negotiations, the course of dealing between the parties, the practice as between them and usages of the trade.

Paragraph 2 further provides that there can be no revocation unless "made in good faith or in conformity with fair dealing", concepts which naturally overlap: at all events the distinction is not a crucial one in this context.[82]

These blanket propositions were objected to in the Commission by the delegates of Bulgaria, Hungary and Yugoslavia. The subject is certainly not exhausted, and even at the New York colloquium of the International Association for Legal Science, held from 7 to 10 September 1964, it led to a lively controversy, Honnold's account of which (*Unification*, pp. 369 ff.) should be required reading. During this discussion Professor Mentschikoff observed that, among businessmen at least, offers are made so that a transaction can be arrived at through their acceptance.

Another pointer to the future lies in Schmitthoff's observation that the State-trading countries exhibit certain divergences among themselves in regard to formal requirements, so that there may well be, somewhere, opportunities for reaching a compromise. It is thus important to bear in mind that the binding effect of offers is precisely one of those points which such countries,

---

81. Chloros, 'The doctrine of consideration and the reform of the law of contract", 17 ICLQ, 1968, says in conclusion: "In this article it has been suggested that English law would lose nothing if the doctrine of consideration were to be abolished." Graveson/ Cohn (p. 115) would evidently like to exclude the consideration doctrine for the international transactions governed by the Hague Contract Formation Rules—which would certainly not come amiss—but only for those.

82. *Sic* Graveson/Cohn, p. 115.

with their planned economies, approach on different premises from those prevalent in the private-enterprise system.[83]

Difficulties arising from divergences of this kind are hardly susceptible in any essential way to the influence of general notions of fairness or good faith, as commonly understood by businessmen everywhere and incorporated in transnational commercial law. It is moreover obvious how the undeniable vagueness of the blanket clause under discussion worries jurists from countries where owing to recent legislative history there has been less occasion to come to grips with the practical effects of such clauses than in England or Germany, where they have developed furthest and have proved themselves in practice. In this connection Goldstajn's spirited remark that tradition should play the smallest role in this domain (Honnold, p. 54) merits emphasis. It is thus essential that further efforts should not all be devoted to showing up any small holes there may be in the fabric of the clause—and whenever possible enlarging them.[84] Instead, they should rather be concentrated on pinpointing the economic exigencies in each case and on seeing how best they can be met with the aid of the blanket clause.

At the fourth session in The Hague (Conf./CR/Com.F/4) these problems were treated with understanding in a discussion thus summed up by Von Caemmerer (p. 120):

"The binding effect of offers was demanded by the economic facts of life. Within the time of which the offeree disposed for acceptance, he had to be in a position to make preparations, negotiate, or contract if need be with suppliers or customers, and in general proceed with such inquiries as might be requisite to enable him to make up his mind. He ought not to be exposed to the risk of seeing his expense of time and money wasted through the receipt of a telegram withdrawing the offer before he has sent off his statement of acceptance. Damages for culpa in contrahendo in the event of unwarranted and reprehensible revocation would be an insufficient remedy."

Even before this felicitous compromise solution, national jurisprudence had in most countries already taken the path to the formation of corresponding transnational law.[85] A decision reported in the 1969 U.C.C. Cumulative Supplement (E.A. Coronis Associates v. M. Gordon Construction Co.) appears, at least, to represent a step backwards, inasmuch as the key sentence reads as follows:

83. Pointed out by Lagergren in Unification ..., p. 63.
84. Cf. Folke Schmidt, pp. 15 and 35, and Eörsi in Unification ..., p. 370.
85. Cf. the much-discussed judgment given by the Norwegian Supreme Court on 11 November 1924, and the comments of Werner Lorenz, 159 Archiv zivilistischer Praxis, 1960, p. 214, with further references. Cf. also the decision given by the German Reichsgericht on 6 July 1934, and the American, French and Italian decisions adduced in Zweigert/Kötz, pp. 34 ff.

"The subcontractor's letter to a general contractor, making an offer to furnish certain materials and perform certain work, which contains no terms giving assurance that it would be held open, does not fall within this section, and the offer could be withdrawn at any time prior to its acceptance."

The rule here excluded is Section 2-205 UCC which itself is at bottom a noteworthy sign of the gradual turning-away from the consideration doctrine which is evident in the USA. It states:

"An offer by a merchant to buy or sell goods in a signed writing which by its terms gives assurance that it will be held open is not revocable, for lack of consideration, during the time stated or if no time is stated for a reasonable time, but in no event may such period of irrevocability exceed three months; but any such term of assurance on a form supplied by the offeree must be separately signed by the offeror."

As Ernst Rabel wrote:

"The binding of an offeror appears, in fact, most clearly justified when he has declared himself bound by the offer for a specified period of time." [86]

The Hague Commission did not debate this point, but the possibility of presuming the firm and binding character of the offer on account of other circumstances, or on the test of good faith. [87] Ernst Rabel (*loc. cit.*) rightly insists that offers should be binding, because a mere duty to compensate would be inadequate. There is one important difference between the Hague rule and Section 2-205 UCC in that the latter requires the offer to take specific, written, form. Bearing in mind, however, the non-compulsory character of the American rule, there can be no objection to regarding Article 5 of the Contract Formation Rules as transnational law. Here attention should be drawn to the observation of Professor Mentschikoff, who devised the famous Hague compromise, to the effect that only a very small minority of offers were revocable in contemporary practice, and that the compromise had in reality been concluded in favour of irrevocability. [88]

On the occasion of the New York symposium it was pointed out that revocability was judicially admissible only for a reasonable period and that one of the factors determining the length of such reasonable period could be the type of merchandise: thus it would be shorter in respect of perishable goods than, for example, the sale of a Rembrandt. [89]

The effect of paragraph 4 of Article 5 is to impose an absolute *terminus ad*

86. *Warenkauf* I, p. 88.
87. Cf. especially Folke Schmidt, pp. 13 ff., and the English decision of 2 December 1958 (*Rapalli*).
88. Mentschikoff, in Honnold (ed.), *Unification* ..., p. 369.
89. Graveson, in *Unification* ..., p. 371.

quem on revocability. Revocation is only possible so long as the offeree has not sent off his acceptance or done any act to be treated as acceptance. This rule, at which only Belgium and France demurred in the Commission, may be regarded as transnational law. It does not say anything about the time of conclusion of the contract, but only refers to the time as from which no withdrawal of the offer is possible. For the contract to be concluded, it is necessary that the declaration of acceptance should reach the offeror (Art. 6, para. 1, of the Contract Formation Rules, read with Art. 12, para. 1) and that it should do so within the time-limit for acceptance imposed by the law or the offeror (Art. 8, para. 1). Thus the risk of the declaration's getting lost or being delayed is normally to be borne by the acceptor, as the sender of it.

Von Caemmerer (p.122) adds to this observation the proposition that if the acceptance has not arrived in time, the offeror may proceed upon the assumption that the contract has not come into being. From the viewpoint of transnational law, however, with the special priority it accords to good faith, a rider must be added. If the offeror can surmise that the offeree must have taken account of a normal risk of the acceptance going astray, whereas the actual risk was for some special reason abnormally large, he may not remain inactive but must take steps to inform the offeree that owing to unusual circumstances his declaration of acceptance arrived too late and is therefore not binding. The well-known English "mail-box" doctrine of 1818 may, therefore, be transposed onto the international plane and incorporated into transnational law only with that qualification.[90] The comment of Graveson/ Cohn (p.114), to the effect that the rule embodied in paragraph 4 conflicts with English law, rests on a misunderstanding, for the *Dickinson* v. *Dodds* decision cited relates to a transaction in real estate, not the sale of goods.

Clauses stipulating that an "offer" is made "without obligation" are frequent in practice, but in fact they entirely negate the nature of the communication as an offer in the exact sense, and reduce it to a mere invitation to the addressee to make an offer himself. Cases of this sort have intentionally been ignored in the Contract Formation Rules.[91]

90. Thus by transnational law the above-mentioned judgment given on 11 November 1924 by the Norwegian Supreme Court, which decided by 5 votes to 2 to regard an acceptance which had arrived late as a new offer that must be taken as accepted on account of the silence of the original offeror, merits in the event our concurrence, and this idea has also found expression in Article 9 (2) of the Contract Formation Rules. Furthermore, it may not be superfluous to point out that both the "mail-box" rule and the provisions of Article 5 (4) are of a dispositive nature (see Lorenz, *loc. cit.*; Von Caemmerer, p. 122).

91. Von Caemmerer, p. 117; cf. also Zweigert/Kötz, p. 38; German case-law in Baumbach-Duden, *ad* § 346 HGB, n. 5.

C. *The acceptance of the offer*

The Hague Contract Formation Rules can be taken as a model for transnational commercial law insofar as they do not, in the manner of continental laws, regard the concordance of wills between the parties as the critical test of the formation of a contract, but look much rather to the respective declarations of offer and acceptance, as external and objective signs which are essentially easier to observe. These evidential facts must therefore be established with great care. Articles 6 to 10, i.e. nearly half the 13 articles of the Rules, are devoted to this purpose is respect of the acceptance. The declaration of acceptance is especially important, because it brings the contract into being and, at the same time, though the Rules say nothing explicit about this, enables the place and commencement of the contract to be determined.

The first provisions in regard to the acceptance are contained in Article 6, which lays down that it must be conveyed, whether by express declaration or by equivalent act. Article 7 deals with cases where the terms of the acceptance do not exactly coincide with the offer, Article 8 with the time during which acceptance may be intimated, Article 9 with the effects of a belated declaration of acceptance and Article 10 with the possibility of revoking acceptance.[92]

The questions of the time and place of conclusion have been treated exhaustively in all the textbooks of private international law.[93]

Article 6 is so worded:

"1. Acceptance of an offer consists of a declaration communicated by any means whatsoever to the offeror.

2. Acceptance may also consist of the despatch of the goods or of the price or of any other act which may be considered to be equivalent to the declaration referred to in paragraph 1 of this Article either by virtue of the offer or as a result of practices which the parties have established between themselves or usage."

Owing to the energetic participation of the American delegation in the work of the Conference, the provisions of this text were influenced in no small degree by Section 2-206 of the Uniform Commercial Code:

"(1) Unless otherwise unambiguously indicated by the language or circumstances

(*a*) an offer to make a contract shall be construed as inviting acceptance in any manner and by any medium reasonable in the circumstances;

(*b*) an order or other offer to buy goods for prompt or current ship-

---

92. For comparative law on the declaration of acceptance, see in particular Rabel, *Warenkauf* I, pp. 90 ff.; Folke Schmidt, pp. 15 ff.; Lagergren in *Unification* ..., pp. 63 ff.
93. Cf. also Francescakis, note on Colmar 27 March 1957.

ment shall be construed as inviting acceptance either by a prompt promise to ship or by the prompt or current shipment of conforming or non-conforming goods, but such a shipment of non-conforming goods does not constitute an acceptance if the seller seasonably notifies the buyer that the shipment is offered only as an accommodation to the buyer.

(2) Where the beginning of a requested performance is a reasonable mode of acceptance an offeror who is not notified of acceptance within a reasonable time may treat the offer as having lapsed before acceptance."

The meaning of these provisions is made particularly clear in the accompanying official comment:

"Any reasonable manner of acceptance is intended to be regarded as available unless the offeror has made quite clear that it will not be acceptable. Former technical rules as to acceptance, such as requiring that telegraphic offers be accepted by telegraphed acceptance, etc., are rejected and a criterion that the acceptance be 'in any manner and by any medium reasonable under the circumstances' is substituted. This section is intended to remain flexible and its applicability to be enlarged as new media of communication develop or as the more time-saving present day media come into general use."

The acceptance has in some way to be expressed, whether linguistically or implicitly through an act. The use in Article 6 of the term "communicated" is controlled by the provisions of Article 12. The communication may therefore "be made by the means usual in the circumstances" and then satisfies the requirements of Article 6. It is not however absolutely necessary that it should be made in the usual form, for Article 6 states expressly that the declaration may be communicated "by any means whatsoever". It is therefore conceivable that even where the written form is usual, oral communication may be sufficient in a particular instance, provided the requirements of fairness are not infringed.[94] In all cases, however, the expression of acceptance must be unambiguous. This is confirmed by case-law in all the major trading countries,[95] and by the actual use of the word "unambiguously" in the official comment on Section 2-206 UCC.

Silence coupled with sheer inactivity cannot count as a declaration of acceptance. That is the rule in all national laws and is the converse corollary of paragraph 2 of Article 6.[96]

We have already ascertained the state of the law in regard to letters of confirmation. A letter of confirmation postulates an entirely different situa-

---

94. *Sic* Graveson/Cohn, p. 116.
95. Cf. e.g. House of Lords, 3 February 1960.
96. *Sic* Graveson/Cohn, p. 116.

tion from a mere offer, and commercial ethics or good faith therefore require in many instances that the recipient should contest the contents of the letter if he realizes that they do not correspond to the terms of his declaration of acceptance.[97]

A clear distinction must be drawn between tacit acceptance and implicit acceptance as evidenced by conduct within the meaning of paragraph 2 of Article 6. As such implicit acceptance is sufficient, it follows that no explicit declaration is exigible when, for example, goods are sent in response to an offer. This in practice is the most common form of implicit acceptance; nevertheless the despatch of goods is not tantamount to a declaration of acceptance in every case, but only when the special conditions of paragraph 2 are fulfilled, i.e. when the action in question is to be expected by virtue of the offer or as a result of practice between the parties or of usage.[98] So far no discrepancy of any consequence has come to light between the case-law of the various countries and the transnational rules embodied in Article 6.[99]

A problem which arises quite frequently in practice is that the goods sent do not correspond to what was agreed. The official comment on Section 2-206 UCC has the following to say on this subject:

"Subsection (1)(b) deals with the situation where a shipment made following an order is shown by a notification of shipment to be referable to that order but has a defect. Such a non-conforming shipment is normally to be understood as intended to close the bargain, even though it proves to have been at the same time a breach. However, the seller by stating that the shipment is non-conforming and is offered only as an accomodation to the buyer keeps the shipment or notification from operating as an acceptance."

97. Rabel, *Warenkauf* I, p. 96; Von Caemmerer, p. 125, with extensive report on the course of the deliberations in The Hague; Lagergren in *Unification* ..., p. 65; Paris 27 January 1955 concerning tacit acceptance of general conditions of business.

98. Folke Schmidt, pp. 17 ff. He describes the contrast between the continental and the American conception, but finally comes to the conclusion that Article 6 embodies a correct solution to the problem.

99. Cf. *Bundesgerichtshof* 14 March 1963, holding that when the owner of a house under construction agrees to the building works he recognizes by the same token the general terms of business of the building firm. Also the American *Associated Hardware Supply Co.* decision (355 F. 2d., p. 114): "Even in the absence of a written agreement with respect to every term of a contract, great weight attaches to the course of dealing of the parties, and where it appears from the conduct of the parties that their mode of calculating prices, although not accepted formally by signature of a written instrument, was adhered to both parties during an extensive course of dealing, during which the purchaser received, accepted and paid for over $800,000 worth of merchandise, this course of dealing must be held applicable and governing with respect to any merchandise which was received, accepted, but not paid for."

It cannot be denied that whenever an explicit declaration of acceptance is dispensed with, as under paragraph 2 of Article 6, and acts alone must be relied on, a somewhat disquieting uncertainty must persist for the offerer until he can be quite sure of the implications of the offeree's actions. In this connection Von Caemmerer reports (p. 125):

"The Rome draft further provided that in cases governed by paragraph 2 the acceptor should be required to inform the offeror promptly of the despatch of the goods or other manifestation of acceptance. Failure to comply with this requirement would expose him to a claim for damages. The deletion of this provision was moved by the English, Danish, German, Finnish and Greek representatives and carried by 11 votes to 3. It is a rule which lends itself to misunderstandings in the context of the law on the formation of contracts. Such a duty of notification may in many ways be normal and imperative. But it is a subsidiary obligation arising out of the contract once concluded, and one which belongs to the law of sale (Articles 55 and 70). Only there is provision made for damages for the breach of such subsidiary obligations."

While one cannot regard the Hague Sales Rules as a model for transnational law to the same extent as the Contract Formation Rules, these comments merit close attention and ought probably to be taken as indicative of the state of the law from the transnational point of view.[100]

When the acceptance takes the form of an explicit declaration, this declaration must have reached the other party. What is to be understood by this emerges from Article 12. There is general agreement that the risks of the transmission period are to be borne by the declarer.[101] This is a particularly important point in the age of the teleprinter,[102] as has already been frequently confirmed by the courts in international cases.[103]

---

100. Folke Schmidt appears to concur (p. 22); likewise Lagergren, in *Unification* ... (p. 65), with special emphasis on the importance of notification.

101. Cf. Zweigert/Kötz, pp. 37 ff.; Lagergren, in *Unification* ..., pp. 64 and 67; Folke Schmidt, p. 22.

102. Von Caemmerer (p. 123) reports that the Commission did not reach any agreement on teleprinter communication. A problem seems to arise, however, only if one clings, in the teeth of the transnational rule in Article 6, to the obsolescent English "mail-box" doctrine whereby the confiding of the written acceptance to the post was enough—this goes back to the ancient *Adams* v. *Lindsell* decision of 1818 (IB and Ald. 861), but so far as the teleprinter is concerned a decision on the lines of Article 6 has already been given in the *Entores* judgment of 17 March 1955, a decision, greeted with universal approval, which concerned a teleprinter offer emanating from London and its acceptance from Amsterdam.

103. Cf. the decisions given by the Italian Court of Cassation on 3 May 1954 and by the German *Bundesgerichtshof* on 14 February 1958.

By way of precaution, it should however be emphasized that paragraph 2 of Article 6 clearly allows the parties entire freedom to proceed as they wish in regard to the acceptance of an offer. This is confirmed by Von Caemmerer (p. 126) and Folke Schmidt (p. 16).

Article 7 of the Contract Formation Rules deals with discrepancy between the acceptance and the offer, paragraph 1 enunciating the principle, and paragraph 2 describing the exceptions in general terms:

"1. An acceptance containing additions, limitations or other modifications shall be a rejection of the offer and shall constitute a counter-offer.

2. However, a reply to an offer which purports to be an acceptance but which contains additional or different terms which do not materially alter the terms of the offer shall constitute an acceptance unless the offeror promptly objects to the discrepancy; if he does not so object, the terms of the contract shall be the terms of the offer with the modifications contained in the acceptance."

The rule fortunately coincides with the pertinent rules in the laws of most of the world's major trading countries (we discuss below a disparity which in our view can be overcome). [104] The term "other modifications" may be taken to include "conditions", while the word "containing" should not be construed too narrowly: thus it is not a question of whether the modifications or additions constitute an actual part of the declaration and are literally contained in it, or are outwardly independent adjuncts, provided they are conveyed to the offerer by the time of his receipt of the acceptance at the latest.[105]

It is not the rule itself but the exceptions which create difficulties. An exception, according to paragraph 2, can be made for additions or differences "which do not materially alter the terms of the offer". At first sight this formulation looks somewhat vague, but it may be interpreted with the help of Section 2-207 of the Uniform Commercial Code:

"(1) A definite and seasonable expression of acceptance or a written confirmation which is sent within a reasonable time operates as an acceptance even though it states terms additional to or different from those offered or agreed upon, unless acceptance is expressly made conditional on assent to the additional or different terms.

(2) The additional terms are to be construed as proposals for addition to the contract. Between merchants such terms become part of the contract unless:

(*a*)   the offer expressly limits acceptance to the terms of the offer;

(*b*)   they materially alter it; or

---

104. For comparative law see Folke Schmidt, p. 23, and, with reference to State-trading countries, Goldstajn, in *Unification* ..., p. 53.

105. *Sic* Graveson/Cohn, p. 117.

(*c*) notification of objection to them has already been given or is given within a reasonable time after motice of them is received.

(3) Conduct by both parties which recognizes the existence of a contract is sufficient to establish a contract for sale although the writings of the parties do not otherwise establish a contract. In such case the terms of the particular contract consist of those terms on which the writings of the parties agree, together with any supplementary terms incorporated under any other provisions of this Act."

The official comment hereon is also very important for the interpretation of Article 7 and hence for the formation of transnational commercial law. Paragraphs 1 to 3 read as follows:

"1. This section is intended to deal with two typical situations. The one is where an agreement has been reached either orally or by informal correspondence between the parties and is followed by one or both of the parties sending formal acknowledgments or memoranda embodying the terms so far as agreed upon and adding terms not discussed. The other situation is one in which a wire or letter expressed and intended as the closing or confirmation of an agreement adds further minor suggestions or proposals such as 'ship by Tuesday', 'rush', 'ship draft against bill of lading inspection allowed', or the like.

2. Under this Article a proposed deal which in commercial understanding has in fact been closed is recognized as a contract. Therefore, any additional matter contained either in the writing intended to close the deal or in a later confirmation falls within subsection (2) and must be regarded as a proposal for an added term unless the acceptance is made conditional on the acceptance of the additional terms.

3. Whether or not additional or different terms will become part of the agreement depends upon the provisions of subsection (2). If they are such as materially to alter the original bargain, they will not be included unless expressly agreed to by the other party. If, however, they are terms which would not so change the bargain they will be incorporated unless notice of objection to them already been given or is given within a reasonable time."

It should be obvious *a priori* that the benefit of exception cannot be extended to practices whereby such important clauses as that concerning the forum of jurisdiction are not added until after the conclusion of the contract, for example only on the invoice.[106] What may or may not constitute a material alteration is described in the next two paragraphs of the official comment:

"4. Examples of typical clauses which would normally 'materially alter' the contract and so result in surprise or hardship if incorporated without express awareness by the other party are: a clause negating

106. *Sic Bundesgerichtshof* 14 February 1958.

112

such standard warranties as that of merchantability or fitness for a particular purpose in circumstances in which either warranty normally attaches; a clause requiring a guaranty of 90% or 100% deliveries in a case such as a contract by cannery, where the usage of the trade allows greater quantity leeways; a clause reserving to the seller the power to cancel upon the buyer's failure to meet any invoice when due; a clause requiring that complaints be made in a time materially shorter than customary or reasonable.

5. Examples of clauses which involve no element of unreasonable surprise and which therefore are to be incorporated in the contract unless notice of objection is seasonably given are: a clause setting forth and perhaps enlarging slightly upon the seller's exemption due to supervening causes beyond his control, similar to those covered by the provision of this Article on merchant's excuse by failure of presupposed conditions or a clause fixing in advance any reasonable formula of proration under such circumstances; a clause fixing a reasonable time for complaints within customary limits, or in the case of a purchase for sub-sale, providing for inspection by the sub-purchaser; a clause providing for interest on overdue invoices or fixing the seller's standard credit terms where they are within the range of trade practice and do not limit any credit bargained for; a clause limiting the right of rejection for defects which fall within the customary trade tolerances for acceptance 'with adjustment' or otherwise limiting remedy in a reasonable manner (see Section 2-718 and 2-719)."

In practice this rule appears to cause fewer difficulties than is assumed in theory.[107] Particular value can be attached in this connection to experience in Scandinavia, where the legal position very closely approximates to Article 7. Among jurists it is still an open question whether the offerer has not the right to repulse a modified acceptance in such a way that only the alterations are rejected, while a contract which is free of them is duly formed.[108] Paragraph 2 of Article 7 gives the offerer the opportunity of preventing the formation of a contract by promptly objecting to the discrepancy, but whether the objection is to be regarded as directed against the modification as such or against the conclusion of the contract is something which should be decided according to the particular case, bearing in mind that the acceptor,

107. Cf., apart from the decisions elsewhere mentioned, the American decision of 15 January 1962 (*Roto-Lith*), the Prague award of 3 November 1965, Paris 27 January 1955, the English decision of 28 February 1956 (*SCCMO (London) Ltd.*), and the English *Nicolene* decision of 1953 mentioned by Lagergren (*Unification* ..., p. 67, n. 60).
108. Cf. especially Von Caemmerer, p. 127; Folke Schmidt, p. 24; Lagergren (*Unification* ...), p. 68; and, for the concordance with State-trading countries, Goldstajn (*Unification* ...), p. 52.

being responsible for an unclear situation, ought to shoulder a somewhat greater risk.

That the offeror should contest the modified acceptance "promptly" under paragraph 2 goes without saying and holds good in every country.

The American *Bennett* decision of 16 January 1953 dealt with a case of failure to object to a letter of credit which featured alterations.

In the treatment of letters of confirmation Article 7 supplements what was said in Article 2. The writings on the subject, in particular the views of Lagergren, confirm the important distinction we have already made between letters of confirmation which are simply intended as vouchers and those which go farther and possess a substantive contractual content. Article 7 has no revelance for the mere vouchers, but letters of substantive import must be tested for their significance in relation to the contents of the contract as a whole.[109]

Article 8 embodies rules which may fittingly be incorporated into transnational law, of a general nature in paragraph 1, dealing with the time allowed for acceptance, and of a special nature in paragraph 2, which applies only to cases where the offeror himself has fixed the time for acceptance:

"1. A declaration of acceptance of an offer shall have effect only if it is communicated to the offeror within the time he has fixed or, if no such time is fixed, within a reasonable time, due account being taken of the circumstances of the transaction, including the rapidity of the means of communication employed by the offeror, and usage. In the case of an oral offer, the acceptance shall be immediate, if the circumstances do not show that the offeree shall have time for reflection.

2. If a time for acceptance is fixed by an offeror in a letter or in a telegram, it shall be presumed to begin to run from the day the letter was dated or the hour of the day the telegram was handed in for despatch.

3. If an acceptance consists of an act referred to in paragraph 2 of Article 6, the act shall have effect only if it is done within the period laid down in paragraph 1 of the present Article."

The rules of paragraph 1 do not add anything essentially new in relation to national laws; in France they correspond to a century-old tradition.[110] The most important aspect is that the prospective acceptor may not delay unduly in accepting. He is not in particular entitled to play a waiting game, for that amounts to speculating at the offeror's expense on a change of prices or other circumstances in his favour.[111] The length of time allowable may also, how-

109. Cf. Von Caemmerer, p. 127; Graveson/Cohn, p. 117; Folke Schmidt, p. 24; Lagergren (*Unification* ...), p. 68.

110. Cf. Cass. 28 February 1970.

111. Cf. Lagergren, in *Unification* ..., p. 66.

114

ever, be determined by reference to usage, as is expressly stated. Here attention must be paid in the first place to any commercial usage which the offeror had in view in making his offer, and in the second place to any practices or methods of dealing which usually hold good between the parties, as defined in Article 13, paragraph 1.[112] The term "oral offer" must include offers conveyed by telephone, except in the special case of the telephone being used to convey a message which has to be taken down in writing and passed to the offeree.[113] It is generally agreed that an offer made by teleprinter is not oral but written. The appropriate time-limit for acceptance is not necessarily the same for international as for domestic transactions. In certain circumstances it may be longer, for example if the offeror knows that the recipient must first communicate the offer to others or study it with special care.

Paragraph 2 of Article 8 contains a very practical rule of interpretation for international dealings. However, it reduces the protection of the recipient against the deceitful ante-dating of letters to a reliance on the principles of fairness, and saddles him with the onus of proof.

There would likewise appear to be little reason why the rules of Article 9, which deal with late acceptance, should not be adopted as transnational law. They have given rise to more problems in theory than in practice:

"1. If the acceptance is late, the offeror may nevertheless consider it to have arrived in due time on condition that he promptly so informs the acceptor orally or by despatch of a notice.

2. If however the acceptance is communicated late, it shall be considered to have been communicated in due time, if the letter or document which contains the acceptance shows that it has been sent in such circumstances that if its transmission had been normal it would have been communicated in due time; this provision shall not however apply if the offeror has promptly informed the acceptor orally or by despatch of a notice that he considers his offer as having lapsed."

The comparative-law aspects of this problem are discussed in Rabel, *Warenkauf* I (p. 92), according to which all municipal systems leave the offeror the option of regarding the late acceptance as valid or not, while many take the view that it is his duty to state clearly in what sense he is exercising his option.[114]

Paragraph 1, which differs markedly from earlier drafts, was received by jurists which certain misgivings, but these were eventually dropped.[115] With regard to paragraph 2 it is noteworthy that one of the major trading countries, the United Kingdom, had moved for its deletion, on the ground

---

112. Von Caemmerer, p. 128.
113. Von Caemmerer, p. 129.
114. *Reichsgericht*, RGZ 103, p. 13 (cited by Rabel, *loc. cit.*).
115. Cf. Folke Schmidt, pp. 26 and 35.

that is was desirable for the offeror to be always under an obligation to give prompt notice in the event of his not wanting the contract. For the purpose of transnational law, a somewhat cautious approach will therefore be in order, and when in doubt it may be as well to view the offeror as subject to such a time-limit. [116] The question of what is to be understood by "normal transmission" is important in practice. Graveson/Cohn (p.119) discuss the case where postal services are disrupted for a number of weeks, and rightly conclude that the offerer has to take such circumstances into account.

Article 10 deals with the possibility of withdrawing an acceptance:

> "An acceptance cannot be revoked except by a revocation which is communicated to the offeror before or at the same time as the acceptance." [117]

D. *Rules applicable to both parties*

The rest of the Hague Contract Formation Rules (Articles 11, 12 and 13) embody four provisions which are equally applicable to either party. Article 11 expresses transnational law in regard to the effects of the death of one of the parties:

> "The formation of the contract is not affected by the death of one of the parties or by his becoming incapable of contracting before acceptance unless the contrary results from the intention of the parties, usage or the nature of the transaction."

This rule ought to be clear. It coincides, though not perhaps exactly, with most municipal laws in the matter. Bearing in mind the circumstances of international trade, the authors of this text have quite rightly proceeded on the assumption that in the business world declarations are "from the practical point of view, directed to the company." [118]

The Article also refers to incapability of contracting, but this, as is clear from the debate, was not intended to cover bankruptcy. A development of transnational law in this field, where large areas are determined by the public interest, cannot at present be more than hoped for.

Article 12 has a significance extending far beyond the law of the sale of goods, in that it explains what "to be communicated" (or in French: *parvenir*) means for the purposes of the Contract Formation Rules:

116. *Sic* Von Caemmerer, p. 130.
117. Graveson/Cohn mention the case where the buying department of a firm accepts an offer, and another department shortly after notifies the offeror that there are objections to his general conditions while failing to take the previous acceptance into account. On account of this failure Graveson/Cohn refuse to regard the new notification as a retraction of the acceptance. Cf. the treatment of withdrawal of acceptance by Lagergren (*Unification* ...), p. 66.
118. Von Caemmerer, p. 132.

"1. For the purposes of the present Law, the expression 'to be communicated' means to be delivered at the address of the person to whom the communication is directed.

2. Communications provided for by the present Law shall be made by the means usual in the circumstances."

This unfortunately leaves open the parallel linguistic question of such important languages for international trade as Spanish, Russian, German, Italian or Portuguese. Von Caemmerer (p. 135) appears to have made summary use of *zugehen* as the equivalent in his German translation: but in this case it must be borne in mind that the pronouncements of German courts and scholars in regard to this term cannot be employed without more ado for the exegesis of Article 12.[119] Fortunately the seriousness of the language problem is diminished by the fact that Article 12 links the communication of offers or acceptances with certain objective circumstances: it is sufficient if the message has been delivered at the address of the person for whom it is intended. This agrees with the jurisprudence of the Court of Justice of the European Communities.[120]

The drafters of Article 12 have intentionally avoided any closer definition. One will therefore have to distinguish between the factual question of whether a declaration has been communicated and the further question of the time at which the communication became effective, regarding which the Article has nothing to say. Thus once a letter is deposited in the mail-box of the addressee, the communication has taken place even if the delivery was made outside the hours of business. When, however, it is a matter of determining the time at which the communication became effective, nobody with an office mail-box can be expected to consider any earlier moment than the next time at which there would normally be office-staff on duty at his place of business. There is thus an important distinction to be made between mail-box and place of business which Graveson-Cohn (p. 120) have overlooked.

If a person has given an office address and a private address, business communications may only be directed to the former.[121] The only exception is when the message is directly received by the addressee in person at his private address. No other persons who may happen to be staying there may be regarded as his authorized agents for the receipt of business communica-

119. *Sic* Graveson/Cohn, p. 120, and, it would also appear, Folke Schmidt, pp. 34 ff.

120. Decision of the court of the European Coal and Steel Community, 10 December 1957, in case 8-56, Vol. III, p. 200: "It is necessary to apply a principle of law recognized in all countries of the Community, to the effect that a written statement of intent becomes effective as soon as it arrives in the regular way in the sphere of control of the addressee."

121. *Sic* the *Reichsgericht* in the Anglo-German case of the notification of a claim based on a bill of exchange.

tions at his private address—least of all in international business.[122]

There is an important rule for telephone communications which emerges from Article 12, namely that the risks arising from any interruption in the telephone connection during the conversation are to be borne by the person making the communication, since his declaration has to be duly received by the addressee. [123]

Paragraph 2 of Article 12 is word for word the same as Article 14 of the Hague Sales Rules. It ought moreover to be read with the first sentence of Article 8 of the Contract Formation Rules, which means that as rapid a means of communication should normally be used for the answer as for the offer.[124]

It would appear reasonable to conclude that Article 12 does not leave any doubtful loopholes.[125]

After the Contract Formation Rules have referred to commercial usage or practices in Article 4(2), Article 5(3), Article 6(2) and Article 8(1) and (3), Article 13 finally offers the requisite definitions:

"1. Usage means any practice or method of dealing, which reasonable persons in the same situations as the parties usually consider to be applicable to the formation of their contract.

2. Where expressions, provisions or forms of contract commonly used in commercial practice are employed, they shall be interpreted according to the meaning usually given to them in the trade concerned."

Mutatis mutandis, these two paragraphs employ exactly the same language as paragraphs 2 and 3 of Article 9 of the Hague Sales Rules, and in drafting them the Commission drew conscious inspiration from Section 1-205(2) UCC, which according to Von Caemmerer (p. 140) then lay before it in the following form:

"1. Usage means any practice or method of dealing having such regularity of observance as to justify an expectation by both parties that it will be observed with respect to the international transaction.

2. When commercial terms and expressions have been used, they are to be interpreted in accordance with the meaning habitually given to them in connection with such a transaction."

The present wording is somewhat different.

It need scarcely be stressed that commercial usage is something other than custom, as understood in public law—more especially public international

122. *Sic* Graveson/Cohn, p. 120.
123. *Sic* Von Caemmerer, p. 135.
124. Von Caemmerer, p. 135, with reference to the deliberations of the Commission.
125. But see the comments on Article 14 of the Sales Rules by Graveson/Cohn, p. 60.

law—and recognized subject to a host of rather difficult conditions. In its *Right of Passage* Judgment of 12 April 1960 (p. 38) the International Court of Justice satisfied itself that a factual state of affairs had demonstrably persisted for 125 years before recognizing it as custom. Such stringent tests do not apply to commercial usage. Naturally, even in domestic trade it is often disputable whether a usage exists, and the problem of determination will therefore tend to be all the more difficult at the international level. The judge will, however, be able to narrow the scope of inquiry to the question whether a usage exists in, or in relation to, the case before him. Furthermore, he himself is undeniably master to some extent of the decision, for the following applies to courts no less than to the legislator:

> "But in the commercial field at least, legislation must not only reflect usage and refer to it, but must also develop and refine it." [126]

It is not, unfortunately, possible to draw from the genesis of Article 13 any sure argument in favour of its validity as transnational law, for it cannot be read in isolation from Article 9 of the Sales Rules, which was the subject of a lively controversy and in the end was retained only by the small margin of 14 votes to 8, with 4 abstentions including those of France and Israel. [127] Nevertheless, Article 13 offers in itself a strong argument for recognizing the controlling role of usage, an argument which requires testing against the circumstances of each case, in relation to the practices in question and the situation of the parties. If the controlling role of usage can then be shown consonant with transnational law, preference should be given to such practices as the offeror would have had in mind and, in certain circumstances, to those which must likewise have formed part of the offeree's expectations. After that, due account should be taken of such practices as reasonable persons in the same situation usually consider to be applicable to the formation of their contract (so-called normative practices). [128] These practices, in accordance with Article 2, enjoy priority in case of doubt not only over the rules of national statutes, but also over the Contract Formation Rules themselves.

Even without the Hague Rules, the prospects of incorporating commercial usage and practices into transnational commercial law are by no means slim, thanks to the wide area of agreement in the judicial practice and legislation of many countries. [129] The English *Milhem* decision of 26 November 1954 (see

---

126. Berman, *Law and Contemporary Problems*, Duke University 1965, p. 368.
127. Cf. Riese, *RabelsZ* 1965, p. 21.
128. Von Caemmerer, p. 141.
129. For German law cf. § 346 of the Commercial Code; for American law, e.g. the *Griffin* decision of 24 March 1919 and the *Sperry Rand* decision of 17 May 1954; for England, e.g. the *J. Milhem* decision of 26 November 1954 and, with particular reference to Article 13 (2), the *Brown & Gracie* decision of 3 February 1960 and the dictum

119

last footnote) is also worthy of special mention because a contracting party in that case tried to take shelter from the consequences of an unfavourable movement of prices in an abnormal interpretation of the terms of his declaration, and because, characteristically, the arbitral tribunal condemned him whereas the regular judge in subsequent proceedings held that the contract had not been formed.

We have already referred above to Ernst Rabel's conclusion (*Warenkauf* I, p. 58) that there is a virtual concordance among the major trading countries in the legal treatment of commercial usage and practices. If this satisfactory state of affairs be borne in mind, and if the guidelines we have traced are followed, any difficulties which scrutiny may reveal in individual cases will not appear so insurmountable.[130]

III. *Rights and obligations arising out of the contract*

A. *Reciprocal aspects*

With the subject of the interdependence of reciprocal rights and obligations in contracts of sale we return to the domain of reliable transnational rules. Articles 71 and 72 of the Hague Sales Rules agree not only with Sections 28 and 19 of the British Sale of Goods Act 1893 but also with most other systems, assuming as one may that the term *synallagma* used in civil-law countries can be rendered by "concurrent conditions". To the extent that concordance is not directly evident from the various national systems themselves, it can in most cases be attained by reference to commercial usage and practices. This is true in particular with regard to the correct agreement and sequence of performance in the case of sales involving carriage. [131]

The time has only recently become ripe for giving a transnational answer to the question as to who should bear the risk of the loss of the goods purchased, a very important problem in practice. In 1947 Ernst Rabel (*Conflict*, II, p.308) gave a brief account of the various positions of the law hereon in the major trading countries, positions which are by no means clear. According to this account some countries still clung at that time to the Roman-law system, whereby the risk of loss was transferred to the purchaser on the

---

therein of Viscount Simonds (p. 295): "No business can be safely transacted except upon the footing that words are to be given the meaning which they bear to the reasonable man." For French law see Paris 1966, p. 31.

130. The fundamental difficulties with regard to the validity of oral sub-agreements when a different commercial usage is alleged are pointed out by Goldstajn and by Michido (*Unification* ..., pp. 48 and 290).

131. Cf. the further references in Riese, *RabelsZ* 1965, p. 77.

conclusion of the contract. In the realm of French and Anglo-American law, on the other hand, the date on which title in the goods was transferred to the purchaser was regarded as critical. A third system was in operation in the realm of German and Scandinavian law, including certain countries thereby influenced; this regarded the risk as transferred at the moment when the goods were delivered to the purchaser. One has only to imagine the numerous possibilities of confusion among these systems to realize how unsatisfactory the situation was from the viewpoint of international trade. Owing to the influence of classical doctrines, the courts had made virtually no contribution to the removal of these vexations.[132]

The breakthrough towards transnational law had, however, already occurred at Rome in 1951 through the Rabel-influenced draft of the International Institute for the Unification of Private Law, and in 1962 the Uniform Commercial Code of the American Law Institute, prepared under the influence of Karl Llewellyn, proved a happy continuation. Both Institutes decided to take the moment of delivery of the goods as the time of passage of the risk. Today therefore we have in the two codes a gratifying convergence of views, embodied in Section 2-509 UCC and Article 97 of the 1964 Hague Sales Rules. There is moreover little danger that the countries which must now abandon their domestic law in international cases will make difficulties.[133] Kahn's meritorious research into standard practice, even though its initial premises have rightly been criticized, also reaches the same result.[134]

Although there are still many points where the two major codifications need to be brought into harmony, almost complete agreement has fortunately been achieved in their treatment of the risk of loss.[135] Their model effect on this point is therefore especially powerful, and the rule they have established enjoys the advantage of a very wide territory of application.

---

132. Examples: Hamburg *Landgericht*, 24 October 1907, and Swiss Federal Tribunal 11 October 1918. The relevant decisions of the Mixed Arbitral Tribunals now have the air of painful but unavailing endeavours to find the right, and at the same time a legally persuasive solution; cf. e.g. the decision of 7 April 1927, and also the two decisions of 26 July 1922, both noteworthy for an attempt to substantiate the findings by the concordance of the two national legal systems involved.

133. The commentary of Graveson/Cohn explains Articles 96 ff. simply by referring without any critical observation to Section 20 of the Sale of Goods Act. Schmitthoff, however, in *Export Trade* (p. 70) calls Section 20 "an antiquated rule" and recommends our two codifications as models of what a modern text should be. French judges will hardly remain indifferent to what the greatest authority in the field. Professor André Tunc, has to say on this theme in the commentary we reprint below.

134. *La Vente commerciale internationale*, p. 29; critique by Lorenz, 126 ZHR, 1964, p. 156.

135. Farnsworth, *Proceedings*, p. 233; Honnold, 107 *University of Pennsylvania Law Review*, 1959, pp. 317 and 324.

Nevertheless, though quite understandably for so new a rule, it still requires detailed elaboration in many ways.[136]

In the first place, a difficulty arises out of the term "delivery". Both codes make the passage of the risk dependent on the fact that "the goods are delivered" or, to quote Article 97 of the Rules, that "delivery of the goods is effected". Now the meaning of the word "delivery" is not even wholly clear at the moment where it first comes to the fore, namely in connection with the question of the moment when the seller has performed his obligations. Of that, however, more later. But "delivery" does not necessarily have to be understood in the same sense when considering the risk of loss as when the seller's fulfilment of his duty to deliver is in question: the decisive aspects are not entirely the same in either case.

The governing principle behind the regulation of the onus of risk is now, fortunately, everywhere the same; for the present, however, there are still certain differences in the ways in which it is given expression in the various languages. One must pay heed to this before assuming that transnational law lies within one's grasp. In German law what is considered decisive from the outset is whether, and up to when, this or that party had the goods in his *Obhut* ("charge", "care", "keeping" or "custody").[137] The official comment on Section 2-509 UCC observes:

> "The underlying theory of this rule is that a merchant who is to make physical delivery at his own place continues meanwhile to control the goods and can be expected to insure his interest in them."

The semantic problem is not touched upon by Tunc in his French-language commentary on this article (p.388). On the other hand, it emerges in Graveson/Cohn's commentary on Article 96, though here again it is expressed from a different angle:

> "The general rule is that the seller carries the risk while he has care of the goods and while the buyer is not bound to take them into his care."

Honnold provides yet another formulation:

> "The risk should be borne by the party who can thus guard against it. Usually, the one in possession and control of goods is in the best position to guard against their loss and also to insure the goods in standard policies covering buildings and their contents."[138]

When the conditions of possession or control are fulfilled within the meaning of this principle will be a question for decision according to the individual case. This applies especially to what is the normal case for the international sale of goods, i.e. that of their carriage over a more or less considerable

---

136. It is in this sense that one should surely understand the criticisms by Honnold and Berman, in *Law and Contemporary Problems*, pp. 338 and 354.

137. Riese 1957, p. 109.

138. 107 *University of Pennsylvania Law Review*, 1959, p. 319.

distance. Here the question arises, at what precise moment does the delivery take place from the viewpoint of risk of loss? With the aid of the principle of proximity to risk and the basic guidelines for such cases which we have just discovered, it will nearly always be possible to arrive at a transnational decision.

> "The buyer, who is in the presence of the goods and the carrier when the damage is discovered, is usually in a better position to negotiate the settlement of the claim against the carrier or insurer than is a distant seller. If, as is often the case, the damage during transit is minor or relates to only part of the goods, the buyer can more conveniently sell the goods; this result also tends to reduce the grounds for rejection of goods by buyers who find that the transaction has become unprofitable during the period required for shipment, and who could by rejection force the seller into the awkward position of choosing between redisposing of the goods in a distant market and negotiating with the buyer for their redisposition at a disadvantageous price." [139]

Attention must be drawn to the fact that, even within the area where the principle we have outlined is accepted, a number of special cases still obtain. Thus for example, in accordance with Article 9 of the Hague Sales Rules, which confers priority on commercial practices, maritime and inland water transport are governed by special rules which have not yet been completely unified. [140] As compared with the extremely thorough regulation comprised in Sections 2-319 to 2-325 of the Uniform Commercial Code, the Hague Conference of 1964 was fortunately reluctant to place this special domain in a straitjacket of rigid rules. An exception is Article 99 of the Sales Rules, concerning carriage by sea, and it is a moot point whether this provision is succesful (cf. Graveson/Cohn thereon).

In view of the contradictions between national laws, and the well-known propensity of the Sales Rules to err on the side of caution, it is for the present scarcely possible to discern any transnational rule for the event that the seller uses his own equipment or resources for the transport of the goods, though one may find it only reasonable in a given case that the seller should bear the risk so long as equipment under his own control is in use. [141] On the other hand, transnational law can now be posited in respect of the long-disputed question as to whether an agreement by the parties over the costs of transport may effect the apportionment of risk. This question, on the pro-

---

139. Honnold, 107 *University of Pennsylvania Law Review*, 1959, p. 323. See also the extensive treatment given the whole question by Rabel in *Warenkauf* II, pp. 324 ff.

140. American Foreign Trade Definitions 1941, published by International Foreign Trade Council Inc.; Incoterms, published in 1953 by the International Chamber of Commerce, Paris.

141. Cf. Rabel, *Warenkauf* II, p. 331; Riese 1965, p. 34; Honnold, 107 *University of Pennsylvania Law Review*, 1959, n. 72, p. 324.

posal of the International Chamber of Commerce, was answered in the negative by Article 101 of the Sales Rules, which most probably also represents the prevalent American view.[142]

It is also undoubtedly transnational law to understand "loss of the goods" as meaning not only total loss but also diminution and deterioration. [143] Moreover the risk in question is obviously that of loss by chance or *force majeure*, not of blamable loss.[144]

Schmitthoff offers an important rule of interpretation:

"If the contract provides for delivery franco domicile of the buyer, the intention of the parties as regards the passing of the risk can often be gathered from the terms of payment and the arrangements about insurance: if the price is prepaid and the buyer is responsible for insurance, there is hardly any doubt that the goods travel at his risk; the result would be reversed if the price were collected on delivery and the seller had to cover the insurance risk." [145]

One may never lose sight of the fact that the rules governing the allotment of the risk are non-mandatory in the national laws no less than in the two great codes. The field, in fact, remains wide open for interpretation.[146]

There remains a series of important problems which are outside the scope of the present work. They are, however, dealt with most lucidly in the commentary of André Tunc. Bearing in mind that not all readers will have ready access to this important text, we will here reproduce it *in extenso*:

"It follows from this provision [Article 97(1)], by reasoning *a contrario*, that if the seller delivers goods which conform to the contract on a date or at a place other than those provided, risk does not necessarily pass. A distinction must then be made between two cases.

When delivery is delayed, this being covered by Articles 26 to 28, risk passes at the time of delivery if the delay does not amount to a fundamental breach; but if there is fundamental breach it only passes if the buyer waives his right to declare the contract avoided and only from that time. Where delivery is made before the fixed date, this being covered by Article 29, then since this is really a problem of risk, it seemed reasonable to provide that, even if the buyer accepts the goods, risk only passes at the date fixed in the contract. If the goods are delivered at a place other than that provided in the contract, the case

---

142. Cf. Honnold, *op. cit.*, p. 320, with references to standard practice and case-law. Contrast Swiss Federal Tribunal, 11 October 1918.

143. Cf. Riese 1965, pp. 92 and 96; Honnold, *ibid.*; restrictively, Schmitthoff, *Export Trade*, p. 70.

144. Riese, *ibid.*

145. *Ibid.*

146. Cf. e.g. the English *"President of India"* case decided on 28 November 1968.

124

covered by Articles 30 to 32, and the buyer requires the seller to perform the contract, risk only passes when the goods arrive at the agreed place; but if the buyer cannot or will not declare the contract avoided nor does he require performance of the contract, risk passes on his acceptance of the goods.

The second paragraph of Article 97 covers the situation where goods which do not conform with the contract are handed over. In this case there is no delivery. In consequence risk will never pass to the buyer, or not at any rate until the seller has carried out the operations necessary to remedy the defect in the goods, deliver the missing part or quantity of goods or supply other goods which do conform with the contract. Whilst there is nothing extraordinary in risk remaining with the seller when the buyer had declared the contract avoided or has requested that other goods be supplied to replace those handed over, it would not be reasonable to allow this to be the rule beyond these cases. If the buyer does not declare the contract avoided and moreover does not request that replacements be supplied, risk must pass to the buyer at the time of the handing over in accordance with the contract and the Law, except for the fact that the goods do not conform with the contract; this is the rule laid down in the second paragraph.

The putting into effect of this rule, however well-founded it may be, could give rise to difficulties which are not expressly dealt with in the text. Assuming, for example, that the buyer does not in the first instance declare the contract avoided and does not ask for replacements to be supplied, but merely requires that defects be remedied or a supplementary delivery be made and supposing furthermore that he does not obtain satisfaction and eventually claims avoidance of the contract, as he may do by Article 42(2), it would seem that it must be agreed, although the Article does not expressly say so, that risk which passed to him on the handing over of the goods returns to the seller without retroactive effect when the declaration of avoidance is made (Article 79 (2) (d) may suggest a retroactive transfer, but the fact that the buyer had accepted the goods should result in the principle in Article 97 (2) overriding this).

Again it may be asked where the risk lies during the short period allowed by Article 38 (1) for the examination of the goods. If, in spite of the loss or deterioration of the goods, it is still possible to prove that they did or did not conform to the contract, then either Article 97 (1) or Article 97 (2) must be applied. In the converse case, where the goods have not been examined, it seems that it should be presumed that they conform with the contract, from which it follows that risk has passed.

The position is different if the buyer has ascertained a lack of conformity and the risk takes effect in the short period allowed by Article 39 for notification or lack of conformity. It must then be conceded, if the buyer can still prove the want of conformity, that he is entitled to demand avoidance of the contract and can call for replacements, thus negating the passing of risk. The same solution must follow if the risk takes effect after the notification of lack of conformity, but before the buyer has exercised the rights given him by Article 41 and succeeding Articles.

Finally, if, as is envisaged in the second sentence of Article 39, the buyer could not have made known the lack of conformity in the goods even though he carried out the examination prescribed by Article 38 (I), it would appear that his silence up to the time of the discovery of the defect could not amount to a valid acceptance of the goods and of the risk. If he gives notice of the defect promptly upon discovering it, it would seem, by applying Article 97 (1), that the goods were never at his risk. In essence, indeed, the position is little different from that which has just been examined in the preceeding paragraph of this commentary." [147]

In practice, the question of who bears the risk of loss is in virtually every case much simpler than in theory. Nowadays it is almost unheard-of for goods to travel uninsured. Hence the problem is more one for insurance law than for sales law. So far as the parties are concerned, it is transformed from a question of risk to a question of the costs and the price, because the costs include the insurance premium.

The question of who has to bear the loss of the goods is absorbed by the much more difficult question of the circumstances in which a contracting party may seek exemption from performance. At first sight this problem does not appear suitable for solution on a transnational basis. In one part of the world, notably where the influence of German law prevails, even this question is considered in the first place with an eye to *Verschulden*, i.e. culpable intent or negligence; but in other parts of the world, for example the domain of English and American law, this aspect is regarded as secondary, and primary attention is paid to the warranties. [148] Rabel once pointed out that this antithesis was considerably blurred in practice. Today we may venture to say that a transnational principle in answer to the fundamental question does exist, and that the only remaining difficulties confronting the judge concern the ways in which that principle will have to be inflected in application to the

---

147. 1964 *Hague Conference on the International Sale of Goods*, The Hague 1966, Vol. I, pp. 388 ff. Cf., further, Graveson/Cohn; Rabel III, 2nd ed., pp. 93 f.; Farnsworth, *Proceedings*, p. 235; Riese 1965, p. 93; Honnold, *ibid.*, n. 59.

148. Cf. in particular Rabel, *Warenkauf* I, p. 329. Even in 1936 he devoted nearly 40 pages to this question alone.

many and various particular cases. It is articulated in exemplary fashion by Article 74 of the Hague Sales Rules:

"1. Where one of the parties has not performed one of his obligations, he shall not be liable for such non-performance if he can prove that is was due to circumstances which, according to the intention of the parties at the time of the conclusion of the contract, he was not bound to take into account or to avoid or to overcome; in the absence of any expression of the intention of the parties, regard shall be had to what reasonable persons in the same situation would have intended.

2. Where the circumstances which gave rise to the non-performance of the obligation constituted only a temporary impediment to performance, the party in default shall nevertheless be permanently relieved of his obligation if, by reason of the delay, performance would be so radically changed as to amount to the performance of an obligation quite different from that contemplated by the contract.

3. The relief provided by this Article for one of the parties shall not exclude the avoidance of the contract under some other provision of the present Law or deprive the other party of any right which he has under the present Law to reduce the price, unless the circumstances which entitled the first party to relief were caused by the act of the other party or of some person for whose conduct he was responsible."

Should anyone doubt that these terms were worked out with extraordinary care and now represent the best that can be found internationally, let him study the commentaries of the participants in the Hague Conference of 1964.[149]

The difficulties that national courts have experienced with this problem, not to mention the activity of companies and trade associations in promoting standard regulations, throw the progress achieved in the Sales Rules into high relief and reinforce the model effect of Article 74.[150] The thought underlying that text is that the party under obligation can only free himself from accountability in the event of circumstances which he could not be expected to foresee, hence take into account. This satisfies a demand raised long ago by Rabel:

---

149. Riese 1957, p. 91, and 1965, pp. 78 and 83, and more especially Honnold (ed.), *Unification* ..., p. 29, in reply to certain objections: "Can one hope for greater precision in a uniform law proposed for adoption by States with varying degrees of relationship with international trade? If greater precision is needed, should it not be sought through contract provisions specially devised for the situation at hand? "

150. In England the House of Lords decision in the *Fibrosa* case (15 June 1942) led to the enactment of the 1943 Frustrated Contracts Act (see Schmitthoff, *Export Trade*, p. 102). On the standard practice we have the comprehensive report of Philippe Kahn, pp. 99 ff.

"The decisive element in business, as distinct from the everyday life of the community, is calculation, which presupposes a clear apportionment of the risks of the transaction not following a normal course and higher costs being incurred. What the individual contract and the typical situation allot the parties in the way of risk must also be authoritative where the juristic norm of apportionment is concerned."[151]

This consideration is closely allied to the notion that an unforeseen risk ought rather to be borne by the person within whose sphere of influence it lies. To be logical, this also implies that a risk lying equidistant from either party should be shared.[152]

So far as the translation into practice of our transnational principle is concerned, nobody will surely claim that the judge with the numerous decisions of many lands to inform him should find it harder to reach a correct solution than the judge who, as hitherto, had nothing more to go on than the relatively slim volume of his own domestic jurisprudence. In other words, the very fact that a transnational principle is now available as a guiding thread should expedite the decision of the individual case. In the present context we must rest content with the mere enumeration of pertinent decisions, set forth in chronological order so as to render the progress accomplished plain:

16 June 1911, Railway Arbitration Tribunal (*nationalization*);
15 July 1916, Swiss Federal Tribunal (*war*);
7 December 1921, MAT (*war; freight-costs*);
25 January 1922, MAT (*war*);
27 July 1923, MAT (*war, currency-collapse*);
16 June 1925, MAT (*war, export-licence*);
5 September 1930, *Lena Goldfields* award (*concession*);
25 March 1933, Paris (*expropriation in Russia; burden of proof*);[153]
12 June 1942, *Reichsgerichtshof* (Aluminium foil; *war*);
20 October 1944, Berne court of appeal (*US embargo*);

---

151. *Warenkauf* I, p. 343.

152. In his "Nichterfüllung auf Grund ausländischer Leistungsverbote" (14 *RabelsZ*, 1942, p. 283), Zweigert enlarged upon a remark of Franz Kahn's ("Die Lehre vom *ordre public*", 39 *Jherings Jahrbücher*, 1898, p. 108) to the effect that *ordre public* often enshrines private law that is not yet ready to emerge. The *Fibrosa* case exemplifies this. Wengler, in 54 *Zeitschrift für vergleichende Rechtswissenschaft*, 1941, p. 295, observed that the critical point about foreign prohibitions on performance was whether they produced effects within the domestic jurisdiction. This is consonant with the risk or sphere theory. Lately, the production by a law of effects in other countries has been found an important criterion in connection with anti-trust law.

153. Cf. Langen, *Studien zum internationalen Wirtschaftsrecht*, Munich 1963, p. 182.

21 July 1952, England (Brauer; *export-licence*[154]);

17 December 1956, House of Lords (Board of Trade; *infringement of German currency-law*);

21 October 1957, House of Lords (Reggazzoni; *export-prohibition*);

19 June 1958, Moscow arbitration (Israel Oil; *export-prohibition*);

19 October 1960, *Bundesgerichtshof* (wine-merchant; *import-prohibition*);

15 March 1963, *Sapphire* award (force majeure *clause*);

24 June 1965, House of Lords (Hong-Kong Textiles, *quota-system*).

This list is by no means exhautive, and is intended merely as an aid to viewing the progressive concretization of the principle case by case. For additional material the reader is referred to the cases discussed in the official comment to Section 2-614 UCC.[155]

The Hague Sales Rules do not indicate any clear approach to the problem of impediments to performance which already existed at the time of conclusion of the contract. However, the commentaries would suggest that the critical test in this regard is whether the party in question was aware or ought to have been aware of the obstacle.[156]

Changes in the law, even considerable changes, cannot, according to the Rules, normally be relied on as grounds of exemption from performance. This agrees with most municipal systems and would therefore appear to be a transnational principle.[157]

The act of a person for whose conduct a contracting party is responsible can be regarded as a case of *force majeure* only within the scope of Article 74 of the Rules. This emerges from the last sentence of that text.[158] It is also transnational law, as a corollary of the good-faith principle, that a party intending to invoke *force majeure* should inform the other party to that effect without delay, though in view of the importance of such a decision he must be allowed a reasonable time to form that intention.[159] In any case, the

154. The granting of a licence to export from Brazil was made conditional by the authorities on the payment by the purchaser of a considerably higher price than had been agreed, but the seller was not allowed a plea of *force majeure*.

155. On the question of exemption in accordance with Article 74 (3) of the Sales Rules, see also the French decision Cass. 17 May 1939, concerning the delivery of mica from Madagascar to France and the applicability of Article 1147 of the Civil Code.

156. Riese 1957, p. 93, and 1965, p. 82.

157. Riese 1957, p. 92; Tunc, p. 384; Rabel, *Warenkauf* I, pp. 355 and 357; Houin, "Some comparative aspects of the law relating to sale of goods", ICLQ Suppl. 9, 1964, p. 27; Supreme Court of Vermont, 10 May 1924 (*Miles*), p. 564; English *Brauer* decision cited by Schmitthoff, *Export Trade,* p. 106.

158. Riese 1965, p. 79; Graveson/Cohn, p. 96; cf. Rabel, *Warenkauf* I, pp. 329 and 332.

159. A suggestion in this sense was made by the International Chamber of Commerce but was not expressly incorporated in the Sales Rules, probably because the point was thought to go without saying. Cf. Riese 1965, p. 81; Kahn, p. 104; Lorenz, 126 ZHR, 1964, p. 154. The duty to inform the other party can also be inferred from Article 88 of the Sales Rules.

freedom of contract permits great latitude in the framing of a clause to regulate the appeal to *force majeure*, whether in the contract or in the general terms of business.[160]

The knotty problem of the borderline between a negligible transitory impediment and an intolerably persistent one is meticulously parried by paragraph 2 of Article 74. This can unhesitatingly be adopted as a model for transnational law, especially as it already coincides with English law.[161] The rule which transpires from paragraph 3, namely that a plea of *force majeure* leaves all other remedies intact, may also be regarded as transnational law.

The same is true of two other rules, which in final analysis are but good faith in a different guise. One is the rule that a party is not bound to execute his side of the contract if he is justifiably uncertain that the other will execute his. The second is the rule that each party must handle the goods with care and do everything that can be expected in order to reduce any potential damage to the minimum. The first may be inferred from Articles 73, 76 and 77 of the Hague Sales Rules and Section 2-609 to 611 UCC.[162]

Special difficulties for the German jurist arise out of the fact that Articles 77 ff. of the 1964 Sales Rules represent a deviation from one of the

160. Copiously illustrated in Schmitthoff, *Export Trade*, p. 104, and Kahn, pp. 99 ff. Cf. also Riese 1965, p. 81, and 1957, p. 80, likewise Graveson/Cohn on Article 74 and the English *Swiss Atlantic* decision of 31 March 1966 with the reasoning of Lord Wilberforce there cited, pp. 431 ff. Rabel also discusses the question at length, and from the angle of comparative law, in *Warenkauf* I, p. 358. Lorenz, *loc. cit.*, voices justified misgivings at Kahn's excessively one-sided presentation. The bounds of the validity of such covenants are constituted, for transnational law also, by misuse of monopoly, conflict with public policy and like considerations.

161. Graveson/Cohn on Article 74, with case-law. In the Swiss decision of 20 October 1944 an American wartime embargo on dealings in securities was treated as only a passing impediment. Lorenz, *loc. cit.*, in criticizing Kahn, comes out against the one-sided handling of contractual practice to the seller's advantage. There is a lengthy treatment of the question in Rabel, *Warenkauf* I, p. 348.

162. On the first rule, cf. the German *Bundesgerichtshof* decisions of 19 February 1969 and 22 October 1969 (the latter deals in particular with the provision of Article 8 (5) of the ECE conditions) and, for comparative law, on *stoppage* (Section 2-702 UCC), Rabel, *Warenkauf* I, p. 38. The duty of care, preservation or mitigation of damage is discussed in terms of comparative law by Rabel in *Warenkauf* I, p. 517, and has been given manifold expression in decided cases, e.g. MAT 16 June 1925 (*Negreanu*), pp. 215 and 217; *Bundesgerichtshof* 26 February 1969; Paris 15 February 1933 (*Marschak*); the English decisions of 12 May 1953 (*d'Almeida*) and 27 March 1957 (*Federspiel*); the American decisions of 4 September 1942 (*Monarch Brewery*), p. 586, 17 March 1943 (*Delaware*), 13 February 1946 (*Texas Motor*), p. 94, and 17 December 1956 (*Global Commerce*). It is expressed in Articles 91-95 of the Hague Sales Rules and in Section 2-515 UCC. On the duties of care and salvage, see in particular Honnold, 107 *University of Pennsylvania Law Review*, 1959, p. 226, with references to Sections 2-603 and 2-709 UCC, and to Lagergren, *Delivery of Goods and Transfer of Property and the Risk in the Law of Sale*, Stockholm 1954, p. 18.

fundamental doctrines of German law. According to German conceptions it is impossible at one and the same time to repudiate—or "avoid"—a contract and demand damages for its non-fulfilment. The Hague Rules, however, follow the view of the majority of the great trading nations, according to which such action is possible. Probably this contradiction is far less important for the practitioner than for the jurist.[163] At all events, in seeking the transnational law on the subject, it would be as well to begin by clarifying the terminology used, so as to see whether supposed distinctions are real, or synonyms more than apparent. In view of the inconsistency of the terms employed, it would further be advisable to reapply this test to each case that arises and to decide in accordance with each separate set of facts. Here are some of the words which overlap: the Hague Sales Rules speak of "avoidance" and, in French, "*résolution*"; in addition, the Uniform Commercial Code employs "cancellation" and "rescission"; in German we have the word "*Aufhebung*" (literally: lifting or removal) as suggested by Rabel and supported by Riese and others, alongside "*Rücktritt*" (literally: withdrawal or resignation), a term which in this application is surely obsolete. Reference to commercial usage might also be useful for the clarification of the question.

The Hague Rules for damages effective equally for either party possess a particularly strong model effect, because the Uniform Commercial Code was frequently consulted in their elaboration and particular regard paid to its rules.[164] This model effect is particularly important for the realm of German law, because the model grants more remedies than the German rules.

This is true in the first place of the question whether must be fault for a claim for damages to lie. As is well known, German law answers in the affirmative, while the model regulations, following Anglo-American law, ignore the aspect of culpability. The laws of France and the Netherlands also agree with the model rules. The German opposition is in fact no longer very strong,[165] and in appropriate cases, therefore, even a German judge may consider applying the rules as transnational law. Indeed his readiness so to proceed should be the greater in view of the freedom of the contracting parties to regulate the question of fault however they wish, hence even to

163. For that reason Tunc (p. 385) sees no difficulty here in the implementation of the Hague Rules and, if one accepts the analysis of Rabel (*Warenkauf* I, p. 429) and Riese (1957, p. 94; 1965, p. 83), none is to be expected, more specifically, in their application in the sphere of German law. Nevertheless it will not be possible to accept the Hague Rules as here epitomizing transnational law, except as may transpire from emphasis of their model effect and careful testing of the circumstances of the given case. In an award made on 2 November 1954 the Prague Chamber of Commerce refused to apply French law, which allows the imposition of a penalty fixed by the contract in addition to damage, and relied on Czech law, which does not permit such double penalization.

164. Riese 1965, p. 86, and 1957, p. 106.

165. Cf. above all the opinion of Rabel to which attention is drawn by Riese, 1957, p. 61, and also Rabel, *Conflict* III, 2nd ed., p, 102.

exclude the application of the Sales Rules and the above-mentioned national laws (cf. Article 3 of the Rules). What is more, paragraph 3 of Article 74 embodies in its final version an amendment intended to make it clear that while the seller is liable for deficiencies in the goods even when he is not at fault, he nevertheless enjoys a possibility of exemption.[166] However, there is at least one important exception in regard to which it is still far too early to predicate any transnational rule: products liability. In the USA it is apparently possible to find the producer liable even in the absence of fault on his part.[167] In Europe, on the other hand, according to the probably correct view of Von Hippel (op. cit.), the possibility of recognizing products liability is still being explored.

When it comes to the estimation of loss and damage, the German judge is again faced with the embarrassment of having to depart from his domestic law if he wishes to acknowledge the model effect of the Hague Sales Rules. Yet here too experience confirms that the practical outcome, even though reached from different premises, is more or less the same. In German law (§ 347 of the Commercial Code) the aggrieved party has as a rule freedom to choose whether he proves the size of his loss by concrete reference to the peculiar circumstances of the case or by abstract reliance on the quoted or market price of the goods. Only in exceptional cases is he restricted to the second method, i.e. when for reasons of mutual consideration he should have made a covering purchase to avert damage of an unusually high order that would otherwise have threatened.[168] The Sales Rules, on the contrary, following once more the model of most of the major trading countries, set out with abstract estimation as their postulate, but entertain proof of greater damage (Articles 84 and 86).[169]

166. Riese 1965, p. 81; Tunc, p. 384. In the American decision of 10 May 1924 (*Miles*) proof was entertained that the buyer had objected to a consignment of potatoes not on quality grounds, in the last resort, but on account of an intervening drop in prices.

167. Von Hippel, "Internationale Entwicklungstendenzen des Schadenrechts", NJW 1969, p. 682, with further references, n. 15; Markert, "Die Schadenshaftung für fehlerhafte Produkte in den USA", *Aussenwirtschaftsdienst des Betriebsberaters* 1965, pp. 69 ff., with further references; Honnold, in Ziegel/Foster, pp. 6 ff., with further references; Fridmann, *ibid.*, pp. 38 ff., with illustrations from English law; French decision Cass. 24 November 1954 on explosion of gas-bottles; American decisions of 13 February 1946 on accident through defective vehicles, 4 April 1957 on faulty gas-regulator, and 9 May 1960 on defective car; German decision of 26 November 1968 on fowl-pest.

168. Cf. case-law cited by Würdinger in *Reichsgerichtsrätekommentar zum HGB*, 2nd ed. 1961, appendix *ad* § 374, n. 160.

169. This rule, which applies to the special case of avoidance of contract under Article 84, should also apply to the regular case of a contract not yet avoided, within the meaning of Article 82 (Riese 1965, p. 89); on the assessment of damages in the USA cf. Sections 2-713 and 2-708 UCC. In its decision of 8 May 1921 and 18 January 1923 the Swiss Federal Tribunal allowed both methods of estimation, at the option of the

132

To apply the rule embedded in Article 82 of the Sales Rules, to the effect that damages for loss of profit may also be sought, judges have no need to rely on the model effect of the Rules. Even before the Hague Convention this had become transnational law, and indeed it had always held good in public international law. This rule has been set aside in only a relatively small number of exceptional cases.[170] In transnational commercial law, loss of profit includes appropriate default interest, only the computation of which gives rise to difficulty. Fortunately it will henceforth be possible to follow the method set forth in Article 83 of the Sales Rules.[171]

Other rules which have now become more or less established in transnational commercial law are those in Article 82 and 86 limiting the liability of the party in breach to loss which he ought to have foreseen.

The assessment of damages remains however a subject over which controversy is rife. One point of dispute concerns the adequacy of causality as a term of reference for the assessment, another the role of foreseeability in this connection and whether it should not be the decisive consideration. Within this issue, the question arises as to whether the foreseeable should be defined in terms of the subjective capabilities of the party under obligation, or whether a more objective yardstick, derived from the notion of a reasonable businessman, ought not rather to be applied. Then again, it is suggested that causality may be an unsuitable touchstone altogether, so that there is no other solution but to "elaborate a typology of critical cases".[172]

---

creditor. On questions of abstract or concrete estimation, cf. above all Rabel, *Warenkauf* I, pp. 171, 282 and, with special reference to the English distinction between "general" and "special" damages, 283; also the American decision of 10 April 1946 (*Price*), para. 8, and more particularly the English *National Broach* decision of 21 December 1964 (confirmed on 15 June 1965) with the critical observations of Mr. Justice Cross on these concepts (pp. 85 ff.). The English decision of 27 July 1954 (*Kwei Tek*) dealt with the case of the goods having in fact become unmerchantable. On the Sales Rules, cf. further Riese 1957, p. 104, and 1965, p. 88, Tunc, p. 386, and with particular reference to the advantages and increasing use of abstract estimation, Honnold, in Schmitthoff, *Sources* ..., p. 13, together with Von Caemmerer, *ibid.*, p. 96, and NJW 1959, p. 570.

170. Cf., for public international law, the references given by Georg Dahm, *Völkerrecht* III, Stuttgart 1961, pp. 235 ff.; also the Railway Tribunal judgments of 1897, the English *Molling* decision of 20 December 1901, and the American *Bowman* decision of 21 November 1927. In the American *Thrift Wholesale* (27 July 1943) and *Price* (10 April 1946) decisions, and the Prague award of 27 January 1966, indemnity for loss of profits was refused for special reasons.

171. Cf. Riese 1957, p. 103; Tunc, p. 386; Cass. 15 May 1935 with note by Niboyet; Rabel, *Conflict of Laws* II, p. 44, n. 325.

172. Von Caemmerer, NJW 1959, p. 570, taking up Rabel. Cf., further, on *causa proxima non remota spectatur*, a rule widely applied in international maritime law, the *"Havanna"* decision given by the Hamburg *Oberlandesgericht* on 29 November 1962, with further references; also, for American law, the references under that heading in *Black's Law Dictionary*.

But these are theoretical questions. In practice, it has always proved possible to find a way out in the spirit of transnational law, by resort to the principle of good faith, in accordance with the exemplary formulation which we now possess in Article 82 of the Sales Rules.[173] The Uniform Commercial Code does not diverge from this in any essential respect (cf. Sections 2-714 ff. in particular).

With regard to each party's obligations to do his utmost to keep damage to a minimum, the Sales Rules, far from setting any new example, merely express (in Article 88) a longstanding transnational rule which is anchored in all national laws and therefore calls for no further illustration here.

The same is true of the rule in Article 89 which in case of fraud releases the claim from the limitations of the Sales Rules governing damages in general.[174]

It is outside our present scope to discuss the various special kinds of sale for which Section 2-306 UCC, in particular, provides detailed rules, many of which, however, are undoubtedly transnational in character.

So far as the time-limitation of claims in the area of sales-law is concerned, we now possess the report of an Uncitral study-group (A/CN.9/30, 3 November 1969).[175]

The Uniform Commercial Code offers in Section 2-210 something which is not usually to be found in statutes of commercial law, namely a set of detailed rules governing the assignability of rights and obligations arising out of contracts of sale:

"(1) A party may perform his duty through a delegate unless otherwise agreed or unless the other party has a substantial interest in having his original promisor perform of control the acts required by the contract. No delegation of performance relieves the party delegating of any duty to perform or any liability for a breach.

(2) Unless otherwise agreed all rights of either seller or buyer can be assigned except where the assignment would materially change the duty of the other party, or increase materially the burden or risk imposed on him by his contract, or impair materially his chance of obtaining return performance. A right to damages for breach of the whole contract or a right arising out of the assignor's due performance of his entire obligation can be assigned despite agreement otherwise.

(3) Unless the circumstances indicate the contrary, a prohibition of assignment of 'the contract' is to be construed as barring only the delegation to the assignee of the assignor's performance.

173. Cf. Riese 1957, pp. 102 & 107, and 1965, p. 87; Tunc, p. 386; Graveson/Cohn on Article 82.
174. Cf. the English *Kwei Tek* decision of 27 July 1954, concerning a forgery in shipping documents.
175. It has now recommended a four-year period of limitation: see p. 187, n. 48, in Part Four.

(4) An assignment of 'the contract' or of 'all my rights under the contract' or an assignment is similar general terms is an assignment of rights and unless the language or the circumstances (as in an assignment for security) indicates the contrary, it is a delegation of performance of the duties of the assignor and its acceptance by the assignee constitutes a promise by him to perform those duties. This promise is enforceable by either the assignor or the other party to the original contract.

(5) The other party may treat any assignment which delegates performance as creating reasonable grounds for insecurity and may without prejudice to his rights against the assignor demand assurances from the assignee (Section 2-609)."

For a precise understanding of these provisions, the reader is referred to the official Comment thereon. These rules are at all events most realistic and there should therefore be little hesitation in taking them as a model, the more so in view of the useful suggestions they embody in regard to the financing of sale transactions.

B. *Obligations of the seller*

There is a considerable measure of agreement between the Uniform Commercial Code and the Hague Sales Rules where the obligations of the seller are concerned. This is especially so in regard to the concerted step forward recently taken by legal scholarship in all the major trading countries, namely the separation of the duty of delivery from the duty of procuring title of ownership. This is now a settled question.[176] The model effect for transnational law which we may attribute to the two codes in this area is therefore an extremely powerful one, and it will also be possible on any given point to enlist the aid of one code to make good the lacunae of the other.

In view of this great advance, it is purely secondary, as well as wholly understandable, that our two exemplars still diverge in a few details. The rules contained in Articles 18 and 19 of the Sales Rules, and in Sections 2-301 and 2-503 UCC, are essentially the same. In the context of commercial linguistic practice, it is virtually self-evident what is meant is essence by "delivery" in Article 19 and in Section 1-201 (14). Rabel describes it as:

"...the end-term of the activity which is incumbent on the seller in order that possession of the goods may pass to the buyer. This activity, *qua* object of the contractual duty, is to be understood in a purely factual sense, hence with no regard to such acts as may be requisite

---

176. The jurisprudence of the Mixed Arbitral Tribunals reveals their struggle to reconcile divergent international sources of law (see e.g. MAT 25 May 1923). The progress now achieved was specially applauded by Honnold in 107 *University of Pennsylvania Law Review*, 1959, p. 319, and by Eisemann, "Die Incoterms", pp. 21 f.

under the specific national rules for possession and the conveyance of title. Thus envisaged, it is surely amenable to uniform regulation."[177] In the actual world of commerce, and therefore in transnational commercial law, the grasp of the subject possessed by reasonable businessmen experienced in dealing across frontiers certainly takes precedence over any theories excogitated within the four walls of a study on this or that side of border. This is evident in connection with the interposition of third parties who participate in the delivery, and with the case referred to in Article 19 of the Sales Rules, when the "delivery" does not merely consist in the handing-over but comprises an additional element, namely the conformity of the goods. It is true that, traditionally, the word "delivery" (though not necessarily its near equivalents in other languages) does not bear this complex meaning, as is recognized by most qualified commentators, and this is regarded by some writers as a special difficulty. English-speaking jurists who fear semantic difficulties may, however, make it clear when the more complex sense is intended by making use on such occasions of the word which appears in the parallel French text: *délivrance.*[178]

The seller, who is under obligation to deliver, has the burden of proof if the fact of delivery is contested.[179]

Sale involving carriage is the normal case in international trade in goods. As such, however, it is dealt with by the Sales Rules only in general terms (Article 19, paras. 1 and 2). The Uniform Commercial Code, in Section 3-319 to 3-321, lays down more comprehensive rules, which therefore, for the purpose of expanding transnational law, may be viewed in conjunction with commercial usage and practices, including the Incoterms and the corresponding American rules.[180] One of the most important guidelines for transnational law to emerge from all these rules and the case-law thereon is the

---

177. *Warenkauf* I, p. 320.

178. Cf. especially Riese 1957, p. 44; Farnsworth, *Proceedings,* pp. 234 f.; Honnold, *University of Pennsylvania Law Review* 1959, p. 318; also Eisemann, "Die Incoterms", p. 22, and Lagergren, *Delivery of the Goods and Transfer of Property and the Risk in the Law of Sale*, Stockholm, 1954, p. 17.

179. MAT 25 May 1923 (*Stöhr*).

180. *Sic* Riese 1965, pp. 66 and 77. It is certainly no obstacle to thus drawing upon these rules that, as Honnold (*Sources* ..., p. 78) points out, no full harmony has yet been achieved as between the Sales Rules that require supplementing, commercial practices and other rules. Cf. Dölle, "Bedeutung und Funktion der 'Bräuche' im Einheitsgesetz über den Kauf beweglicher Sachen", *Festgabe Rheinstein* 1949-I, p. 448. As against the doubts expressed in respect of certain individual cases by Farnsworth (p. 234), with reference to the report of the American delegation to the 1964 Conference, it is surely more important to note, with Tunc (p. 372), the concordance of these rules with international commercial usage and, with Schmitthoff (comments on Section 32 of the Sale of Goods Act), their agreement with English law. Cf. also Graveson/Cohn, on Article 54 and on the seller's duty of dispatch after receiving the buyer's bank guarantee,

principle that at no time should one and the same party enjoy powers of disposal over both the goods and the money for them. This principle should also enable a solution to be found in cases arising out of carriage by a party's own or third-party means of transport.[181]

Turning to the purchaser's remedies against breach of the seller's obligation to deliver, we will here discuss only the fundamental rules in the matter, leaving the remedies in such special cases as failure to comply with the date or place of delivery, or the non-conformity of the goods, to be dealt with in relation to the special duties of the seller. This distinction is essentially the same as is observed by the two model codes and by scholars in general.

In this area, again, the two codes do not make new law but at bottom merely confirm an existing transnational view to the effect that the purchaser should have the choice either to demand performance of the contract by the seller in breach or to declare the contract avoided. In the special case of non-conformity of the delivered goods both codes confirm the transnational rule that a reduction in price may be demanded (Articles 24 and 41 of the Sales Rules). In addition, and unlike certain trading countries, notably those of German law, the model codes grant an action for damages, as has already been mentioned in the previous section.

The situation when the purchaser requires performance is not construed by the two model codes in the same way as by German jurists, but this makes a smaller difference in practice than in theory. Thus there can be little doubt that Article 25 of the Sales Rules expresses an established rule of transnational law in debarring the purchaser from requiring performance where a purchase in replacement is possible and would correspond to usage. The same undeniable difference between theory and practice emerges in the academically controversial question as to whether and when a purchaser can apply to the courts for an order to secure delivery ("specific performance"). Under English and American law this course is open to him only in quite special and relatively rare circumstances, and in all other cases a claim for damages is his only remedy. The position under German law is the reverse. Both attitudes are very deeply rooted in the national commercial structures concerned: on the continent of Europe, law has not strayed too far from husbandry and local trade, where purchase of ascertained goods is the archetype, whereas the

---

discussed in relation to Article 72. One consequence of the duty of delivery is that it is the seller who has to apply for any export licence that may be necessary (Berman, *RabelsZ* 1959, p. 464, on the *Israel Oil* case, with further case-law); on the other hand, neither party may lose sight of the duty of collaboration which results from the good-faith principle and affects them both equally (for indications from American case-law see in particular Lüderitz, *Auslegung von Rechtsgeschäften,* Karlsruhe 1966, p. 442).

181. Honnold, *University of Pennsylvania Law Review* 1959, p. 323 and n. 72; Riese 1957, p. 45, with reference to the initial carrier in the event of the collaboration of several forwarding agents.

point of departure for English and American law is much rather overseas trade, in which the purchase of commercial goods predominates. Unquestionably, therefore, to adopt the outlook of the model codes corresponds more closely to the facts in the domain of the international sale of goods than to cling to continental convictions. This is moreover tacitly acknowledged by the German courts in the way they apply § 374 of the German Commercial Code. On the other side, in the realm of Anglo-American law, there is an unmistakable trend towards some rational loosening of the narrow bonds within which claims for specific performance had previously been confined. Thus in practice the two theoretically opposed conceptions already meet upon the midline between them. Even if this line is at present somewhat broadly drawn, it can already be treated as transnational law. This, it is true, is but hedgingly indicated in Article 16 of the Sales Rules, with its diplomatic deference to judicial homing instincts, but Section 2-716(1) UCC empowers courts positively in the following terms:

"Specific performance may be decreed where the goods are unique or in other proper circumstances."

In the official Comment, under "Purposes of Changes", and in the New York Annotations of this rule, it is explicitly pointed out how the new text is intended to promote a departure from previous law and, more particularly, a liberalization of judicial practice. If this American rule be taken as a model for transnational law, practically every difficulty should vanish. [182]

We shall now consider the purchaser's right of rescission, cancellation or avoidance of the contract (*résolution du contrat; Aufhebung des Vertrags*). For the purpose of transnational law, the difficulty centres in the determination of the circumstances conditioning this right. For the international lawyer this question is bedevilled with semantic problems, as the English and French expressions are not entirely synonymous, perhaps among themselves, and certainly not with the term which has been customary in German legal parlance: *Rücktritt*—which though finally untranslatable conveys the notion of "withdrawal" or "resignation".[183]

---

182. Cf., on the Sales Rules, Riese 1957, p. 48, and 1965, p. 29; *idem, Z.f.schw. Recht* 1967, p. 27; Tunc, pp. 370 and 373; Graveson/Cohn, p. 61; Honnold, *University of Pennsylvania Law Review* 1959, p. 327; Hellner in Ziegel/Foster, p. 108; for comparative law, Rabel. *Warenkauf* I, pp. 376 ff. On the small difference in practice, see also Lüderitz, p. 79, with reference to Wolfgang Friedmann, *Law in an Changing Society*, p. 91. For English law, see Schmitthoff, *The Sale of Goods*, p. 191; noteworthy decisions: English—17 December 1926 (*Wait*), 24 June 1926 (*Cohen*); American—21 November 1927 (*Bowman*); Swiss—4 July 1953 (*Intra-Handels AG*). That the difference "does not go so deep" in practice is also the view of Von Caemmerer, NJW 1956, p. 570. Cf. also Rabel, *Conflict of Laws* III, 2nd ed., p. 102, with American illustrations, and Treitel, "Specific performance in the sale of goods", *Journal of Business Law* 1966, p. 211.

183. Cf. Riese 1957, p. 94.

One considerable obstacle to the discovery of transnational rules lies in the fact that our two model codes do not agree on the subject. The Sales Rules make the right of avoidance in all cases of breach uniformly conditional on the fundamental nature of the breach (cf. Articles 27, 30 and 43). They have therefore to define fundamental breach, and this they do in Article 10:

" ... a breach of contract shall be regarded as fundamental wherever the party in breach knew, or ought to have known, at the time of the conclusion of the contract, that a reasonable person in the same situation as the other party would not have entered into the contract if he had foreseen the breach and its effects".

Now although this solution is in harmony with English law it has received little support, because in all too many cases it leaves the practitioner in the dark. For this reason, in particular, American publicists have roundly opted for the strict obligation of performance enshrined in Section 2-601 UCC, as being the better model. [184] On the other hand, continental writers have scarcely felt able to recommend the adoption of such stringency. [185] In this area, questions of law tend to find themselves reduced to the trade-policy question as to who should receive the more favourable treatment: the purchaser or the seller. [186] In view of all this, transnational law can only be postulated for cases where it is genuinely possible to reach a solution which accords due weight to the relative merits of the opposing theses yet which has no tincture of partiality. This cannot be done without enlisting the help of the principle of proportionality. Thus it is not solely the gravity of the breach which should be decisive for the avoidance of the contract, nor the traditional English distinction between "condition" and "warranty", except insofar as the parties themselves may explicitly or implicitly have so agreed. The question to be put is much rather whether it is still possible for the seller to repair the effects of the breach for which he is responsible, or, conversely, whether the purchaser might not reasonably be expected to adjust his demands. This is basic to any notion of mutual accommodation. A last-minute proposal on these lines, submitted by the Dutch delegation to the Hague Conference but not taken further by the Commission, sought to distinguish between reparable and irreparable breach (cf. Riese 1965, p. 22). In all cases where adjustment is a feasible proposition, no reasonable judge will allow the avoidance of the contract. The Sales Rules point to this principle in Articles 33 (2) and 44 (1). Even zealous proponents of strict performance, on the lines of the Uniform Commercial Code, concede that a reasonable degree of adjustment

184. Farnsworth, *Proceedings*, p. 231.

185. Von Caemmerer, in Ziegel/Foster, p. 130, with reference to Hellner, *ibid.*, pp. 107 ff.

186. Cf. especially Lorenz, "Formularpraxis und Rechtsvereinheitlichung im internationalen Kaufrecht" (review of Philippe Kahn's book), 126 ZHR, 1964, p. 154.

must be admitted, for example, in the case of long-distance sales, if only because of the high cost of return freight that could otherwise be incurred.[187]

In international commercial practice, as in the entire sphere of the law of contracts, avoidance is *per se* the last resort when all else has failed. As such it is a course which should never be lightly taken. Yet experience shows that it is often employed—notably in cases of unexpected price-changes—as a mere means of pressure to force price-concessions out of the other party. This is particularly true of overseas transactions, because avoidance in this instance may give rise to considerable expense in terms of freight, storage and customs duty. It follows that avoidance of the contract will be more reluctantly admitted in transnational law than within national boundaries.[188]

Intentionally, the Hague Sales Rules say nothing more about the legal consequences of avoidance than what is contained in the general formulation of Article 78. Honnold comments that the text "unfortunately drifts off into language of metaphysical obscurity". [189] Set against the reasons for the Commission's attitude explained by Riese (1957, pp. 96 ff.), this criticism is altogether too harsh and provokes the empirical question whether the parallel provisions on "cancellation" in Section 2-711 and 2-106 (4) UCC constitute any essentially better regulation of the problem, or at all events one closer to practice. In fact, the cautious blanket clause of the Sales Rules deliberately leaves considerable latitude for commercial usage and the courts, which in practice attenuates the antithesis between the codes on which Honnold lays such stress.[190]

We have already discussed the legal question of the assessment and computation of damages insofar as it affects each party equally. In the present context we have to consider the circumstances in which the seller has a claim for damages. Both model codes agree in contemplating such a claim even when combined with avoidance and even where the other party was not at fault.

187. Farnsworth, *Proceedings*, p. 232. Section 2-605 UCC provides for a right of cure in certain circumstances. Schmitthoff, *Export Trade*, p. 86, refers to the necessity that everyone, before strictly exercising his rights, must give the other side an opportunity for "readjustment" and mentions as apposite the English *Tool Metal Mfg.* and *SCCMO* decisions of 16 June 1955 and 28 February 1956 respectively.

188. This consideration (and not the desire to favour the seller) led the drafters of the ECE Conditions to treat avoidance as a step to be resorted to only *in extremis*. On avoidance rules, see also Von Caemmerer, NJW 1959, p. 570.

189. *Law and Contemporary Problems*, 1965, p. 347.

190. Graveson/Cohn's commentary on Article 78 (p. 57) plainly gives no handle to such criticism. Their doubts are addressed not so much to the consequences of avoidance as to the preconditions laid down in Article 10, in particular the concept of "fundamental breach". Reservations are also expressed by Ellwood, ICLQ 1964, Suppl. 9, p. 46, and Farnsworth, AJCL 1965, p. 237. Honnold, in *Law and Contemporary Problems* 1965, p. 344, is even scornful ("stew with many ingredients").

Although this represents a marked divergence from German and other continental laws, the model effect of the codes is here all the greater for their concordance between themselves.[191] Yet transnational law should not be lightly presumed. Rabel's recommendation on the subject (*Warenkauf* I, pp. 434 ff.) is doubtless in itself not enough for this purpose.[192] It will however in many cases be possible to discover a relevant commercial usage, and, over and above that, a German judge seeking a transnational rule may find a useful clue in the principle of good faith and fair dealing.

Once a dispute has reached the courts it may under no circumstances be resolved on the basis of general considerations of trade-policy. Whether this or that rule favours the purchaser or the seller is then no criterion, and the problem remains exclusively that of finding the proper solution to a given legal situation.

Transnational commercial law exists in large measure in respect of all problems to do with the date of delivery.[193] The Hague Sales Rules (Articles 20-22) and the Uniform Commercial Code (Section 2-309) fundamentally agree, inasmuch as both, in the final analysis, allow the principle of reasonableness to decide.[194] What is reasonable in relation to dates of delivery is essentially determined by commercial usage and conventions, the importance of which for the Sales Rules has been expressly acknowledged in this connection.[195] Thus, if the seller should be allowed some latitude in the case of non-fungible goods, this does not mean that the requirement of reasonableness is abandoned by a one-sided exception in his favour. On the contrary, given the special nature of the goods, it is the principle of reasonableness itself which calls for the flexible treatment of the delivery-date.[196]

---

191. Cf. on the whole question, with special references to the controversy in Germany, Rabel, *Warenkauf* I, pp. 434 ff.; Riese 1957, p. 61, and 1965, p. 53; Graveson/Cohn, p. 77; Prague award of 2 November 1954.

192. *Warenkauf* I, pp. 434 f., proposing a theoretical basis for the combination of *Rücktritt* with a claim for damages. In terms of German doctrine, he postulates the residual damages for withheld performance on both sides going to the party having most closely adhered to the contract. ("Die Kombination von Rücktritt und Schadensersatz ist dann theoretisch so zu verstehen, dass der Vertrag aufrecht bleibt, aus dem Vertrag selbst beide Teile das Recht auf Rückstellung der Leistungen haben und gegebenenfalls der vertragstreue Teil den restlichen Schadensersatz erhält. Diese Auffassung bietet in Wahrheit keine sachlichen Schwierigkeiten, freilich aber sprachliche.")

193. For comparative law, see Rabel, *Warenkauf* I, p. 327 and, with particular reference to cases of material time of performance, time-bargains and the like, pp. 389-409.

194. This furthermore agrees with Section 10 of the (English) Sale of Goods Act and long-attested English practice. See Graveson/Cohn on Article 20.

195. Riese 1965, p. 35.

196. Lorenz, 126 ZHR, 1964, p. 153, here concurring in the findings of Philippe Kahn.

It is however not only this principle but also that of good faith which governs the date of delivery. It governs in particular a question which at first sight appears contentious; whether and under what circumstances it may be necessary for one party to impose a time-limit on the other. The complicated provisions of German law in regard to *Verzug* (not wholly congruent with "default") are certainly not adaptable for transnational purposes,[197] but it cannot on the other hand be said to represent transnational law that no such time-limit must ever be imposed.[198] Even the Uniform Commercial Code, though it does not mention the fixing of a limit in Section 2-309, comments on this text that good faith may in certain circumstances require one to be set.[199]

Honnold, it is true, has complained[200] of the somewhat bewildering way in which the remedies for late delivery are interlocked in the Sales Rules with those for delivery at the wrong place, and this may indeed be a hindrance in applying the Rules, but our other model code has often been criticized by continental jurists for the same drawback. One must look to practice for a way through the maze, and there are indeed many decisions which already provide a guide.[201]

Where the place of delivery is concerned, there is virtually complete agreement between Section 2-308 UCC and Article 23 of the Sales Rules. The

197. Riese 1957, p. 47.

198. Which Schmitthoff would seem at all events to imply on p. 66 of *Export Trade*.

199. Hellner refers to this in Ziegel/Foster, p. 107, n. 39, rightly drawing attention to a fact which continental lawyers must find remarkable, namely that this important rule is not embodied in the text of the Code but in the official comment thereon. This discovery compensates one in some small degree for Honnold's at times downright sarcastic aspersions on the drafters of the Hague Sales Rules (*Law and Contemporary Problems* 1965, pp. 341, 344 and 347).

200. *Loc. cit.*

201. English decision of 24 June 1965 (*Rosenthal*), holding that where shipping-space was rationed (in Hong Kong) the supplier was entitled in good faith to adjust the delivery-date according to the shipping possibilities and to dispatch the goods in two consignments. Swiss Federal Tribunal 4 July 1953 (*Intra-Handels AG*): the buyer who put up a letter of credit did not *ipso facto* place the seller in default. Swiss Federal Tribunal 31 August 1953 (*Künzle*): where there are import difficulties known to both sides, the seller may in certain circumstances presume the consent of the buyer to the seller's breaking down the shipment into smaller quantities and to the corresponding delay in delivery. English decision of 26 November 1954 (*J. Milhem*): inadequate agreement between the parties as to the date of delivery had prevented the formation of the contract (not unobjectionable, because the case involved quite exceptional price-changes). Arbitration tribunal of the Bremen Wool-Trade Association, 10 June 1958, concerning the "immediate replacement" clause of a CIF contract. American decision of 17 March 1943 (*Delaware*): oral alteration of time-limit for delivery by a commercial traveller not thereto empowered. MAT 25 May 1923 (*Stöhr*): when railway-traffic was disrupted, the seller should have delivered by motor-van.

Code also contains a rule on the place of delivery for documents, while the Sales Rules provide for the event that the goods still have to be manufactured or produced. Both agree in essentials with national laws on this subject, e.g., Section 29 of the English Sale of Goods Act. [202] The case-law on place of delivery should be approached with a certain caution, for it is not uninfluenced by conflicts-law theory on the connection of the entire contract to the place of performance. On the whole, however, it is doubtless transnational law that agreements on costs and insurance may not be regarded as automatically implying an agreed place of delivery. [203] Unfortunately the Hague Conference was unable to reach the same degree of unification and agreement over the remedies for breach of obligations regarding place of delivery as in the case of the date of delivery, and herein lies an acknowledged weakness of Articles 30 and 32 of the Sales Rules. [204] But this does not mean that there is any fundamental difference between these provisions and Section 2-711 of the Uniform Commercial Code, which also deals with these remedies.

The seller has to deliver conforming goods, i.e., goods which in kind and quality correspond to the contract. That is part of his duty to deliver, as explained above. This duty is an integral constituent of any contract of sale, whether expressly stated or implicit. Surveying from the transnational vantage-point the broad and variegated realm of the seller's duty to deliver conforming goods, one cannot fail to observe two salient features. Even before the second World-War, Ernst Rabel had drawn frequent attention to the first of these, finally with these penetrating words:

> "Many writers and judges have felt disquiet over the uncertainty of the nature and limits of that institution of law which is known as warranty against material defect. Here practical, everyday questions are involved, yet to the jurist they appear full of unresolved difficulties. I am more than ever convinced that the irregularities and obscurities of the teachings hereon are basically due to the irrational survival of an antiquated doctrine with very deep roots... If the synoptic insight of comparative law be mentally combined with the very clear history of this institution, it will scarcely be possible to avoid seeing how insistent the tendency to simplify it and then implant it in the theory of contracts has become." [205]

---

202. For comparative law, see Rabel, *Warenkauf* I, p. 321.

203. Swiss Federal Tribunal 4 July 1953 (*Intra-Handels AG*), concerning sale on FAS terms by a stateless person of no fixed abode.

204. Riese 1965, p. 42, and 1957, p. 47; also the American opinions mentioned above. Cf. also Ellen Peters, "Remedies for breach of contracts relating to sale of goods under the UCC", 73 *Yale Law Journal*, 1969, p. 199.

205. *Warenkauf* II, p. 101.

To this authoritative utterance we may now add a second observation, concerning the stage now reached by the trend which Rabel had noted. This stage can be shown in two ways. First, by following the course we have already so often taken, that of comparing the two great model codes and relating them to national laws. Second, by ignoring all endeavours at codification or doctrinal controversy and simply collating the relevant case-law.

Nobody seems so far to have expressed any doubt that the model codes do in fact seek to conform to the trend towards simplification and realism noted by Rabel, and therefore have something better to offer than the national legal orders which are so bedevilled by outmoded concepts.[206] As for the case-law on the obligation to deliver conforming goods, it is unfortunately not possible within the scope of this work to give anything more than a very incomplete picture, but reference may be made to 27 decisions which are frequently cited in studies of private international law. Ten of them are American, eight English, three French, three German, one Swiss, one Czech, and the other is the award of a Mixed Arbitral Tribunal. These proportions more or less correspond to the relative importance of the sources of law, but the total number is, needless to say, not sufficient for the purpose of deducing rules of transnational law. Nevertheless, even this incomplete survey should reveal how practice long ago freed itself from doctrinaire considerations and historical fetters and how the decisions derive their persuasiveness from their conformity with the categories of the reasonable businessman. And any rules founded on what is reasonable can scarcely help being transnational.

Duty to deliver conforming goods: Select Repertory of Decided Cases

1. 23 May 1900 France (*Desrée*). According to commercial practice, an insignificant qualitative inferiority justifies a reduction of price but not avoidance of the contract (the case concerned dealings in grain).

2. 20 December 1901 England (*Molling*). There was a contract for the supply of books by a German seller to an English purchaser. The books were destined partly for England and partly for the USA. A consignment meant for America was sent to England and then forwarded unexamined to the USA, where it was rejected as unsuitable for American use and returned to England. A claim for the purchase-price was refused, but damages were awarded the purchaser for the return freight to the USA, because it was only there that the inspection could have been carried out.

3. 24 March 1919 USA (*Griffin Tool Metal*). The seller had delivered "high-speed steel" which turned out to be ordinary steel and was therefore useless for tool-production. The seller knew for what purpose the purchaser had bought the steel, and was condemned to pay damages even for the expense of the buyer's fruitless efforts to use it.

---

206. Cf. the articles in Ziegel/Foster, *Aspects of Comparative Commercial Law*, and, more particularly, with reference to English law, Fridmann, p. 38; also the articles in Honnold, *Unification of Law governing International Sales of Goods*, Paris 1966.

4. 10 May 1924 USA (*Miles*). The purchaser had bought "branded potatoes". The price having fallen, he refused to take delivery, alleging poor quality, and denied formation of contract on the ground that no place of delivery had been agreed. However, that place was clear from a custom of eight years' standing and was therefore recognized by the judge.

5. 16 June 1925 MAT (*Negreanu*). The Romanian party had bought and paid for leather in Germany before the outbreak of war. The goods were sold in Germany as enemy property. The proceeds of the sale were depreciated by inflation. After the war the purchaser demanded delivery or damages. The tribunal found for him: it was true as far as it went that wartime conditions had provided the seller with a plea of *force majeure*, but after the German occupation of Romania he had not paid due regard to the interests of the purchaser.

6. 10 March 1929 USA (*Wilson*). Strawberries of "best stock" had been sold. In the case of warranted quality, taking delivery does not preclude complaint. In commercial usage, "best stock" signifies sorting as well as quality, so both were warranted. The damages exceeded the purchase-price.

7. 6 September 1929 France (*Provençale*). A sold car had an engine-defect which was only evident after a fair amount of use. This could not be regarded as latent defect. On the other hand, the dealer was not entitled to sell with a disclaimer of such defect.

8. 4 September 1942 USA (*Monarch Brewing Co.*) A bottling machine did not work as verbally promised. The buyer sued for damages. The seller successfully relied on his written disclaimer.

9. 10 April 1946 USA (*Price*). "The Supreme Court avoids consideration of academic complaints leading to a pursuit of abstract principles." The "used steel road forms" sold were unusable for the buyers' purposes, which were unknown to the seller. "Only these damages may be awarded for a breach of contract which are within reasonable contemplation on the parties as a natural and probable consequence of breach and which are, therefore, foreseeable. Special or extraordinary damages cannot be recovered unless the person sought to be charged is at the time of making the contract informed of the special circumstances out of which such damages will probably arise and they are thus brought within the principle of reasonable foreseeability."

10. 19 February 1948 England (*Groupement*). Argentinian cattle-fodder was sold FOB Buenos Aires. The point at issue was whether a certificate of quality and acceptance of the Argentinian branch of the Geneva Société de Surveillance, for which provision was made in the contract and which was made out after inspection of a sample, disposed of the question of quality. This was denied in the circumstances of the case.

11. 29 July 1948 USA (*Atlas Trading*). The delivery of purchased trucks was rendered impossible through official intervention in wartime. The defendant was held in breach of his obligation to refrain from any act which would hinder the plaintiff's efforts to remove these difficulties.

12. 9 July 1951 USA (*Fairbanks*). A diesel motor was sold with specification of a maximum fuel-consumption figure. The points at issue were whether this constituted a warranty or merely a description, and whether the buyer, by confirming that the motor "was operating in a satisfactory manner", had renounced his claims.

13. 28 April 1953 USA (*Charles*). In the case of a sales-monopoly contract between an American and a French vermouth-producer, the quality of the liquor delivered was complained of. The court held American law applicable and found that there was an implied guarantee that the quality would be suitable for American taste.

14. 31 August 1953 Switzerland (*Künzle*). "In the summer of 1951 the importation of agricultural products from Germany to Switzerland was hampered by the prevalence of foot-and-mouth disease in Southern Germany, and it was necessary to take specially

into account the fact that the possibilities of importation would be further restricted if the disease should spread. This was known to the Appellant, as he had already had to put up with delivery-delays in previous transactions... If he nevertheless concluded further contracts of sale, this shows that he had been willing to reckon with the possibility of late delivery. In these circumstances it is necessary to assume a tacit agreement between the parties that delivery would be effected as and when possible, it being understood that the seller was entitled to distribute the procurable merchandise to all his Swiss customers in accordance with a private quota-system, which is in fact what he did." The decision also held that occasional toleration of late payment could not be construed as a contractual understanding.

15. 17 May 1954 England (*F.E. Hookway*). In a dispute over the standard conditions of the London Shellac Trade Association, it was submitted that according to the usage of the trade only visible defects were of account, and not defects which could not be detected without chemical analysis. Devlin, J., held that such an unusual restriction could not be recognized as a usage of trade without special proof.

16. 2 November 1954 Prague Arbitration Tribunal (*S.A.C. Tanger*). The case concerned a contract for the exchange of Czech motor-lorries against Moroccan products. It proved impossible to procure for the lorries a Moroccan traffic-licence. The point at issue was whether not only damages but also a penalty under the contract should be paid. This was allowed, as French law was applied. (On the absence of official permits, cf., for motor vehicles, the German jurisprudence mentioned by Rabel, *Warenkauf* II, and, for the importation of wine, No. 20 below.)

17. 5 January 1955 USA (*United States*). On the requirements to be satisfied in adducing proof of the unsuitable quality of oil delivered for use in trucks.

18. 16 November 1955 France (*Gélabert*). More spring vegetables were delivered than bargained for. Held that the buyer was entitled to place the surplus at the seller's disposal but was obliged to take the quantity agreed.

19. 10 January 1958 Germany (*Canned Meat*). After a sample had been sent, spoiled canned meat was delivered to England. The purchaser claimed return of purchase-price and damages. The seller relied on the fact that the sample and the delivered goods had been produced not by himself but by a third firm; furthermore, the claim was time-barred. The decision of the Hamburg *Oberlandesgericht*, which had applied German law and accepted the plea of limitation, was quashed by the *Bundesgerichtshof*. As it was common ground that the institution of German law known as *Wandlung* (annulment of sale for material defect) was unknown in English law, the *Oberlandesgericht* should have construed the application as a claim for damages on account of warranty.

20. 19 October 1960 Germany (*Importation of wine*). Some French wine was turned back at the German frontier as unfit for carriage. The claim for refund failed, but the buyer was awarded damages for non-fulfilment. A claim for substitute delivery, as under § 480 of the German Civil Code, does not exist in statutory form in French law, but could be agreed.

21. 13 January 1961 England (*Mash*). Cyprus potatoes intended, as the seller knew, for human consumption were sent from Lisbon to England CIF but arrived spoiled. "The necessary and inevitable deterioration during transit, which would render goods unmerchantable on arrival, was normally one for which the seller was liable."

22. 12 December 1961 England (*Abraham Dawood*). The bargain was for 50 tons of galvanized metal plates of various dimensions, CIF Mauritiu͡s, "assorted, equal tonnage per size". All 50 tons were delivered in one and the same dimension. The buyer successfully claimed a refund of the purchase-price on account of "breach of condition".

23. 20 December 1961 England (*Hong Kong Fire*). An unseaworthy ship was chartered out. Diplock, L.J., observed that in this special area there was something which was neither condition nor warranty. Cf. Schmitthoff, *Export Trade*, p. 122, n. 30, on Article

146

10 of the Hague Sales Rules: "This change in the emphasis is in harmony with modern English developments."

24. 5 October 1964 USA (*Sperry Rand*). Dealt with the *caveat emptor* rule and guarantee questions in relation to a compound system of ten machines. For the rest it followed the lines of the *Tool Metal* decision of 24 March 1919, above, No.3. A tacit guarantee could not be assumed if the goods were sold below their commercial value.

25. 27 July 1966 England (*Phoenix Distributors*) Northern Irish Class A potatoes were sent from England to Poland, accompanied with a certificate of freedom from disease issued by the Northern Irish Minister of Agriculture. Notwithstanding, Poland refused to allow the potatoes entry on the ground of their being diseased. The buyer's claim for repayment was allowed, because the potatoes were merchantable and could be sold elsewhere.

26. 26 October 1967 England (*United Dominions*). Concerned the sale of a used aircraft, which after a time was only good for scrap. Diplock, L.J., confirmed and enlarged upon his reasoning in *Hong Kong Fire* (No. 23 above, q.v.). Cf. also Schmitthoff, *loc. cit.*

27. 4 December 1968 Germany (*European Scrap*). If it is expressly mentioned in a contract for the delivery of imported goods (scrap) that goods of domestic origin are to be excluded, and if the seller nevertheless delivers goods of domestic origin, the case is then in principle one of misdelivery, and not of delivery of non-conforming goods. Thus the short time-limit for claims arising out of qualitative defect is inapplicable.

It can safely be said that where liability for conformity is concerned, transnational law is in rapid process of formation. Even if no coherent system is yet discernible (and the transnational rules already visible, being at various stages of development, are not all equally convincing) the two great model codes and the practice of the courts will already be found to offer sufficient material for the decision of many cases. The concordance of the codes is recognized even by American critics of the Sales Rules, [207] while many rules treated by scholars as showing some divergence have already to a great extent been "synchronized" by practice. This applies for example to the various, doubtless important distinctions made in national laws with regard to apparent or latent defects, express or implied warranty, warranted qualities, merchantability of the goods, etc. [208] Other rules may undoubtedly be already regarded as transnational, e.g., the treatment of non-material or easily remedied deficiencies, which had already been regulated in Section 2-508 UCC and was subsequently dealt with on the lines of *de minimis non curat praetor* in the new version of the last sentence of Article 44 of the Sales Rules. [209]

207. Farnsworth, *Proceedings*, p. 233: "In sum, then, there is a considerable similarity between the Uniform Law and the Code with regard to the seller's responsibility for quality, the buyer's obligation of salvage of rejected goods, and the buyer's remedies against the seller after a proper rejection."
208. Here we must content ourselves with referring the reader to Fridmann, in Ziegel/Foster, p. 38; Riese 1965, p. 46; Graveson/Cohn, p. 73; Philippe Kahn, p. 132.
209. Cf. Riese 1965, p. 45; also Honnold, *University of Pennsylvania Law Review* 1959, p. 316; Graveson/Cohn, p. 73; above-cited decisions of 4 September 1942 and 29 July 1948.

Where the two codes do not agree, this does of course create special difficulties for the development of transnational law, but even here some paths towards the transnational solution of particular cases have already been signposted. Let us consider for example an antithesis to which we drew attention above: that between Section 2-601 UCC and the avoidance provided for under the Sales Rules. Hellner observes:

> "This seems to be a point on which it will be difficult to arrive at a solution acceptable to both parties." [210]

Von Caemmerer [211] agrees with Hellner's comment that the American outlook would be "hardly acceptable to a European lawyer", but neither author draws attention to the practical possibilities for compromise pointed out by Riese (1965, p. 44). The same may well apply, for example, to Honnold's sharp criticism of Article 38 and 39 of the Sales Rules, dealing with notification of damage-claim and or rejection of the goods, as compared with the treatment of the same topic in Section 2-602 (1) UCC: [212] these problems have by no means been overlooked. [213] Article 38 of the Sales Rules was adopted only by a majority-vote. Hence it is not excluded, bearing Article 3 of the Sales Rules in mind, that transnational law on this point may develop in the direction of the Uniform Commercial Code.

It is also still open for transnational law to develop in two further areas of importance, those of products liability and of disclaimers of warranty (*Freizeichnungen*). The absence of a rule for the former has already been discussed in the passage on damages above. Unfortunately, no transnational rule on disclaimers has fully evolved either, probably on account of the preponderant national interests in this area. Possibly it is a mistake to expect one to do so; at least, so long as the necessary distinction between commercial transactions and private purchases remain unmade and codifiers persist in what looks like the doomed attempt to subsume an infinite variety of goods and potential transactions under the same detailed rules and attach the same meaning to specific words in all cases. [214]

Here too, history points the way into the future. Rabel (*Warenkauf* II, pp. 182 ff.) has shown how, at the beginning, the boundless freedom of contract in national laws allowed the seller almost any kind of disclaimer, then how the courts in various countries (in Germany, from 1929 on, through the initiative of Ludwig Raiser) began to protect the buyer from the excessive power of banded or monopolistic sellers, and how this occurred in the most

210. In Ziegel/Foster, p. 108.
211. In Ziegel/Foster, p. 130.
212. *Law and Contemporary Problems*, 1965, p. 346.
213. Riese 1965, p. 50.
214. Cf. especially Honnold's critique of Sections 2-316 and 2-719 UCC, in Ziegel/Foster, p. 9.

varied ways in accordance with the possibilities offered by each national legal order: for example by invoking public policy, misuse of monopoly, fair dealing, or the strict interpretation of contracts (in particular with reference to textual obscurities or inadequate disclosure), or by placing the greater burden of proof on the seller. This is the present position, and unification is devoutly to be wished. It is likely to be achieved rather by the careful alignment of decisions than by continuing the endeavour to set up general rules.

From the viewpoint of that endeavour the two model codes have fallen short of succes and therefore been criticized. Americans have reproached the Sales Rules with unfairly favouring the seller by altogether abstaining from regalating the matter. [215] This criticism might seem justified if one confines onself to Riese's comment (1965, p. 44) that Article 3 enables claims for damage to be excluded without restriction. To be accurate, however, the Commission never expressed itself in this sense, but merely decided, with reference to Article 8, that the problems outside the scope of the Uniform Law of Sale should be judged for the time being in accordance with the national law applicable to them.[216]

In Sections 2-316 and 2-719 the Uniform Commercial Code attempts to lay down provisions to regulate the matter. The detailed formulations of Section 2-316 have aroused the misgivings even of a leading American authority. [217] Section 2-719 is interesting, and more closely akin to German thinking, in the possibility it opens up to judges:

"(3) Consequential damages may be limited or excluded unless the limitation or exclusion is unconscionable ...".

The preferred field of application of this provision can already been seen from post-1962 American case-law. It has been invoked in cases involving abuse of inexperience or rash innocence, hire-purchase transactions, restrictive jurisdictional clauses and the like.[218]

In sum, this problem, and the treatment it has received internationally, afford a textbook example of the adage that *le mieux est l'ennemi du bien*. In supinely waiting for it to be regulated by supranational legislation, time has been wasted which would have been better spent in eliciting transnational law by the careful collation of the decisions in particular cases.

215. Criticism in Farnsworth, *Proceedings*, p. 235, and Daw, *Proceedings*, p. 244.

216. Riese 1965, p. 19 and, with special reference to damages for material defects, 1965, p. 15.

217. Honnold, in Ziegel/Foster, p. 9.

218. Cf. the illustrations in the 1969 *Cumulative Supplements to the Uniform Commercial Code*, republished by the Lawyers' Co-operative Publishing Co., Rochester N.Y.

C. Conforming goods: inspection and notification

The purchaser is entitled to inspect the goods before he pays for them. If he has claims to raise against the seller for defective goods, he has to notify him accordingly. The model codes agree not only on these two principles but also on all the basic rules which flow from them. But the UCC, here again, contains provisions (Section 2-513) which go into greater detail than the Sales Rules (Articles 38 to 40). This however does not hinder the extraction of transnational rules. Many American objections against the Sales Rules concern the regulation of special questions and allege conflicts or obscurities which could probably be eliminated in the careful handling of individual cases.[219] More weight is to be attached to the objections raised by the British and American delegations at the Hague Conference to the effect that Articles 38 to 40 unduly favour the seller as against the buyer. The majority by which, as already mentioned, Article 38 was adopted was primarily composed of jurists from the civil-law countries.[220] In the quest for transnational law this difference of opinion may not be disregarded. Yet at the same time it should not be over-rated. It should not be forgotten that, however admirable the Uniform Commercial Code may be as an achievement in law-unification, it remains a work of regional, intra-American scope, whereas the Convention on the Law of Sale aspires to a far wider and truly international realm of application. To achieve or restore the appropriate balance of advantage between buyers and sellers is naturally another and indeed an easier exercise within one country or economic region than in a context which transcends the regional. Moreover the American delegation, in particular, had not had the time necessary to prepare an adequate response to problems of this kind. In fact one has only to look behind their dislike of Articles 38-40 in general, and test their specific objections in particular cases, to discover that the divergences are not unbridgeable.[221]

There would appear to be agreement on all the rules concerning inspection and they may therefore be taken as transnational.[222] Nor do the courts seem to have had any particular difficulty over them.[223] There is no serious discrepancy between the Sales Rules' requirement that the goods should be examined "promptly" and the Code's requirement that an inspection be

219. Cf. e.g. Honnold, *Law and Contemporary Problems*, 1965, pp. 346 ff., on the treatment of goods on-forwarded by the buyer.

220. Cf. Riese 1965, p. 50.

221. Cf. also Graveson/Cohn (p. 75) according to whom Article 38 imposes a far heavier burden on the purchaser than English law.

222. Cf. especially Goldstajn, "The Contract of Goods Inspection", 14 AJCL, 1965, p. 382, with examples.

223. Cf. e.g. the American decision of 5 October 1964 (*Sperry Rand*), according to which the inspection may in certain circumstances take place before the delivery.

carried out within a reasonable time. No judge will suppose that Article 38 imposes an "unreasonable" time-limit, while conversely no upholder of the Code will regard an interval as reasonable if it exceeds the scope of "promptly" without reasonable cause. Hitherto the courts have proved themselves fully capable of coming to sensible decisions in the related matter of time allowed for notice of defect, no matter what terminological controversies may have raged. [224] Certain rules are to be found in only one of our two model codes, which of course does not exclude their being enlisted to swell the ranks of transnational rules. One of them, however, ought not to be so enlisted, namely the rule in Article 38 (4) which provides for the methods of examination to be governed, in the absence of agreement, by the law or usage of the place of examination. Only in a case of extreme necessity should it be applied. It is all the more open to objection in that the original draft of the Rules, in Article 47 (4), obligated the buyer to give the seller notice to attend, with a view to obviating any abuses that might arise from reliance on inadequate local usage. [225]

If the seller has acted in bad faith, he is not entitled to rely on any error which the buyer may have committed in regard to the inspection or notification. This express rule of Article 40 "does no more than sanction a rule of good faith", [226] and it is not merely transnational law but also exemplifies

224. MAT 9 July 1922 treated as out of time a notice of defect which had been served some four weeks after the delivery. In a case decided in the USA on 17 November 1937, an abbreviation of the time-limit for notice of defect was embodied in the delivery-terms but was ruled non-effective because the defect could only ,be discovered after microscopic inspection. The German decision of 14 August 1958 was on the other hand dubious, finding as it did "that the question whether a foreign purchaser can be expected to notify defect 'forthwith' (*unverzüglich*) can naturally only be determined in accordance with the law of his own place of performance". The German decision of 4 December 1968 is interesting in that the short period of limitation imposed by § 477 of the Civil Code, which seemed unfair in the circumstances, was excluded by the finding that it was not non-conforming goods but quite other goods —*aliud*—which had been delivered. See also the German decision of 23 October 1969 interpreting Article 9 (8) of the ECE Conditions for the export of plant and machinery.

225. Riese 1957, p. 59. By way of illustration one may refer to the German decision of 28 April 1920, in a case where, after an inspection in Hamburg, by one party, the other was able to claim that the timber inspected was not even that which had been delivered. In the German decision, already mentioned, of 14 February 1958 the court eventually came to the right solution by applying the test of good faith: the plaintiff company should concede that no inspection of the goods was needed any longer, because the absence of the quality allegedly agreed upon had long been known to it; furthermore, it could in good faith have taken the requisite steps for the completion of delivery, even if that had implied payment of duty, yet it had not even approached the defendant for an advance on such costs.

226. Tunc, p. 376. Riese (1965, p. 53) rightly points out that the wording of this article should have referred not to "facts" but to "circumstances".

international *ordre public.*[227]

The costs of the inspection are to be borne by the purchaser. He is however entitled to claim them from the seller if the goods are returned for defect. This is absent from the Sales Rules but is to be found in Section 2-513 (2) UCC. It may be viewed as transnational. This rule has been expanded by jurisprudence in the sense that the reimbursement may also be sought of the costs incurred by the purchaser in trials to determine and/or efforts to restore the fitness of the goods for use.[228] Somewhat surprisingly, the American delegation in The Hague expressed misgivings in regard to Article 39 (2), on the ground that it failed to make clear to what extent the notice of non-conformity must specify every detail of the deficiency. Yet it should be self-evident that the details to be given are dictated by commercial usage and the requirements of good faith.[229] It does at least emerge from the attitude of the American delegation that the duty of specification in notifying lack of conformity may be regarded as transnational law.

The special case of the redespatch of goods objected to does not seem to be clearly covered by Article 38 (3) of the Sales Rules. Criticism has therefore indicated Section 2-602 (2) UCC as a superior treatment of the problem.[230] Why should the judge not treat the latter provision as the better concretization of a transnational rule? Neither of the model codes seem to have paid attention to the carrying-out of the inspection, and issuing of a certificate of acceptance, by third persons, questions which play a considerable role in practice, and which are also governed by general legal principles over and above the law of sale. The decisions of national courts show a wide area of agreement on these matters.[231]

227. Cf. the German decision of 28 April 1900, referred to by Rabel (*Conflict* III, 2nd ed., p. 102f., n. 93): "That in the case of fraud the seller may not put up the defence of notification of defect out of time is a rule, closely connected with the principles of public policy which prevail in our country, which is absolutely mandatory and is always to be applied by the German judge, even if in the given case the foreign law which otherwise governs the contract contains no such rule."

228. American *Tool Metal* decision of 24 March 1919.

229. Riese 1965, p. 52. The same answer covers the questions raised by Graveson/Cohn, p. 77. Cf. also the Austrian decision of 8 May 1912, according to which the mere notification that the machine purchased "is not suitable" does not constitute adequate notice of defect.

230. Honnold, *Law and Contemporary Problems* 1965, p. 347.

231. French decision of 28 October 1953 (*Blum*): the Société Générale de Surveillance had taken delivery of plum jam, bought in Algiers, on behalf of the purchaser, who was subsequently not allowed to rely on a concealed deficiency. Awards of 2 November 1954 by the Prague Chamber of Commerce: trucks from Czechoslovakia for delivery in Morocco were accepted in Paris, but that was insufficient, because the trucks were not granted a permit to circulate in Morocco, nor did it suffice to render French law applicable to the contract. Award of the same Chamber on 5 August 1965: after conclusion

The seemingly irreconcilable conflict between the two model codes on the subject of the time allowed for notification of defects can probably, in individual cases, be overcome at transnational level with the aid of considerations which we set forth in Part Four, on Limitation. [232] Such time-limits are not absolutely mandatory law, elsewhere or in the two codes. This if the time-limits set in the national laws of the parties, or even in model codes, do not agree, the judge may reach a decision within the given span from the viewpoint of reasonable expectation and, if need be, that of fair apportionment of risks. In certain circumstances the intra-Comecon delivery-conditions may be taken as a model. [233]

In the light of the foregoing it should be evident that, if only because of the differences between the two chief models, the time has not yet come for the elaboration of detailed transnational rules for this important area of law. [234] Yet if the tangle of clashing or divergent national rules be stripped of

---

of contract, a company purchasing cotton altered with the seller's consent the place of delivery; this made it impossible to execute an agreement for the acceptance of the goods at a third place; the purchaser unilaterally chose the person to accept the goods at the new place, and that person found fault with them; the seller denied the legal validity of his criticism, on the ground that the acceptance had not been effected by a party authorized by seller; the award found that there was no possible doubt about the defects and that the same conclusion would have been reached anywhere and by anyone; nevertheless the damages were shared, on the ground of blame on either side.

232. See in particular p. 187 below and especially note 48 in Part Four.

233. General Conditions of Delivery of Goods between Organizations of the Member Countries of the Council for Mutual Economic Assistance 1968, *Register of Texts of Conventions and Other Instruments concerning International Trade Law* I, UN New York 1971 (*Sales No.* E.71.V.3.), p. 72. See especially § 72 on p. 94:

"1. Claims may be presented:

(*a*) in relation to quality of the goods, within six months from the date of delivery;

(*b*) in relation to quantity of the goods, within three months from the date of delivery;

(*c*) in relation to goods for which a guarantee is granted, not later than 30 days from the expiration of the guarantee period, provided that the defect is discovered within the guarantee period,"

For the 1958 Conditions, see (in German) 6 *Zeitschrift für Ostrecht*, 1960, pp. 49 ff., and (in English) 7 ICLQ, 1958, p. 659.

234. Hellner (Ziegel/Foster, p. 102) describes the system of Árticles 41 to 49 of the Sales Rules as "so exceedingly complex that it is hard to see how it can work in practice", while Honnold (*Law and Contemporary Problems* 1965, p. 347) sums up in these words: "The Uniform Law on the International Sale of Goods makes the common error of laying down detailed rules that fail to fit the complex facts of commercial life." Even if the criticism by continental jurists of the Uniform Commercial Code is far more restrained, and even if one may concede the greater closeness of this code to the realities of commercial life, it has not at the time of writing been so much as suggested that its rules could be extended beyond the territory of the United States.

historic and polemical deadwood,[235] it is already possible to elicit a few transnational rules, thanks notably to judicial practice:

1. Non-material defects produce no legal consequences.
2. The seller may replace non-conforming with conforming goods by the original delivery-date.
3. When non-conforming goods are delivered, the price may always be suitably reduced.
4. The principle of freedom of contract entitles the seller to limit within reason his liability arising out of non-conformity.
5. The buyer's right, when non-conforming goods are delivered, to place them at the seller's disposal instead of paying a reduced price, i.e., to avoid the contract, is undoubtedly established as transnational law, but the time, preconditions and modalities for the exercise of this right remain uncertain. It will at least be a transnational rule that the buyer may not take such action without giving the seller adequate notice.[236] It is already generally recognized that under certain special circumstances—which however have still not been precisely delineated—to avoidance of the contract may be sought for non-conformity. In this respect the distinction between "warranty" and "condition" developed in English law is important, as is also the situation of "fundamental breach" covered by the Sales Rules. Thirdly, avoidance is justified in transnational law when the worth of the goods is so diminished that the buyer cannot be expected to turn them to account, so that he is entitled to place them at the seller's disposal and leave him to do so. This is quite irrespective of the question of fault, or the importance of the breach or the legal construction of the contract. It is simply the fair mercantile solution and derives from the principle of reasonableness which is basic to transnational law. But it can also be derived from a principle which is established in the sales law of every country, namely that each party must do his utmost to ensure that any damage is kept to a minimum. Hence a buyer receiving goods so defective that he cannot be expected to keep them or turn them to account is not merely entitled but is even in a sense duty-bound to place them, after due notice, at the seller's disposal. It will however never be possible to decide exactly when this is to be expected of a buyer on the basis of any general rule, let alone juristic considerations. Whether the loss of value exceeds half the price may be a useful test, but many other factors may also be material, for example whether the goods can still be utilized at this or that place, or at this or that time. At all events, it is transnational law in view of the circumstances that the buyer must allow the seller adequate time to take the goods back.
6. Rights derived from the delivery of non-conforming goods may never be exercised in such a way as to throw back on the seller the price-risk the buyer accepted on conclusion of the contract.
7. The rights of the buyer may be exercised in respect of the whole of the delivered goods or only parts thereof, if this can be done under a supplementary settlement for mitigation of damage.

The relevant case-law is too abundant for any comprehensive treatment, but we may end this section by mentioning a number of cases which are particularly interesting:

235. Cf. especially Rabel, *Warenkauf* I, p. 420, and Philippe Kahn, pp. 148 ff.
236. Cf. in particular Honnold, *Law and Contemporary Problems* 1965, p. 347.

1. Germany 16 June 1903 (planks): place of annulment for material defect, and regard had to situation concerning interest.
2. Germany 26 April 1907 (sheepskins): place of diminution.
3. USA 14 April 1922 (*Shofi*): inadmissibility of merely partial avoidance.
4. USA 10 May 1924 (*Miles*): notice of defect in potatoes on fall of market-price.
5. USA 4 September 1942 (*Monarch Brewery*): costs of mending a machine.
6. Prague Chamber of Industry and Commerce 14 August 1953: forced sales.
7. Germany 10 January 1958 (c anned meat): damages in place of avoidance.
8. Bremen Wool-Trade Arbitration Tribunal 10 June 1958: substitute delivery.
9. Germany 19 October 1960 (wine-importation): substitute delivery.
10. Switzerland 16 November 1965 (lining-silk): partial avoidance.
11. Germany 19 December 1968: avoidance (*Rücktritt*) of contract after expiry of additional period, on account of unreliability of seller.

D. *Documents: shipment clauses*

Our two model codes adopt different approaches to these questions, but that does not mean that their conclusions are in conflict. The difference stands revealed as soon as we seek their answers to the first question that arises: does the seller have to deliver the documents relative to the transaction? The Sales Rules (Article 50) leave the answer to the contract and the usage of trade. With the words "unless otherwise agreed" the Uniform Commercial Code (Section 2-323) does this also, it is true, but it proceeds on the explicit assumption that in case of doubt such a duty does exist. [237] The next basic question, as to which documents must be delivered, receives no answer in the Sales Rules, whereas the Code contains quite detailed rules, above all in Section 2-325 concerning letters of credit. On the consequences of any breach of an obligation to deliver documents, the Sales Rules get into an unfortunate tangle by referring to the remedies for lack of conformity, [238] so that the rules of the Uniform Commercial Code are therefore to be preferred.

The most significant point is probably that both codes agree in their constant references to the contract and the usage of trade. This places this whole complex of problems on the brink of transnational law. But caution is evidently called for in considering whether the relevant commercial practices agree. Similarities of usage may be discernible from case to case, but in principle it would be wrong at present to presume harmony, and that caveat, surprisingly enough, holds good for the most important standard clauses, such as CIF and FOB. [239]

---

237. For comparative law, though somewhat cursory, see Rabel, *Conflict* III, 2nd ed., p. 100, and *Warenkauf* II, pp. 27 and 347.
238. Riese 1965, p. 72.
239. On the concordance between the rules of Section 2-329 ff. UCC, the Revised American Foreign Trade Definitions 1941 and the Incoterms 1953, see especially Eisemann, *Die Incoterms im internationalen Warenkaufrecht*, Stuttgart 1967; Michido, in

E. Title in the goods

It is undoubtedly transnational law that the seller is under obligation not merely to deliver the goods to the buyer but also to procure him title of ownership. Despite differences of phraseology, the two model codes are at one upon this (Article 18 and 52 of the Sales Rules; Section 2-301 UCC). Unless otherwise agreed, the obligation cannot in good faith be interpreted to mean anything other than the conveyance of the title unencumbered by any charges or liens. This is transnational law and also emerges from Section 2-312 UCC and Articles 52 and 53 of the Sales Rules.[240]

At present, unfortunately, it is not possible to discern any transnational rule on the important question as to the way in which the title is to be transferred. Property is still a reserved area of national laws. This is expressly confirmed by Article 8 of the Sales Rules, and Riese (1965, p.64) has given an account of the fruitless efforts to reach international unification on this branch of law. On the other hand, in the case of the Uniform Commercial Code, designed to operate within a single national region, it proved possible to achieve a set of unified rules, embodied in Section 2-401 ff. These rules can however scarcely claim model status for transnational law outside the sphere of American and English law.[241]

A series of legal questions which are particularly important in the world of trade arises from the practice of delivering goods while reserving ownership. In view of the above, it is only logical that transnational law hereon has not passed the embryonic stage, at least so far as the relations between the contracting parties are concerned. The Sales Rules, in Article 5 (2), expressly declare themselves inapplicable where mandatory national provisions protect a party to an instalment-sale. In this field, the principle of the protection of the weak penetrates right down into the contractual relationship of the parties. National legislators have increasingly made the legal validity of any reservation of ownership dependent on some kind of publication, most through registration (Article 715 of the Swiss Civil Code). The Uniform Commercial Code takes a similar course in Section 1-201 (37), read with Sections 9-203

Honnold (ed.), *Unification* ..., p. 255; Honnold, in Schmitthoff (ed.), *Sources* ..., p. 77. *Law and Contemporary Problems* 1965, p. 340, and *University of Pennsylvania Law Review* 1959, p. 301.

240. Hence the uncertainty about the freedom from encumbrance of foreign patents which so worries Daw (*Proceedings*, p. 245) ought surely not to subsist, especially as no doubt as to the existence of liability for defective title exists in the major trading countries (see e.g., Section 12 (1) of the English 1893 Sales Act).

241. Notwithstanding the praise rightly lavished on the UCC rules of property for their progressive character by Honnold (Ziegel/Foster, p. 14) and Schmitthoff (*Sources* ..., p. 13). For comparative law, see Rabel, *Warenkauf* I, p. 28, and *Conflict* III, 2nd ed., p. 78.

ff. and 9-302, which require written agreement and registration. [242] As the protection of the weak is a transnational principle, it may at least be said that the spirit of transnational law exercises no small influence even in this field, and that in itself may be regarded as a movement in the right direction. [243] To conclude this section we would enumerate a selection of decisions which are illustrative of the difficulties involved, but also show the progress made towards transnational law.

1. Austria 2 October 1902: sale of hire.
2. England (Prize Court) 17 December 1920 ("*Kronprinzessin*"): ownership.
3. The difficulties are particularly well brought out in a whole series of decisions by the Mixed Arbitral Tribunals of the 1920's, in particular by MAT 7 December 1921 (ownership in the case of sale over a distance, equal rights).
4. MAT 30 April 1923: questions of ownership are governed by the place where the goods are situated.
5. MAT 16 June 1925 (*Negreanu*): transference of ownership taking place automatically on conclusion of contract of sale.
6. MAT 11 June 1926 (*Charles Semon*): ownership should be transferred only after arrival and inspection, but actual course of dealing is determinant.
7. MAT 7 April 1927: against a general presumption that it is the intention of parties to transfer ownership at the earliest possible moment.
8. USA 21 November 1927: transfer of ownership, specific performance.
9. USA 3 April 1933 (*Jewett*): reservation of ownership.
10. England 7 March 1945 (*Glenroy*): the making-out of documents in the buyer's name does not necessarily prove the seller's intention to transfer ownership.
11. France 18 December 1950: alienation and contract of sale.
12. England 27 March 1957 (*Federspiel*): transfer of ownership.
13. France 19 June 1957: reservation of ownership.
14. England 17 October 1958: transfer of ownership conditional on conformity of goods.
15. USA 1 May 1959 (*Shanahan*): reservation of ownership.
16. Germany 20 March 1963: recognition of French mortgage.
17. England 2 June 1964 (*Cheetham*): transfer of ownership, in accordance with contract; Section 17 of Sale of Goods Act.

---

242. For comparative law, see Rabel, *Conflict* III, 2nd ed., p. 85; for USA, especially Eisner, "Eigentumsvorbehalt und Security Interests im Handelsverkehr mit USA", NJW 1967, p. 1169; Drobnig, "Eigentumsvorbehälte bei Importlieferungen nach Deutschland", 32 *RabelsZ*, 1968, p. 450; Mertens, *Eigentumsvorbehalt und sonstige Sicherungsmittel des Verkäufers im ausländischen Recht*, 1964; Coing, "Probleme der Anerkennung besitzloser Mobiliarpfandrechte im Rahmen der EWG", 8 *Z.f.Rechtsvergleichung*, 1967, pp. 65-82; for France; Féblot/Mezger, "Eigentumsvorbehalt und Rücktrittsklausel bei Lieferungen nach Frankreich", 20 *RabelsZ*, 1955, p. 662, and Philippe Kahn, *La Vente commerciale internationale*, pp. 203 ff.
243. Kronstein, in *Festschrift Hallstein* 1966, pp. 283 ff., at p. 303; Honnold, in Ziegel/Foster, p. 15, with references to Section 2-403 UCC; on the Hague Sales Rules, see Riese 1965, p. 18. The relevant national decisions rely heavily on the special principle of the protection of confidence, i.e., the requisite clarity in legally dubious convenants; cf. especially the German decision of 2 June 1965 and the discussion of it by Drobnig, *loc. cit.*

18. Germany 2 June 1965: ownership in bankruptcy.

19. England 1 December 1965 (*Ginzberg*): change of ownership on shipment.

20. Germany 2 February 1966: reservation of Italian ownership on machines delivered to Germany.

F. *Duties of the purchaser*

All laws agree as to the two basic duties of the purchaser. One may therefore unhesitatingly conclude that they also prescribed by transnational law. They are treated in the same way by the Sales Rules (Article 56) and the Uniform Commercial Code (Section 2-301): the buyer must take delivery from the seller, and pay for the goods, in accordance with the terms of the contract. By their wording the codes both give one to understand that the taking of delivery is just as important as the payment, and is thus not just a subsidiary obligation—a point which has at times given rise to academic controversy. The two codes differ only in their treatment of the seller's remedies in the event of breach of these obligations. This a subject to which we shall return below.

The essential questions bound up with the duty of paying the price are the following: what is meant by "the price" and how is it arrived at? At what place is payment to be effected? At what time is payment to be effected? In what way is payment to be made? All the world over, the price is expressed by a figure relating to units of some national currency. [244] The price may therefore alter in two ways, by a change of figure while the currency remains stable, or by a change in the purchasing-power of the currency while the figure remains unchanged. Only in the first case will one normally speak of a price-change. Such price-changes are as a rule to be ignored, for neither the seller nor the buyer is entitled to take advantage of them. [245] Riese gives an account (1957, p. 91) of the debate at the 1951 Conference on the Law of Sale. Well may there be differences in the degree of rigour with which the courts of different countries have disallowed unilateral references to price-changes, they all agree at bottom in rejecting them, and this rejection is accordingly transnational law. [246]

244. We have already discussed the somewhat different treatment of barter or exchange of goods in Section 2-304 UCC.

245. In earlier times this matter was judged on another basis in various national laws, i.e. from the standpoint of *laesio enormis*, deriving from late Roman law. This standpoint is however unsuitable for international transactions (*sic* Rabel, *Warenkauf* II, p. 6: "The considerable price-variations between individual countries cannot be compensated by legislation in the field of civil law. Indeed, it would be advisable to have an explicit provision to the effect that claims in that sense cannot be entertained. That of course would not affect the general rules of protection against exploitation, menaces and fraud."). The American *Yusupov* decision of 20 July 1927 found in the same sense.

246. The French decision (Tourcoing) of 6 December 1927 declared a fall in price irrelevant (p. 283); the American decision of 10 May 1924 (*Miles—"Vermont Potatoes"*)

Changes in purchasing-power can only be taken into account if they occur between the date on which the price becomes payable and the date of actual payment. National courts have in the past sought to solve the problems hereby presented in terms of damages, [247] or *force majeure* (cf. the discussion of exemptions above). These are suitable categories where transactions within a single territory are concerned. In international transactions, however, it is only the purchasing-power of the domestic currency which can be taken as a legal fixture; any foreign currency must be regarded as an exchange-commodity which has first to be sold against the domestic currency if it is to be turned to account for the payment of the price.[248] Legal theory seems to be ahead of practice in discriminating between price-changes and changes in purchasing-power.[249] The drafters of the 1964 Sales Rules did not, it would seem, find it either possible or useful to regulate the questions arising in this connection.[250]

In any case, law has for some decades now been lagging behind the facts in this domain. Meanwhile the factual position itself has been complicated by the tendency of governmental policies to substitute creeping diminutions in purchasing-power for obtrusive devaluations or revaluations. Should the parties expressly or tacitly have made a specific degree of purchasing-power a basis of their contract, it is doubtful at international level how large any change must be to have legal effect. In recent times, it has however been decided under German law that creeping inflation should be treated as a process in its own right and ascribed a corresponding significance. [251] On the international plane, a guideline may be found in the principle that the brunt of a risk is to be borne by the party in closest proximity. For the present, however, this is scarcely a transnational rule.

A price the size of which is unknown cannot be paid. If, therefore, it is not determined in the contract, it must at least be determinable with the aid of other circumstances and considerations. All laws, then, agree that no contract has been formed unless the price has either been determined or become

---

admitted evidence that the notice of defect served by the buyer had been solely inspired by a drop in price.

247. Rabel, *Warenkauf* II, p. 46, with references.

248. French decision of 15 January 1962: the sterling debts of a Frenchman for purchases in a London department-store were to be converted into francs not as on the date of invoice but as on the day of payment.

249. Cf. note by Würdinger, *Reichsgerichtsräte-Kommentar zum HGB*, 2nd ed., Berlin 1961, *Anhang, ad* § 374, n. 28; Arthur Nussbaum, *Money in the Law*, Brooklyn 1950, pp. 481 ff., with reference to the English *Arcos* case of 1935; F.A. Mann, *The Legal Aspects of Money*, Oxford 1953, p. 142. Also the statements of F.A. Mann, Duden, Sieveking, Lorenz and Würdinger at the *Deutsche Juristentag* 1953; reliance on the basis of the transaction was regarded as a sufficient plea in law.

250. Tunc, p. 380.

251. *Bundesgerichtshof* 30 September 1970, NJW 1970, p. 103.

determinable. This is therefore a rule of transnational law.

It thus remains to be decided under what circumstances the price can be regarded as determinable, and when not. Here there is a twofold difference of opinion between the two model codes which at first sight appears very important, but is not really insuperable. According to Section 2-305 (1) of the Uniform Commercial Code, a "reasonable price", more specifically "a reasonable price at the time of delivery", may do duty for a stipulated price if the parties "so intend". The Sales Rules, on the other hand, in Article 57, stop the gap with "the price generally charged by the seller at the time of the conclusion of the contract". At the Hague Conference the French delegation demurred at this formula, more especially because of the wholly different method of calculating the "economic price" applied in socialist countries. This apart, it is also a well-known feature of international trade that the home price and the export price are seldom the same, on account of the utterly different marketing conditions abroad. At all events, that must be kept in mind when interpreting Article 57. On the other hand, the official comment on Section 2-305, as also sub-section 2 itself, reiterates that the entire article is governed by the general principle of good faith. Hence it is only rarely that a difference will subsist in practice between the Code's "reasonable price" and the "price generally charged" of the Sales Rules; when this does happen, the seller, despite Article 57, may not demand the "price generally charged", nor for that matter may the buyer insist on paying it, if that would contravene the principle of good faith which rules both model codes alike. [252] From this principle, the mediatory effect of which is here particularly in evidence, there also emerges not only the requisite curbing of arbitrary acts on either side but also the buyer's duty to exercise due concern for clarity and certainty in regard to the price: he must for example take care not to make use of superseded offers or catalogues. [253]

Of recent years, as a consequence of government practice and creeping inflation, it has become increasingly frequent to agree on sliding price-rises, a phenomenon the validity of which in international trade it would by now be

252. Thus Graveson/Cohn (p. 86) are certainly wrong in assuming that the seller's price is valid even when unfair.

253. This is sharply, but rightly emphasized by Tunc (p. 379) and Graveson/Cohn (p. 86).In the American *American Sand* decision, 198 A. 2d., p. 68 (adduced in the UCC 1969 Cumulative Supplement *ad* Section 2-305), the buyer had accepted the price only after a wait of two years and after an approximately 20% price-rise, and was condemned to pay this price obtaining on delivery. On the basic question, the Austrian decision of 20 February 1952 is particularly apposite, as witness the headnote: "A contract conditional on subsequent final determination of the price ... is in itself permissible, as the strict provisions of the General Civil Code with regard to the fixed nature of the price, which derive from Roman law and now no longer obtain in any other modern law, are, in accordance with customary commercial law, not applicable to commercial sales."

scarcely realistic to challenge. To recognize it, in what is *par excellence* the field in which the buyer can reasonably be expected to take variables in his stride, would surely not be inequitable.[254]

Both model codes, and the municipal courts, [255] all agree that during any transitional stage of uncertainty as to whether a price may be fixed, and if so how, a valid contract of sale exists.

G. *"The debtor must seek the creditor"*

This principle of English and American law, which is also to be found in continental statutes, is embodied in Articles 59 and 60 of the Sales Rules and undoubtedly represents transnational law. (It also corresponds to international usage that payment against documents must take place where they are handed over. [256]) One consequence of this principle is that the risk of loss of the remittance is to be borne by the purchaser, [257] but for the present there appears to be no transnational rule on his liability for its late arrival. The two model codes leave the matter open. On the municipal plane there is a contradiction between, on the one hand, Germany and Austria, and, on the other, Scandinavia (where there is specific liability for dilatoriness). [258] In most cases this problem will very likely be absorbed in the question of liability in the event of *force majeure*.

The time at which the buyer must pay is as a rule prescribed by the contract or results from the usage of trade. Article 60 of the Sales Rules expresses transnational law in providing that no formality or declaration is needed for the price to fall due. The obligation to pay takes effect without notice, just like the obligation to deliver (Aticle 20), [259] a rule which is moreover derived by Graveson/Cohn (p. 87) from the principle of reasonableness.

Unless otherwise agreed the buyer must pay for goods delivery-by-delivery:

254. Cf. Rabel, *Warenkauf* II, p. 17.

255. Swiss decision of 11 February 1952 (*Chevalley*); German decision of 11 March 1970 concerning a guarantee-transaction regarded as "hovering" and non-effective; French decision of 18 December 1950 on the purchase of a car in Vienna with a receipt signed by only one party in place of a contract of sale giving the price; MAT 19 June 1925 (*Negreanu*) on transactions without mention of price in the case of longstanding business-relations.

256. Cf. the decision of 27 January 1955, in which the Paris domicile for the bill of exchange also determined the applicable law. For comparative law, see Rabel, *Warenkauf* II, pp. 24 ff.

257. This became a burning issue at the time of the German collapse in 1945. The extensive case-law on the theme of abortive bank-transfers still awaits evaluation.

258. Rabel, *Warenkauf* II, p. 25.

259. Cf. the English decision of 1 March 1955 (*Ets Chainbaux*) on belated provision of letter of credit (cf. Section 2-310).

"performance for performance". The presumption to that effect in municipal law is *a fortiori* valid in international trade. [260] If payment is not made when due, the buyer automatically incurs interest on the price, without any need of notice to that effect or any other declaration or prerequisite circumstances. [261] In the international context, however, it would lead to immeasurable complications to bind up the question of payable interest with the earning-capacity of the goods, as is still undertaken under many national laws. These two questions should on the contrary be kept strictly apart. A debtor must pay interest on what he owes as from the due date, and the applicable rate of interest in international transactions is not the statutory rate of this or that country but should simply be reckoned on the basis of the loss of interest which the creditor could not be expected, even by careful management, to avoid sustaining as a result of not receiving the payment.[262]

The type and method of payment in international commerce is determined virtually in full by the contract and the usage of trade. The Sales Rules, therefore, while acknowledging this situation in Article 69, contain no specific provisions on the subject. Under Section 2-511 UCC the purchaser is *a priori* entitled to pay by cheque or bill of exchange unless the seller has expressly demanded cash payment and provided that payment by cheque or bill of exchange corresponds to commercial usage. It may of course be wondered whether so liberal a rule, applicable on the regional scale of the Uniform Commercial Code, may also be regarded as transnationally valid, bearing in mind how often dispute has arisen in recent times over a usage in point. At all events, it may be taken as transnational law that payment by cheque or bill of exchange represents a conditional tender for discharge of the debt, i.e. that it does not automatically destroy the seller's claim under the contract. On this point the Code, in Section 2-511 (3), and continental law are in basic agreement.[263]

In contrast to the general allusions of Article 69 of the Sales Rules, Section 2-325 UCC defines and regulates the effect of letters of credit. Involving general commercial usage as they do, these rules, irrespective of the territorial scope of the Code, possess considerable significance for the development of transnational law, especially insofar as they can be shown to harmonize with the guidelines first laid down by the International Chamber of Commerce in

260. American decision of 10 May 1924 (*Miles*).
261. Rabel, *Warenkauf* II, pp. 20 and 22 ff.
262. Our two model codes do not regulate this question; more specifically, it is not covered by Section 2-710 UCC. Courts tend either, as in the *Sapphire* award of 15 March 1963 (p. 1021), to take a customary 5% interest as their working-norm, or to refer to national laws, in doing which they sometimes have to cope with considerable differences, e.g., that between legal interest of 6% in France and 9% in Morocco (French decision of 17 May 1939). Cf., further, Rabel, *Warenkauf* II, p. 44, for comparative law.
263. For more detailed treatment, cf. Rabel, *Warenkauf* II, p. 30.

1953 as Uniform Customs and Practices for Documentary Credits. [264] Quite rightly, municipal courts are particularly inclined in this field to decide after establishment of an international commercial practice, hence by transnational commercial law, without concerning themselves overmuch with the question of which national law is applicable. [265]

The rules concerning the purchaser's obligation to take the goods into his possession may be regarded as transnational without hesitation. Here Article 65 of the Sales Rules and Section 2-606 UCC agree in essentials, however much they differ verbally. Particularly important is the stress laid in the former on the necessity of enabling the seller to hand the goods over. [266] The obligation to take delivery may be made subject in the contract to whatever the parties may wish to stipulate. For example, the buyer may be given an option, whereby he is allowed an agreed period within which to make up his mind whether he wishes to take delivery or not. He may also be given another kind of option, whereby, although he must eventually take all the goods he purchased, he may take them piecemeal and not all at once. [267]

In Articles 69 and 70 the Sales Rules lump together, under the head of "other obligations of the buyer", a number of rules which are but tenuously interconnected. For the rest, all the remaining obligations of the buyer, as also of the seller, emerge from the same principle: that of good faith, by virtue of which, for example, the buyer has to take as much care over the goods in receiving them as the seller has to take over any advance-payment the buyer may have entrusted to him. [268] As, in transnational law, each party in case of doubt is responsible for those steps in the discharge of the contract to which he stands in the closer relation and may more easily carry out, it is

264. Cf. in particular Zahn, *Zahlungsmittel und Zahlungssicherung im Aussenhandel*, 1959, pp. 171 ff.; Schinnerer, *Bankverträge* I, 1961, pp. 74 ff., and II, 1958, pp. 116 ff.; Jackson, "Contract guarantees abroad", 79-80 *Journal of the Institute of Bankers*, 1958, pp. 100 ff. and 304 ff., and 1959, pp. 38 ff.; Schmitthoff, *Export Trade*, 5th ed., 1969, pp. 189 ff.; Von Caemmerer, "Bankgarantien im Aussenhandel", *Festschrift Riese,* Karlsruhe 1964, p. 395.

265. Cf. e.g. the English decision of 10 December 1957 (*Hamzeh Malass*), concerning the principle that a bank-certified documentary credit creates an absolute duty to pay, irrespective of any question arising out of the contract of sale.

266. Riese 1965, p. 73, and Rabel, *Warenkauf* II, p. 75.

267. Cf. the rules in Section 2-311 UCC, and Article 67 of the Hague Sales Rules, on sale by specification. The latter was consciously modelled on American law. Cf. also Riese, 1957, p. 85. On the point that the granting of an additional period by the seller is not prejudicial to him vis-à-vis a purchaser who is dilatory in the acceptance of the goods, cf. the Swiss decision of 18 January 1923 (*Renold*). A German decision of 19 February 1949 deals with the proven unreliabillity of the seller in an international sale, which entitled the buyer to cancel the contract without extending the time-limit.

268. For an example of the former case, cf. the English decision of 12 May 1953 (*J. d'Almeida*) on the coincidence of English and Portuguese law; for an example of the latter, cf. MAT 16 June 1925 (*Negreanu*), p. 216.

163

for the buyer to obtain any import-permit necessary in his country of business and for the seller to obtain any requisite export-licence.[269]

For the moment, there are no specific transnational rules governing the, in practice, important and recurrent question as to which contracting party should bear the cost of customs duty and similar levies. It is significant that the authors of the 1964 Sales Rules left this question aside, despite the endeavour to regulate it which had been embodied in Article 69 of the 1951 draft. With all respect to Graveson/Cohn (p. 86), the problem can hardly be solved by reference to national law. In suitable cases it will much rather be possible to rely on the transnational concept of proximity to risk.

Commenting on Article 69 of the (1964) Sales Rules, Tunc writes:

"As the buyer is obliged to pay the price he is also certainly bound to obtain the necessary currency and to carry out all the steps required by any system of controls. The wording of Article 69, by which the buyer must take the preparatory steps provided for in the contract to effect payment, leaves no doubt in this regard. But the variety and impermanence of municipal systems of control bar any more precise rule."[270]

Subsequent to taking delivery, the purchaser may be under a prohibition to re-export the goods, this constituting a subsidiary, negative obligation of separate importance. The civil legality of agreements to such effect is no longer open to doubt and, given their raison d'être, is very much in line with transnational law. At the present time, however, it is very difficult to find any unified assessment of their standing from the viewpoint of *ordre public*.[271]

The objections raised above against the excessive fragmentation resulting from the Sales Rules' treatment of remedies for seller's breach have now to be echoed with respect to their handling of the seller's remedies for any acts of the buyer in breach of the contract. Honnold has expressed these objections from the American viewpoint,[272] but converse objections against the treatment of the same subject in Section 2-709 ff. UCC have been forthcoming from Europe.[273] It is however precisely contradictions of this kind which

---

269. The American and English decisions cited by Rabel, *Warenkauf* II, p. 20, n. 153, should be investigated. A special kind of difficulty exists in regard to State-trading countries, where it behoves the private party to the contract to exercise particular care in view of the high degree of economic identity between the other party to the contract and the import-export department concerned. Cf. the *Israel Oil* case of 19 June 1958 and the relevant literature on international foreign exchange law.

270. 1964 Conference, *Records*, p. 380.

271. Cf. Rabel, *Warenkauf* II, pp. 98 ff.; Philippe Kahn, *La Vente commerciale internationale*, pp. 214 ff.; more especially the material on Article 85 of the Treaty of Rome.

272. *Law and Contemporary Problems*, 1965, p. 343.

273. Hellner, in Ziegel/Foster, p. 108.

facilitate the pinpointing of transnational law. The most material contradiction, as Hellner has pointed out, [274] derives from the fact that in the United States it is possible to sue for the whole price only in exceptional circumstances, it being the rule to resell the goods and claim for any difference; this conflicts with many continental systems, and even English law, insofar as these allow a seller injured in his rights an option between action for the price and resale. [275] The Sales Rules offer the sole possible escape from this dilemma by making resale obligatory only when it is practicable and corresponds to the usage of trade. This may and surely should be viewed as transnational law, neither does it conflict with the Uniform Commercial Code so far as international transactions are concerned.

For the rest, it will be necessary to exercise particular caution in determining what constitutes transnational law with regard to breaches of contract by the buyer, given the somewhat sketchy and none too solidly voted character of the Sales Rules on the subject and their occasional discrepancy with the rules of our other model. If the transnational principles abstracted in Part Five of this study are used as a filter, it must be borne in mind that breaches of a duty to pay money can more easily be repaired than breaches in the delivery of goods. From this it follows for example that where payment is overdue, and the seller can without risk to himself notify the buyer to pay within a brief delay, avoidance of the contract for late payment will not be possible in transnational law unless justified by special circumstances. In all other cases, despite the American objections referred to above, the distinction between "fundamental" and "non-fundamental" breach, made by the Sales Rules with reference to breaches of contract by either party, will be found to offer a not unsatisfactory contribution to transnational law.

274. *Loc. cit.*
275. Graveson/Cohn, p. 87.

Part Four

THE LIMITATION OF CLAIMS

I. *The general principle of lapse by time*

Before speaking of limitation, or prescription, one must first distinguish between the general principle of time-lapse[1] and its embodiment in particular cases. It would be extremely hard for anyone who neglected this distinction, and immediately devoted all his attention to the national laws wherein that embodiment takes place, to discern any intrinsic principle of transnational law, for the great number and variety of contradictory rules would be bound to bewilder and distract him. At present both jurisprudence and doctrine, having failed to exercise such preliminary caution, find themselves in a position whose uselessness for practical purposes would be difficult to surpass. Professor Alex Weill of Strasbourg has pointed out, with reference to French writings on the subject (notably J. Michel's monograph of 1911), that the proposed solutions now number no less than fifteen (note on Cass. civ. 31 January 1950), and has described the question of the applicable law in limitation cases as one of the most "academic" issues of private international law. Niboyet, in his note on Cass. civ. 9 January 1934, gives vent to his despair with "What is one to make of this proliferation of systems? ", while the American judge Montgomery, in a decision concerning a licensing agreement (23 May 1905; 74 NE, p. 524), had long ago remarked on the "irreconcilable conflict and hopeless confusion" reigning among the courts of different States. Ernst Rabel uses the following words to describe the situation:

> "Too much in the debates going on for so many centuries has been a strange mixture of obsolete legal terminology and concealed policy considerations; the policies have been too often one-sided or confused;

---

1. In the present Part, the German word *Verjährung*, which suggests the natural erosion of a claim with the passage of the years, much rather than the positive institutional bar of *limitation*, is rendered by "(the general principle of) time-lapse" when to use "limitation" would do violence to the sense or mask the difference between the English procedural theory of limitation and the substantive doctrine of *Verjährung*. The slight play on words in "time-lapse" (lapse by time, lapse of time) is intended as a reminder of the dual import of *Verjährung*: the organic process and its legal effect. It is felt unlikely that any reader will be led astray by it. (*Translator.*)

and the provincial lawyer's thinking has usurped undue privilege. The subject, thus, has become an outstanding illustration of the necessity for an unbiased and supernational discussion."[2]

However, anyone who first becomes clear in his mind as to the scope and substance of a transnational principle of limitation will then find it easier to solve the problems of its embodiment in particular cases.

The decisive question of whether any universal transnational principle of limitation exists may be answered by its converse: is there any civilized nation in which this principle is unknown? Has it not, in fact, been part of the cultural heritage of the civilized world for nigh on two thousand years, since the time of the first Christian emperors in Rome? When the question is put in this way, the answer cannot be in doubt. For detailed corroboration, may it suffice to refer to two fairly recent works of comparative law: Ernst Rabel's *Conflict of Laws*, Vol. III, 2nd ed., pp. 487-536, for private law, and Bin Cheng's *General Principles of Law*, pp. 370-386, for public international law. Both these writers adduce evidence that limitation is one of the "general principles". According to Rabel, it has "the same structure under all the statutes of the world", its features including lapse of time from the moment of completion of the cause of action, the possibility of waiver, and the effect of so extinguishing the claim that only a weak, ethical remnant of the debt remains, known everywhere as natural obligation.

Decisions explicitly confirming this principle are hard to seek, but this of course is due to the fact that the courts, through their allegiance to classical doctrine, find occasion to resort to it only in exceptional cases. The Mixed Arbitral Tribunals set up after Versailles found themselves in an exceptional situation, and thus it is that the interesting observations which follow are to be read in one of their awards:

"Positive international law has not yet established precise, generally approved rules either as to the principle or as to the theory of limitation ... Nevertheless, limitation appears to be a rule of positive law accepted by every delegation; it is no more than the expression of a major principle of thought which underlies general law and every civilized system of jurisprudence ... As an integral and necessary part of every legal system, limitation merits admission by international law."[3]

Naturally enough, those who concern themselves with public international law, where reference to national laws is of little assistance, have had more occasion to seek a general principle of time-lapse. Judicial practice in this

---

2. *The Conflict of Laws* III, 2nd ed., p. 488.
3. Greco-Bulgarian MAT, 14 February 1927. The Greek plaintiff claimed damages arising out of the Greek pogroms which took place in Bulgaria in 1906. Bulgaria pleaded limitation. Though the tribunal took up a position of principle on this point, it declared itself incompetent to hear the merits.

sense has, significantly, a far longer history than doctrine, for it was only in 1925 that, thanks to the Institute of International Law, the theoreticians really came to grips with limitation and reviewed the practice in the subject.[4] Since then, both judges and scholars have in their great majority come to share the view of the Institute that, in the interest of legal stability, limitation should be treated as one of the legal principles acknowledged by civilized nations. There is no need here to go into the copious illustrations of this provided, for example, by Bin Cheng, for there is in fact only one decision of importance in which the tribunal took a contrary line, refusing to treat certain arrears as time-barred, on the ground that "the rules of prescription, belonging exclusively to the domain of civil law", were not applicable as between States.[5] It remains to be seen whether this award was not perhaps superficial in its reasoning and ignored the fact that limitation is a "general principle" even in civil law.

Admittedly, such a general principle, while yet so vague in substance, so indefinite in scope, may appear to present a typical defect of its kind: a tendency to uselessness. Yet even the mere recognition that it poses one of the "minimum requirements addressed by international law to every branch of municipal law" points directly to a cardinal inference, namely that "to disregard these minimum requirements means to incur State responsibility for denial of justice".[6] It could create, as it were, a form of *ordre public international* whereby no court would henceforth be entitled to conclude that any claim was imprescriptible. Such a principle, even if it formed no more than a minimum standard, would still yield good service when the issue revolves on certain matters of juristic interpretation which are still far from clear, for example on the question whether in the given case one should refer not so much to limitation as to customary law, presumption of payment of debt, forfeiture, estoppel, renunciation or whatever.[7] Even a minimum standard, moreover, has the important effect of furnishing a uniform yardstick for the underlying resemblances in different sets of facts. Thus, however national laws may differ in their treatment of limitation, this minimum standard will enable one to elicit a single, uniform international situation, the legal assess-

4. "La prescription libératoire en droit international public", 32 *Annuaire*, 1925, pp. 1 ff., 466ff., 558 ff.

5. *Pious Fund* decision of the P.C.A., 14 October 1902, in 2 AJIL, 1908, p. 901, and *The Hague Court Reports* 1916, pp. 5 f.

6. Lipstein, "Conflict of laws before international tribunals", 27 *Trans. Grotius Soc.*, 1942, p. 175.

7. The question of renunciation was raised in the *Williams* public international law case (Moore, *International Arbitrations* IV, pp. 41-81 ff.) and in the *Borel* award of 18 April 1924 concerning the Turkish national debt (UNRIAA I, p. 529). The relationship of limitation and estoppel is left open in Judge Learned Hand's decision of 4 August 1930 (USA), p. 943.

ment of which admits of variance only in extraordinary circumstances.

Once our "general principle" is viewed teleologically it acquires an immediate accession of strength. In this respect the French have not gone far enough, for they regard the protection of the debtor to be the principal purpose of limitation, whereas behind this notion there stands another, much more important: peace and security (*Rechtsfrieden*). It is not merely the debtor who is protected from a negligent and tardy creditor, but the debtor's other creditors too. The general principle of limitation must be envisaged in this light if it is to be applied correctly and where, appropriate, and this, France apart, appears to have been the universal conviction ever since the days of the Roman emperors. A much-cited award of the Mixed Arbitral Tribunals was expressly founded on the purpose of limitation as thus conceived:

In a dispute with Romania, Germany submitted that its opponent had not observed the time-limits fixed by the Treaty of Versailles for the filing of applications by allied powers, and the tribunal upheld this submission on the ground that even States are under obligation to avoid uncertainties prejudicial to the private persons affected by their treaties.[8]

The vagueness of our principle is no excuse for disregarding it. Principles are always vague, only some are strong while others are weak. Ours is a strong one, on account of its connection with the public weal, and it can be set to work, despite its vagueness, provided that two points be borne in mind. The first is that its embodiment in national statutes has to be viewed in the context of time and place. Thus we know from the history of Roman law that in the beginning *obligatio* was endowed with perpetuity.[9] Only gradually, as law was refined, notably in the commercial field, were the shorter periods of limitation introduced. Nowadays, when we come up against decisions in which the choice lies between a thirty-year prescription and a shorter limitation, this historical consideration will often lead to treating the longer period as obsolete and no longer in harmony with our transnational principle.[10]

Recently Coing has pointed out what a breakthrough is possible in comparative law once it is realized that certain discrepancies between national laws

---

8. *Negreanu* decision of 16 June 1925, pp. 208-210. Cf. my study "Völkerrechtliche Verträge vom Standpunkt der Betroffenen", *Annales Universitatis Saraviensis* 1960, p. 217.

9. Dernburg, *Pandekten*, 3rd ed., 1892, I, p. 338.

10. The older English decisions are the most interesting in this connection. Thus in the *British Linen* case of 1830 there was a conflict between English 6-year limitation and the Scottish period of 40 years. The House of Lords decided in favour of the shorter period, but on a ground that would no longer be acceptable in comparable circumstances, namely that English law was the applicable law. In the *Don* decision of 26 May 1837, on the other hand, Scottish 6-year limitation was opposed to a 40-year French period, and the shorter limit was preferred for the same outdated reason.

are merely due to the fact that each of the systems concerned has reached a different stage of development in relation to the general principle common to all.[11]

The second point to be borne in mind is that principles necessarily call, as such, for elasticity in their practical application. This has so frequently been stressed by courts and commentators that to single out particular authorities would surely be superfluous. [12] Such elasticity is especially important when dealing with cases of contradictory time-limits in national laws. Here an example may and must be sought in public international law, according to which periods of limitation may never be established as general rules but must be determined in conformity with the circumstances of each case. [13] Those who equate principle with rigidity may feel that its elastic application to the particular case must cost a principle its virtue, but, on the contrary, this approach renders it not worthless but useful—a point which will receive further illustration below.

In the past it has not been customary to regard the prescriptibility of claims as a standing tenet of transnational law. It did however receive recognition whenever identified as an element in one of the positive national laws concerned. Not surprisingly, therefore, the German *Reichsgericht* decision of 4 January 1882 aroused general criticism:

Suit had been brought in Germany on a promissory note issued in and subject to the laws of Tennessee, although the German three-year period of limitation had expired. However, the period laid down under Tennessee law, to wit six years, was still running. The court dismissed the plea of limitation, arguing that the German statute was inapplicable because, in the German conception, limitation was part of substantive law, so that the (American) law governing the bill-debt as such was also the law of reference where limitation was concerned; but since in American conceptions limitation was an institution of procedural law, the American statute in question must also be disregarded, because an established norm of German conflicts law prohibits German courts from applying any foreign procedural law. In consequence, the claim for execution of the bill was imprescriptible—in contradiction to both the national systems of law concerned!

What is of special interest for present purposes is the key sentence of this decision, which ran as follows:

"For the prescription of claims as such does not lie in their juridical nature, but belongs to positive law."

<hr/>

11. Cf. Coing, address to the Berlin convention of the *Gesellschaft für Rechtsvergleichung, RabelsZ*, 1968, p. 1.

12. Cf. Philippe Kahn, *La Vente commerciale internationale*, Paris 1961, p. 144, with examples from the French courts; cf. also the American decision of 4 September 1942 regarding the appropriate fixing of a time-limit when the parties have meanwhile been jointly engaged in endeavouring to remedy a defect in the object sold.

13. Cf. the above-mentioned resolution of the International Law Institute (1925).

To this error may be traced the defectiveness of the judgment, not to mention a string of similarly faulty decisions—not all of them German. The court's finding was in itself enough to prompt such descriptions as "notorious blunder" (Nussbaum, p. 47), while Ernst Rabel referred to an "outcome amazing even to the hard-boiled specialists of conflicts law" (III, 2nd ed., p. 532). Yet despite this rejection of the outcome, the defective basis of the judgment has, unfortunately, been not merely upheld but even reinforced by publicists. Three years after the case Franz Kahn made the following comment upon it:

> "It was beyond doubt from the outset that the prescription problem could be judged only in accordance with one of two laws, either American law or German.[14]

The *via media* which offered a solution, namely the application of transnational principles, went for a long time unperceived. Even a generation later, when the German *Reichsgericht* handed down its judgment of 19 December 1922, it still remained hidden:

In 1909 a Swiss firm in Winterthur had obtained, against a defendant then resident in Switzerland, orders to pay a certain commercial debt. Following non-compliance and fruitless distraint, the firm eventually acquired a "certificate of loss" (*Verlustschein*) such as is only known to Swiss law. Under Article 149 (5) of the Swiss Debt Recovery Act, claims in respect of which such certificates are issued are imprescriptible. The suit subsequently brought in Germany by the creditor was rejected in the courts of first instance and appeal, on the ground that the imprescriptibility of the claim would be contrary to German *ordre public*. The *Reichsgericht* quashed this decision and referred the case back, not, however, because of the reliance on *ordre public*; that, it said, was correct in itself, only it should not lead to the arbitrary substitution of German limitation provisions for Swiss ones. It was, rather, the duty of the German judge "to ascertain among German statutes that particular provision which most closely approximated to the juristic thought of the foreign law".

Hereby the *Reichsgericht* set up a signpost to the future. Only a short step was now needed for the transnational principle to be discovered in the process of correlating law with law. At all events, the first hurdle had been taken, in that the German courts had met the threatened introduction of imprescriptibility with recourse to *ordre public*. The same happened in France.[15] But as the final step to transnational thinking was still to be made, the ill-starred method of juggling with two national legal systems still persisted in the practice of the Mixed Arbitral Tribunals.[16] Witness the decision given by the Anglo-German tribunal on 31 May 1926 in *Cook* v. *Kutscher*, when an English creditor had laid claim, through the clearing-office set up under Ar-

14. "Gesetzeskollisionen", *Abhandlungen* I, p. 105.
15. Cf. the post-1933 references in Batiffol, No. 615, n. 74.
16. Cf. references in Rabel, *Conflict* III, 2nd ed., p. 533, n. 124.

ticle 296 of the Versailles Treaty, for payment of various goods supplied between 1905 and 1907 to a German debtor:

"The Debtor was resident in Portuguese Guinea during several years before the middle of 1907. During visits which he then made to Germany, he ordered [certain articles] from the Creditor ... These orders were given partly to a representative of the Creditor, then visiting Germany, partly by letter to the Creditor. The Debtor further ordered articles ... from the Creditor during a stay of some weeks in London in the middle of 1907 on his way to Germany from Portuguese Guinea.

The Debtor ... contests the claim as barred by prescription.

Under the interpretation of paragraph 4 of the Annex to Article 296 in the Treaty of Versailles given in the decision of this Division in the case *G.B. Livingston & Findlay* v. *William Graaff* (Case 3025) the law of prescription to apply shall be determined by German private international law.

Under German private international law the domestic law to apply to the contractual obligations of the Debtor would be the law of the place of fulfilment of the Debtor, that is under German law the law of the country of the domicile of the Debtor at the time of the contract.

To apply the domestic law of Portuguese Guinea to any of these orders would however, the Tribunal holds, be against the intention of the parties.

English domestic law would seem to be the proper law to apply, as the fact that some of the orders were given during a temporary visit of the Debtor to Germany could not be in itself sufficient reason to apply German domestic law to these orders.

In adjudicating under German private international law on a claim based on a contract governed by English domestic law the difficulty arises that the English domestic law applicable to contracts contains no provisions of prescription. The English law of prescription is part not of the English law of contracts but of the English law of procedure. Accordingly if the Tribunal adjudicating under German private international law should apply English law of contracts no rules of prescription could be applied. See decisions of the Reichsgericht (*Entscheidungen des Reichsgerichts in Zivilsachen*, Band 7, page 21 ff., and Band 24, page 383 ff.).

This result however would be in such contradiction to the principles governing prescription in German Law that the Tribunal, acting according to the rule laid down in paragraph 4 of the Annex to Article 296 as a Court sitting in the country of the Debtor, cannot accept it.

The German Law of prescription in matters of debts is based on the conception that prescription is not a question purely of private law but also a matter of public policy. The prescription serves not only the debtor but the public welfare, the purpose of the rules of prescription being peace and security in matters relating to claims and debts. The German Law therefore disapproves on principle of the excluding of prescription in matters of debts. See decision of the Reichsgericht (*Entscheidungen des Reichsgerichts in Zivilsachen*, Band 106, page 83 ff.)

In this case the application of German private international law must therefore be set aside, as it would lead to a result contrary to a principle of public policy accepted in German domestic Law.

Accordingly the Tribunal acting as a Court sitting in the country of the Debtor has to apply German domestic law of prescription and under this law the claim is barred after the expiration of two years from the end of the year in which the debt became due."[17]

---

17. Walther Lewald, JW 1926, p. 2818.

Considering that the underlying fact of the whole case was merely the failure of a German farmer in Africa to pay his London tailor's bill, it is not surprising that Ernst Rabel should have commented: "But how awkward is a treatment that requires such precarious counteractions!" (III, 2nd ed., p. 533). Later on we shall return to this case and discuss the correct solution which transnational law would yield.

If there is recognized to be a general principle of time-lapse in all civilized laws, it cannot be held merely to take effect whenever a specific rule of limitation is lacking in a given national law. On the contrary, it must also be allowed effectiveness as a signpost and arbitrator where two national systems exhibit conflicting rules of limitation. This point, however, has not hitherto been grasped. The views of English and American jurists, in particular, are still based on precedents dating back to an age when other modes of thought and social structures prevailed. Thus one of the great American judges, in a much-cited decision of 4 August 1930, which we shall encounter again below, still thought fit to concern himself with the century-old English *Huber* v. *Steiner* judgment of 17 June 1835, wherein Lord Chief Justice Tindal relied principally, and explicitly, on a work of the celebrated Dutchman Ulrich Huber (1636-1694), and on the even older *British Linen* judgment of 1830, in which Lord Chief Justice Tenterden bolstered the authority of the venerable Ulrich Huber with that of his no less famous contemporary Johannes Voet (1647-1714); as Lord Tindal loftily observed:

"It is unnecessary to cite more; the authorities are collected in the case of *The British Linen Co.* v. *Drummond* ..., which case itself furnishes an authority for the position."

Thus a direct connection can be traced between contemporary jurists and predecessors who lived 300 years ago, whose mentality was permeated with the sovereign categories of the up-and-coming national State. In a well-known decision of October 1820, Joseph Story obviously considered himself bound to follow the traditional precedents, even though he himself was personally unable to suppress certain misgivings. [18] Our only concern for the time being is to make the point that English and American decisions have been all too closely bound up with the past. Later we will have to come to grips with the peculiar nature of this bond, and its dependence on the controversial question of whether limitation is a mere defensive remedy or the content of a substantive right. Be it however mentioned in passing that one English authority, at all events, has made the following comment on the traditional view:

---

18. *Leroy* v. *Crowninshield*, 2 Mason 151, 152 Fed. Cases 362, No. 8269. Cf. Schlinck, "Die international-privatrechtliche Behandlung der Verjährung in den Vereinigten Staaten", 9 *RabelsZ*, 1935, p. 418.

"This is another example where English law, through its failure to interpret a foreign rule in its context, has gone astray."[19]

All decisions on the subject of limitation necessarily contain an element of nationalism to the extent that they are based on the outlook of that bygone era. The judge must find it almost a matter of course to apply his own domestic limitation law, and the doctrine of the procedural nature of limitation cannot but offer him welcome incitement to do so. By its agency, any idea of applying in the field of limitation the idea that conflicting rules deserve to be treated *a priori* on a plane of equality is helpfully kept submerged.

This idea, in fact, belongs to more recent times. It had long been a feature of domestic criminal law, notably in the case of conflicting statutes (*Konkurrenzen*),[20] and from there it was transplanted into the law of civil procedure by Hellwig. At length Franz Lent devoted a two-volume study to the conflict of domestic laws. Yet not even the examples he cited deal with the question of limitation, let alone private international law. The first exhaustive treatment of the problem was in fact undertaken by Franz Kahn in 1891.[21] Of course the solution of the problem becomes a more exacting task when, instead of granting from the outset a certain priority to one national law, one treats two conflicting national laws on a basis of equality. Hence Franz Kahn was driven to a somewhat pessimistic forecast:

"The attempt to construct a uniform private international law out of the trend and sense of the individual territorial laws is, we consider, doomed to fail of its own accord through the unnatural and inextricable overlapping of laws and irrational legal vacua to which it must lead if consistently pursued."[22]

As he expressly states in his closing words,[23] it was not Kahn's intention to oppose the attempt to win ever more ground from dangerous conflicts of law for the benefit of harmonization. But way back in 1891 he was unable to perceive any other road to this goal than the gradual emergence of an internationally similar territorial legislation. Experience has since taught us what a

19. Cheshire, *Private International Law*, 6th ed., p. 685.
20. If someone breaks several criminal laws with one and the same deed, a decision has to be taken as to whether the penalties prescribed are to be added together or only one applied and, if so, which? In German law (§ 73 of the Criminal Code) the decision is based on the notion that the lighter penalty is fully "absorbed" in the heavier. It is thus taken from a superior viewpoint. A similar course should be followed when two different periods of limitation are in question, but then of course the superior viewpoint will belong to civil and not criminal law.
21. *Abhandlungen zum internationalen Privatrecht*, Vol. I: "Gesetzeskollisionen", Munich and Leipzig 1928 (first appeared in 30 *Jherings Jährbücher*, 1891, p. 1).
22. *Abh.*, p. 110.
23. *Ibid.*, p. 122.

disproportionately lengthy and weary road that is. In the specific field of limitation, the laws and the decisions of the one State and the other are every bit as contradictory now as they were then. In so desperate a situation every conceivable attempt must be made to find an exit. These efforts may be begun with a series of observations which are necessary for the purpose of marking off wrong turnings and assisting recognition of the possible way out.

In these circumstances, the distinction which scholars have developed between "limitation" (*Verjährung, prescription*) on the one hand, and "preclusion" (*Ausschlussfrist; déchéance, delai fixe*) on the other, will be intentionally disregarded in what follows. In land law, family law and many other contexts it may well be significant, but in commercial law it is of less consequence. [24] A businessman is not concerned with nice distinctions between the different entries he has to make in case he loses out through overlooking a crucial date. It is all one to him at the outset, and any discrimination he may make as between the decision of one instance and another depends upon the peculiarities of each case in point. Thus cases of failure to comply with specific time-limits—especially, in sales law, those for the notification of defects—will, as Batiffol points out (para. 703), be more intimately connected with contracts than will general periods of limitation. But Ernst Rabel (III, 2nd ed., pp. 500 ff.) was surely right in arguing that any decision on time-bars must be supported by considerations which follow the same guidelines. It is in the interest of social stability that a peaceable situation should not be exposed to belated disturbance. A debtor should not be compelled to respond to claims of obscure provenance. He should not be expected to rummage out proof after an unlimited lapse of time, when both witnesses and evidential documents may reasonably have become untraceable. Neither should courts be obliged to undertake laborious inquiries. Negligent creditors, or those who make unreceipted payments, cannot be protected for ever. Thus although we should certainly, from case to case, take the difference of circumstances into account, it would be wrong to belittle from the outset the material offered by decided cases; we shall find that the essential considerations are similar, whether long or short periods of limitations were involved, or non-statutory time-limits.

Respect for the general principle of time-lapse ought in future to rule out the severance of limitation questions from the case as a whole and the isolated treatment of them in accordance with the national law of one contracting party, while other legal questions touching the same agreement may perhaps be dealt with according to some other national law. This is the so-called "splitting" of contracts which is now overwhelmingly rejected (cf.

---

24. On the German efforts at the Hague Conference to get limitation replaced by preclusion, see Riese, in *RabelsZ* 1965, p. 60.

Introduction). In this respect, a decision given by the German *Bundesgerichtshof* on 14 February 1958 merits criticism:

> An Italo-German contract of sale failed to specify the applicable law. The Italian purchaser demanded the return of the price paid on account of deficiencies in the delivery. The German defendant objected that the deficiencies had not been notified "without delay" (*"unverzüglich"*), in accordance with § 337 of the German Commercial Code, as the purchaser had made use of the eight days' notice permitted in Italian law. The *Bundesgerichtshof* opined, albeit as an *obiter dictum*, "that the question whether a foreign purchaser can be expected to comply with the requirement of notification 'without delay' is, in the nature of things, one that can only be addressed to the law of his own place of performance".

"In the nature of things"? Hardly! This decision has already been criticized by Von Caemmerer (JZ 1959, p. 363) as a product of the "splitting" theory, and also for its inadequate exposition of the facts. The question whether defects have been notified in time, and what time-limits are appropriate under transnational law, will be dealt with below. The point to be made here is that this question cannot in any case be answered if it is divorced from the overall contractual relationship and allocated to this or that domestic law—which has always regulated the matter in accordance with the circumscribed national outlook of the legislators of the day.

II. *Limitation as an instrument of national policies*

In dealing with questions of limitation in international trade, one may never lose sight of the fact that in a fairly large number of cases they are closely bound up with considerations of public policy or with blatant trade politics. Now this is something which is openly admitted among legal scholars in every land, and it is discernible in both legislative materials and diplomatic instruments. [25] Yet no awareness of it transpires in decided cases, for courts endeavour to embroider or even smother politico-commercial or public policy motives (which in fact have influenced the decision) with purely legal arguments. Such decisions are dangerous for the development of law and should in future be cited only with corresponding reservation. That is true, for example, of the English decision of 26 May 1837 in *Don* v. *Lippman*, which even today is constantly cited:

---

25. As a persual of the materials of the Hague International Sales Law Convention will confirm. Cf. furthermore the position adopted on 20 February 1956 by the German private international law council towards the 1951 draft uniform law on the international sale of goods (*RabelsZ* 1959, p. 151).

"The late Sir Alexander Don, the father of the Appellant, happened to be within the French territory in 1802, when hostilities recommenced between this country and France after the peace of Amiens, and with many other British subjects was tyrannically detained in France. He remained a prisoner until February 1810. Upon the 13th of November 1809, Charles Fagan, merchant in Paris, drew two bills upon him, which are dated 'Versailles', ordering him, as acceptor, to pay to the Respondent Lippmann, who was named in the bills as payee, the sum of 20,000 francs, each bill being for that amount. These bills were drawn upon the acceptor at the 'Hôtel de Richelieu, Paris', his place of residence, were made payable on the 1st of March; and were drawn and accepted in the [French language by the baronet].

Before the bills became due, Sir Alexander Don left Paris, and was in England in the month of February 1810. When the bills became due they were dishonoured, and protested for non-payment against the acceptor, and the dishonour was intimated to Charles Fagan, the drawer.

M. Lippman then commenced proceedings according to the law of France, against both the acceptor and the drawer of the bills, and, in the action raised before the Tribunal de Commerce of the department of the Seine, Charles Fagan, the drawer, made appearance, but he did not deny the validity of the debt. He requested the Court, however, to give him time, in order that he might arrange as to payments of the bills. On the 25th July 1810, judgment was pronounced against both the drawer who had made appearance, and against Sir Alexander Don the acceptor in absence. All the requisites of the law of France were stated to have been complied with in these proceedings. The decree of the Court was for payment of the contents of the bills, and fifty-nine francs of expenses, exclusive of the expense of registering the judgment. This judgment was, in the pleadings in the present suit, alleged to have been intimated on the 22d October 1810, by the proper officer, and according to legal form, at the former residence of Sir Alexander Don; and it was stated, that he had left the Hotel Richelieu about six months before, and was believed by the servants at the hotel to have gone to England. Execution then followed against the effects of Charles Fagan, as his person could not be found. That person afterwards died, and about the month of March 1813 his effects were sold at the instance of M. Lippmann, and the sale was reported by the auctioneer as having produced 434 francs, after deducting expenses, for which credit is given. A claim was made on Sir Alexander Don, but he positively declared that he had remitted to France ample funds to pay all his just debts, and after a correspondence on the subject, which took place in 1814, no further claim was made on Sir Alexander Don in his lifetime. He died in April 1820. The action, now the subject of appeal, was

177

commenced on the 3d of April 1829, and it was founded both upon the bills and the judgment. The defendant, who, being an infant, appeared by his tutor, set up in defence the Act of 1772, by which it is declared, 'that no bill of exchange, etc. shall be of force in Scotland unless diligence shall be raised and executed, or action commenced thereon within six years from and after the terms at which the sums in the said bills shall become exigible.' The question therefore which was raised, was whether the law of Scotland or that of France was applicable to the case. If the former, then the Act of 1772, which limits the right of suing to within six years after the bill, etc. becomes due, had taken effect, and the action was barred by prescription; if the latter, then the bar by prescription would take effect at five years from the date of the instrument, unless proceedings were taken in a French court on such instrument, but if such proceedings were taken, then after judgment therein obtained, the prescription would not be a bar for thirty years after the date of the judgment, and consequently the decree in the French court might properly be made the ground of the present suit."[26]

We will have occasion to revert to Lord Brougham's closely reasoned summing-up. The defendant's defence of limitation was allowed. The only point of immediate interest is the following:

"In reversing the most material part of the interlocutor appealed from, you do not introduce the law of England or of the commercial world into Scotland, but you are renewing in Scotland the principles of the old law of that country. The Appellant was an alien enemy in France, and could not appear in the French courts; he was, too, out of the country, and he could not possibly possess any property, real or personal, by which he could be rendered amenable."[27]

This passage, read with that concerning the tyrannical detention in France, throws a special light on the whole decision. What is more, the facts of the case are but vaguely given. One is not told the original reason for the late baronet's presence in Paris, whether he was staying there for family reasons, as a tourist, for political reasons—or may-be as some businessman trying to circumvent the French continental system. Neither does one learn anything direct about the circumstances of his arrest or the conditions of his eight-year detention, which cannot at all events, given the hotel address mentioned, have been very harsh. Another matter on which no light is shed is that of the business relationships of the three persons concerned in the bills. Lippmann was most probably a banker—connected, it may be, with the Amsterdam

26. 5 Cl. & F. 1, HL, p. 303.
27. *Ibid.*, p. 310.

banking-house of Lippmann and Rosenthal—and Fagan an impoverished Frenchman or naturalized Irishman. It must certainly have been Sir Alexander who cashed the countervalue of the two bills, for he himself declared that he had remitted to France ample funds to pay all his "just" debts. Beyond that, all is obscure—for example, where exactly the funds went, how they managed to get to France through the net of the continental system, and what the baronet meant by "just" debts. Neither is it known to what purpose he applied the proceeds of the bill, or under what circumstances and with what intentions he quit France shortly before it fell due. This much, however, does seem sure, that Lippmann helped the baronet out of a hole with his money, that suit for payment in Scotland was hardly possible until the conclusion of peace in 1815 and that Sir Alexander's heir took advantage of the fact to claim limitation, in which he found the help of the English judge.

Such a case should never have been generalized and cited as a leading decision—as still happens—so long as so many aspects of it remained obscure. Actually, we are not even told what exactly passed in regard to the claim and correspondence of 1814, and the position might even have been the reverse of our first conjecture: Lippmann could very well have received the countervalue of the bill, at a correspondingly low exchange-rate, outside France and in contravention of the continental system, in which case his claim would have been a wrongful attempt to cash it twice. The appellant may have felt for some reason inhibited from exposing this side of the affair to the light of day and preferred in the event to resort to the plea of limitation. Now it is known that, to no inconsiderable extent, the immense wealth of the banking-house of Rothschild was due to the astute exploitation of the continental system. Without knowledge of this background, the precedential value of *Don v. Lippmann* is minimal.

Again, the *Braugerste* judgment given by the Hamburg *Oberlandesgericht* on 29 October 1958 is scarcely an appropriate model. In this instance a German purchaser had complained of short weight and inferior quality in the brewer's yeast delivered by a French supplier. Here also we are not given all the facts—nothing is conveyed of the actual point at issue or the submissions of the parties, and all that can be deduced is that the case concerned the time-limit for notification of defects. The court argues that where such time-limits are concerned each party would opt for his own domestic law every time, and that this held good even when the parties had said nothing as to the applicable law. In our opinion, the maintenance of any such *parti pris* would totally inhibit the conclusion of any contract. This decision, too, is unfitted for the role of precedent by its exaggerated nationalism.

In other cases, to be found in all countries, courts have set themselves against biassed measures passed by foreign States in furtherance of trade and currency policies, and have at all events ignored them when they have had the possibility of applying their own domestic law instead. [28] For some indication of the relationship between limitation and national commercial policies, the reader is referred to an article written by Schlink in 1953.[29]

It is wholly possible, however, to avoid the one-sided preference of domestic law in limitation cases or the injection of nationalistic purposes. This was achieved, for example, in the above-mentioned *Verlustschein* decision of the *Reichsgericht* (19 December 1922), which directed the lower court to seek out those rules of German law which most closely approximated to Swiss law.

As for *Don v. Lippmann*, we have seen how the judge found in favour of his fellow-Briton in accordance with domestic law, despite the fact that all the material considerations—place of conclusion of contract, place of performance, language of agreement—spoke in favour of the application of the foreign law. This judgment was substantiated by a purely formal consideration, deriving from the theoretically procedural nature of limitation.

This procedural theory of limitation has been used for centuries to protect the debtor. It has hardened to a veritable dogma. It is typical that in *Société Anonyme Métallurgique de Prayon* (2 November 1933) an English judge, Roche, could content himself with the words:

"It was clear from those authorities that English law regarded the law of limitation as a matter of procedure, and the English courts were unable to apply any law of procedure other than the law of England."

However this has not gone undoubted, unchallenged. We have already quoted the remark of Cheshire: "This is another example where English law, through its failure to interpret a foreign rule, has gone astray".[30]

In American case-law we have the much-cited note with which the celebrated Learned Hand concluded his decision of 4 August 1930 in *Wood & Selick*, where he concerns himself with Judge Shipman's decision in *Canadian Pacific Railway* v. *Johnston* (29 May 1894). In the latter case, a railway employee had sued the company for compensation in respect of an industrial accident which had occurred on 6 September 1890. In April 1891 the plaintiff had gone home to his mother in Vermont and on 6 November of the same year brought his suit in that State of the Union. The company raised in defence the one-year limitation existing in Canadian law. The United States judge rejected this on the basis of the well-known precedents and specifically relied on the authority of Story. Thirty-six years later Judge Learned Hand commented:

---

28. Cf. House of Lords, 25 November 1957 (*National Bank of Greece* v. *Metliss*), where it is held that a foreign extension of a period of limitation must be treated just like a foreign moratorium.

29. 9 *RabelsZ*, 1935, p. 418.

30. *Private International Law*, 6th ed., p. 685.

"It is not necessary therefore to decide how far the rule adopted by us in *Canadian Pac. Ry.* v. *Johnston*, 61 F. 738, 25 L. R. A. 470, is still the law. It has indeed the support of considerable other authority, and, being fathered by Story, it has possibly become too strong now to be overruled. We cannot forbear saying, however, that except in so far as, in application to a given situation, it results in the correct interpretation of the *lex loci contractus*, it is extremely difficult to defend in principle. We leave that question open for the future when it shall arise, for the time being wishing to do no more than disclaim any intention of approving *Canadian Pac. Ry.* v. *Johnston*, by our citation of it in another connection."[31]

So great an authority as Ernst Rabel (III, 2nd ed., p. 534) has also remarked that this doctrine should unquestionably be reformed.[32]

The French courts have adopted another course to justify the preferential treatment of their compatriots. They assume that the limitation statutes of French law, *qua* provisions for the protection of the debtor, are invariably applicable when the debtor is domiciled in France, even when the statute governing the debt itself is a foreign one.[33] This assumption, however, can be overruled in suitable cases:

The subject of the decision of 31 January 1950 was a Norwegian bank's claim against the liquidator of the Paris subsidiary of a former Petrograd bank. As Norwegian law entered the picture, the French defendant had been able to plead the shorter Norwegian term of two years' limitation. This the lower court denied, on the ground that the law of the place of performacence (Paris), with its thirty-year period of prescription, must prevail. The Court of Cassation annulled this decision, because it deprived the debtor of the right of choice inherent in such an international contract.

The case is noteworthy, because the debtor is allowed to rely even on the law of the land of his creditor. As we have already pointed out, the general principle of time-lapse derives from the need for peace and security and confronted with this overriding object the favouring of this or that debtor or creditor pales into triviality. What, then, would the French courts say if this practice of theirs reared its head in the case-law or legislation of other lands?

No less to be condemned, however, as incompatible with the uniform international principle of time-lapse, is a German practice which, where limitation is concerned, consists of splitting the contract between two different national laws, applying one to one part, the other to another. Typical

31. 43 F. 2d., p. 944.
32. In note 127b (*ibid.*) Rabel refers in this connection to J.A. Carnahan, "The full faith and credit clause–its effect on statutes of limitation", 4 *Duke B.J.*, 1954, p. 71.
33. Cf. the authorities cited in Batiffol, No. 615; but also the critical remarks from a German viewpoint by Wengler, 54 *Z.f.d. vergleichende Rechtswissenschaft*, p. 176, and Raape, p. 499; further, the notice by Weill, JZP, 1950-II, p. 5541.

of such decisions is that given by the Hamburg *Oberlandesgericht* on 28 April
1920, reported as follows by Rabel (III,2nd ed., p. 535):

"A German buyer sued an Austrian seller for rescission on the ground of implied warranty and for damages on the ground of express warranty. According to the splitting method, the Appeal Court of Hamburg applied German law to the rescission and Austrian law to the damages, In consequence, the question whether the time of limitation was interrupted by a formal expert inspection of the goods, was answered affirmatively as respects rescission, under the German BGB., § 477 par. 2, and negatively, with respect to the damages, under the Austrian Allg. BGB., § 1977, and an Austrian Supreme Court decision."
Rabel comments:

"With a better choice of law, only Austrian law would have been applicable; under the common law approach, only German law." (*Ibid.*)
Even today the *Bundesgerichtshof* still employs this "splitting" method, [34] one the very principle of which, as already observed in our Introduction, should be rejected in regard not only to limitation but to transnational commercial law in general. Neuhaus too has shown (pp. 85 and 174) how the "homing instinct" in this connection is an unmitigated hindrance to progress.

We have seen how every consideration which leads to divorcing limitation as an institution of law from the factual context in which the question of prescription arises bears the taint of nationalizing the universal principle of time-lapse. Yet even when the dominant international view is followed and limitation questions are assessed in the light of the contract-law with which they are particularly connected (e.g., the law of sale, loan, hire or whatever) the danger of "nationalization" is still not entirely averted. For example, if the underlying contractual relationship, following a very widespread practice, is tested in accordance with the law of the place of performance, this in most cases proves to be the domicile of the defendant and *lex fori* once more wins the day. [35] Certainly, the place of performance may well be a significant element of decision in limitation cases, but in view of the doubtful outcome to which it can lead, it cannot be accepted as the only criterion.

For the purposes of transnational commercial law, reference to the place of conclusion of the contract is more valuable than reference to the place of performance; for one thing, being unequivocal, it neutralizes the "homing instinct". On the other hand, it should not be granted all the significance bestowed on it by French jurists. [36] In the above-mentioned *Don* v. *Lippmann* case, greater weight should have been given to the circumstances of

34. Cf. the decision of 14 February 1958 and the notice thereof, criticizing this method, by Von Caemmerer, in JZ 1959, p. 363, with further references.
35. As Neuhaus pointed out (p. 174).
36. Cf. Weill's note on Cass. 31 January 1950, with further references.

the conclusion of the contract in Paris, detailed above, and this would perhaps have led, despite the English procedural theory, to a different finding. The same applies, in the English *Huber* v. *Steiner* case judged on 17 June 1835, to the fact that the two parties, one of whom had gone off to Switzerland and the other to England, had concluded their agreement in France before setting out on their travels. In this affair the creditor, as a careful businessman, ought to have brought his claim within the French prescriptive period of five years, otherwise he ran the risk of the altered circumstances created by the change of domicile of both parties; moreover, in this particular case, where neither of the parties to the conclusion of the contract had any connection with England, there could not be the slightest doubt that the limitation involved ought to have partaken of substantive, not procedural law.

In a decision of 15 March 1949 concerning a licensing agreement for *Suchard chocolate*, the Swiss *Bundesgericht* took the logical course and held the contracting parties to the American law agreed upon between them, even though they had returned to Switzerland. Judge Learned Hand, on the contrary, in his decision of 4 August 1930, clung to the procedural theory and refused to recognize an agreement as to limitation, even though there was every reason in this case also to view it as a covenant of substantive character.

In the conflict between the *lex loci contractus* and the *lex loci executionis* it is the practice in France, as we know, to allow the debtor a right of choice. This can lead to a dubious under-estimation of the former, as is seen for example in the case decided by the Court of Cassation on 9 January 1934, in which a French party owing a sum for carriage was allowed to invoke the shorter French prescription even though the bill of lading embodied the New York / Antwerp Rules, had been signed in Liverpool and specified Liverpool as the port of destination of the merchandise. Instance are also to be encountered, especially in American and older decisions, where preference was given to the place of performance over that of the contract even when the debtor had changed his domicile. Story's *Leroy* v. *Crowninshield* decision of 1820 [37] is a case in point.

The Prussian case-law of almost as long ago strikes me as more consonant with transnational conceptions. Thus for example, in a case judged by the Royal Prussian *Geheimes Obertribunal* on 15 January 1845, a man in debt to a tailor had moved out of the territory of (Roman) common law, with its 30-year prescription, into the territory of general *Landrecht*, where two-year limitation applied. Sued before the Prussian court, he relied on the latter and alleged the claim barred. The court (which by the way styled the plaintiff an "alien") called upon the defendant for proof of whether—and when—the plaintiff had had cognizance of his new domicile, for the limitation could only have begun to run as from the time of his having so known. There

37. Cf. the American *Leroy* decision of 1820 (Story).

emerges here, therefore, a new and, in my opinion, an important consideration for cases of change of domicile.

Of the various classical methods of resolving conflicts of laws, it is the method which consists in seeking out the "centre of gravity" of the case, or better still, its characteristic make-up, which comes nearest to transnational commercial law. In investigating the characteristic make-up, relations of mere propinquity are not the only consideration. The laws involved are also examined from the practical viewpoint. Once a case is no longer situated in a national, but in the international domain, it becomes like a space-ship in the gravitational fields of two celestial bodies and it is then a question not only of distance but also of power of attraction. The question, furthermore, may concern the properties not merely of two laws, or forces of attraction, but of three or even more.

Hence the right and just solution of an international limitation case demands a comparative approach and can only be found by the duly weighted application of all the laws concerned. This technique having been described in general terms in the Introduction, it will be appropriate at this point to show, with reference to limitation cases, how it works out in practice.

But first an important caveat: haste to construct a general proposition out of individual cases is likely to lead one astray. [38] This of course holds good for all contemporary private international law. Such precipitation is especially dangerous when the necessary distinction between statutory and contractual obligation has not been made at the outset, and also, where appropriate, between contract law and e.g. family law. In the present context we are concerned only with commercial debts and for the most part only with the law of contracts, where each decision is *a priori* significant only for the case itself and can make no claim to significance for a wider circle of third parties. [39]

Another point to be borne in mind is that cases involving limitation are as a rule exceptional cases. For a debtor to be able to refuse performance on an entitled claim is rare, and is as a rule justifiable only by exceptional circumstances. This, experience teaches and a glance at decided cases will confirm. The actual source of limitation cases is very often some wartime complication. A line of such cases can be traced out, from *Don* v. *Lippmann* with its origin in Napoleonic times, through the Mixed Arbitral decision of 21 June 1927 (on a case arising from the first World War and the Versailles Treaty) down to decisions of the Bremen *Landgericht* (8 December 1952) and Munich *Oberlandesgericht* (15 April 1952; 1 October 1959) occasioned by

38. Neuhaus, p. 137, referring to Kleinstein, 26 *University of Chicago Law Review*, 1958, p. 186.

39. *Sic* Neuhaus, p. 63.

the second World War. Other exceptional circumstances favouring the oc-currence of limitation cases are currency upheavals and revaluations, an example being offered by the *Reichsgericht* judgment of 22 October 1929.

Thus cases involving limitation are pre-eminently cases to be treated as exceptional or isolated instances. On the whole, English-speaking courts are more fully alive to this necessity than those of France or Germany and handle such cases accordingly.[40]

On the other hand, despite the dependence of each decision on the peculia-rities of the case, the application of the transnational method to limitation cases is unlikely to succeed if the factual details are allowed to obscure the above-developed principles of time-lapse. Whoever succumbs to the lure of seeking the "seat" of the obligation, is bound to come to grief. Unless some such factor as the sequestration of enemy property is involved, there is never any need in limitation cases to determine the "*situs*" of a claim—and it is in fact not permissible to do so: in considering limitation, a claim must be neither localized, nor immobilized, nor nationalized. The principle of time-lapse can never be pinned down in this way. It is not subservient to national laws. Only, it does not subsist everywhere in exactly the same guise. It has been said of comparative law in general, by one of its most perceptive and experienced teachers, that it will hardly ever lead to a finding of total con-gruence. [41] That is also true of limitation law. That, however, need not deter us from seeking resemblances to the farthest bounds of the possible, and seeing on every possible occasion just how far the decisions of individual cases can be founded on such similarities.

The most frequently recurring difficulty arises out of differences in the period of limitation laid down by the various national laws concerned in the case. These differences can be enormous. In *Don* v. *Lippmann*, for example, the periods were 6 and 30 years, in *British Linen* (1830) 6 and 40, and in *Huber* v. *Steiner* (1835) 5 and 40; in the Dutch-German case of 22 November 1912 they were 2 and 30 years, whereas in the German *Dosenfleisch* case of 10 January 1958 the figures were 6 and 36 months. Once indeed, in the famous German decision of 19 December 1922 on the Swiss *Verlustschein*, the difference was that between 2 years and eternity. Such immense discre-pancies at least make the difficulty clearer than when the difference is relati-vely slight, as for example in the Austro-German case on lawyer's fees decided on 20 March 1936, where it lay between 2 and 3 years, or that decided by Judge Learned Hand on 4 August 1930, where the point at issue was whether the time allowed for complaint was exactly one year or a little longer.

40. Cf. Mr. Justice Holmes in the decision of 16 May 1904 (p. 1071): "We do not go beyond the case before us." In this way the judge clearly separated the case of limitation before him from all others.
41. Nussbaum, p. 48.

At bottom, however, the problem is the same, whether the gap is large or small. As a consequence of classical doctrine, judges have hitherto known no better solution than to nationalize the case and apply one of the periods of limitation on offer, instead of seeking a way to bridge the gap or resolve the difference. It is significant that such a way has been trodden only in the single instance of the *Verlustschein* case, where it would otherwise not have been possible to arrive at any kind of logical solution.

A judge having to decide an international case of limitation will therefore be well advised to take as his premise the notion that, of the national rules of limitation, only a small proportion, which has moreover yet to be established by research, constitutes *jus cogens*, and that apart from these compulsory rules the way nearly always lies open to the adoption of a middle course. In all laws, the same situation prevails in regard to the agreed prolongation of a statutory time-limit: it is admissible and is as a rule treated as a contractual guarantee. In regard to the curtailment of periods there is less general agreement. There would seem to be no relevant case-law, but some academic authorities consider it no less admissible to shorten than to prolong. In Dicey, for example, we find the following comment:

"... a contract may itself provide a period of limitation shorter than that imposed by the general law. Such a provision is analogous to one limiting or agreeing damages and should be regarded as substantive."[42]

This appears to me to ignore the reason why the curtailment of periods of limitation is frowned upon in national laws. Where German law is concerned, an indication of the reason is given in Palandt-Danckelmann on the Civil Code, 27th ed., *ad* § 225, n. 1, according to whom the freedom of contract in respect of periods of limitation is subject to certain exceptions in the case of the very short periods for which the law provides in some instances. Here reference is made to the principle, also valid in the international field, that limitation as such may not be entirely done away with. Something of this nature would occur not only if imprescriptible claims were created but also if a period of limitation were reduced beyond a certain minimum—for example if it were to consist of but one hour. Though it is not permissible to transfer into the international field such national rules concerning periods which cannot be further shortened by agreements, they yet contain a kernel of sense which is worthy of consideration. That the German rules in question are not rigidly conceived can be seen from the fact that they are not applicable to commercial transactions; in this domain, curtailment and prolongation are always admissible.[43] Furthermore, quite a number of countries admit the

---

42. Cf. also Staudinger's *Kommentar zum BGB*, 9th ed., *ad* § 477, n. 3e, which regards the admissibility of shortening as "natural".

43. Brüggeman, in *Reichsgerichtsräte-Kommentar zum HGB*, 2nd ed., 1961, *ad* § 377, n. 188.

shortening of periods without reserve.[44]

In considering these questions, as we have remarked above, there is no need to discriminate between limitation and preclusion. For one thing, the distinction is immaterial in the present context and, for another, its practical feasability is open to doubt, as was shown in discussions over the Convention on the International Sale of Goods. [45] Moreover, one is probably not entitled to premise of an international contract that the parties regarded limitation questions as so remote that they would have signed regardless of the theoretical possibility of such questions one day coming into prominence. Still less may a judge assert that each party to a synallagmatic contract would normally wish to be bound only by his own legal order. [46] The attempt must rather be made, once a broad framework for intermediate solutions is clearly available, to fit the solution of the particular case into this framework.

A first guideline may often be found by studying the genesis of the national statutes in question and the reasons for their adoption. Admittedly, little is to be gained from one consideration which crops up nearly everywhere, namely that the businessman cannot be expected to keep his books and vouchers indefinitely, [47] for it is overshadowed by the more important practical consideration that there must in any case be limits within which the general principle of time-lapse is realized in particular cases. If, in the notorious *Promissory notes* case of 4 January 1862, the *Reichsgericht* had established such limits, something useful might perhaps have resulted. Not only must the motives for the national statutes be fathomed but regard must also be had for the position of jurisprudence and custom. Here there is also room in certain circumstances for a so-called *lex mercatoria*. Often, it is true, little else than an astounding superficiality, or a blatant compromise between material interests, will be found to characterize limitation and time-limits in general.[48]

What one encounters in respect of this question is therefore anything but impressive. From the outset, little scientific value can be attached to the actual periods laid down in national laws, for the purpose which they serve is much rather that of procuring some kind of order than that of promoting international justice. Needless to say, they are conceived and enacted for the

44. Examples in Rabel, *Warenkauf* II, p. 282, n. 86.
45. Riese, 29 *RabelsZ*, 1965, p. 61. See note 48 below.
46. Hamburg *Oberlandesgericht*, 29 October 1958 (*Braugerste* – brewer's yeast).
47. *Sic* Hawkland on UCC, p. 270.
48. It is characteristic that the only information Rabel (9 *RabelsZ*, 1935, p. 345) was able to convey about Article 52 of the draft uniform law of sale, regarding the length of the preclusive time-limit, was that the Council of the Rome Institute had decided it and had considered that two years were necessary. However, at the time of writing, Uncitral, as its fifth session (10 April to 5 May 1972) has approved a draft convention on the limitation of claims which provides for a four-year time-limit.

realm of national, not international law. They come into being under the influence, if not with the actual participation, of combinations of interests in which external trade may well be represented, but only as one voice in the choir. Herein may be found the deeper-lying causes of the fact that the limitation of claims has been made an element of the terms of business in international trade. This familiar fact alone is a powerful counter-argument against those who without closer inquiry would regard rules of limitation as *jus cogens*.

Perceptive judges have always approached each case—not only, of course, in the domain of limitation—with the aim of respecting, rather than appearances, its underlying reality. We have already met the example of the prolongation of a limitation period which, being as such of doubtful validity, was construed as a contractual guarantee.[49] The American judge Sutter, in the *Harrisburg* judgment of 15 November 1886, used a particularly striking interpretation in order to avoid an unsatisfying outcome which could have resulted from the procedural theory of limitation, construing the contract in such a way as to find that a resolutive condition had been agreed instead of, or in addition to, a limitation of claims (see the further discussion of this case, below).

More particularly, where there are permanent business-relations between the parties, it must be presumed that they intend to resolve any disputes that may arise by mutual accommodation. If therefore any inadvertent disagreement over a period of limitation, or other time-limit, should occur between them, the matter should be decided on the basis that appeal to their separate domestic laws is less consonant with the business relationship than for them to split the difference and share the loss. This, as a general guideline, will require to be nuanced according to the facts of each case, a process in which the further considerations dealt with below may have a part to play.

In reflecting on such older decisions as those in the *British Linen* (1830) and *Don* (1837) cases, with their enormous disparities of time-limits, one may well call to mind the old and tested empirical maxim of the model effect of better-quality law (see Introduction). In the law of limitation, this is borne out by the fact that, from the age of Roman law right down to the present, the extremely long periods of limitation which were originally the rule have in all legal systems given place to shorter ones, to meet the needs of

---

49. In the "canned meat" (*Dosenfleisch*) decision of 10 January 1958, the *Bundesgerichtshof* rescinded a decision of the Hamburg *Oberlandesgericht* and said that the parties were agreed as to the absence from English law of any remedy of annulment of sale on account of material defect (*Wandlung*) as known to German sales law; however, the claim could be understood in the sense that damages corresponding to a guarantee were demanded, and to that the time-limit laid down in § 477 of the Civil Code would not apply.

commerce where certain trades or occupations are concerned. Thus the shorter periods are the more modern. Now no judge can be called upon, in the absence of some exceptional indication from the parties in that sense, to remain behind the times in the doctrine he applies and, hence, the findings he may reach. *A fortiori*, in the international field, where he is bound only by the mandatory provisions of national law and is otherwise free, the judge must decide in accordance with contemporary law and in favour, moreover, of the party able to rest his case on the more contemporary law. It would have been up to the other party, if he wished to rely on outdated law, to secure an agreement for its use.

It is not possible to achieve such results by the "nationalization" of the contract, and the classical method, as evinced for example in the decision handed down by the *Reichsgericht* on 22 November 1912, has therefore no future:

In this case, a German in business in Rotterdam as a forwarding agent, under his German company name, was sued in Germany for some "compensation" unspecified by a Dutchman who had been working for him in Rotterdam. The defendant put up as a defence the two-year limitation period provided for by § 196 (15) of the German Civil Code, but the plaintiff relied on Dutch law, which barred the claim only after 30 years. Choice of law was not an element in the case. The court "nationalized" the contract in favour of the plaintiff from Rotterdam and 30-year prescription.

Now here the periods of limitation differed in the proportion of 15 to one, and the Dutch prescription of 30 years scarcely corresponded (as it would have been for the plaintiff to demonstrate) to modern law. Substantive justice, therefore, was rather on the side of the defendant. The report of the case unfortunately contains no indication as to the reasons for overruling the shorter period or by how much it was exceeded (though there is some mention of conciliatory negotiations). Having already raised the test of good faith in the context of a preliminary question, the *Reichsgericht* would here have had a good opportunity of applying the same test in the matter of limitation. (It is true that the *Reichsgericht* stated on 12 February 1913 that periods of limitation were formal in nature, must be uniformly applied and could not, for reasons derived from the facts of a given case or on equitable grounds, be maintained in one case and disregarded in another. However, that was in the context of an entirely domestic case, where both parties were subject to, and must have been familiar with, the same statutes of limitation.)

The model effect of a law may rest on its contemporaneity, but may also in certain circumstances be derived from the fact that it represents the law of the wider circle of humanity. This is a fair presumption when rules of a more or less technical nature, such as rules of limitation, are involved. The Munich *Oberlandesgericht* could have taken such considerations into account in arriving at its decision of 15 April 1953, which was founded instead on somewhat specious grounds of place of performance and *bona fides*:

189

A State-owned company in Berlin had during the second World War sold a Munich firm army-huts with the fixtures and delivered them through another Munich firm. Choice of law did not arise. The Munich defendant pleaded 4-year limitation under § 196 (1), subparagraphs 1 and 2, of the German Civil Code. In Bavaria, where the wartime limitation-freeze remained in effect up to 31 March 1951, a suit interrupting limitation had been brought in the nick of time on 28 March 1951, but this was not the case in Berlin, where in the absence of extended wartime legislation the suspension of limitation had come to an end on 31 December 1945, so that the bar was already operative at the time of claim. The *Reichsgericht* found itself driven to declare: "It was not bad faith on the plaintiff's part not to take the view in this legal situation that Berlin was the place of performance."

It would have been more convincing to say that it had been equally impossible for either party to foresee the situation that would develop. The risk it represented could not be apportioned according to the parties' relative proximity to the risk, for both were equally near. Nor was any other dissection of the risk a possibility. This being so, the proper limitation-law to apply was the law which had been established with effect for three of the four occupation-zones, while no corresponding regulations had been introduced in Berlin. The regulations in the three occupation-zones were therefore endowed with model effect vis-à-vis the comparative legal vacuum in Berlin. The report of the case unfortunately does not indicate why the State-owned company had been so tardy in bringing suit.

A further aid to right judgment is to be found in the impermissibility of unreasonable decisions, even if this is only a means of obviating gross injustice. We find this principle underlying limitation-decisions in every country. Thus Lord Tindal observed as long ago as 17 June 1835, in *Huber* v. *Steiner*: "To maintain a position so contrary to reason, very strong authority must be expected" (p. 85). There are numerous statutes which speak of "reasonable time" and cases of courts applying the test of "not unreasonable" results to determine what time-limit is appropriate. [50] Conversely, American judges sometimes apply the test of constitutionality to statutory limits, that is to say, they examine the law to see whether it is compatible with the requirement that decisions must not be unreasonable. [51] If this can be done in the context of a closed system, how much more should it be done in the open context of international contracts!

If the parties themselves have merely agreed with regard to some time-limit that it must be reasonable, it is for the judge himself to determine the limit. [52]

The principle of the impermissibility of unreasonable decisions is especially appropriate for application to cases where the general circumstances have

50. Cf. for the American decision of 13 February 1946 (*Texas Motor Coach*).
51. *Sic* Judge Holmes in the *Davis* v. *Mills* decision of 16 May 1904, p. 171.
52. House of Lords, 16 May 1955 (*Tool Metal*).

undergone an unforeseen change. Such cases are particularly frequent in matters of limitation. An argument in this sense is to be found in the House of Lords decision of 25 November 1957, when the question was whether a Greek statute could influence the limitation of claims arising out of an Anglo-Greek loan contract. Viscount Simonds said: "If I have to base my opinion on any principles, I would venture to say it was the principle of rational justice" (p. 525). On the continent of Europe, where it is less customary to invoke the principle of reasonableness, similar results are achieved by other means—in Germany, above all with the aid of the good-faith principle. [53] Changes of domicile by one or both parties also represent altered circumstances, though not when they were due to *force majeure*. They will be further discussed below, in connection with the subject of good faith.

Municipal rules of limitation are of a formal nature. In principle, therefore, they cannot be applied in different ways according to the facts of each case. [54] In the international domain this is naturally not so. Mandatory provisions have of course to be respected once the national system to which they belong is adopted as the proper law, but apart from that there is only the general principle of time-lapse, which on the international plane cannot very well be applied other than elastically. This means that in the individual case it may be given a slant which benefits either the creditor or the debtor. At the present stage in the development of transnational law, there is not the remotest possibility of embodying such variations in a system with the solidity of municipal legal structures. Nevertheless, the most prominent aspects can already be discerned and certain guidelines laid down.

It is the agreed view internationally that certain special circumstances should be regarded as working in the creditor's favour. Thus in a case of fraud there can be no limitation under civil law until the criminal limitation has run its course. There does not appear to be any explicit jurisprudence on this point, but it would appear to be implicit in the widespread case-law (particularly American) which exists in regard to concealed defects in purchased goods. In such cases, as is well known, any agreed time-limit for complaints or statutory bar becomes inoperative. [55] Again, it is also regarded as a consideration in favour of the creditor if the point at issue between the parties has been the subject of negotiations or other efforts to reach a solution, or if a

53. On suspension of limitation: during the war, see e.g. Bremen *Landsgericht*, 8 October 1952, and Munich *Oberlandesgericht*, 15 April 1953; on account of uncertainty over revaluation, *Reichsgericht* 22 October 1929; on account of misjudgment, *Kammergericht* 28 February 1931. On the other hand, refusal of legal aid and ignorance of the law were not recognized as sufficient cause for a suspension of limitation: *Reichsgericht* 22 October 1929, Treves *Landgericht* 20 December 1955.

54. *Sic*, for Germany, Soergel/Siebert *ad* § 194 BGB, n. 6, with reference to *Reichsgericht*, JW 1913, p. 485.

55. Cf. e.g., the American *Catsup* decision of 17 November 1937.

so-called *pactum de non petendo* has even been signed.

In connection with the proper time-limit for notification of defects, the following was stated in the American decision of 5 October 1964 in the *Sperry Rand* case (p. 370):

"Industrial Supply did not know and could not be expected to ascertain, except by use and experience, the functional abilities and capa-
cities of the electronic equipment, with its transistors, tubes and diodes,
its varicolored maze of wiring, its buttons and switches, and the supplementing of machines and devices for the punching of cards and
others for the sorting thereof. And, of course, the personnel of Industrial Supply could not be expected to understand the processes by
which a set of these modern miracle-makers perform their tasks.
Whether the trial use of the equipment was an inspection or its
equivalent we need not decide. We see no merit in the contention that
the termination of the lease by the purchase of the equipment operated
in some fashion as a rejection of the opportunity of continuing the
inspection. The substantial rights of the parties, we think, were the
same as if there had been no intervening lease. An inspection, if required, could have been made after the sale had been completed as well
as before."

Here, even though the case was purely national, we encounter a very clear statement of something which would be all the more likely to apply in an international case. The time allowable for submission of complaints, which the law requires to be notified without delay, is here deemed to be particular-ly long on account of the peculiar nature of the case. The American decision of 4 September 1942 affords an illustration of the taking into account of common remedial efforts and of a technically somewhat imperfect filling-machine. Conciliatory talks or resumed negotiations also enter into the factual background to the two *Reichsgericht* decisions of 22 December 1912 and 20 March 1936; unfortunately the report does not make it clear in either case whether due weight was given to these circumstances. It is however noteworthy that even in German law, according to Palandt-Danckelmann on the Civil Code (*ad* § 194, n. 3), the statutory periods of limitation are not conclusive in such cases, unless they are consonant with "the requirements of honest trade and the circumstances of the case".

In all countries, the notion of misuse of law plays a part in matters of limitation, though under various conceptual guises and often not pinpointed by any name—sometimes, for example, it is subsumed in a general reference to bad faith. [56] Instances of *prima facie* misuse of law would include the case of the debtor who changes his domicile and then claims the benefit of a

56. It is so in German law. Cf. especially Soergel/Siebert *ad* § 194 BGB, n. 17, and
more particularly *ad* § 242, n. 167, with reference to the international principle of *venire*

shorter limitation-period effective there. This does not occur in English or American law, on account of the procedural doctrine of limitation. On that same account, such older English decisions as *Huber* v. *Steiner* (1835) and *Don* v. *Lippmann* (1837) have no contemporary validity. The decision handed down by the Prussian *Geheimes Obertribunal* on 15 January 1845 is less open to objection, as it did at least place on the defendant the burden of proving whether and when the plaintiff had knowledge of the former's new domicile, so that the limitation could be computed as from that date. The *Obertribunal* did not give any special reason for this decision.

The decision was criticized by Nussbaum (p. 235) for another reason, namely its obsolete application of the domicile principle. It is correct that the debtor may adduce his own change of domicile if in the final analysis the cause of it is imputable to the creditor. A comparable situation arose in the American *Canadian Pacific* case decided on 29 May 1894, where the plaintiff had left Canada for his mother's home in Vermont following injury in an accident at work. Judge Learned Hand, it is true, dissociated himself from that judgment in his own of 14 August 1930, but that was on wholly other grounds; and even *Canadian Pacific* does not embody the considerations here put forward, but relies on the procedural doctrine of limitation. Quite apart from that, it should be borne in mind that the case concerned damages in tort, thus not the limitation of contractual claims. What difference this makes is a question we must leave aside. Judge Learned Hand declared:

> "While there are exceptions when the defendant has misled the plaintiff who has acted upon the strength of a promise, in such cases the question is really whether these facts create a contract not to use the defense, though this is usually disguised under the term 'estoppel' " (p. 943).

It is the strict decision of the Swiss Federal Tribunal in the *Suchard* case (15 March 1949) which corresponds the most closely to the internationally agreed view. Not only did the court definitively reject the procedural doctrine but it also stated (p. 64):

> "The Federal Tribunal has held that it is the will of the parties at the moment of the conclusion of the contract which is decisive: 'In fact, the applicable law cannot change. A legal relationship exists by virtue of the law on the basis of which it came into being ... The foundation of its existence cannot be modified after the event. At the most one might admit a change when the parties have provided for it from the outset' (RO 62 II 126). There is good reason to abide by this jurisprudence, except that one may also reserve the position in the event that,

---

contra factum proprium; also, with special reference to the treatment of time-limits, *idem, ad* § 252, n. 170. See also the jurisprudence in Palandt/Danckelmann, *ad* § 194a, n. 3.

in the case of a long-term contract, the circumstances of its execution undergo a radical transformation in the course of time. In any event, moreover, for a clause indicating the applicable law to be modified while the contract is in force would require a formal declaration of the parties, above all if the dispute to be settled has already risen."

It is a pity that the Swiss court did not, in this decision, come to terms with the old American decisions in *Leroy* (1820) and *Bulger* (1831), with Story or with Schlinck's article in *Rabel's Zeitschrift*, 1935, p. 418.

In this connection there are also certain German cases to be mentioned because, instead of getting at the underlying transnational principle, the courts in question unfortunately reached their decisions either by outright dismissal of one side of the argument or through tortuous and barely intelligible expedients:

On 18 April 1956 the Hattingen *Amtsgericht* allowed a German soldier to put up a defence of limitation against a claim for maintenance brought against him by the Dutch child he had illegitimately fathered during the occupation, because Dutch law was applicable and the objection of guile (*Arglist*), with which it was possible in German law to parry limitation, could not be permitted since, according to advice received from the Netherlands Consulate-General in Düsseldorf, there was no rule to that effect in Dutch law.

Here counsel for the plaintiff could certainly have obtained a more favourable result if he had not rested content with the Consulate-General's advice. For that matter, the court itself should not have contented itself with that advice, considering the unhappy result to which it led.

On 6 July 1934 the *Reichsgericht* had to decide a complicated case, involving the procurement of funds through the discounting of a bill in England, in which the debtor alleged that a certain notification had not reached him in time. Now the debtor was domiciled both in Poland and in Germany, but only the German address was apparent from the bill. The *Reichsgericht* rightly held the debtor responsible, but only on account of this lack of clarity for which he himself had been to blame.

The decision given by the German *Bundesgerichtshof* on 9 June 1960 in a case concerning the consignment of chocolate from Chicago to New Orleans has been exhaustively analysed. [57] This dispute still remained unsettled after three years, on account of the complex questions of *renvoi* involved. The *Bundesgerichtshof* sent the case back to the *Oberlandesgericht*. If the no-nonsense approach of the Swiss Federal Tribunal had been adopted, the case could have been settled simply and rapidly on the basis of transnational law.

There are some cases in which the misuse of law is particularly plain to see, because the party making use of the law in question has at the same time to expose himself to the countercharge of having, by some positive gesture,

57. By Kegel, in *Die Grenze von Qualifikation und Renvoi*, Opladen 1962.

194

given the other side reason to believe he would not avail himself of that law. In all legal systems, such cases form a special group denoted by different terms and given various doctrinal explanations. Thus in Germany they are denoted by references to *Treu und Glauben* (good faith and fair dealing), *Vertrauensschutz* (protection of confidence), *Arglist* (deceitful guile or dishonest cunning), *Schutz des Rechtsscheins* (protection of persons trusting in the semblance of legality; protection of good-faith judgment) or *Verwirkung* (forfeiture or defeasance). In France the reference is to *pouvoirs apparents*, and in England and the United States to "estoppel" or "laches". The Latin expression *venire contra factum proprium* is also found. The principle holds good in private as in public law,[58] and it is not merely a question of equity. A limitation case involving the estoppel principle was that decided by the American judge, Learned Hand, on 4 August 1930 (see above).

In certain special cases the additional requirement of positive conduct should not be pressed too hard. For example, if the parties are in constant business relations it may be permissible in an international commercial case to regard silence as signifying the acceptance of an agreement, even if this would not be possible in the context of the national laws concerned.[59] Usually, however, a case of this kind will be treated directly from the general angle of misuse of law and not as a case of forfeiture.

While the concept of misuse of law may in blatant cases lurk behind estoppel or forfeiture, in less obvious cases it may don the simple garb of the test of good faith. It is, at any rate, a most elastic concept where international commerce is concerned;[60] and, significantly enough, in public international law also, to the extent that the law of nations admits the time-lapse principle, the absence of statutory prescription leaves no other course in the fixing of time-limits than to proceed according to the merits of each case as tested against the requirement of good faith.[61]

As is well known, use of that test as a basis of judgment is particularly in keeping with juristic thought in Germany, and it accordingly is so used there in cases of limitation. An example is the *Dosenfleisch* judgment given by the *Bundesgerichtshof* on 10 January 1958. It is however striking that in the

58. See English *Volcaan* decision of 27 March 1958 and the German decision of 12 May 1928. For further German private law references, see Soergel/Siebert, *ad* § 194 BGB, n. 2. For American law, see under "estoppel" in *Black's Law Dictionary*. For public international law, see article on "estoppel" (by Eberhard Menzel) in Strupp-Schlochhauer (ed.), *Wörterbuch des Völkerrechts*, and more especially Bin Cheng, *General Principles of Law*, London 1953, pp. 141 ff.

59. Germano-Romanian MAT, 16 June 1925 (*Negreanu*), p. 203.

60. The special requirements of international trade are discussed by Philippe Kahn, *La Vente commerciale internationale*, Paris 1961, p. 144, and Rabel, 17 *RabelsZ*, 1952, p. 224, in connection with periods of limitation. See also Weill, note on the decision of 31 January 1950.

61. *Cf. Ambatielos* decision of 6 March 1956.

strictly contemporary Italo-German case decided on 14 February 1958 the same court, after having held that in international commerce it was not possible to assume that a foreigner under different domestic law was bound to notify defects without delay, failed to apply the good-faith test which the case then called for. In another case involving a time-bar the Munich *Oberlandesgericht*, on 15 April 1953, applied the test of good faith when the facts would have permitted solution on a different basis. Outside Germany, as most cases turn on the relative immediacy of notice of defect, the notion of "reasonable time" has enabled courts to reach decisions without recourse to the concept of good faith.[62]

We have so far taken as our premise that the principle of time-lapse, while transnational, is effective not in the absolute but only relatively speaking— that is to say, only when a party invokes it. But does the right to invoke it repose in all respects on national law? And can such national law be so much part and parcel of the *ordre public* of the country in question that the judge may neither effect nor countenance any deviation? Leaving aside the sphere of the Anglo-American procedural doctrine, which will remain to be considered, the answer must be negative. This has undoubtedly been recognized in Italy, where the Court of Cassation, as quoted by Rabel (III, 2nd ed., p. 527), observed on 13 November 1931:

> "Although it cannot be denied that limitation of action is founded also on considerations of public order (which are, however, joined by other, not less important, reasons), this does not mean that it belongs to the international public order. Therefore, limitation is not considered by the court without party request; it can be waived after the time has lapsed; and the time is suspended if impossibility to sue is proved."

The Italian party had submitted that a provision of Soviet law regarding the interruption of prescription conflicted with Italian *ordre public*. The court, on the contrary, held that the Soviet rule expressed an international principle and therefore could not stand in conflict with the *ordre public* of Italy. The Italian supreme court further held, in a decision of 3 March 1933, that concern for Italian *ordre public* would not in itself be sufficient to justify maintaining a 5-year Italian period of limitation as against an Argentinian period of 3 years.

The intrinsically justified reluctance of judges to integrate statutes of limitation with *ordre public* may even upon occasion be taken too far. This was so in the case of the *Reichsgericht* decision of 22 November 1912, when the

---

62. Cf. the American decision of 13 February 1946 and the decision of the Franco-German MAT of 9 July 1922 in *Albert* v. *Gerstle*. On the concept of *"unverzüglich"* or "promptly", cf. in particular Rabel, *Warenkauf* II, p. 213; Knapp-Kalinsky, in Honnold (ed.), *Unification ...*, p. 101; Hawkland, p. 233, and Graveson/Cohn, *Uniform Laws on International Sales Act 1967*, London 1968, *ad* Article 11 of the Hague Sales Rules.

preference given to the Dutch 30-year limitation over the more sensible German period of two years was accompanied with the explicit rider that the 15-times longer period did not offend German *ordre public*. We have already pointed out that this decision itself offended against the transnational principle that the better law has model effect.

It would step outside the scope of the present work to enter thoroughly into the question of when limitation periods are matters of *ordre public* and when not. The decision given by the Regensburg *Landgericht* on 10 September 1954 may serve as an example of a case in which a foreign time-bar was examined in terms of *ordre public* and its application therefore refused, the court holding that the 2-year time-limit allowed in French law for the submission of maintenance claims on behalf of natural children was incompatible with German *ordre public*. The model for the ascertainment of the right *via media* between conflicting national statutes of limitation remains the *Reichsgericht* decision of 19 December 1922 in the case of the Swiss *Verlustschein*, when the court declared:

> "Having, on the basis of Article 30 of the Civil Code Introductary Act, ruled out application of the specific provision of Swiss law which in itself would have been competent, the appeal judge should have gone on to ask himself whether the competence of Swiss law in general fell to the ground with the exclusion of that one directly competent provision, or whether he should not rather revert to Swiss law for the purpose of stopping the legal gap thus created. Only if he found that the gap could not be stopped from Swiss law was he entitled to apply German law. But even then it remained his duty to ascertain among German statutes that particular provision which most closely approximated to the juristic thought of the foreign law."

Ever since the days of the Mixed Arbitral Tribunals, with their significant jurisprudence, there has been an increasing number of references in theoretical writings to the necessity of recognizing an *ordre public international* over and above the various national *ordres publics*. [63]

The Anglo-American doctrine, according to which the plea of limitation is a procedural remedy and not a substantive right, has the automatic consequence of making all limitation law a constituent part of the *ordre public* of the countries in question, so that it can be discarded only for the sake of an overriding *ordre public international*—which seems possible solely in certain favourable circumstances. Yet is this procedural doctrine really so impregnable as it has appeared for so long? We have already, in earlier pages, drawn attention to certain signs of the contrary, and it should also be recalled that

---

63. Gutzwiller, *Internationales Jahrbuch für Schiedsgerichtswesen* (Nussbaum) III, p. 151; Cavaglieri, note on the decision given by the Italian Court of Cassation on 13 November 1931 (Col. 29).

even in England and the United States the publicists are anything but certain on the point. [64] In jurisprudence, the procedural doctrine has at times been to blame for decisions which have incurred almost unanimous disapproval. [65] The series of English or American judges who for all their allegiance to precedent have seen fit to qualify their decisions begins with Story and includes such names as Blackburn and Holmes. [66] In 1949 the Swiss Federal Tribunal, in a carefully reasoned decision, rejected the procedural doctrine outright.[67]

There have also been several attempts in judicial practice to overcome the doctrinal antinomy between continental law on the one hand, and English and American law on the other. It will be necessary to return to one or other of the approaches used in these attempts, according to the nature of the case. In every case it will be possible to find a way. The guiding thread will be the understanding that the lapse of claims with time is a uniform principle, whether it is crystallized in substantive or in procedural law. [68] Particularly striking is the dictum of Celsius quoted by Rabel (III, 2nd ed., p. 491): *nihil aliud est actio quam ius quod sibi debeatur iudicio persequendi.* Thus in the two thousand years since Celsius it is merely two variant translations of the same principle that have exercised the jurist. They should not be accorded such importance that the principle itself can, thanks to the procedural variant, be "nationalized" and its transnational character sacrified.

This can be avoided if limitation is wherever possible, without prejudice to its procedural character, construed at the same time as a resolutive condition of the obligation. Starting from the statutory periods of notice which

64. In Dicey-Morris/Treitel, 8th ed., p. 1094, the problem is laid bare in all its confusion and the writer's own uncertainty thereby revealed. Cheshire (6th ed., p. 685) even goes so far as to say in this connection that "English law, through its failure to interpret foreign rules in its context, has gone astray"; cf., above all, Rabel, *Conflict* III, 2nd ed., pp. 520 ff.

65. As in the case of the German *Reichsgericht's* decision of 4 January 1882 on the limitation of Tennessee promissory notes, and the English decision of 7 June 1869 on limitation in the Isle of Man (see next footnote).

66. Cf. Story, in the *Leroy* decision of 1820, and Schlinck, 9 *RabelsZ*, 1935, pp. 418 ff. Blackburn, in the English *Harris & Adams* v. *Quine* decision of 7 June 1969: "If the plaintiffs could have shown that the law of the Isle of Man extinguished the right as well as the remedy, and this had been the issue determined by the Manx court, that would have been a different matter." Holmes in the American *Davies* v. *Mills* decision of 16 May 1904: "In cases where it has been possible to escape from that qualification ('procedural') by a reasonable distinction, courts have been willing to treat limitations of time as standing like other limitations and cutting down the defendant's liability wherever he is sued."

67. *Suchard*, 15 March 1949.

68. Certain pronouncements of Nussbaum (p. 48), Batiffol (No. 615, with Italian case-law) and Rabel (*Conflict* III, 2nd ed., p. 491) are surely to be understood in this sense.

always have this character, American courts have already taken this course. In this connection, special mention should be made of the decision given by Judge Learned Hand on 4 August 1930 (p. 942), when he took up the arguments whereby Chief Justice Waite broke new ground in the *Harrisburg* judgment of 15 November 1886. It may very well be a mistake, however, to base one's decision on whether the right is actually extinguished by limitation or not. For the transnational principle itself is concerned not with extinction but with extinguishability through objection. To that extent one may adopt Ernst Rabel's conclusion (III, 2nd ed., p. 506):

> "In fact the right of a debtor to bar the action of his creditor, by invoking its limitation by lapse of time, is always a substantive right, even though the lapse of time does not extinguish the claim and is not inherent in the debt."

The shorter the periods of limitation in international commerce, the more critical is the date on which the period begins to run. In the old easy-going days, it was taken more or less for granted that the period could not begin to run until the opposing party had knowledge of the circumstances making limitation possible. Witness the decision given by the Royal Prussian *Geheimes Obertribunal* on 15 January 1845, already cited above, which did not even think it necesssary to refer to good faith. Today, however, in the particular sphere of international commerce and more especially the sale of goods, it is most probably transnational law that the limitation begins to run independently of knowledge. The German *Reichsgericht* decision which was the first to hold knowledge immaterial relied for the purpose on the explanatory preamble to the Civil Code.[69]

The Uniform Commercial Code stipulates in Section 2-725 (2):

> "A cause of action accrues when the breach occurs, regardless of the aggrieved party's lack of knowledge of the breach. A breach of warranty occurs when tender of delivery is made, except that where a warranty explicitly extends to future performance of the goods and discovery of the breach must await the time of such performance the cause of action accrues when the breach is or should have been discovered."

Hawkland (I, p. 271) comments thereon:

> "At first blush this rule seems unduly hard. It is justified, however, by the philosophy that commercial interests are best served by quickly bringing finality to commercial transactions."

However, the basic transnational rule requires to be carefully nuanced in particular cases. Here national regulations may serve as a model. For example, the limitation of a claim for annulment or reduction of price runs from the date of knowledge if the seller has deceitfully kept silent about the defect

69. *Reichsgericht*-Warn. 1911, Nr. 369.

(§ 477 (1), German Civil Code). A similar rule is to be found, for example, among the Hague Sales Rules (Art. 49). [70]

What is certainly transnational commercial law is the principle that a period of limitation which has already begun to run may be interrupted under certain circumstances, and that when the interruption comes to an end the whole period begins afresh. That being so, it would be wrong to leave it to a national legal system to spell out the rules governing the interruption (or the suspension, in certain cases). [71] The decision whether the limitation is interrupted or not should not depend on whether the case is referred to a national legal system with stringent requirements or to one allowing more latitude. In transnational law it will be sufficient if the creditor has served some probative form of notice or reminder. [72] Rules as stringent as the German, which make interruption conditional on the institution of legal proceedings and in international commercial cases further require that the foreign court proceedings should be recognized by the German courts, are inappropriate for transnational law, and the question of referring to them need not arise, unless the parties have expressly or tacitly agreed that German law shall apply. Even in German law, moreover, a certain trend to the facilitation of trade is discernible, for example, in the admission of a proposal for the preservation of evidence as a ground of interruption (Civil Code, § 477 (2)); it is satisfying to note that on 28 April 1920 the Hamburg *Oberlandesgericht* decided an Austro-German case as if, according to the Austrian law applicable to it, the interruption of limitation through a proposal for the preservation of testimony would have been possible in Austria too. The court could have spared itself the tortuous process of setting off one law against the other if it had applied transnational commercial law.

As has already been suggested, the famous English decision of 26 May 1837 in *Don* v. *Lippmann* must be considered erroneous. Here a French creditor had obtained from a French court a regular judgment by default against his British debtor, a judgment which applied at one and the same time to a loan debt and to the bill of exchange made out to cover it. This necessarily interrupted the limitation. It is quite another question whether, in transnational law, the period of limitation was not also suspended on account of the state of war between France and Britain.

It is doubtless also a rule of transnational law that the course of a period of limitation is interrupted if the debtor acknowledges the claim. However, what constitutes such an acknowledgment is not a question which ought to be answered in terms of a single national legal system: what is decisive is what is

70. Cf. Graveson/Cohn, p. 81.

71. A doubt expressed by Schnitzer II, 3rd ed., p. 591.

72. *Sic* Bremen *Landgericht* 8 October 1952, following an earlier decision of the Bremen *Amtsgericht*, 22 November 1951.

regarded as acknowledgment as between the participants in international commerce. The Munich *Landgericht* was therefore right, in its decision of 1 October 1949, to refuse to see an acknowledgment in the letter written by a German purchaser to inform his Austrian supplier that payment was blocked through a prohibition imposed by the American occupation authorities (Military Government Law No. 53).

An independent transnational rule must be found with regard to suspension no less than interruption. If certain treaties have taken the course of referring questions of interruption and suspension to the law of the country where suit is brought, [73] this is certainly no path to the future. How badly international practice is served by this stopgap can be seen from Hawkland's wry comment (I, p. 272) on Section 2-725 (4) of the Uniform Commercial Code:

> "This provision permits the continuation of the common-law rule that stops the statute of limitations from running while the defendant is out of the State and the like."

Furthermore, we can easily do without such an expedient. For centuries the maxim *contra non valentem non currit praescriptio* has been accepted in every country. Although, like every principle, this maxim does not provide instant and definitive solutions but requires flexible application to the particular case, [74] that by no means disqualifies it as transnational commercial law. On the contrary: various leading decisions have expressly mentioned it.[75] In particular, the Italian Court of Cassation declared, in a decision cited with approval by Rabel (III, 2nd ed., p. 527), that *contra non valentem* was a general principle and that its application in accordance with Russian civil law did not offend Italian *ordre public*. In a note on this decision (col. 29) Prof. Cavaglieri suggests that the principle should even be accounted part of international *ordre public* and as such capable of overruling any national *ordre public*. *A fortiori*, when in a given national legal system this principle belongs to *ordre public*, it may overrule conflicting national law.[76]

In the absence of statutory provision for the suspension of limitation, *contra non valentem* may also be treated as an extension of the good-faith principle. On 22 October 1929 it was so treated by the German *Reichsgericht*

---

73. Cf. the references in Rabel, *Conflict* III, 2nd ed., p. 536.

74. In the last century the celebrated German pandectist Dernburg gave a similar caution (*Pandekten* I, Berlin 1892, p. 347).

75. Cf. the illustrations from public international law in Bin Cheng, p. 384. In German law the principle has been enshrined in § 302 of the Civil Code. For French commercial law, see Philippe Kahn, *La Vente commerciale internationale*, p. 144, and the French decision of 16 March 1949 (Paris: concerning a gift between spouses) and 28 June 1970.

76. *Sic* German jurisprudence on wartime statutory suspension of limitation, e.g., Bremen *Landgericht*, 8 October 1952.

in favour of a commercial agent from Łwow (Lemberg) who was suing for his commission, "considering that the idea of revaluation had not yet materialized in German jurisprudence and the enforcement of claims was therefore legally impossible". A similar line was taken by the Prussian *Kammergericht* on 28 February 1931, in deciding that a Polish worker might rely on an—erroneous—judgment of the Potsdam *Landgericht* concerning the legitimacy of a child and that the case was one of *force majeure* whereby the period allowed for the filing of disclaimer was suspended on account of misjudgment. On 15 April 1953 the Munich *Oberlandesgericht* had to deal with the rare event of a difference in the rules of suspension due to the partition of Germany; it decided in accordance with the test of good faith but, as is explained above, it could have reached the same conclusion more directly by applying the transnational principle of model effect.

Part Five

THE PRACTICE OF TRANSNATIONAL ADJUDICATION
("Binomial Adjudication")

I. *Language and interpretation*

Faced with the problem of deciding which law he should hold applicable to an international case, a careful judge will take heed not to solve it *à la* Procrustes through overhasty "nationalization". For, unless it corresponds to the parties' valid choice of law, to consign such a case *in toto* to a single municipal system deserves no better epithet than Procrustean. The "nationalization" of the international is only apposite when that is what the parties want; in all other cases the judge must keep steadily in view the goal of reaching a decision which is compatible with the national laws of both parties—a "binomial" decision,[1] as we may henceforth call it. On the one hand this requirement facilitates his task, inasmuch as he may begin to seek this compatible decision by the lights of his own domestic law, without prior immersion in a foreign system. On the other hand it aggravates it, because the critical aspects of the case will necessitate his drawing upon foreign law for comparative purposes—a chore he could avoid if he could give his homing instinct free rein and subordinate the whole dispute to his own law. It would in any case be a misconception to suppose that there is any one technique of

---

1. The literal meaning of "binomial", in its Greek derivation, is "two-law" (*bi* + *nomos*: see e.g. *Webster's New Collegiate* Dictionary, 1959 edn.), and it is borrowed for present purposes not from Linnaean botany and zoölogy (where the sense is influenced by the Latin *nomen*), but from mathematics, where it denotes expressions of the $(a \pm b)$ type. Moreover, just as the "binomial theorem" enable such expressions to be raised to any power without actually performing the intervening operations, so "binomial adjudication" enables a transnational decision to be reached without actually plumbing the depths of both national laws. The ease with which classically derived terms can be slotted into different languages was also a factor in the choice of this expression.

The Greek word *nomos* was probably introduced into German legal studies by James Goldschmidt (JW 1924, p. 245) in the word *Nomomachie* (literally "conflict of laws"!) which he coined to denote the misapplication of concepts in the process of law-making. Carl Schmitt subsequently alluded to this neologism when he himself, in the later part of his career, published a work on *Der Nomos der Erde im Völkerrecht des Jus publicum Europaeum*, Cologne 1950 (cf. also his *Verfassungslehre*, 3rd unaltered edn, Berlin 1957, p. 142).

binomial adjudication which is preferable above all others: sometimes one approach will produce the right result, sometimes another, and what matters in the final analysis is that the decision should convince.

Now it cannot be denied that a judge applying his own law stands *a priori* a better chance of producing a convincing decision than one who is obliged to work in foreign categories, just as a judge speaking his own language is likely to express himself better and more persuasively than one having to use a foreign tongue.[2] However, any judge who wishes to argue from his own domestic law must test the compatibility of the outcome with the other national law involved. In other words, he must verify the transnational substance of his decision. He is therefore not entitled to steer such a radical course as modern American scholarship recommends. To carry the right force of conviction, his decision must be truly binomial.

In this endeavour, language is the first hurdle. For it is not what is thought but what is said which is legally material. As Lord Asquith said, in the *Abu-Dhabi* award of 28 August 1951:

> "Chaos may obviously result if ..., instead of asking what the words used mean, the inquiry extends at large to what each of the parties meant them to mean ...".[3]

Language is form to law's substance, and with the pure substance severed from the form a judge can do nothing. The difficulty is aggravated by the fact that there is, on the one hand, no single invariable expression corresponding to each idea, while on the other there is no guarantee that a given term will have but one invariable meaning. On the contrary, in any international case the judge is confronted with two languages which, even if not wholly foreign to each other, will represent two different sets of linguistic usage, and he has therefore to put their congruence to the test. Notoriously, they will exhibit few absolute synonyms outside the mathematical or scientific domain. In regard to certain technical expressions the judge will therefore have to enlist the aid of translators, and frequently of experts in the field concerned. It may be supposed that this semantic problem is less acute within the sphere of an international business language like English than elsewhere. One would therefore expect to find more indicative material in the legal vocabulary of bilingual or polyglot States, and that is in fact the case. An early source is Jus-

---

2. Speaking from the special experience of a judge in a country with four languages, the Swiss federal judge Stauffer wrote in "Bundesgericht und Parteiautonomie", *Festschrift für Hans Lewald* (p. 398), that parties obliged to conduct a case in a given country mostly wished the judge to apply the local law: "That is greatly to be welcomed, for it is always somehow unnatural and, indeed, bears the taint of amateurishness when a judge has to apply foreign law. At all events, the application of the judge's own domestic law must, in the sphere of international contract law, appear the ideal situation and *bonum summum* of all national conflicts laws."

3. *International Law Reports* 1951, p. 149.

tinian, and more recent examples are afforded by Austria-Hungary, the Baltic provinces of Russia, Finland, Switzerland, South Africa, Canada, Belgium, the Soviet Union, Czechoslovakia and Yugoslavia.[4] An even richer mine of material is offered by international treaties,[5] and what little has so far been reported of the experience of international tribunals is especially instructive and important.[6]

Even when the judge is ostensibly confronted with only one language, he cannot be sure that a word used by one party will be understood by the other in the same sense. Oxford English and American English are not congruent, for example, and, to give but two examples, the legal German spoken in the two parts of Germany now differs in the meaning attached to such elementary terms as *Eigentum* ("property") and *Preis.* The way in which the vocabulary of statutes, and documents in general, can age and acquire dangerously altered connotations is also familiar to every lawyer, and will be evident to every layman who compares an old translation of the Bible with a modern one. Hence on-one should be surprised when, for example, the translation of the GATT regulations into just one other language appears to take a disproportionate length of time: it is an arduous and extremely responsible undertaking. Nor is it to be wondered at that on 13 July 1959 the German *Bundesgerichtshof* should have warned a tribunal that apparent linguistic similarity was an insufficient ground for construing an Austrian statute by the lights of German rules.[7]

The linguistic problem is especially critical for a judge who adopts the transnational approach and abjures the expedient traditional method of preliminary allocation of the case to a single national system. However, this extra burden is more than offset by the opportunity he has, while remaining within the principles of his own domestic law, of clarifying the facts without

4. Cf. in particular Dölle, "Zur Problematik mehrsprachiger Gesetze und Vertragstexte", 26 *RabelsZ*, 1961, p. 1. The first part has also been printed in the *Festschrift Yntema, Twentieth Century Comparative and Conflict Law*, 1961, p. 277.

5. Cf. in particular De Vries, *Choice of Language in International Contracts* (Parker School Studies ed. W.S. Reese), New York 1962. For public international law, see also Dölle, *loc. cit.*

6. Cf. Swiss federal judges Bolla, "Il testo italiano nella interpretazione della legge svizzera", *Rechtsquellenprobleme im schweizerischen Recht* (Berne *Festkommentar* for the Swiss Jurists' Union, 1955), p. 56, and Stauffer, *loc. cit.* Also cf. Otto Riese, President of the Court of Justice of the European Communities, "Einheitliche Gerichtsbarkeit für einheitliches Recht", 26 *RabelsZ*, 1961, p. 604; *idem*, "Das Sprachenproblem in der Praxis des Gerichtshofs der Europäischen Gemeinschaften", and Hans G. Ficker, "Zur internationalen Gesetzgebung", both in *Vom deutschen zum europäischen Recht (Festschrift Dölle)*, II, Tübingen 1963, p. 507 and pp. 38 ff. Further, barrister Alfred Werner, "Linguistisch-juristische Bemerkungen zur Rechtsprechung in Rückerstattungssachen", *Juristische Rundschau*, 1954, p. 168.

7. The use of a German commentary with regard to a question of Swiss law was, rightly, treated as unobjectionable in the German decision of 4 April 1928.

having to deal with any points of law. In this, at least initially, he is likely to require the help of translators and experts. In this connection, what Lord Esher M.R. had to say in the *Chatenay* judgment of 25 October 1890, concerning a written authority in Brazilian Portuguese, remains exemplary:

"... this writing was a business document, written in Brazil in the Brazilian language, and with the formalities necessary according to the Brazilian law and custom, by a man of business carrying on business in Brazil. An English Court has to construe it, and the first thing, therefore, that the English Court has to do is to get a translation of the language used in the document. Making a translation is not a mere question of trying to find out in a dictionary the words which are given as the equivalent of the words of the document; a true translation is the putting into English of that which is the exact effect of the language used under the circumstances. To get at this in the present case you must get the words in English which in business have the equivalent meaning of the words in Brazilian, as used in Brazil, under the circumstances. Therefore you would want a competent translator, competent to translate in that way, and, if the words in Brazil had in business a particular meaning different from their ordinary meaning, you would want an expert to say what is that meaning. Amongst those experts you might want a Brazilian lawyer—and a Brazilian lawyer for that purpose would be an expert. That is the first thing the Court has to do. Then, when the Court has got a correct translation into English, it has to do what it always has to do in the case of any such document—either a contract, or such an authority as this—that is to say, determine what is to be taken to be the meaning of the party at the time he wrote it, and what is to be inferred from the language which he has used."

Publicists echo this opinion. Rabel (*Conflict of Laws* II, p. 533) writes:

"Indeed, in all cases of party statements and agreements, the true meaning must be discovered under full observation of all circumstances. This may be supposed to be provided for in practically all municipal laws and does not touch conflicts problems."

Batiffol writes (No. 604):

"Rules and interpretation are matters of law, but the meanings of terms, intrinsically, are not."

In practice, the difficulty of the semantic problems which arise varies greatly according to whether the terms in question, e.g. "to ship" or (as in the *Leningrad-Ice-Clause* decisions of 10 March and 4 November 1933) "supply", denote a factual process or object, or legal concepts are involved. Thus for example the English legal term "limitation" cannot be translated without qualification into French or German. An additional intellectual effort is called for. But from whom? The translator, an expert or the judge? To simplify, we may answer: so long as the matter can be settled by familiarity with general linguistic usage and terminology and, if need be, the consultation of ordinary dictionaries, a translator will suffice; if it calls for technical knowledge and technical glossaries, an expert may have to be called in; between them, the expert and the translator will be equal to the task so long as the question is one of comparative terminology and linguistics. However, if the question goes beyond language and involves developed legal concepts, only the judge may perform the comparison. That is his highest and hardest task. For speech and law are living things, and of that the judge may never lose sight. His comparison of law must grasp the subjects of comparison in their living reality and must leave them alive when he has done. The effects of both disparities and resemblances have to be studied in depth. Only a comparison of this kind will enable the transnational substance of different national rules to be elicited.[8]

It will already be clear that an international case involves interpretation on two planes—not one, as in adjudication within a single legal order. As the latter kind of adjudication is by far the most frequent and represents the normal, it is generally presumed that the interpretation is primarily determined by whatever rules of interpretation hold good within a given jurisdiction. But this is to overlook the fact that ostensibly national rules of interpretation belong for much the greater part to a category which sets them far above the particularities of any one municipal system. There are rules and methods of thought which have remained, and probably will remain, the same at all seasons and places. Rules of interpretation are by nature transnational. Only in special circumstances are they supplemented by specific national rules of interpretation. This however has not yet been acknowledged by the bulk of opinion, which tends to view the national rules of interpretation as a basis and starting-point, and the transnational rules only as an adjunct. This is understandable on the part of national supreme courts, but something surprising from legal scholars. In a decision given on 6 April 1911 (JW 1911, p. 532: unfortunately without a report of the facts) the German *Reichsgericht* said

8. Ernst Forsthoff, *Recht und Sprache*, 1940 (reprinted, Darmstadt 1964), recalls, on p. 9, Schiller's beautiful line on language, "that endights and thinks for Thee" (*"die für Dich dichtet und denkt"*), and, on p. 11, Novalis: "True communication takes place only among like-minded, like-thinking persons". In Rosenstock-Huessy, *Die Sprache des Menschengeschlechts* I, Heidelberg 1963, p. 40, we read: "To speak means to condense different experiences divided among different persons as if they were undergone by one and the same subject: speech—language—is unifying in its effect." The same idea is expressed by Werner Weber, "Sprache im technischen Zeitalter", *Laudatio auf Emil Staiger*, 1967, p. 88, as follows: "The equation should not run, German equals Greek. German and Greek are, rather, both bound together in a third and overriding authority, in that spiritual, intellectual matter to which they both from time to time lend utterance in words." An American voice, likewise, that of De Vries (*Choice of Language*, p. 22), points out that "not enough attention is directed to the deeper perspective and understanding reached because of having to work in more than one language".

that it was never possible to undertake the interpretation of a contract otherwise than "from the standpoint of a particular positive law". The *Bundesgerichtshof* upheld this same view even in 1959, as witness its decision of 13
July regarding the textual similarity of German and Austrian statutes:

> "As the constant jurisprudence of the *Reichsgericht* confirms, it is
> also irrevelant that the foreign statute applied by the appeal court
> coincides with a German law. This conception must be adhered to. The
> foreign statute must be interpreted in harmony with the whole of the
> foreign legal order, which is a unified whole and is not to be torn apart
> by sundering individual provisions from their context."

Before the court narrowed the circle of rules of interpretation to the
pertinent rules available in Austrian law, it could easily have discovered that
transnational rules of interpretation, especially in view of the textual similarity of the two laws, would have enabled what we have termed a "binomial"
decision to be given. Among scholars, Batiffol[9] would appear to share this
view, while Raape (p. 124) and Cheshire (p. 247) are of the same opinion as
the German supreme court.

Arbitral practice, and that of lower courts not so far removed from the
facts, present a clearer picture, showing in particular how recourse to national
rules of interpretation is not necessary so long as the solution of the case can
be achieved through the construction of terms which are used in particular
business-circles, on particular occasions or at particular places.[10] The great
majority of commercial adjudications make irreproachable use of transnational rules of interpretation in matters of construction and turn to national
rules only by way of exception and when the case demands it. A model

9. "La sentence Aramco et le droit international", *Revue critique* 1964, pp. 647 ff.
(at p. 661).
10. Much has already been said concerning the interpretation of the English word
"supply" in the German *Leningrad-Ice-Clause* decisions of 10 March and 4 November
1933. An example of an English decision may be found in the case of *Mowbray, Robin-
son & Co.* v. *Rosser* (1922), 21 *Law Journal*, K.B. 524 (Court of Appeal), dealing with
the different significance of "to ship" in England and the USA. The *Miles* case of 10 May
1924, on "branded potatoes", may be taken as an example for the USA. Another
interesting American decision is that of 8 July 1955, which hinged on whether inventory
values and tax reserves could be included in an estate-valuation in regard to which it had
been agreed that the last audited book-values would obtain. Judge Desmond, in his
dissenting opinion, said that it was common knowledge that book-values never coincided
with actual net values and that it was precisely on that account that the parties had
agreed upon book-values, so as to avoid all discussion. The existence of this dissenting
opinion is significant if only because it shows how, even in so important a question,
there is no agreement even within a single legal system. As one may note from the
decision given by the Hamburg *Oberlandesgericht* on 13 November 1929, Rule XVII of
the 1924 New York / Antwerp Rules treated the concept of "actual net value" as
amenable to interpretation independently of all national laws.

decision in this respect was the *Aramco* award of 23 August 1958, wherein it was observed (p. 66):

> "Problems of interpretation are solved mainly by using methods, evolved by doctrinal writings, which are the same in all the legal systems of the world."

Now it should be borne in mind that this award concerned a dispute between a State and a private party. The quoted sentence should not, therefore, be taken to mean that the rules of interpretation of any municipal system must also hold good for the realm of public international law. It is, on the contrary, the generally held view that the national rules of interpretation which are valid in matters of private law do not automatically apply as between States or other subjects of public international law.[11]

The implication of the sentence in this realm is much rather that the rules of interpretation for public international law are everywhere the same. As a corollary of this, it surely follows that if uniform rules of interpretation already subsist on the higher plane of inter-State law, they may also lay claim to validity in respect of disputes between private persons, except where some national legal system prescribes some different rule for the specific situation. This presumption is but reinforced if we consider the source of these uniform rules for all States. To be precise, they are based neither on customary law nor on treaty law, but derive, since the age of Grotius, from the ancient Roman rules of interpretation. And the application of these latter is recommendable "in so far as those rules of Roman law are full of common sense".[12]

The objection which may here be raised is of course that of the absence of the requisite legal certainty, more particularly in international commerce; even the necessary uniformity must be lacking so long as there is not a single supreme tribunal to decide such a question. Yet one of our most experienced practitioners is impelled to remonstrate against such objections:

> "It is decidedly exaggerated to deny all value to the substantive unification of law just because uniform interpretation remains unassured."[13]

The whole range of these rules of interpretation which are already uniformly valid for public international law, and can therefore be treated as rules of

---

11. Oppenheim/Lauterpacht, *International Law* I, 7th ed., London 1948, § 554, 14, with further references. Reference should also be made here to the Vienna Convention on the Law of Treaties, 23 May 1969, especially Part III, Section 3, on interpretation, A/CONF.39/11/Add. 2 (Sales No. E.70.V.5), pp. 293f.

12. Oppenheim/Lauterpracht, § 553.

13. Otto Riese, "Ueber die Methoden der internationalen Vereinheitlichung des Privatrechts", *Z.f.schw.Recht* 1967, p. 26.

transnational commercial law, can easily be gathered from the writings on the subject.[14]

In recent times it has become possible to supplement the transnational rules of interpretation gleaned from Roman and public international law by the exemplary provisions of Article 9 (3) of the Hague Sales Rules and Section 2-208 of the Uniform Commercial Code. Together these two models supply us with an additional rule of the most modern variety, especially when we consider that the Sales Rules, in Article 17, instead of referring to the conflicts rules of private international law, declare the principles of the Uniform Law of Sale itself to be the guideline for purposes of interpretation. This additional rule may be formulated somewhat as follows: *In doubt, that interpretation is to be preferred which best serves the unification of law.*[15]

Below, we will have to confine ourselves to a selection from those rules of interpretation which are of particular importance for international trade. But first a warning is needed against any arbitrary misuse of the three well-known methods of interpreting a contract: i.e., according to its wording, its history (both before and after conclusion) and its purpose. In this connection, an experienced jurist has referred to an "almost cynical-looking co-existence of judgments" wherein the choice among these methods appears to have been nicely calculated to produce the "right" outcome.[16] With due respect to Neuhaus (p. 281), however, one cannot very well institute a kind of democratic majority-vote system among these three methods. Instead, the result to which the use of each method leads must be evaluated in itself and along with the other results.

One English decision of quite some time ago formulated one of the most important rules of interpretation in a manner which even today reveals it as transnational:

> "The only certain guide is to be found in applying sound ideas of business, convenience and sense to the language of the contract itself, with a view to discovering from it the true intention of the parties."[17]

This still represents good English practice,[18] and indeed the same guideline

---

14. For a conspectus of the jurisprudence, see Oppenheim/Lauterpacht, *loc. cit.*; Edvard Hambro, *The Case Law of the International Court*, Leyden 1952, pp. 27-59; Hartwig Bülck, article "Vertragsauslegung" in Strupp/Schochhauer (ed.), *Wörterbuch des Völkerrechts*, Berlin 1962. Cf. also the Cavin award of 10 June 1955 and, for private international law, the three basic rules laid down by Neuhaus (pp. 280 ff.), also the comparative study of Lüderitz, *Auslegung von Rechtsgeschäften*, Karlsruhe 1966.

15. This rule would in particular correspond to the views of the American delegate Richard D. Kearney at the 1964 Hague Conference on the Law of International Sale (cf. Riese, *RabelsZ* 1965, p. 30).

16. Ernst Hirsch, JZ 1961, p. 300.

17. *Jacobs v. Crédit Lyonnais*, 1884 (12 QBD, pp. 589 ff., at p. 601).

18. Cf. Lord Denning in *Fluflon* (11 May 1965) and, more especially, Viscount Simonds in *Brown* (3 February 1960).

may be found everywhere, notably in America too.[19]

There is however no perfect agreement among national legal systems in regard to the relevance attributable to materials and events located in time before or after the signature of the contract. The more, therefore, will it be advisable to recognize in this connection the rules which hold good in public international law. It would not occur to any reasonable judge to construe a contract contrary to the parties' true intention just for the sake of excluding the evidence afforded by events preceding or subsequent to its conclusion. [20]

In regard to the treatment of unclear contracts and the significance of the *contra proferentem* rule, we must refer the reader to the special literature. [21] One important German decision[22] even applied the rule on obscurities against the law-makers themselves.

Finally, it should be almost superfluous to emphasize the special prudence with which all matters of interpretation are normally handled in national decisions, but which is *a fortiori* requisite and observed in international cases.[23]

II. *Comparison before choice of law*

Once the judge has completely and accurately ascertained the facts with the aid of translators and transnationally valid rules of interpretation, his work of law-comparison begins. In this, both the legal systems to be compared have equal worth and status. At this stage a conflicts-law decision is neither necessary nor permissible. For it makes no difference to the outcome of the comparison whether the judge says "I am now going to compare system A with system B", or, in the reverse order, "system B with system A". The

19. Cf. the caustic dictum in *Roto-Lith* (15 January 1962): "But businessmen cannot be expected to act by rubrics."

20. From the wealth of relevant decisions we must confine ourselves here to mentioning the *Abu-Dhabi* award of 28 August 1951 (p. 251), MAT 11 June 1926 (*Charles Semon*) and, although it did not concern private international law, the German decision of 8 May 1935 concerning the activation of an older contract.

21. For Germany, especially from the comparative viewpoint, Lüderitz: *op. cit.*; Schmidt-Salzer, "Geltungsgrund und Anwendungsbereich der sog. Unklarheiten-Regel", *Versicherungsrecht* 1966, p. 910; and Weber, *Allgemeine Geschäftsbedingungen*, n. 324.

22. *Apotheke*, 30 May 1956, NJ 1956, p. 1025.

23. Cf. for example the German decision of 21 June 1912 on the interpretation of articles of association (*GmbH-Vertrag*), and especially the House of Lords decision of 12 October 1940 on a broker's commission alleged to have been tacitly agreed. See also "longstanding business-relations" in the subject-index, and an interesting observation in Proells, *Rückversicherung*, p. 57: "It is a matter of experience that reinsurers, who generally set store by a lasting association, ... have declared that restraints demanded of them, whether consonant with the contractual position or not, had their consent."

difference lies only in the standpoint of the comparer. So long as the judge abides by the rule of treating the law of either party as equal, it does not matter if one of them happens also to be his own domestic law. This does not mean that the judge will be prejudiced, only that he will be an expert in regard to one of the two laws. The usual three-member arbitral tribunal presents the advantage of having an expert on the bench for each of the laws to be compared, so that the domestic-law problem simply does not arise.[24] A conflicts-law decision becomes inevitable only when there is a conflict of laws; that is, when the comparison does not reveal a concord pointing to the solution of the case. In international trade-law, such cases are the rare exception.

A decision thus founded on comparison of laws, a binomial decision therefore, carries particular conviction. The statement of grounds, however, should itself be full and cogent. Many past decisions which were otherwise on the right path show unfortunate deficiencies on that score. As indicated in the preceding section, it is not enough just to compare statutes and ascertain their similar wording. Yet this was not infrequent in the early days of comparative law. [25] On the other hand, a given statute might actually coincide, or at least be presumed to coincide, with jurisprudence, and therefore be given normative status. The relative unpersuasiveness of certain decisions may be traced to this factor.[26]

The rapid strides made in this field can be seen from the jurisprudence of the Mixed Arbitral Tribunals. Only three years were required in order to advance from the decisions discussed in Section III of the Introduction to a progressive outlook:

> "With few exceptions, the Mixed Arbitral Tribunals have so far dispensed with determining the applicable law, inasmuch as they acted on the hypothesis that the legal systems in conflict embodied the same rules. There is a certain risk inherent in this solution, for in not a few cases a more thorough investigation of both legal orders reveals differences which are not discernible at first sight. Yet in principle, at all events, this tribunal is of the opinion that it would be as well to expound and resolve the difference, for it is always in this way that the

24. As expressly stated in the *Aramco* award of 23 August 1958, p. 310.

25. E.g. the Franco-German MAT decisions of 26 July 1922 (*Rumeau* and *Alcan*), also 13 July 1925 (*Gutberlet*).

26. In the English *British Nylon* decision of 16 October 1952 the similarity of all patent laws in the Commonwealth was presumed. The French decision of 27 January 1955 postulates the freedom of form in contract-formation equally obtaining in both France and Germany. In the American *Pennsylvania Co.*, decision of 9 December 1960, a conflict decision was first reached as between the laws of Pennsylvania and Delaware, but the court then went on to note the identity of the law in the two States.

Mixed Arbitral Tribunals may by their jurisprudence make their contribution to international law."[27]

For a binomial decision to be convincing, the way in which the transnational rules behind it were elicited from both the national laws compared must be clearly recognizable. A bald statement that both laws led to the same result will therefore be inadequate. [28] Neither will any decision which leaves open the question whether this or that national law was applied carry conviction (quite apart from the question of its exposure to revision by the national supreme court). Uncertainty as to what legal order the judge chose as the basis of his decision is intolerable. The judge ought therefore never to relinquish his firm basis by saying that this "or" that legal order shall apply. He may on the other hand say that this "and" that legal order can simultaneously apply because the rule governing the outcome is to be found in both, or emerges at all events from an idea basic to both. The former course either fails utterly to carry any conviction or at best but half convinces of the rightness of the judgment. The latter, on the other hand, is doubly persuasive.[29]

Also inadequate are those hybrid decisions which employ law-comparison only as an adjunct to conflicts-law adjudication. This is to set off on the

27. Franco-German MAT 16 June 1925 (*Negreanu*), p. 210. Cf. the decision given by the German *Bundesgerichtshof* on 13 July 1959, regarding similarity of law between Germany and Austria.

28. Cf. Anglo-German MAT 7 April 1927. Identity of result can at all events provide an adequate ground in purely internal cases (German decision of 1 December 1964) or in the event that several different conflict rules all point to the application of the law of the same State (American *Sperry Rand* decision of 5 October 1964, p. 369).

29. For the older German case-law, cf. the references in Kegel, *Einführungsgesetz*, nn. 86 and 114 *ad* Art. 7. The procedure was used many times by the Mixed Arbitral Tribunals: cf. MAT 7 December 1921, 9 July 1922, 26 July 1922, 24 November 1922, 13 July 1925; of these, the decisions of 7 December 1921 and 24 November 1922 expressly leave the question open while the others pass over it in silence. In most decisions the question remains open because the court refers in its reasoning to a general principle of law which is in its opinion of equal validity in all legal systems. To this kind of decision belongs that given by the German *Reichsgericht* on 29 June 1915, which hinged on the test of good faith: "It is alleged that §§ 133 and 157 of the German Civil Code were misapplied, inasmuch as the contract provided for the competence of English law. This challenge must fail, if only because it is neither contended nor may be assumed that the principles enshrined in §§ 133 and 157 of the German Civil Code are foreign to English private law. But if it is to be posited that both laws coincide in these principles, it is self-evident that even if the court of appeal had applied English law it would not have arrived at a different construction of the contract." Cf. also the decision given by the Railway Arbitration Tribunal on 20 December 1922, holding that a unilateral mistake could be ignored; the American *Obear* decision of 26 February 1926 on the subject of fraud; the Greco-Bulgarian MAT decision of 14 February 1927 on limitation as transnational law; and the European Court's decision of 10 December 1957, concerning the communication of a statement of intent.

213

wrong foot. The right sequence of consideranda is not choice of law, then enlistment of comparative law for the sake of substantiation, but the reverse: first, law-comparison, and then—but only if necessary—a choice of law. [30]

III. *Transnational law through comparative law*

The part which comparative law has hitherto been allotted in the substantiation of international decisions is a variable quantity. It is but seldom that a decision has been exclusively founded on the presence of identical rules in both systems of law, e.g. such general principles as good faith. In the majority of cases, this presence is accorded a merely auxiliary significance. However, alongside the cases in which an appreciable identity is established but relied on only as a corroborative argument, there are those relatively rarer cases in which, though this identity provides the whole *ratio decidendi*, there is a failure to demonstrate it to the hilt; the court, in other words, contented itself with noting a legal similarity without showing its presence to the extent necessary for the decision to carry conviction. The group of decisions invoking general principles of law is so wide-ranging and important that we deal with it in a separate section below. Both it and the smaller class of decisions founded on points of similarity may however be included within the body of international decisions in which comparative law plays a part: a category which has not hitherto been statistically surveyed.

Among scholars, meanwhile, it has become settled teaching that a comparison of the pertinent rules of law is admissible and relevant in the motivation of international decisions. Here theory is confirmed by practice. Merely within the relatively narrow field of the present study we have discovered at least 30 decisions founded upon comparative law, ranging over the jurisprudence of all the major trading countries and international arbitral tri-

---

30. Naturally enough, it was the Mixed Arbitral Tribunals which, although they were initially concerned to seek the proper law by the classical method, first employed the substantial identy of laws as a subsidiary ground of decision: cf. MAT 25 May 1923 (*Stoehr*) on burden of proof and 24 May 1923 (*Goldschmidt*) on place of performance, also the *Negreanu* decision detailed above (16 June 1925) and 7 April 1927 (*Düsse*). Whenever the forum itself is international there is a strong tendency to rely on substantial identity as well as on the finding of the proper law: see the decision of the German *Bundesgerichtshof*, 5 December 1966, on newspaper reports of the Le Mans motor race; the American decisions of 24 March 1919 (*Griffin*), with a reference to the substantial identity of law achieved by the Uniform Sales Act, 26 January 1953 (*Bennett*) on the similarity of the law relating to letters of credit in the USA and Iran, and 9 December 1960 (*Pennsylvania Co.*) regarding the similar results of different conflict rules; for England, cf. for example 12 May 1953 (*d'Almeida*) on the existence in both England and Portugal of the same legal duty of minimization of damage; for France, the decisions of 15 February 1953 and 27 January 1955.

bunals.[31] The matters covered by these decisions include sales-law, patent-law, maritime navigation, damages, limitation, concessions, leasing, *force majeure*, the formation of contracts, and unilateral mistake. This demonstrates that the range of the quest for transnational rules is more or less unlimited, both potentially and in practice.

When the comparison of laws does not divulge a complete identity of the pertinent rules, but merely a strong resemblance, the judge's task is hard. How perfect a match must there be before he may found his judgment upon the results of his comparative research? In the jurisprudence of every country, as also in arbitral case-law, instances can be found of judges' contenting themselves with a certain degree of resemblance.[32] Such decisions are fraught with danger. They may be unsound; and in any case they carry little conviction, because they positively advertise the fact that differences in the national laws concerned may have been overlooked or under-rated. In 1927 Ernst Rabel referred to "the thorny question of the full congruence" of rules of law. Admittedly, he then went on:

> "At one point or another we come to an abyss which is spanned by no bridge. For between the two legal systems directly involved there is absolutely no community of civil law, and neither as a rule do 'tried doctrine and tradition' offer any foothold, for these too are divided, and the decision becomes a matter of national or individual taste. Who will venture to judge by objective principles ...?"[33]

31. American decisions: 24 March 1919, 26 February 1926, 29 July 1948, 26 January 1953, 5 January 1955, 4 April 1957, 9 December 1960, 15 January 1962, 2 October 1964. German decisions: 29 June 1915, 13 October 1931, 10 March 1933, 10 June 1933, 18 February 1965, 5 December 1966. English decisions: 16 October 1952, 12 May 1953. French decisions: 15 February 1933, 27 January 1955. Arbitral awards of 1897 (s.d.), 1 September 1905, 7 December 1921, 1 December 1922, 20 December 1922, 16 June 1925, 14 February 1927, 10 December 1957, 15 March 1963.

32. We will content ourselves with some German decisions, for example *Reichsgericht* 4 April 1928: "Considering the similarity of the provisions on gaming and betting in §§ 762-764 of the German Civil Code and Art. 513-515 of the Swiss law of obligations, the fact that the application of Art. 513 of the latter is not excluded by Art. 30 of the German Civil Code Introductory Law requires no further substantiation."; or *Reichsgericht* 25 April 1932: "The failure of the appeal court to pronounce as to the applicable law does not necessitate rescission of its judgment, because that question has no influence on the decision ... For both Italian ... and English law ... regulate the position and functions of executor essentially in agreement with German law"; more recently, *Bundesgerichtshof* 10 January 1958 (canned meat), in which the institution of annulment for material defect (*Wandlung*), being unknown to English law, was replaced by a guarantee as representing the nearest equivalent; also *Bundesgerichtshof* 19 October 1960 (importation of wine) in which French law was supplemented by the institution of substitute delivery, featured by German but not French law.

33. *RabelsZ* 1927, pp. 43 ff.

As late as 1961 Raape still referred to this "abyss", adding that the sole recourse was for the judge "to cling tightly to the legal order ... of some State or other".[34] But is this not to behave as if a whole generation, and a world-war, had come and gone without any change or development having taken place?[35] One need only recall how permanently irreconcilable the conflicts over "limitation" and "specific performance" were thought to be at the time when Rabel wrote, to show how the "abyss" has since been bridged at many points, though certainly not everywhere.

There are above all two lines of thought which should help the judge who discovers that the national rules investigated, though not identical, present a certain similarity. One is to remember that though absolutely pure chemical substances are extremely rare, existing rather in theory than in practice, yet in practice, i.e. in industrial technology, people have learned to work with very slightly impure substances. On this analogy, the judge has to carry out the comparison of laws to the point where the smallest irreducible difference between two rules stands revealed in the sharpest possible focus. Once this point is reached, a new set of considerations enters into play; for example, whether one of the two rules of law, which now differ only in a non-essential way, can serve as an exemplar for the other; or whether both rules may be regarded as equidistant, on opposite sides, from the ideal point for the given case, so that the solution can be reached by splitting the difference.

At bottom, nobody will deny the possibility that one of two competing rules may be held up as a model to the other and will therefore deserve preference.[36] There is however a difficulty, namely by what criteria the exemplary nature of the rule vis-à-vis the other may be ascertained. Only *in extremis* should the judge employ a personal yardstick of his own. It will certainly be more reliable and convincing if he can appeal to the judgment of a number of experienced and knowledgeable persons, just as the founding of a decision on an established legal order will always be preferable to any innovation by the judge, because the established legal order "expresses the experience of many".[37] It is probably on similar grounds that continental jurists have certain reservations over the great reverence accorded to "leading cases" in English and American law.[38]

34. *Internationales Privatrecht*, 5th ed., p. 561.
35. Cf. Schmitthoff's Vienna address on the influence of extra-legal factors on the shaping of principles in English private international law, *Z.f. Rechtsvergleichung*, Vienna 1970, p. 81; also Drobnig. "Rechtsvergleichung und Rechtssoziologie", 18 *RabelsZ*, 1953, p. 295.
36. The "better rule" approach is often used in American practice, even though it is disputed in theory. Cf. Siehr, *RabelsZ* 1970, pp. 607 and 617 ff.
37. Kegel, "Leo Raape und das internationale Privatrecht der Gegenwart", *RabelsZ* 1966, p. 7.
38. Cf. the article on "leading cases" in *Black's Law Dictionary*.

It is however not merely the legal orders embodied in statutes or constant jurisprudence which are endowed with special authority because they reflect the experience of many, but also the great conventions whether of private or of public international law. In the case of a convention between States, the extent to which it has been ratified makes only a difference of degree to its model effect, which may be greater or smaller, but never negligible. This model effect is recognized by scholars and the courts alike, and countless illustrations of this could already be given.[39] Naturally, not each part of a convention will necessarily have an equivalent model effect,[40] but on the other hand its model effect will be doubly powerful if it can be shown to concord with provisions either of other conventions or of national laws.[41]

The effect of such models is particularly strong in relation to legal systems which are incomplete or undeveloped in the relevant fields. It would however

39. Even Savigny (1849, pp. 30 f.) suggests that treaties or conventions do not establish anything new in a fully positive sense but are the expression of a general community of law. Eisemann (p. 26) sums up the Incoterms as a "guiding image" to the interested businessman. Von Caemmerer (Ziegel/Foster, p. 126) points to the Geneva Convention on the Law for Bills of Exchange as a model, in particular, for developing countries. He has also drawn attention to the fact that in Scandinavia mere bills of accession are used as sources of law even without ratification (*Festschrift Hallstein*, p. 93).

On the model effect of the Bretton Woods (IMF) Agreement, cf. articles by Bold in 19 *RabelsZ*, 1954, pp. 601 ff., 22 *id.*, 1957, pp. 601 ff. (in particular as regards the decision of the Office of Alien Property in the US Dept. of Justice *in re* Eddy Brecher-Wolff, Title Claim No. 41668, p. 620) and 27 *id.*, pp. 606 ff.

On the model effect of IATA as only a private international convention which in the case in point had not even been ratified, see the English decision of 2 March 1939.

In American case-law the Restatement is constantly treated as a model, and so was the Uniform Commercial Code even before it had been put up for ratification in every State of the Union: cf. Mentschikoff, *RabelsZ* 1965, p. 313, and Broches, *RabelsZ* 1967, p. 592, and *Louisiana Law Review*, 1966, p. 196 (both with numerous references); from case-law, *Fairbanks Morse & Co.* 9 July 1951 (190 F. 2d., pp. 817 ff., at p. 822), *Rotolith Ltd.* (15 January 1962, 297 F. 2d., p. 497), *Williams* (11 August 1965, 350 F. 2d., pp. 445 ff., at p. 448), *United States* v. *Wegematic* (5 May 1966, 360 F. 2d., p. 674), *Alkins-Dell* (13 May 1966, 253 F. Suppl. pp. 854 ff., at p. 871), *Frosty-fresh* (15 November 1966, 374 N.Y. Suppl. 2d., p. 757), *Natus Corp.* (20 January 1967, 372 F. 2d., pp. 450 ff., at p. 456), *Baffinland* (13 June 1967, 425 Pac. 2d., pp. 623 ff., at p. 627).

On the model effect of the Hague Sales Rules, see Von Caemmerer (*Festschrift Hallstein*, p. 83). It was surely this model effect which won over the skeptics in the controversy as to whether the validity of these Rules could unreservedly be agreed (cf. Riese, *RabelsZ* 1965, p. 16, on Article 4). For a broad treatment of such conventions see also Honnold (*Unification* ..., p. 36).

40. Cf. the challenge to the rules of the International Chamber of Commerce regarding letters of credit in the American decision of 12 September 1944 (*Dixon*).

41. Cf. in particular Part III above, on contracts of sale, especially where differences between the two model codes concerned are discussed.

nowadays no longer be possible to follow the course taken in 1951 in the *Abu--Dhabi* case and, without thorough investigation of an allegedly undeveloped system, to take another as model.[42]

In certain cases, it will even be necessary to ascribe a model effect to ordinary bilateral treaties.[43]

A rule may also be exemplary because it is more well-tried than another. To counter vagueness, this test should never be applied on a general basis, but always in relation to the particular case which has to be decided. Although it will normally involve ascertaining which rule has better proved itself over the years, it may sometimes be wrong to draw favourable conclusions from past performance, as one rule may in fact be all too influenced by the past whereas the other is undoubtedly the more contemporary. Unless he feels statutorily bound to do so, a judge is not entitled to give an obsolescent rule preference over a more modern one.[44] The more proven rule may also be ascertained with the help of a merely quantitative comparison of fields of application, but that of course should not be the only method employed for the purpose.[45]

---

42. Cf. Zweigert's criticism of the *Abu-Dhabi* award in *Berichte der deutschen Gesellschaft für Völkerrecht*, Karlsruhe 1964, p. 214, and on the other hand the careful arguments of the *Aramco* award of 23 August 1958, pp. 311 and 314. In the Dutch decision of 15 March 1921 the more comprehensive law of the Netherlands was brought in to supplement the law of the Dutch East Indies. Cf. also MAT 31 May 1926, in which the law of Portuguese Guinea, which strictly speaking was applicable, was set aside as evidently unwanted by either party. As Cohn has pointed out (ICLQ 1957, p. 389), the more comprehensive or meticulous law is often preferred when choice of law is made in arbitration agreements, e.g., English law in matters of maritime navigation, or Swiss law in agreements with trading-partners from Socialist countries.

43. That might have been worth considering in the case decided on 4 August 1950 by the Supreme Court of Israel, which dismissed the claim of a lender even though his legal case had already been confirmed by a treaty signed in March of the same year; the law of application, however, was not to be passed until 26 February 1951. I have already criticized this judgment in my article "Völkerrechtliche Verträge vom Standpunkt der Betroffenen", *Annales Universitatis Saraviensis* 1960, pp. 217 ff., at p. 246.

44. One decision which may be criticized on this score is that of 22 November 1912, in which the *Reichsgericht* needlessly preferred the antiquated 30-year limitation period of Dutch law to the modern two-year limit laid down by § 196 of the German Civil Code—a period well suited to the everyday dealings to which it applies. In BYBIL 1957 (p. 19) Lord McNair offers an interesting indication of the preferring of the more modern law when he says that the law of the opposing party could also be expected to develop in its direction. In any case, in the absence of any specific agreement between the parties a judge is probably justified in presuming that both would from the outset share the view that a contemporary rule should apply rather than one out of date.

45. In its decision of 15 April 1953 the Munich *Oberlandesgericht* had to grapple with the unusual situation of different rules for the suspension of limitation applying because of the partition of Germany. It decided in accordance with the test of good

218

Now when a judge thus compares the empirical performance of two rules, he is already asking himself which of them is in fact the better rule of law. This question is not wholly unexceptionable, for it carries the danger that his judgment will be clouded with subjectivity. Yet it is certainly not an impermissible question, and in the last resort it will often turn out to be the only one enabling a choice to be made between two rules. It is impossible to exclude value-judgments of this kind, if only because it is the supreme duty of a judge to work out the best solution for the case he has to decide, and therefore to apply the best legal rules. This duty was enshrined in the very formula with which the oath of office was administered to judges in ancient Rome: *debet enim iudicare secundum melius ei visum fuerit.* [46] Moreover, in the narrower field of commercial law the introduction of considerations concerning the better quality of certain rules is far less open to objection than, say, in matters of family law, because all the rules involved are of a more or less technical nature; indeed, in this connection the law of contract, according to all we learn from legal history, is of pioneer significance.[47] Understandably enough, such considerations are not clearly discernible in the jurisprudence of municipal courts, but they can be detected by inference from the findings.[48]

---

faith, but might have done better to point out that in three-quarters of the divided territory a sensible regulation of the problem had been introduced, whereas no such regulation existed in the far smaller remaining part.

46. On the survival of this formula in the private international law of the Middle Ages and in Magister Aldricus, cf. Kegel, p. 358, where recourse to model systems is expressly recommended and illustrated from German case-law.

47. The reception of Roman law has to an overwhelming extent consisted of the appropriation of obligation or contract law, and is to be explained by the superior quality of the Roman rules in this field. Cf. Coing, "Die Bedeutung der europäische Rechtsgeschichte für die Rechtsvergleichung", *RabelsZ* 1968, p. 21, where "the solution which may lay claim to respect by virtue of its quality, and not only by virtue of its institutional authority" is referred to. Here we glimpse an interesting parallel between the reception of Roman law in the Middle Ages and the gradual consolidation of transnational commercial law in the present era. In this connection the words of Zweigert deserve to be taken to heart: "The general principles of law would become practicable and, above all, acquire the crisper outline they need for scientific knowledge, if the term general principle of law could be understood as indicating that key to a concrete problem which a survey of the world's leading juridical systems reveals to be the least fallible. There are numerous problems in respect of which that key can be identified with a high degree of scientific accuracy. In other instances it turns out that the leading systems solve the problem concerned in ways which, though different, are all equally valid. Now in the first case, it is the best key which is the general principle. In the second, it is what the judge may gather or distil from the equi-valent solutions." (*Berichte der deutschen Gesellschaft für Völkerrecht*, 1964, p. 213, freely translated.)

48. It is by this channel that the typically Anglo-American institution of the trustee has found recognition in Austria and France (Austrian *Oberst-Gerichtshof*, 3 March 1967; Cass. 4 June 1941, annotated by Batiffol). Cf. also the Swiss Federal Tribunal's

Far more frequently than the superficial observer may think, two disparate rules can on closer inspection be traced back to the same basic idea, as Savigny pointed out so long ago.[49] It often happens that at the moment of comparison the two rules, having set out from the same basis, find themselves at different stages of what is nevertheless a parallel development. The discrepancy observed will therefore be attributable to a mere difference of tempo.[50] This is especially true of the overall development of law in Europe and America, which has only in recent years been receiving a proper structural reassessment.[51]

While it is primarily in the restricted field of contract-construction that the "return to the original draft"[52] is advocated and practised among jurists, this technique is at bottom but the perceptible externalization of a far wider methodological complex. Instead of "the original draft", one might equally speak of "the original idea", in returning to which the judge engaged in law-comparison accedes to the higher vantage-point which alone will enable

---

decision of 13 September 1935 on third-party motor-vehicle insurance "for the sake of *ordre public* and public policy".

49. Treaties between States are often the expression of "the general community of law" rather than the institution of new law (1849, p. 30).

50. Not only have the major codes emanated from different national traditions, "they must also be understood as different stages of a common tradition" (Coing. "Die Bedeutung der europäischen Rechtsgeschichte für die Rechtsvergleichung", *RabelsZ* 1968, p. 14). In the celebrated American case of *Milliken* v. *Pratt*, decided on 12 September 1878 (125 Mass., pp. 374 ff., 28 Am.Rep., pp. 241 ff.), the problem lay in the fact that, while both Maine and Massachusetts law protected commercial transactions, the latter made an exception, in that married women could not serve as guarantors on a debt transaction. Notwithstanding the fact that Mrs. Pratt was domiciled in Massachusetts, the court applied the law of the place where the guarantee was made, i.e. Maine, and therefore allowed an action for execution of the guarantee she had given. Currie (*Selected Essays on the Conflict of Laws*, Duke University 1963, pp. 77 ff. and 597 ff.) made a thorough analysis of this case, and Kegel, who in 112 RdC, 1964-III, pp. 95 ff., concerns himself on no fewer than 19 pages with Currie's analysis, calculated that the number of possible conflict situations involved could be 2100 (p. 129; Currie, *op. cit.*, p. 142, n. 58). Now it is to be noted that at some time between the guarantee transaction (1870) and the judgment (1878) the law of Massachusetts was brought into line with that of Maine by the removal of the disability of married women. This shows that the law of Maine was the model law of the two. Hence the court of Massachusetts could have substantiated its (correct!) decision more convincingly by reference to the model effect which may legitimately be taken into account in an international–or inter-State–case.

51. As sensitivity to this kind of phenomenon is more a feature of the artistic than of the juristic temperament, perhaps we may be allowed to quote what the celebrated art-historian Wilhelm Pinder wrote nearly fifty years ago: "Today there is ... something like a stabilized European national character ... All those from outside agree that this is so, and we ourselves, despite our frightful political divisions, are beginning to realize it more and more." (*Das Problem der Generation*, 1926; reprint Munich 1961, p. 61.)

52. Dölle, "Zur Problematik mehrsprachiger Gesetze und Vertragstexte", 26 *RabelsZ*, 1961, p. 37.

him to attain what is expected of him: the best solution. He proceeds in accordance with the law of logic that when two quantities are equal to a third they must also be equal to each other, with this difference, of course, that it is not mathematical equality which is involved but the equivalence of underlying legal ideas. [53] Without the imperceptible yet powerful workings of a persistent undercurrent of community, such great achievements in unification as the Uniform Commercial Code in America or the Hague Sales Rules in Europe would scarcely have been possible.

For the present, there is, understandably enough, little evidence of the application of the above-described method to be found in the jurisprudence of municipal courts; first echoes of it, on the other hand, are to be found in such great arbitrations as the *Aramco* award of 23 August 1958.

IV. *Striking a balance between irreducible differences in national rules of law.*

When a judge is unable to discover the transnational rule applicable as between the two national legal systems, must he turn at once to one of the two competent national rules or is there still an intermediate solution?

The attempt to find such a solution even in an impasse of this kind will, however difficult, be worth making, for it would at all events be deplorable to have to abandon an international case to a national legal order.

The best-known device for extricating the case from the impasse, and one to which judges frequently resort, is to seek the parties' authority for a decision *ex aequo et bono,* [54] not to be confused with a judgment "in equity" in the Anglo-American sense:

53. This method of proceeding is regrettably being lost sight of. Franz Wieacker remarks: "Both the natural division of labour and the lack of communication between national juristic disciplines have for a long time distracted attention from the unity of the history of private law in Europe. Above all, the eminent jurists who at the beginning of the last century recast the various branches of legal history in the now familiar moulds failed to give the period of unity its due." (*Privatrechtsgeschichte der Neuzeit*, Göttingen 1962, p. 4). It must be said, however, that there has been some improvement in Germany in recent times, if only because the collapse in 1945 eventually resulted in a more outward-looking tendency. Cf. Hülsen: "The nearer the legal principle to the underlying idea or the more fundamental the norm, the more cogent is the reference to what has been derived from that principle in some other legal system." ("Sinn und Methode der Rechtsvergleichung besonders bei der Ermittlung übernationalen Zivilrechts", JZ 1967, pp. 630 f.). Hülsen also speaks of the "existence of a body of civilian law, sustained by the values of comparative law, outside the existing municipal legal order" (p. 632).

54. Probably the most significant instance of this in recent times is to be found in Article 43 (3) of the Convention on the Settlement of Investment Disputes between

"The difference between equity and a decision *ex aequo et bono* lies in the attitude towards rules of law. The judge who refers to equity stays within the borders of existing laws. The judge deciding *ex aequo et bono* wins a greater freedom which dispenses him to some extent from the legal order."[55]

An objection which weighs heavily against decisions *ex aequo et bono* lies in the still unresolved dilemma concerning the borderline between law and arbitrary judgment.[56] On this question, even less clarity prevails in regard to international adjudication than within national legal orders. The basic theoretical and comparative research has only recently been undertaken;[57] while the courts of State which must keep a watchful eye on the enforceability of decisions are most wary of all cases giving rise to the slightest suspicion of arbitrary decision, with or without the prior consent of the parties.[58]

States and Nationals of other States, submitted to Governments by the Executive Directors of the International Bank for Reconstruction and Development, 18 March 1965, to which dozens of States have acceded. So far, however, no use seems to have been made of the arbitral tribunal set up under the Convention. See article by A. Broches on the Convention in the *Festschrift Domke*, 1967, p. 12. In earlier times some important arbitral tribunals appear to have decided *ex aequo et bono* even without being thereto empowered by the parties. At all events, no mention of such power is discernible in MAT 16 June 1925 (*Negreanu*) and the Railway Arbitration Tribunal 10 November 1910 and 20 December 1922.

55. Scheuner, "Decisions *ex aequo et bono* in international courts and arbitral tribunals", *Festschrift Domke*, 1967, p. 282. Earlier in Jessup, *Transnational Law*, p. 77. Less clearly: Wengler , *Völkerrecht* I, p. 891.

56. This problem of delimitation appears to have emerged as early as Roman law and to have continued unresolved into the continental legal systems. Cf. Schirmer, "*Arbitrium merum* und *arbitrium boni veri*", 91 *Archiv f.d.ziv.Praxis*, 1901, p. 136; also German commentaries on § § 317-319 of the German, and French commentaries on Article 854 of the French Civil Code.

57. Cf. W. Habscheid, "L'expertise-arbitrage", *Festschrift Domke*, 1967, p. 103.

58. Cf. for example the German decision of 22 September 1949: "although the parties, in a legally effective compromise on the vacation of a dwelling, had agreed that in the event of a dispute over the suitability of alternative accommodation the court of execution could at the request of either party decide the matter after viewing the premises, this court may not act in the dispute either as a referee or arbitral tribunal, nor decide as a court of execution". Mr. Justice Megaw was particularly emphatic in the English decision of 31 October 1962: "If the parties chose to provide in their contract that the rights and obligations shall not be decided in accordance with law, but in accordance with some other criterion, such as what arbitrators consider to be fair and reasonable, whether or not in accordance with law, then, if that provision has any effect at all, its effect, as I see it, would be that there would be no contract, because the parties did not intend the contract to have legal effect—to affect their legal relations ... It must remain a firm principle of the law governing arbitrations that that which is, in English law, a question of law, shall remain in all respects and for all purposes a question of law; and it cannot be turned into something other than a question of law by any agreement of the parties in the agreement to arbitrate or otherwise." Cf. also the French

222

To obviate such difficulties, experienced judges or arbitrators often aim at seeing the parties reach a compromise with their assistance. Such a settlement before the court or arbitral tribunal is a genuine judicial decision. It is one valid solution of the problem of striking a balance between two conflicting national rules of law in the absence of any transnational rule.

For it to be possible *a priori* to strike any such balance in the given case, the judge must first establish that neither party entered into the contract with the tacit reservation that only his own domestic law should be applied in case of dispute. If there had in fact been any such reservation, no contract, given the importance of this aspect, would presumably have been concluded. Hence the fact that a contract was concluded justifies a presumption that no such reservation was made.

It is also conceivable that there was no choice of law because each party tacitly conceded to the other that the point would be settled positively once a dispute arose. In that case the judge would be obliged to give a decision in accordance with the classic rules of conflicts-law, both parties having taken a speculative risk herein.

A third possibility which is certainly not improbable is that the parties had not expressed themselves with regard to the applicable law because they wished from the outset to treat all risks that might arise from any subsequently emerging differences in their laws as risks common to them·both. For parties are no less entitled to divide or share a risk arising out of the absence of competent transnational law than to divide or share economic risks. In such a case the judge has to ascertain the size of the risk and divide it equitably between the parties. Just as in the interpretation of two differing contract-texts, so he must ascertain the appropriate mid-term between two rules of law, always with reference to the particular case before him. [59] In both cases it is the hypothesis of a median line to be drawn which is the judge's chief aid to arriving at a fitting solution. This device is part of the oldest and most respectable stock-in-trade of the judificial art, for the con-

---

decision of 4 February 1966, particularly the note thereon. It is frequent contract practice to provide for this situation with a general indication to the arbitral body to take care that its award is enforceable against the losing party with due regard for his national law; cf. the reference to Article 17 (3) of the SAS airline consortium agreement in Goldmann, "Arbitrage international de droit privé", 109 RdC, 1963-II, p. 400; also the reference to Batiffol, *Revue d'arbitrage*, 1957, p. 112, in Tallon, *Sources* ..., p. 158.

59. Cf. Dölle, "Zur Problematik mehrsprachiger Gesetze und Vertragstexte", 26 *RabelsZ*, 1961, n. 101: "On the other hand, this argument in favour of an interpretation which best brings the rights and duties of the contracting parties into mutual harmony has reason so strongly on its side that it can surely be followed in cases of doubt." In the same article, though in the expansion appearing in the *Festschrift Yntema*, 1961, Dölle draws attention to the opinion of the Swiss federal judge Bolla, to the effect that in the case of such textual differences, the reading which renders the "*senso migliore della legge*" should be preferred (p. 285).

ception of the judge as a *mediator* is part of our ancient cultural heritage and is found in the Nicomachean *Ethics* of Aristotle (V, 7):

"And the judge is sought as the man who stands in the middle, and in many places he is called 'mediator' in order to indicate the expectation that one will be justly dealt with if one receives the mean."

This acute and fruitful insight still plays a part in Greek law today, as Bender-macher-Geroussis has pointed out.[60]

Nevertheless, it is not so much in the field of national adjudication that the judge plays the mediator's role as, *par excellence*, in the international domain. It is, in the highest degree, a creative role.[61] It is intrinsic to international cases, with their manifold possibilities of linkage to national legal orders, that the judge has to mediate between two or more systems—and by definition, or etymologically at all events, that indicates a search for middle ground. The judge is always justified in embarking on this search whenever there is so much as a reasonable presumption that his doing so accords with the mind of the parties. At the same time he will, for the sake of an equitable solution, allow his search to be guided by the specific principles which govern the division of risk in international transactions and have long been recognized as worthy of judicial respect.[62]

---

60. "Ermessensfreiheit and Billigkeitsspielraum des Zivilrechters", *Arbeiten zur Rechtsvergleichung* XXIV, Frankfurt am Main 1964, p. 128.

61. Hence it ought not to be assumed lightly and played mechanically. "The person who shows alacrity to turn his hand to everything succeeds only where a mechanical solution is possible. Any higher relationships involving genuine moral niceties will simply be sent awry by his mechanical intervention." (Paul Stöcklein, *Einführung in Goethes Wahlverwandtschaften*, Artemis ed., p. 711.) Zweigert refers to "the most fruitful way of practising jurisprudence, because it betrays feeling for measure and the golden mean" (*Festschrift Raape*, 1948, p. 36).

62. Cf. above all Philip C. Jessup, *The Modern Law of Nations: an Introduction*, New York 1949 (German ed., Vienna 1950, p. 149), who in turn referred to Dunn, *The Protection of Nationals*, 1932, pp. 133 ff., and even at that early date called for further thorough research in the matter. I myself applied the same line of thought to the solution of private international cases in my *Studien zum internationalen Wirtschafts-recht*, Munich 1963, p. 15, and pursued it in a subsequent lecture in London, reported in *Arbitration, the Journal of the Institute of Arbitrators*, 1964, p. 68; later in my report in *World Peace through Law: the Washington Conference*, Minneapolis/St. Paul, 1967, pp. 311 ff. ("International commercial arbitration most energetically supports the develop-ment of supranational law and thus world peace through law") and my *Kommentar zum Aussenwirtschafsgesetz*, Munich 1968, (loose-leaf ed., § 6, paras. 29 ff.); further, "Some thoughts about transnational commercial law for the use of judges and arbitrators", writings of the German section of the *Association des Auditeurs de l'Académie de droit international de La Haye*, Series No. 3, Vol. III, Baden-Baden, 1968, pp. 31 ff.; the relevant articles in NJW 1969, pp. 358 and 2229; and "From private international law to transnational commercial law", *Comparative and International Law Journal of Southern Africa*, 1969, pp. 313 ff.

V. Reliance on general principles of law

A judge who wishes to decide an international case by applying the yardstick of general principles of law can nowadays do so with less hesitancy than at the beginning of the century. For the last 50 years "the general principles of law recognized by civilized nations" (*ICJ Statute*, Art. 38, para. 1 (*b*)) have been recognized at the highest level as a source of law. We have furthermore been witnessing:

"... the unfolding of autonomous international trade-law, transnational law, the basic norms and principles of adjudication, and whatever other labels may have been given to the stealthy advance of law-analogizing, unification of law and conflict-avoidance in general".[63]

There are in fact three sources or springs of law which it is necessary to distinguish, with this proviso that they well up in close proximity and immediately commingle. The distinction is not unimportant when considering the operative effect of a general principle and the overall hierarchy of such principles.

The first and most important source of law, but also the vaguest, is constituted by the general principles of civilized nations. This is a concept of public international law. Seeing that it would not nowadays occur to anyone to exclude any Member State of the United Nations from the category of "civilized", the principles referred to must obviously be those which are uniformly valid over virtually the whole world. It has frequently been pointed out that, if this is so, only a handful of principles of the most elementary kind qualify for inclusion.[64] In the field of international trade the general principle "*pacta sunt servanda*" is of particular importance. Its operative force is not always uncontested in the law of nations. In trade-law, on the contrary, the judge need only put the reverse question, "are compacts not to be kept?", in order to realize what principle must underlie his decision: only on that basis may he examine whether any special circumstances justify a derogation.

---

63. Wiethölter, "Zur Frage des internationalen *ordre public*", *Berichte der deutschen Gesellschaft für Völkerrecht*, Heft 7, Karlsruhe 1967, p. 158. Kötz ("Allgemeine Rechtsgrundsätze als Ersatzrecht", *RabelsZ* 1970, p. 663) has misunderstood the significance of general principles of law in considering that they form a kind of substitute law. On the contrary, they are directly valid in both legal systems involved in the case. The issue is no longer whether such general principles exist, but what are their sources, effect and hierarchy. These are still questions with which the judge must come to grips if he should wish to rely on general principles in coming to his decision.

64. Kollewijn, *Nederlands Tijdschrift voor internationaal Recht*, 1961, p. 171; Langen, *Studien zum internationalen Wirtschaftsrecht*, Munich 1963, p. 20; Rabel *Conflict of Laws* II, p. 582.

The second source of law yielding general principles is to be found, its controversial nature notwithstanding, in what, for want of a better name, has become known as *ordre public international*.[65] This interesting concept for the judge in quest of transnational rules cannot be made fully intelligible without a glance at the legal history of the last 40 years. With the proliferation, especially on the mainland of Europe, of saving clauses forbidding application of foreign law contrary to local *ordre public*, it was inevitable that the query should arise as to whether these many reserved areas, in all their variety, might not in many respects be traced back or reduced to similar principles. It is only logical that this thought should first have become insistent in connection with the Mixed Arbitral Tribunals set up under the Versailles Treaty;[66] but it is also logical that the attempt to produce something common to all out of such vague concepts as the individual *ordres publics* should have resulted in nothing better than yet another vague concept. It is particularly curious, not to say bizarre, that a synthesis of reservations from several national laws, hence of negative values, should be expected to give rise to a positive value on the world community level. Be that as it may, when a judge has to come to terms with *ordre public international* he will have to remind himself that it is a concept which has its uses in the historical development of law (for which reason we ourselves have used it at the points in this study where it was apposite) and that its importance for the unification of trade-law ought not to be underestimated.[67]

One factor which should not be overlooked is that both the sources already mentioned are replenished by comparative law. In relation to the first it is the highest values of mankind, wherever they may have manifested themselves, which are compared; in relation to the second, the reservations which are made by national legal systems in order to protect the public good. In both categories, it is certain distinctive values, mostly of a higher order, which are sought out and then compared.

One may however also ask: what do the national legal systems include in the way of commercial rules the comparison of which may be instructive from the transnational point of view?

The usual procedure in comparative law is to compare definite rules of law, but the comparison of such relatively indefinite norms as the general principles of law is an essentially more difficult undertaking, and the passage

65. This concept should not be confused with another of the same name, employed chiefly in French and Italian private international law, which forms a necessary subdivision of mandatory national law in its relationship to *ordre public* (on this, more below).
66. Cf. the references given by Wiethölter, *loc. cit.*, n.51.
67. Cf. In this sense Neuhaus, p. 263, and Batiffol, *Aspects philosophiques du droit international privé*, 1956, p. 229: "The special interests of international society will be borne in mind, however embryonic they may be, for these relations are one of the constituent elements of private international law" (as cited by Kegel, p. 68).

from one task to the other roughly corresponds to the transition from calculation with fixed figures to calculation with indeterminate quantities. Thus, despite the particularly valuable results to be expected in this domain, it remains relatively under-explored.[68] Principles are something other than fixed rules. A certain vagueness and uncertainty is part of their characteristics. For that very reason, principles are to be found in all national legal systems and industrious use is made of them. For what they lack in fixity is made up for by their utility, not to say indispensability. This however would appear to be true only at national level, for on the international plane one finds constant references to the legal uncertainty created by the use of principles derived from law-comparison.[69]

Now as we have already suggested, the comparison of indistinct rules of law can scarcely produce anything else than further uncertain rules. How can one insist on transnationally firm rules where only unfirm ones exist at national level? But solid substances are often useless, because inert: they become active only in the liquid or gaseous state. Every natural scientist knows this, but not every practitioner of the legal science is willing to believe that a similar situation exists in his own domain. Finally, there is one historical consideration which should be kept well in mind, namely that when general principles begin to crystallize they are often the sign of progress in the evolution of law.[70]

---

68. But cf. in particular Graveson, "Comparative aspects of the general principles of private international law", 109 RdC, 1963-II, pp. 7 ff. See also the comprehensive work of comparative law on *Contracts* published by Rudolf B. Schlesinger and the Cornell Law School, reported on by Lorenz, "Rechtsvergleichung als Methode zur Konkretisierung der allgemeinen Grundsätze des Rechts", JZ 1962, p. 269; Schwarzenberger, "The fundamental principles of international law", 87 RdC, 1955, p. 372; Friedmann, "The uses of general principles in the development of international law", 57 AJIL, 1963, p. 279. According to the Franco-Algerian arbitration treaty on the mineral resources of the Sahara, it is the "general principles of law" which will be decisive in the last resort (cf. Jean Robert, "De la place de la loi dans l'arbitrage", *Festschrift Domke*, 1967, p. 234).

69. Cf. in particular Langen, NJW 1969, p. 2230, and Joseph Esser, "Realität und Ideologie der Rechtssicherheit in positiven Systemen", *Festschrift für Theodor Rittler*, Aalen 1957, p. 13.

70. As Sir Arnold McNair pointed out in BYBIL 1937, p. 19. European law constitutes a particularly impressive example of the connection between a law in process of formation, or re-formation, and the employment of principles; cf. Von Caemmerer, *Festschrift Hallstein*, p. 91, and Von Brunn, NJW 1962, p. 985. Cf. also Heldrich, *Die allgemeinen Rechtsgrundsätze der ausserverträglichen Schadenshaftung im Bereich der EWG*, Frankfurt am Main 1961: the author considers that the development of law in the individual States lags behind changing needs, apart from which the points on which reforms are brought to bear vary from one State to another; consequently, a community of law does not so much arise out of reforms as subsist in what is already on the brink of obsolescence. Hence, says Heldrich, Article 215 of the Treaty of Rome has

How widespread an effectiveness may a judge nowadays expect of transnational principles? The survey of decided cases which we give below will reveal the great extent to which general principles are already relied upon. While it is true that the yield from each source of law, taken separately, may be sparse and impure, in combination they already provide a considerable body of effective material, and there is no need for a judge to be over-concerned with the identification of the particular source of law to which the competent transnational principle may be traced.

More particularly, a word of clarification is needed in regard to the distinction made in France and Italy between the *ordre public interne* and *ordre public international*. This distinction has never been recognized in England and, according to a recent German opinion, is "practically dead".[71] But this controversy is beside the point. The important thing is to recognize what lies behind it, and that is the variance of mandatory national law according to whether it is to be upheld against the contrary will of the parties or against a conflicting foreign law.[72] A mandatory national rule cannot very well be over-ridden by the will of parties, but the position is different when it is a general principle which is in some way opposed to the mandatory provision — especially when it is also a principle of transnational law.[73]

That there must subsist a certain hierarchy among transnational general principles will scarcely be denied, though there is precious little to be found on the subject. Certainly, in the case of a conflict between one general principle and another, principles of any other kind must bow before the general principles of civilized nations. The next highest principle after these is surely the inadmissibility of passing unreasonable judgments, to which category inequitable decisions also belong. Then must follow the principle of good faith, which in turn has the power of over-riding even the principle of *pacta sunt servanda*. A hierarchy of this kind is in itself transnational law.

---

proved wide of the mark, providing as it does in its second paragraph that "As regards non-contractual liability, the Community shall, in accordance with the general principles common to the laws of Member States, make reparation for any damage caused by its institutions or by its employees in the performance of their duties" (*United Nations Treaty Series*, Vol. 298, p. 87: translation made by the Interim Committee for the Common Market and Euratom and transmitted by the Italian Government). On 26 April 1955 the ILO Administrative Tribunal decided the case of *Duberg* v. *Unesco* in accordance with general principles of law.

71. Graveson, 109 RdC, 1963-II, p. 44. Wiethölter, *op. cit* ., p. 134.

72. Cf. Nussbaum, p. 64, and Eugen Ehrlich's work of pioneer research. *Das zwingende und das nicht-zwingende Recht im Bürgerlichen Gesetzbuche*, Jena 1899.

73. From the case-law, cf. *Reichsgericht* 29 June 1915 (good faith), the Italian decision of 31 December 1931 and the French decision of 28 June 1870 (limitation); also the German decisions of 29 June 1959 (good faith in the reorganization of operations) and 6 July 1961 (preferential claim of social insurance).

A judge, furthermore, must never lose sight of the fact that the rightness or at all events the cogency of his decision depends on his working inductively, from the circumstances of the case, demonstrating from both national laws concerned the applicability of any general principle on which he relies, and not deductively, placing summary reliance on an allegedly over-riding general principle. This inductive demonstration is essential if only because general principles bearing similar labels may turn out to be two different norms, while an unfamiliar foreign label may conceal a familiar precept. For example, a literal translation of the "rule of reason" so important in English and American law means nothing in French or German law, but can make sense once its meaning in the circumstances of the case is explored.[74]

In a domain where everything is still in a state of flux and evolution, one should not even attempt to present a complete picture. In what follows, consequently, we merely outline the present situation with regard to the employment of general principles in the adjudication of international commercial cases.

Although the general principles of civilized nations constitute in origin a category of public international law and are thus primarily intended to operate between States, they also, as a blanket-clause of political, ethical and cultural content, have some normative relevance for the citizens of these States in their international dealings. However, as need hardly be explained, this only applies to a relatively limited body of rules which can lay reasonable claim to universal recognition. The prohibition of the slave-trade would undoubtedly qualify for inclusion hereunder, but the prohibition of polygamy scarcely would, still less a ban on traffic in alcohol or other trade-restrictions. Such interdicts may well be instances of the application of a national *ordre public* or public policy, but they cannot be erected into transnational principles, not even when they are recognized by a wider circle of nations by means of an international convention like, for example, that of Bretton

---

74. The much-praised *Reichsgericht* decision of 29 June 1915 is open to criticism, in this connection. It was submitted that the court of appeal had not been entitled to apply §§ 133 and 157 of the German Civil Code, because according to the contract English and not German law was competent. The *Reichsgericht* observed: "This challenge must fail if only because it is neither contended nor may be assumed that the principles embodied in §§ 133 and 157 of the German Civil Code are foreign to English private law." The court ought not simply to have said that it could not be assumed that the German principles of *True und Glauben* were foreign to English law. If it had wanted to ascertain a transnational principle, it ought first to have demonstrated it. In so doing, given the lack of absolute congruence between the English good faith and the German *Treu und Glauben*, it ought to have established the concordance of the two principles in relation to the particular case. If the decision is no misjudgment, that is only due to its making the point that it had not even been contended that there was a difference between the English and the German principle. It was solely on that ground that the court was entitled to argue from the concordance of the two laws in these principles.

Woods; this is without prejudice to any special impact that the model effect of such a convention may have upon a particular case.

Hence there is only a few specific rules to be extracted for international trade practice, and the development of transnational commercial law, from "the general principles of law recognized by civilized nations". Their universal validity can be traced back to the rules which the great religions—Christianity, Islam, Buddhism, Confucianism, Shintoism—set up for the conduct of man towards man. In the more limited field of commerce, they include the rule that fraud merits no protection,[75] the prohibition of compound interest,[76] and the principle that no-one may cause loss or damage to another, whether intentionally or by negligence, without incurring an obligation to indemnify.[77] Within transnational damage-law the general principle that contributory fault must be taken into account probably falls into this category.[78] The protection of social stability (*Rechtsfrieden*) may also be accounted a general principle, as may be seen from the concordant jurisprudence noted in Part Four on Limitation.[79] Two other principles which are generally recognized, but are very much dependent on the circumstances of the particular case, are the prohibition of racial discrimination[80] and the prohibition of expropriation without compensation.[81]

As we have suggested above, the principle of *pacta sunt servanda*, though developed in public international law and, within that domain, not wholly uncontested, is especially important for transnational commercial law, and not only for wholly private international transactions but also in dealings between private persons and States.[82] In private law this principle is wholly uncontested; otherwise no national laws of contract would exist and an international contract-law would be downright impossible. When the execution of a contract is in issue before a court, it is never the basic obligation of honour-

75. American decision of 26 February 1926 (*Obear*).

76. MAT 22 March 1924.

77. Railway Arbitration Tribunal 20 December 1922, and MAT 27 July 1923 (Vienna Waterworks); also the rapidly accumulating case-law on international traffic-accidents.

78. Railway Arbitration Tribunal 10 November 1910 and 16 June 1911.

79. Cf. also MAT 14 February 1927; French Cass. 28 June 1970; Italian Cass. 31 December 1931.

80. German decision 11 February 1953, NJW 1953, p. 544.

81. On the disputed validity of this prohibition in public international law, and the problems therefrom arising for private international law, cf. especially the decision given by the Bremen *Oberlandesgericht* on 21 August 1959 in the Bremen tobacco dispute, and the *Lena Goldfields* award of 3 September 1930. For more, see Langen, *Studien*, pp. 102 ff.; Veith/Böckstiegel, *Der Schutz von ausländischen Vermögen im Völkerrecht*, Baden-Baden 1962; and Schwarzenberger, *Foreign Investments and International Law*, London 1969.

82. On the derivation of this priciple from the invocation of God in the preamble of such treaties, cf. the *Sapphire* award of 15 March 1963, p. 1016.

ing contracts which is the subject-matter of the dispute but only the special circumstances in which exoneration from that obligation may be obtained.

From *pacta sunt servanda* emerges the transnational rule of interpretation that contracts should be so construed as to preserve, where this can be done, the possibility of their being maintained.[83] It is not so much the validation of *pacta sunt servanda* which gives rise to difficulty as determining the special circumstances under which some degree of derogation may be allowed. In international commerce especially, all these circumstances are encompassed by the transnational principle of good faith. Even a cursory comparison of laws will suffice to demonstrate the presence of this principle in the law of all the major trading countries. Witness § 242 of the German Civil Code:

"Der Schuldner ist verpflichtet, die Leistungen so zu bewirken, wie Treu und Glauben mit Rücksicht auf die Verkehrssitte es erfordern."

or Article 1135 of the French:

"Les conventions obligent non seulement à ce qui y est exprimé, mais encore à toutes les suites que l'équité, l'usage ou la loi donnent à l'obligation d'après sa nature."

or Section 62 (2) of the English 1893 Sale of Goods Act:

"A thing is deemed to be done 'in good faith' within the meaning of this Act when it is in fact done honestly, whether it be done negligently or not."

or, more recently, Section 2-103 (1) (*b*) of the US Uniform Commercial Code:

"Good faith in the case of a merchant means honesty in fact and the observance of reasonable commercial standards of fair dealing in the trade."

A detailed examination of these texts, and more particularly of the characteristics of the "reasonable standards of fair dealing" which the American code adds to "honesty", will not be possible here, nor will it be necessary, as we are only concerned with the recognition of the principle.[84]

---

83. English decisions: *Campbell* 11 November 1931, and 1 May 1935, 52 LLR 16 (1935), *Maritime Insurance*. MAT 30 June 1928 (*Thames and Mersey*), VIII, p. 64. In the award given by the Prague Chamber of Commerce on 3 November 1965 it was established that the principle of *pacta sunt servanda* held good in both Czechoslovakia and the Federal Republic of Germany.

84. Cf. especially Farnsworth, "Good-faith performance and commercial reasonableness under the Uniform Commercial Code", 30 *University of Chicago Law Review*, 1963, pp. 666 ff.; Mentschikoff, "The Uniform Commercial Code", *RabelsZ* 1966, p. 406; Honnold, in Ziegel/Foster, p. 12, with further references; also Lüderitz, *Auslegung von Rechtsgeschäften,* Karlsruhe 1966, pp. 418 and 356, with further references. From Switzerland: Heini, *Z.f.schw.Recht,* 1967, p. 280, with references to the Americans Leflar and Rheinstein on the "reasonable expectations of the parties". From German case-law: *Reichsgericht* 29 June 1915 on German and English law, 10 June 1923 on German and Austrian law.

When international cases are solved by the classical method of "nationalization", there is little call to recognize the transnational character of the good-faith principle. In public international law, on the other hand, where such a procedure is impossible, this recognition becomes an urgent necessity. In this domain, therefore, the concept of *bona fides*, which is substantially congruent with the Germanic principle of *Treu und Glauben*, was part of the judge's equipment even in the heyday of Roman law.[85] But as the circumstances of each case will show what can be expected of the parties on grounds of good faith, it is useless and would be risky to attempt too close a definition of this principle:

> "Compliance with the letter, but defiance of the spirit of an engagement is no less incompatible with the standards of a *bonae fidei*, as distinct from a *stricti juris*, transaction. The purpose of the rule is more exacting. It is to exclude arbitrariness, capriciousness, contradiction, unresonableness and absurdity. Good faith serves as the measuring rod by reference to which it can be tested whether, in any individual case, subjects of international law have lived up to these standards in the relations governed by the *lex inter partes* of a consensual engagement.
>
> Observance of good faith, then, becomes equivalent to the infusion of considerations of equity in the moral sense into the treaty superstructure of international law."[86]

We shall confine ourselves below to enumerating a few instances of the application of the good-faith principle in decided cases.

The question, so important in commerce, as to the circumstances in which one party has a duty to enlighten and inform the other, and those in which the neglect of such a duty is tantamount to wilful deceit, can only be answered in reference to the particular case:

> "The law requires disclosure to be made only when there is a duty to make it, and this duty is not raised by the mere circumstances that the undisclosed fact is material, and is known to the one party and not to the other, or by the additional circumstances that the party to whom it is known, knows that the other party is acting in ignorance of it." [87]

---

85. Verdross, article *"bona fides"* in *Wörterbuch des Völkerrechts*; not to mention Grotius, who writes delightfully: "Justice, it is true, in its other aspects often contains elements of obscurity; but the bond of good faith is in itself plain to see, nay more, it is brought into use to so great an extent that it removes all obscurity from business transactions." (*De Jure belli ac pacis*, III, Ch. XXV, tr. Kelsey.) Since those early days, as we read in Verdross, *"bona fides"* has been inserted in important international treaties down to our own times—witness Article 2 (2) of the United Nations Charter, for example.

86. G. Schwarzenberger, "The fundamental principles of international law", 87 RdC, 1955-I, pp. 300 f.

87. *People's Park* v. *Bogard* (1880,81), N.Y. 101, 107, 37 Am.Rep., pp. 481 ff., approved in *Green Lac Holding Corp.* v. *Kahn* (1951), 106 N.Y. Supp., pp. 83 ff., cited by Newman, "Equity and comparative law", ICLQ 1968, p. 816. Cf. also the American

This sensible and careful formulation may surely be considered as a transnational rule, the connotations of which differ from case to case; for example, there will be a special duty to inform when a a special relationship of confidence has been built up through longstanding business relations.[88]

Frequently the good-faith principle will offer guidance for the conduct of the parties when the performance of an obligation has become impossible, for example on account of circumstances beyond their control. The case-law on this is relatively copious:

On 27 July 1923 a Mixed Arbitral Tribunal ruled that the execution of a water-supply contract dating from 1906 between a Belgian company and the municipality of Vienna had in accordance with § 1147 of the Austrian Civil Code become quite impossible on account of the total collapse of the Austrian currency, and added that a creditor who insisted on performance in such conditions would be acting contrary to the supreme principle of good faith which governed every contract. A similar situation underlay the *Lena Goldfields* arbitration of 5 September 1930, and here too the tribunal referred to good faith. The Russian revolution of 1917 gave rise to a whole series of decisions where the tribunal had in the end to invoke good faith, e.g. the French decision of 15 February 1933 in the case of the jeweller, *Marschak*. Here we can do no more than draw attention to the abundance of material concerning nationalizations and expropriations.

Even as between the three related legal systems of France, Germany and Switzerland, we are still, where the treatment of accident and *force majeure* is concerned, "far removed from any kind of unity".[89] All the greater, therefore, is the importance of the good-faith principle in this field.

Often the same principle will enable cases to be decided where performance by one party was based on a *bona fide* but misplaced belief in the soundness of the other's claim.[90] Furthermore, as a principle of transnational law, it may well provide a convincing solution to cases in which the alleged liability of a party is based on his having allowed another person to act as his authorized agent.[91] Then again, there have been countless decisions, all over

---

Krantz decision of 5 September 1958 cited in Part Two, on Licensing Agreements, above.

88. Cf. Müller-Erzbach, "Die Interessen- und Marktanlage beim Kauf", *Festschrift für Heinrich Lehmann*, Berlin 1937, pp. 141 ff., and the decisions there cited. More especially, on longstanding business-relations cf. Müller-Erzbach, DJZ 1904, p. 1158.

89. Kaden, *RabelsZ* 1967, p. 606.

90. Extensively discussed, with references, by Rabel in *Conflict of Laws* III, 2nd., pp. 427 ff.

91. Cf. the German decisions on "*Anscheinsvollmacht*" of 22 November 1912 in a Germano-Dutch, and 9 December 1964 (strawberry pulp) in a Germano-Bulgarian case. The definition in Section 1-205 UCC may doubtless serve as a starting-point for the American view: "A course of dealing is a sequence of previous conduct between the parties to a particular transaction which is fairly to be regarded as establishing a common basis of understanding for interpreting their expressions and other conduct." Cf. further the German decision of 27 April 1933, the English decision of 12 October 1951 (*Bank Melli Iran*), and the American decisions of 27 July 1943 (*Thrift Wholesale*) and 17 March 1943 (*State of Delaware*).

the world, in which the court, on grounds of good faith, gave protection to a party whose ignorance of legal phraseology was exploited by the other. [92] There can be no doubt that the obscurity-rule, to which we have already referred in another connection, is also related to the principle of good faith. [93] There are likewise many decisions concerning the careful treatment of contested goods which, insofar as the requirements do not result directly from the contract, derive from the same principle. [94]

The applicability of the good-faith test in flagrant cases of inconsiderate behaviour is surely obvious. [95] However, it is only in exceptional instances, for example where something like an association or other long-term relationship exists between the parties, that considerations of good faith entitle one party to expect to be consulted before the other takes any major decisions, as already holds good in public international law between members of e.g. GATT or the OECD. [96]

In many highly complicated cases it may be simpler and more convincing to found the judgment rather on good faith than on some over-sophisticated construction.

One case which springs to mind here is that decided by a German tribunal on 18 February 1965: during the war a contract had been concluded in contravention of foreign-exchange regulations between a German and a Polish woman; both subsequently left Poland, he becoming a refugee from the Eastern territories while she acquired Swedish nationality, and the problem was to decide what claims each had against the

---

92. See the American decision of 15 November 1966 ("*Frosty-fresh*") concerning an English-language contract with a Spaniard. See also the German decision, of 19 July 1962 concerning an Anglo-German contract in English: the Englishman was ignorant of German, but the sale was confirmed on a German standard form with German-language delivery-conditions in fine print on the back, the blanks being filled out in English; the court decided that there was no call on the Englishman to regard the finely printed German delivery-conditions as essential or, therefore, to have them translated in full. The *Bundesgerichtshof* gave a decision in the same sense on 9 February 1970. Honnold (Ziegel/Foster, p. 11) draws attention to the links between these considerations of *Treu und Glauben* and the English concept of "unconscionability".

93. Cf. for example the English decision of 2 March 1939 (*Imperial Airways*).

94. English decision of 12 May 1953 (*d'Almeida*).

95. For example, in the *Sapphire* award of 15 March 1963 it was found (on p. 1018) that in good faith one party was no longer obliged to give the other special advice or notice, because the latter had already clearly withdrawn from the contract. In the German decision of 16 November   , it was said in regard to the manner of conducting an inspection of books: "It would however be a contravention of good faith if the respondent company were to have itself represented by a personage who was particularly obnoxious or objectionable to the applicant."

96. See Hahn, "Das Wirtschaftsrecht der OECD", *Archiv des Völkerrechts*, Tübingen 1967, p. 177; and Granow, articles on "*Konsultation*" in the *Wörterbuch des Völkerrechts*.

other in view of the devaluation which had taken place in both Germany and Poland. One may add that the Ripert-Panchaud award of 2 July 1956 had expressly applied the test of good faith to problems arising out of revaluation.

Here of course considerations of good faith are bound up with the general desirability of striking an equitable balance and fair division of risk as between the parties.

A connected principle, that of the protection of confidence, is useful in judging cases where it is doubtful which party should bear the risk of nullity of the transaction on account of some statutory prohibition. Here § 64 (3) of the German Foreign-Exchange Act of 12 December 1938 is still a model:

"Nullity may not be relied upon to the disadvantage of persons who

1. at the time of closing the bargain were unaware of the nullifying circumstances or

2. are domiciled abroad, unless they were aware of the nullity of the bargain."

Thus the bargain remains void, but the statute provides a right of objection to the *bona fide* party, who however must prove his ignorance under subparagraph 1, whereas the burden of proof is reversed in favour of those domiciled abroad.[97] If the protection of confidence principle is more carefully observed in future, many a decision will be easier and prove less controversial.[98]

To become clear in one's mind about the protection of the individual from another person's misuse of power, and to get a proper grasp of the way law has so far developed in this field, one must go back to the beginnings of our

97. Cf. *Reichsgericht*, JW 1938, p. 230, and Langen, "Währungspolitische Massnahmen im internationalen Privatrecht", JW 1936, p. 1869. Cf., further: "The debtor must be protected against the danger of having to pay twice in the event of his having paid a wrongful creditor who had been certified as the creditor for the claim by documents emanating from the public authorities and binding upon the debtor (cf. *Reichsgericht* JW 1932, p. 346)." (*Bundesgerichtshof* 11 February 1953, NJW 1953, p. 544, concerning Jewish insurance claims on Swiss insurers that had been sequestrated or impounded by the Nazi régime). In the same sense, Supreme Court of New York, *New York Law Journal*, 27 December 1943 and 25 June 1947, and in NJW 1949, p. 920; see also Swiss Federal Tribunal, 72 III, p.2, with further references. For English law, see the headnote in the decision of 15 December 1960 (*Archbold*): "That the contract was not *ex facie* illegal, and public policy did not constrain the court to refuse aid to the plaintiff, who did not know that the contract would be performed illegally." Cf., further, my *Studien zum internationalen Wirtschaftsrecht*, p. 73, and the general references in my *Kommentar zum Aussenwirtschaftsgesetz*, pp. 50 ff., § 30, n. 7, and § 12, n. 14; also the numerous references under "*Vertrauensschutz*" in Lüderitz, *Auslegung von Rechtsgeschäften*, Karlsruhe 1966.

98. Cf. The celebrated Russian award of 19 June 1958 in the *Jordan Investments* case and the criticism thereof by Martin Domke (AJIL, Vol. 53) and Harold J. Berman (*RabelsZ* 1959, p. 449). As appears from the account of the facts given in the award, the parties to the contract had already carried out an oil-deal together in 1955, so that the foreigner must have been aware of the legal position.

legal history. The first authority to which man could complain of misuse of power by a fellow-man was the deity. Not only has the stranger stood from time immemorial under the particular protection of the gods, but more generally speaking, and in all religions, it was in the first place God who assured protection and refuge to the weak, *in extremis* before the altar. In the Old and New Testaments this relationship is described by the image of the shepherd who protects his flock. It was a genuinely transnational state of affairs, yet it did not give rise to any principle of public international law. It is no part of the "general principles" governing inter-State relations that the weak must be protected from misuse of power, though the faint stirrings of a development in that sense may perhaps be detected in the practice of the United Nations. The principle of protection from misuse of power has however shifted from the religious domain to that of the administration of justice by the State insofar as the power of the State has become the guarantor of the law within its jurisdiction. Today we find it clearly expressed, subject to linguistic nuances and varied formulation, in the written law of every nation. Practically every national law condemns taking advantage of inexperience, thoughtlessness or distress, the use of menaces or duress, or however else the reprehensible conduct may be termed, and it will surely not be necessary here to engage in any special law-comparison to establish the protection of the weak from misuse of power as a principle of transnational law. [99] However, attention may be drawn to one particularly emphatic directive to judges not to treat the weak worse than the powerful, coming as it does from a State which in 1945 was dismantled as a public menace by the paladins of the general principles of civilized nations.[100]

99. Cf. for example Braucher, *Louisiana Law Review* 1966, p. 204, on Section 2-302 UCC. Cavers, *The Choice-of-Law Process*, 1965, p. 181, counts such rules of protection among the "principles of preference". Heini, *Z.f.schw.Recht* 1967, p. 275, agrees with this, refers to Article 65 of the Swiss Insurance Act (p. 278) and also makes special mention of instalment-sales (p.279).

100. By a letter of 12 December 1779 Frederick the Great sent the government of the principality of Halberstadt, which at that time belonged to Prussia, a copy of the hearing which he had himself conducted in the celebrated case of Arnold the miller. In this protocol we read: "... His Royal Majesty will ... hold up a compelling example as a mirror to each and every board of justice ..., for they must learn that the meanest peasant, nay more, the very beggar, is as much a human being as His Majesty ... By that they will be well advised ... to take their direction; and should they ever fail to pursue the straight course of justice, without any regard for person or for rank, and set aside natural equity, then they will have to reckon with His Royal Majesty. For a board of justice that practises unrighteousness is more dangerous and wicked than a band of thieves. From the latter one can defend oneself, but from rogues who use the cloak of justice in order to give rein to their evil passions, no man can take cover; they are worse than the greatest rascals in the world and deserve a double punishment." (" ... Seine Königliche Majestät werden ... ein nachdrückliches Exempel statuieren, damit sämtliche Justizkollegia ... sich darin spiegeln ..., denn sie müssen nur wissen, dass der geringste

Meanwhile the principle of protection from misuse of power continues its progress, and is beginning to make inroads into the international legal domain. Its most striking incursion is in the special area of so-called anti-trust law. Now that one has to reckon with Article 86 of the Treaty of Rome, it is necessary to come to terms with a supranational concept of the misuse of power and to integrate it as far as possible into one's thinking on the principle, [101] which is quite obviously still in the throes of mutation into its supranational guise. In consequence, considerable uncertainty prevails over the whole subject at present, and the drafters of contracts have no alternative but to insert careful saving clauses designed to maintain or if need be transform the agreement in the event that a court might view it as a case of misuse of power. [102] At the present juncture it is scarcely possible to give a complete picture of the position with regard to the principle of protection from misuse of power as it gradually evolves into transnational status. In what follows, however, we adduce some of its more important guises for commercial law.

The case-law on misuse of power and the exploitation of weakness is superabundant. In Part Two, on Licensing Agreements, we have already noted a number of interesting decisions concerned with quality-protection. Modern American case-law centres on Section 2-302 of the Uniform Commercial Code and the official Comment thereon. Dealing with the notion of unconscionability, this says:

> "The principle is one of the prevention of oppression and unfair surprise ... and not of disturbance of allocation of risks because of superior bargaining power." [103]

Bauer auch, ja was noch mehr ist, der Bettler ebensowohl ein Mensch ist, wie Seine Majestät sind ... Danach mögen sich die Justizkollegia ... zu richten haben; und wo sie nicht mit der Justiz, ohne alles Ansehen der Person und des Standes, gerade durchgehen, sondern die natürliche Billigkeit beiseite setzen, so sollen sie es mit Seiner Königlichen Majestät zu tun kriegen. Denn ein Justizkollegium, das Ungerechtigkeit ausübet, ist gefährlicher und schlimmer, wie eine Diebesbande; vor der kann man sich schützen, aber vor Schelmen, die den Mantel der Justiz gebrauchen, um ihre üblen Passiones auszuführen, vor die kann sich kein Mensch hüten; die sind ärger, wie die grössten Spitzbuben in der Welt sind, und meritieren eine doppelte Bestrafung".)

101. A first venture on these lines was my *Marktbeherrschung und ihr Missbrauch nach Artikel 86 des EWG-Vertrages*, Baden-Baden 1959, a study which was brought to fruition with the friendly advice of Messrs. Batiffol, Minoli, Nebolsin, Nouel, Wertheimer and Lord Wilberforce. In many of the reviews received, the difficulty of the problem was not even recognized.

102. Upon occasion, even a judge in these circumstances has no other course than to incorporate such a saving clause into his judgment: cf. Lord Denning in *British Nylon Spinners*, 16 October 1952, p. 295.

103. See, above all for the further references, the American decisions of 13 May 1966 (*Elkins*) and 15 November 1966 ("*Frosty-fresh*"), and, for a case which dealt with a difference between the laws of Pennsylvania and New York, the decision of 16 May 1927 (*Joseph Seeman*). Especially typical of the application of the protection-of-the-weak principle was the American decision of 17 April 1909 (*Critcher*).

When a judge seeks the transnational element in national laws providing for the protection of the weaker party to a contract, he must make an especially thorough appraisal and at all cost avoid precipitate resort to the saving clause of *ordre public.* [104] The considerations expounded in the German decision of 6 July 1961, concerning the conflict arising between a private hypothecary lien on a ship and the statutory lien of the social insurance institutions in the event of the judicial sale of the vessel, deserve close attention even though they have not yet ripened into transnational law.

The unfortunate, because over-constrictive development undergone in recent years by the principle of protection from misuse of power is especially evident in the field of anti-trust law. There, jurists have been far too obsessed with its *anti* aspect, i.e., its effect against power and the powerful, and this has therefore usurped the place of its positive aspect, i.e., its effect in protecting the weak, which would have offered an essentially more straightforward line of approach. Ernst Rabel took the point of this development very well in 1947 when he wrote (*Conflict of Laws* II, p. 300):

"Such repression of monopolistic conspiracies is intended to protect the domestic commerce rather than the individual interests involved."

Signs of an initially tentative counter-movement, one more concerned with the general good, can be seen in what Jessup wrote in his *Transnational Law* of 1956 (p. 77):

"By way of clarification and to get away from preoccupation with the rules obtaining in the courts of any one particular country on any given subject matter, it may be useful to consider certain fora where jurisdiction is not an issue, but where there is a problem of choice of law in the broad, not technical sense of that term."

A year later, in two important British works, the anti-trust problem was viewed squarely from the standpoint of protection from power. [105] But it does not appear to have been formulated in really clear terms by German writers until about 1962, when one of them, hoping to be able "to recommend a new, universal principle for the solution of conflicts of laws in the domain of private cartel law", alluded to the "solid private interests" involved and concluded:

"For the time being, private cartel law is so tainted with the odium of industrial politics, and there is such a lack of *communis opinio* on

104. The not-uncriticized German decision of 14 June 1960 has exemplary value here. It concerned the validity of the choice of Dutch law in a contract with a German commercial representative, which excluded the terminal indemnity provided for in § 89 (b) of the German Commercial Code; cf. the note by Maier, AWD 1960, p. 216, and his article in NJW 1959, p. 1471.

105. Lord MacDermott, *Protection from Power under English Law*, London 1957; Wilberforce/Campbell/Ellis, *The Law of Restrictive Trade Practices and Monopolies*, 1st ed., London 1957.

policy towards trusts, that one cannot speak of there being a common juristic conviction in respect of any international conflicts-norm for private cartel law.[106]

The controversy over the extraterritorial applicability of national anti-trust law, falling increasingly under the influence of trade-politics, has enveloped the protection from power principle, which is the sole unifying element, in such a thickening smokescreen that it has been almost lost to sight and is scarcely ever mentioned nowadays.[107]

It is a lesson of common experience that it is easier to make progress by speaking of what and whom one wishes to protect than by quarrelling over what or whom wishes to combat. Unification will be made easier if one recalls to mind a principle such as that of the protection of the weak than if each one strives to get his own national anti-trust law enforced in foreign countries, or, what is an even harder endeavour, to distil one supranational anti-trust law out of the various national laws. To follow the last of these courses is to suscitate irresistibly a struggle of conflicting national power-interests, because it is precisely at these that the legal measures to be enacted are directed, whereas the first course enables one to build upon traditions which are extant in every land and everywhere derive from notions which have belonged from the beginning to the supreme principles of law.

It may be wondered whether there might not also exist, alongside such paramount general principles as that of good faith, a number of less important general principles, of a more or less technical character, which would approximate to the usages of a given branch of trade and in most cases emerge from a basic comparison of laws. For the time being this question, given its predominantly theoretical nature, may remain open, and if we now go on to mention some principles of this kind, our intention is not so much to say anything final as to hold the door open for further developments.

106. Ivo E. Schwartz, *Deutsches internationales Kartellrecht*, Cologne 1962, pp. 223 and 225; concurring, Kegel, *Internationales Privatrecht*, Munich 1964, p. 409. The same view is evidently shared by Fikentscher, "Die Warenzeichenlizenz im Recht der Wettbewerbsbeschränkungen", in *Die Warenzeichenlizenz, Festschrift für Eugen Ulmer*, Munich 1963. On p. 417 he writes: "Economic power as such is no service (*Leistung*) and therefore deserves in principle no protection in the competition. On the contrary, the law has to watch over the fundamental equality of opportunity in the competition and must therefore often check the strong competitor and help the weak."

107. To dispense with many detailed references, let us here refer to the Lausanne 1966 and Tokyo 1970 proceedings of the International Bar Association, *International Bar Journal* 1966, p. 112, and 1970, p. 46; also the reports on the 52nd Conference of the International Law Association, Helsinki 1966, p. 26, also The Hague 1970. Cf., further, the excellent short survey by Ellis, "Extra-territorial application of anti-trust legislation", XVII *Netherlands International Law Review*, 1970, p. 51, and Kronstein, *Das Recht der internationalen Kartelle*, Berlin 1967, especially pp. 506 ff.

For example: the fact that different national laws do not regulate the question of interest for late performance in the same way can probably be overcome with the help of the transnational rule that each party is liable for any damage suffered by the other as a result of his late performance.[108]

The recognition of saving clauses should be transnational law, as emerges from law-comparison.[109]

Historical jurisprudence, in particular that of Roman law, supplies justification for a transnational rule whereby, in the event of novation, the debtor is not released from the original liability.[110]

It frequently happens even in leading cases that the court purports to draw this or that conclusion from generally recognized principles, when the conclusion is really a product of comparative law, only the process of law-comparison has been omitted because the court took the result for granted.[111]

We have placed frequent reliance on one prominent principle of English and American law, namely that decisions must not be unreasonable; but is this to be unreservedly regarded as a transnational principle? This is a necessary question, for one of the forms taken by this principle, the "rule of reason", bears connotations that are quite special to American law and, if only on that score, is scarcely amenable to absorption into the German legal system—even though that is precisely what had to be attempted for a number of years on account of the allied decartelization laws.[112] Quite apart, however, from this special field of application, the continentally trained jurist will wish to ask his

---

108. *Sic* Rabel, *Warenkauf* II, p. 44, with further references and, emphatically, the Swiss *Ripert-Panchaud* award of 2 July 1956 (in which, however, the arbitrators were acting as *amiables compositeurs*). Typical of the difficulties which can arise from an anxious clinging to classical doctrine is the French decision of 15 May 1935, which, understandably enough, is annotated by Niboyet in a very critical manner.

109. See *British Nylon Spinners* (16 October 1952), p. 295.

110. *Sic* the Swiss *Ripert-Panchaud* award of 2 July 1956 and the English decision of 8 December 1958 (*United Railways*).

111. In this group of elliptical utterances we may cite a reference to the dispatch of a declaration in the decision given on 10 December 1957 by the Court of Justice of the European Communities and a finding as to the legal irrelevance of a unilateral mistake in that given by the Railway Arbitration Tribunal on 1 September 1905.

112. In its decision of 16 March 1954 (WuW/E/BGH, pp. 70 ff.) the *Bundesgerichtshof* placed the English word "unreasonable" in brackets immediately after the German "*unvernünftig*", and in that of 10 December 1957 (WuW/E/BGH, pp. 205 ff., at p. 213) it stated in regard to certain marketing tie-ups, and with reference to the "rule of reason", that their admissibility depended on "whether in a just weighing of the interests of those concerned, which includes society at large, they are shown to be economically reasonable" (*vernünftig*). Cf. the vigorous rejection of the "rule of reason" by Möhring, in WuW 1955, p. 7 , the material in the Frankfurt *Kommentar zum Einleitungsgesetz*, Anh.A, paras. 28 ff., and in Wilberforce/Campbell/Ellis, *The Law of Restrictive Trade Practices and Monopolies*, 1st ed., London 1957, para. 1608.

240

English and American colleagues what possible legal substance there can be in a principle of reasonableness, since we all purport to live and act in the light of reason and the notion of the reasonable is therefore too subjective, nebulous and shifting to provide a norm of lawful conduct. No general rule can be laid down to define what is reasonable:

"Nothing is more unreasonable than universal detailed definition of the reasonable. What is reasonable has to be determined with reference to time and place and circumstances."[113]

It does not greatly enlighten the continental jurist, and can scarcely prompt him to the recognition of a transnational principle, when English decisions speak of a "standard of reasonableness"[114] or even when a law-lord, Viscount Simonds, alludes with eloquence to the 2000-year-old tradition of Greek philosophy, saying:

"If I have to base my opinion on any principle, I would venture to say it was the principle of rational justice."[115]

The utter instability of this standard is revealed by all the partial synonyms given under "unreasonable" in *Black's Law Dictionary* (4th ed. 1951): irrational, foolish, unwise, absurd, silly, preposterous, senseless, stupid, immoderate, exorbitant, capricious, arbitrary, confiscatory. As a tool of law, therefore, this concept can only be compared to an adjustable spanner, not forgetting that a spanner is known as an "English key" on the continent of Europe.

Notwithstanding, there are at least two ways in which this standard is transnationally applicable. First, whenever, instead of reasonableness being treated as a substantive category and self-sufficient criterion, the adjective of "reasonable" is applied in conjunction with the noun expressive of the point in issue in order to furnish a concrete, even if not a mechanical yardstick, thus: a "reasonable time-limit", a "reasonable royalty", a reasonable requirement".[116] In this way the concept of reasonableness is itself controlled by and qualified for the circumstances of the case and its spectrum of applica-

---

113. Pound, "Some thoughts about comparative law", *Festschrift Rabel* I, 1954 p. 11.

114. *Terrell*, 31 July 1952, p. 237.

115. House of Lords, 25 November 1957 (*National Bank of Greece and Athens*), p. 525.

116. Cf. the English *Tool Metal* decision of 16 June 1955, and the decisions given on 2 November 1954, 17 January 1955 and 21 February 1955 by the German Patent Office in regard to the fixing of commensurate royalties: these cases also illustrate the theme of the "midway solution". As we have already seen, the concept of reasonableness is of great importance in the comparison of periods of limitation. Also to be borne in mind is Section 2-207 (1) UCC with its reference to the expression of acceptance sent "within a reasonable time". Many contracts provide that consent should "not be unreasonably withheld" (see the English *Advance* decision of 11 July 1958). "Reasonable notice" also featured in the English decision of 10 June 1945 (*Martin Baker*).

tion is narrowed, without loss of essential elasticity, to the extent requisite for its normative effect.

Moreover, comparative law demonstrates that, situation for situation, there is a common denominator between the Anglo-American principle and continental conceptions, though a German jurist, for example, may prefer to stress the element of good faith (*Treu und Glauben*) rather than of reason (*Vernunft*). Then again, the notion of honest good sense or understanding (*Verstand*) is enshrined in a normative figure of law, "*der verständige Mann*", which is for all practical purposes synonymous with that of "the reasonable man", so that when we ask what *der verständige Mann* would do in a given situation we automatically bridge the semantic gap between "reasonableness" and the continental blanket clauses which operate in the same sense.[117]

Thus the transnational applicability of the "standard of reasonableness" can be effectively demonstrated if only one brothers one's head a little less over its meaning *in abstracto* and examines its practical application in concrete cares. Almost without exception, these will be found to consist of cases in which a decision could on grounds of strict law have been taken in a given sense, but was not so taken because it would have been "unreasonable" to do so. And within this category by far the largest group is formed by cases in which the rejected decision would have exhibited a considerable degree of exaggeration, characterized by some such word as "absurd" or "unrealistic".[118] For ever since the *Perry* v. *Skinner* decision of 1837 (150 E.R. 843) the golden rule has been as follows:

> "The rule by which we are to be guided in construing Acts of Parliament is to look at the precise words, and to construct them in the ordinary sense, unless it would lead to any absurdity or manifest injustice."

Now it goes without saying that, even outside the sphere of English and American law, no judicial pronouncement may be absurd, even if the vocabulare used to say so does not exactly correspond to the English idiom.[119]

---

117. Lüderitz (p. 419) has drawn attention to this. Cf. also Joseph Esser, *Grundsatz und Norm*, Tübingen 1964, pp. 46, 68, 80 and 225.

118. English decisions of 11 May 1965 (*Fluflon*), p. 563; 8 April 1959 (*Matthews*), p. 179: "beyond anything reasonable"; 25 June 1958 (*London Transport*); 25 November 1957 (*National Bank of Greece*): "what sense is there ...? ". The American decision of 10 June 1955 (*Tramontana*) is criticized in Pound's article, "Some thoughts about comparative law", as "unreasonable" (*Festschrift Rabel* I, 1954, p. 41, n. 4). "Absurdity" is to be found in *inter alia* the reasoning of the American decision of 15 January 1962, p. 500, and qualified as "unrealistic" in the *Fairbanks* decision of 9 July 1951; also in *Rose* v. *Chrysler Motors*, 28 Calif. Rep., p. 185 (APP 1963), according to Lüderitz, p. 363. It was also used by Lord Atkin in the English decision of 23 May 1927.

119. "Absurd" also crops up in MAT 16 June 1925 (*Negreanu*), p. 209, while MAT 27 July 1923 (Vienna waterworks) chooses to refer to the "impossibility" of performance. Cf. the celebrated decision given in France by the Conseil d'Etat on 30

Often a court will merely find, not that a given decision would be absurd, but that the outcome would be so anomalous that it would be unreasonable so to decide.[120] Another kind of decision which would be regarded as unreasonable is one which is disproportionate in its effects, i.e. which decides more than is called for or affects more rights than is necessary.[121] The rule of contemporaneity, which prohibits flagrantly anachronistic judgments, may also be regarded as a subdivision of the principle of reasonableness.[122]

Finally, one should not overlook the possibility that a choice may have to be made between two possible decisions on grounds of reasonableness, without either of them being intrinsically unreasonable. In the absence of other criteria, it may be necessary to determine which of the two possibilities is the more reasonable. Here we enter the area of "model effect" which we have discussed elsewhere, whereby the better—in this case the "more reasonable"—law or decision is to be preferred.[123]

However, even if one is prepared, over and above the sphere of English and American law, to erect the prohibition of unreasonable decisions into a transnational principle, there can be no gainsaying that it is a principle of the second rank. For nowhere, not even (apart from a few exceptional cases) in English and American law, does this principle carry the whole weight of a

---

March 1916, requiring an "*interprétation raisonnable*". On the other hand, the no less celebrated *Reichsgericht* decision of 28 November 1923, which broke with the "*Mark gleich Mark*" dogma, is an example of the employment of the good-faith principle in place of the inadmissibility of unreasonable decisions.

120. Among such cases we may cite the English *Huber* decision of 17 June 1835, and even that of 24 February 1961 (*Bristol Repetition*), where we read (on p. 226): "It certainly does not seem very reasonable that one particular person should be obliged to pay for the use of an invention after the monopoly granted to the inventor has expired and the rest of the world can use it free of charge. There is, however, nothing to prevent people entering into an agreement to this effect, if they choose to do so." Section 1-205 (6) UCC also postulates "reasonable usage".

121. As an example we may refer to the above-mentioned *Rose v. Chrysler Motors* decision, in which the excessive extension of a right of redress which in itself was guaranteed was described as unreasonable; likewise the finding in the *Sapphire* award of 15 March 1963 (p. 1017) that when a breach of contract by one party is to be expected with certainty, or is already declared, the other party no longer needs to honour his contractual commitment. Further illustrations from German law are given in Gentz, "Die Verhältnismässigkeit von Grundrechtseingriffen", NJW 1968, p. 1600, and more particuarly in my *Kommentar zum Aussenwirtschaftsgesetz, Einl.*, paras. 62 ff., and *Studien zum internationalen Wirtschaftsrecht*, pp. 16 and 100, with regard to the practice of GATT.

122. This plays a role in the rapidly accumulating case-law on international air-accidents; thus the American decision of 12 January 1961 (*Kilberg*) used the expression "unfair and anachronistic".

123. One such would appear to be the American decision of 12 September 1944, which dealt with the commercial concept of a "full set of documents".

243

decision as the primary *ratio decidendi*; álways it serves in a merely secondary role as a cross-check on the rightness of the decision. Quite clearly, it corresponds with the principle of continental law which requires a judge, having rationally worked out his findings, to test them for their intrinsic fairness. This control is an acknowledged necessity within every municipal system, however differently it may be designated. How indispensable it must be, *a fortiori*, in the quest for what is transnationally right amid competing national legal orders!

VI. The procedural dilemma

A judge who has to develop and work with transnational propositions sees himself faced with new and difficult tasks. Whereas familiarity with his own domestic law, including its conflicts rules, used to be sufficient, he must now be capable of comparing two different laws and attuning or synchronizing them. Hence it would seem that he must be familiar with both of them. This is an almost impossible assignment. Impossible, at all events, if the maxim of *iura novit curia* is to apply, as in public prosecutions or judicial investigations in Germany. However, where commercial law is concerned, this exclusive maxim does not hold good to anything like the same extent as it may in other fields of law. In view of the trend towards trade-law unification, it cannot be ignored that in the greater part of the world this maxim does not apply, because foreign law is there considered to form part of the facts which have to be shown by the party seeking to rely on them. Hitherto no-one has suggested that findings in these parts of the world are inferior to those reached in Germany under *iura novit curia*. The fact that this contrast in methodology concerns procedural law, a domain in which the judge is constrained to adhere to his own domestic law, does not preclude a German judge from placing a broad construction on § 293 of his Code of Civil Procedure, which certainly lends itself to flexible interpretation.

Here it must be borne in mind that the main trend of opinion in Germany has up to the present concentrated wholly on cases involving the application of a foreign national law in its entirety. But if individual foreign rules are adduced for the purpose of determining transnational law, the position is different. In this event, the judge does not have the responsibility of applying a complete foreign system in place of his own, but only of comparing and evaluating particular rules in one law and another. For this purpose no more material is required than what the parties or the judge's own science may provide. [124] Of late, the relevant legal issues have been so admirably thrashed

124. That is also the opinion of Schütze, NJW 1965, p. 1652, with which I concurred in NJW 1969, p. 2232, whereas Müller (see next footnote) merely noted

out that a mere reference to the literature should suffice. [125] These discussions plainly show how the trend towards unification has set in even with the procedural aspects of private international law.

The parties to an international legal dispute will undoubtedly set greater store by the realism of having the presentation of the facts, including the exposition of foreign law, in their own hands, than by the relatively faint hope that the judge, in the unaided application of foreign law, will somehow, in his wisdom, hit upon the right solution. The judge, for his part, need fear the reproach of having jeopardized legal certainty only if he fails to substantiate his judgment convincingly. For the rest, he may answer his critics:

"That is the tribute of legal uncertainty which every jurisprudential innovation has to pay in its early days." [126]

Schütze's opinion (p. 68, no. 6) and Kegel disagrees (*Einführungsgesetz zum BGB*, Soergel/Siebert, 10th ed., 1970, *vor Art.* 7, no. 92).

125. *Die Anwendung ausländischen Rechts im international Privatrecht*, special project and colloquium in celebration of the 40th anniversary of the Max-Planck-Institut, ed. Dierk-Müller, Berlin and Tübingen 1968, with reports from major trading countries—France (Zajtay), Germany (Müller), England (Schmitthoff), USA (Hay)—and two general reviews, by Kegel (ascertainment of foreign law) and Zajtay (doctrine of factual character of foreign law, and its revisibility).

126. Joseph Esser, *Grundsatz und Norm*, 2nd ed., Tübingen 1964, p. 80. On the theme of legal certainty, cf. the references given in notes 3-11 of my article on transnational commercial law in NJW 1969, p. 2229.

TABLE OF DECIDED CASES

Date	Country	Tribunal	Case-title and/or description	Subject of case	Reference
1 October 1820	U.S.A.		Leroy v. Crowninshield	limitation	(1820) 2 Mason 151, 15 Fed. Cases 362 No. 8, 269
17 June 1830	England		British Linen	limitation	10 B.C. 901, 683
26 May 1835	England		Hubert v. Steiner	limitation	2 Bing. (N.C.) 203, 80
1837	England	House of Lords	Don v. Lippmann	limitation	V Cl. & F 303
15 January 1845	Germany	Geheim-Obertribunal, Prussia		limitation	E 11, 232
7 July 1854	Germany	Geheim-Obertribunal, Prussia		limitation	E 11, 232
7 June 1869	England		Harris v. Quine	limitation	1869 LR 4 QB 653
28 February 1870	France	Cassation		sale	Dalloz 1871, 61
28 June 1870	France	Cassation		limitation	Jur. Cass 1871, 136
1878	U.S.A.		Milliken v. Pratt	limitation	125 Mass. 375 = 28 Am. Rep. 241
4 January 1882	Germany	Reichsgericht		limitation	RGZ 7, 21
15 November 1886	U.S.A.	Supreme Court U.S.A.	Harrisburg	limitation	119 US 358
1886	U.S.A.		Pope Manuf'g Co.	licence	27 F 100
1 March 1889	France	Bordeaux		sale, lim.	Clunet 19 (1892) 990
25 October 1890	England		Chatenay	licence	1 QB (1891) 79
2 February 1891	U.S.A.	Supreme Court U.S.A.	Waterman	licence	138 US 924
6 October 1892	U.S.A.		Brush Electric	licence	52 F 945
27 October 1893	U.S.A.		Ball & Socket Fastener	licence	58 F 818
10 May 1894	England	House of Lords,	Hamlyn	limitation	AC 1894, 202
29 May 1894	U.S.A.		Canadian Pacific		61 F 738
1897		Railway Arbitration		award	Z. int. Eisenbahntransp. Vol V 1897, 912
22 June 1898	U.S.A.		Burton	licence	50 NE 1029

Date	Country	Tribunal	Case-title and/or description	Subject of case	Reference
28 April 1900	Germany	Reichsgericht		sale	RGZ 46, 193
23 May 1900	France	Cassation		sale	Dalloz 1901, 269
10 November 1900	England		A.G. für Cartonnagen	licence	18 RPC 6
28 June 1901	U.S.A.		New England Phonograph	licence	110 F 26
20 December 1901	England	House of Lords	Molling	sale	TLR XV111, 217
14 May 1902	England		Spurrier	insurance	AC 1902, 446
20 October 1902	Austria	Oberst-Gerichtshof		sale	Östr. OG Sammlung Vol 39, 651
14 October 1902	U.S.A.		Pious Fund	award	Am JIL 2 (1908), 898
24 April 1903	U.S.A.		Bates Mach. Co.	licence	66 NE 1093
16 June 1903	Germany	Reichsgericht	(Planks-"Bretter")	sale	RGZ 55, 105
16 May 1904	U.S.A.	Supreme Court U.S.A.	Davis v. Mills	limitation	194 US 1067
24 February 1905	England		Frost v. Dairy	sale	1 KB (1905) 608
20 April 1905	U.S.A.		New York Phonograph	licence	136 F 600
23 May 1905	U.S.A.		Garrigue	award	74 NE 523
1 September 1905		Railway Arbitration		award	Z. int. Eisenbahntransp. Vol X111 (1905), 332
9 September 1905	France	Trib. comm. de la Seine		sale	Revue 1909, 582
19 October 1906	Switzerland	Commercial Tribunal, Zürich		licence	Bl. Zürch. Rspr. Vol. V1 (1907) 185
26 April 1907	Germany	Reichsgericht		sale	RGZ 66,73
24 October 1907	Germany	Oberlandesgericht, Hamburg		sale	Hans. Gz 1907, 309
14 November 1907	Belgium	Trib. civil de Liège		sale	Revue 1909, 961
4 April 1908	Germany	Reichsgericht		transport	RGZ 68, 203
17 April 1909	U.S.A.		Critcher	licence	169 F 653
10 November 1910		Railway Arbitration		award, private international law	Bull. Transport Vol. 18 (1910), 375

Date		Country	Tribunal	Case-title and/or description	Subject of case	Reference
9 January	1911	U.S.A.		Foster Hose Supporter Co.	licence	184 F 71
14 February	1911	U.S.A.		Rowland	licence	185 F 515
1 March	1911	Germany	Reichsgericht		licence	RGZ 75, 400
16 June	1911		Railway Arbitration		award	Bull. Transport Vol. 19 (1911), 221
3 November	1911	England	House of Lords	E. Clemens Horst Co.	sale	AC 1912, 18
18 May	1912	Austria	Oberst-Gerichtshof		sale	Östr. OG. Sammlung Vol. 49, 359
21 June	1912	Germany	Reichsgericht		interpretation	RGZ 79, 418
22 November	1912	Germany	Reichsgericht		responsibility limitation	LZ 1913, 550
12 April	1913	Germany	Reichsgericht		licence	JW 1913, 861
30 July	1913	France	Lyons			Gaz . Pal. 1913 II, 347
2 December	1914	U.S.A.		Gray Engine Starter	licence	224 F 723
2 January	1915	U.S.A.		W.G.Ward Lumber Co.	sale	93 A 470
29 June	1915	Germany	Reichsgericht		good faith	Warn. Rspr. 1915, 337
30 March	1916	France	Conseil d'Etat		contract	Sirey 1916, 17
15 July	1916	Switzerland	Federal Tribunal		sale	BGE 42 II, 379
9 March	1917	Switzerland	Federal Tribunal		sale	BGE 43 II, 80
26 July	1917	France	Trib. civil de la Seine		licence	Annales 1926, 353
13 April	1918	Germany	Reichsgericht		licence	LZ 1918, 1216
18 June	1918	Germany	Reichsgericht		sale	RGZ 93, 166
10 October	1918	U.S.A.		Bird's Eye Veneer Co.	licence	259 F 266
11 October	1918	Switzerland	Federal Tribunal		sale	BGE 44 II, 416
28 December	1918	Switzerland	Federal Tribunal		sale, war	BGE 44 II, 519
2 January	1919	U.S.A.		Martin	licence	255 F 93
24 March	1919	U.S.A.		Griffin	sale	107 A 713
20 May	1919	U.S.A.		Rosenthal Paper	licence	123 NE 766
11 November	1919	England	House of Lords	Johnson	sale	AC 1920, 144

Date		Country	Tribunal	Case-title and/or description	Subject of case	Reference
28 April	1920	Germany	Oberlandesgericht, Hamburg		sale, limitation	Hans. GZ. 1920, 182
17 december	1920	England	House of Lords	The "Kronprinzessin"	sale	AC 1921, 486
22 december	1920	U.S.A.		Pressed Steel Car	licence	270 F 518
3 March	1921	Netherlands	Kantongerecht, Amsterdam			Nederlandsche Jurisprudentie 1921, 713
3 May	1921	Switzerland	Federal Tribunal		damages	BGE 47 II, 190
5 December	1921	Switzerland	Federal Tribunal		sale	BGE 47 II, 549
7 December	1921		MAT	Chausson	award	Rec. I, 587
9 December	1921	U.S.A.		Cook Pottery	licence	109 SE 744 = SO 89
25 January	1922	France	Cassation	Gruning	force majeure	Dalloz 1922, 71
17 February	1922		MAT	Universal Rim	award	Rec. I, 726
16 March	1922	U.S.A.		Shohfi	licence	21 F 346
14 April	1922	U.S.A.			sale	135 NE 141
22 May	1922	France	Strasbourg		sale	Clunet 49 (1922), 1022
1 June	1922		MAT	Brinon	award	Rec. II, 219
9 July	1922		MAT	Albert	award, sale	Rec. II, 284
26 July	1922		MAT	Alcan	award	Rec. II, 328
26 July	1922		MAT	Rumeau	award	Rec. II, 326
24 November	1922		MAT	Munzing	award	Rec. II, 747
12 December	1922	Germany	Reichsgericht	"Verlustschein"	contract	RGZ 106, 82
20 December	1922		Railway Arbitration		award	Bull. Transport 1923,1
20 December	1922	France	Marseilles		sale	Journal (Clunet) 1923, 280
18 January	1923	Switzerland	Federal Tribunal		sale	BGE 49 II, 28
5 March	1923	Switzerland	Federal Tribunal		sale	BGE 49 II, 70
27 April	1923		MAT	Loy et Marcus	award	Rec. III 998 (1004)
30 April	1923		MAT	Bartelous	award	Rec. IV, 277
24 May	1923		MAT	Goldschmidt	award	Rec. III, 1020
25 May	1923		MAT	Stoehr	award	Re.. III, 286

Date		Country	Tribunal	Case-title and/or description	Subject of case	Reference
27 July	1923		MAT	Comp. des Eaux de Vienne	award	Rec. III, 578
1 November	1923			The "Lusitania"	damages, award	UNRIAA V, 532
28 November	1923	Germany	Reichsgericht		good faith	RGZ 107, 78
8 January	1924	France	Cassation	Lautaro Nitrate Co. ("Vienna Loan")	sale	Gaz. Pal. 1924 I, 405
20 February	1924		MAT		award	Rec. IV, 37
3 March	1924	France	Cassation	London Rice Brokers	sale	Sirey 1924, I 252
22 March	1924		MAT	Marie Lutz	insurance, award	Rec. IV, 390
12 April	1924		MAT	Freiherr von Türcke	award	Rec. IV, 179
10 May	1924	U.S.A.		Miles ("Vermont Potatoes")	contract	124 A 559
23 May	1924	U.S.A.		Carver-Beaver Yarn	sale	143 NE 919
27 May	1924	Germany	Reichsgericht		sale	IPRspr. 1926/27 No. 43
22 July	1924	England		Jones		2 KB 1924, 730
11 November	1924	Norway	High Court		contract	Norsk Retstidende 1924, 1181= Rabels Z 2, 873
8 December	1924	U.S.A.	Supreme Court U.S.A.	Westinghouse Electric	licence	266 US 317
18 December	1924		MAT	Alfred Stern	award	Rec. V, 278
24 December	1924	France	Rouen		sale	Clunet 1925, 968
16 June	1925		MAT	Negreanu	sale-contract, award	Rec. V, 200
13 July	1925		MAT	Gutberlet	award	Rec. V, 790
26 February	1926	U.S.A.		Obear Nester Glass	licence	11 F 2nd 240
30 March	1926		MAT	Zeppenfeld	award	Rec. V, 243
12 April	1926		MAT	Levi	deposit, award	Rec. VII, 256
31 May	1926		MAT	Charles Harbord Cook	limitation, award	Rec. VI, 540
31 May	1926		MAT	Livingstone, Case 3025	limitation, award	Lewald JW 1926, 2815

Date	Country	Tribunal	Case-title and/or description	Subject of case	Reference
11 June 1926		MAT	Charles Semon	award	Rec. VI, 75
23 June 1926	Germany	Reichsgericht		sale	RGZ 114, 155
24 June 1926	England		Cohen	sale	1 KB (1927) 169
3 November 1926		MAT	Antippa	award	Rec. VII, 28
26 November 1926		MAT		limitation, award	Rec. VI, 632
17 December 1926	England		Wait	sale CIF	1 CH (1921) 606
14 February 1927		MAT	Sarropolous	award	Rec. VII, 47/51
7 April 1927		MAT	Büsse	sale, award	Rec. VII, 345
16 May 1927	U.S.A.	Supreme Court U.S.A.	Joseph Seeman	sale	274 US 1123
23 May 1927	England	House of Lords	Kwik Hoo Tong	sale	AC 1927, 604
20 July 1927	U.S.A.		Yusupov		158 NE 64
28 September 1927	Germany	Reichsgericht			RGZ 118, 140
21 November 1927	U.S.A.		Bowman	specific performance	261 P 679
22 November 1927	U.S.A.		Allegheny College	consideration	159 NE 173
23 November 1927	U.S.A.		Montreal Cotton	sale	158 NE 795
6 December 1927	France	Tourcoing		sale	Gaz. Pal. 1928 I, 282
13 March 1928	Germany	Reichsgericht			Warn. Rspr. 1928 No. 56 = IPRspr. 1928 Vol. 2 No. 1
4 April 1928	Germany	Reichsgericht			IPRspr. 1929 No. 31
12 May 1928	Germany	Reichsgericht	Horvath	limitation	LZ 1928, 1550
25 June 1928	U.S.A.		Thames	licence	27 F 2nd 148
30 June 1928		MAT		award	Rec. VIII, 64
13 December 1928	England		Foster v. Driscoll	sale	1 KB (1929) 470
23 January 1929	U.S.A.		Monsanto	licence	31 F 2nd 188
2 March 1929	U.S.A.		Wilson	sale	165 NE 408
8 April 1929		MAT	Chemins de fer du Nord	award	Rec. IX, 67
5 June 1929	France	Cassation		sale	Gaz. Pal. 1929 II, 433

Date	Country	Tribunal	Case-title and/or description	Subject of case	Reference
12 July 1929		Permanent Court of International Justice	Serbian Loans		Ser. A., Nos. 20/21
20 September 1929	U.S.A.		Ruby	licence	36 F 2nd 244
22 October 1929	Germany	Reichsgericht		limitation	IPRspr. 1930 No. 32
13 November 1929	Germany	Oberlandesgericht, Hamburg			IPRspr. 1930 No. 58
19 December 1929	France	Paris	Mouriaque	licence	Annales 1930, 143
12 February 1930	Germany	Reichsgericht		licence	RGZ 127, 243
19 February 1930	France	Cassation			Sirey 1933, 41
19 February 1930	England		Huntoon	licence	RPC Vol. 47, 403
4 March 1930	Germany	Oberlandesgericht, Hamburg			IPRspr. 1930 No. 57 = Hans. GZ. 1930, B 207
4 April 1930	Germany	Reichsgericht		limitation	RGZ 128, 76
30 April 1930	England		Fuel Economy	licence	RPC Vol. 47, 346
5 May 1930	U.S.A.		Western Electric	licence	42 F 2nd 116
4 August 1930	U.S.A.		Wood & Selick	limitation	43 F 2nd 941
3 September 1930			Lena Goldfields	award	Cornell L.Q. Vol. 36 (1950), 42
27 January 1931	France	Cassation	London Corn Trade Ass.		Sirey 1933, 41
28 February 1931	Germany	Kammergericht		limitation	IPRspr. 1932 No. 82
19 March 1931	U.S.A.		Gerly v. Cunard		48 F 2nd 115
29 April 1931	Germany	Reichsgericht		licence	Markenschutz und Wettbewerb 1931, 441
27 July 1931	France	Colmar		sale, import	Clunet 60 (1933), 682
11 November 1931	England		Campbell	licence	RPC Vol. 49, 38
13 November 1931	Italy			limitation	Foro Ital. 1932 I 23
27 April 1932	Germany	Reichsgericht			IPRspr. 1932 No. 32
29 April 1932	England		Suhr	licence	RPC Vol. 49, 359

Date	Country	Tribunal	Case-title and/or description	Subject of case	Reference
4 May	1932	Germany	Reichsgericht		unjust enrichment	Seuff. Arch. 86 (1932) 257 No. 141 = IPRspr. 1932 No. 38
11 May	1932	France	Lyons		licence	Annales 1932, 259
26 June	1932	France	Colmar			Sirey 1934, 273
2 June	1932	France	Trib. de la Seine			Sirey 1934, 275
11 February	1933	France	International Chamber of Commerce		sale-import award	Revue 1934, 147
15 February	1933	France	Paris		sale-import	Clunet 60 (1933), 959
3 March	1933	Italy	Cassation		limitation	Rivista Dir. Priv. 1934 II 67 = Clunet 1936, 697
9 March	1933	England		Campbell	licence	RPC Vol. 50, 213
10 March	1933	Germany	Oberlandesgericht, Hamburg	Leningrad Ice Clause		IPRspr. 1933 No.1
24 March	1933	France	Paris		contract	Sirey 1933 II, 201
4 April	1933	U.S.A.		Thomas G. Jewett	sale-import	185 NE 369
16 May	1933	England		The "Kite"	contract	P.D. 1933, 164
10 June	1933	Germany	Reichsgericht		licence	IPRspr. 1933 No. 22
26 June	1933	France	Trib. de la Seine		licence	Annales 1934, 35
29 June	1933	France	Cassation		licence	Annales 1935, 78
29 August	1933	U.S.A.		Radio Corporation of America	licence	66 F 2nd 778
2 November	1933	England		Soc. An. Metallurgique de Prayon	limitation	The Solicitors' Journal 1933, 800
4 November	1933	Germany	Reichsgericht	Leningrad Ice Clause		IPRspr. 1933, 1b
10 November	1933	U.S.A.		Hollidge	sale	67 F 2nd 459
5 May	1934	Germany	Oberlandesgericht, Hamburg	Leningrad Ice Clause		IPRspr. 1934 No. 3
6 July	1934	Germany	Reichsgericht		bill of exchange	RGZ 145, 121 = JZ 1934, 3121 = IPRspr. 1934 No. 29

Date	Country	Tribunal	Case-title and/or description	Subject of case	Reference
14 July 1934	Germany	Reichsgericht		licence	Mitteilungen des Verbandes Dt. Patentanwälte 1934, 236
6 February 1935	Switzerland	Federal Tribunal	"Preolit"	licence	BGE 61 II 59
12 April 1935	England		Vigneron Dahl et Cie	licence	RPC Vol. 52, 303
1 May 1935	England		Maritime Insurance	reinsurance	42 LLR 16
8 May 1935	Germany	Kammergericht	"agricultural machines"	licence	GRUR 1935, 892
15 May 1935	France	Cassation		sale	Rev. Crit. 13 (1936), 463
19 June 1935	Germany	Reichsgericht		licence	GRUR 1936, 57
13 September 1935	Switzerland	Federal Tribunal			BGE 61 II 204
11 October 1935	England		Arcos		53 LLR (1935) 38
29 January 1936	Italy	Cassation		limitation	Foro Ital. 1936 I 1033
15 February 1936	Germany	Reichsgericht		licence	JW 1936, 1522
11 March 1936	Switzerland	Bezirksgericht, Zürich	Vereinigte Stahlwerke	loan (gold clause)	unpublished
19 March 1936	France	Trib. civ. Ribérac		licence	Annales 1939, 185
20 April 1936	U.S.A.		Krell	licence	83 F 2nd 414
7 July 1936	England		National Carbonising	licence	RPC Vol. 54, 41
2 November 1936	England		International Trustee	gold clause	AE 1936 Vol. 2, 408
15 March 1937	England	House of Lords	R.v. International Trustee	gold clause	AE 1937 Vol. 2, 164
18 August 1937	Germany	Reichsgericht		licence	RGZ 155, 306
17 November 1937	U.S.A.		Kansas City Wholesale	sale	73 P 2nd 1272
17 March 1938	England	House of Lords	Vulcaan	limitation	2 AE 1938, 152
12 April 1938	France	Paris		limitation	Gaz. Pal. 1938, 749
14 May 1938	U.S.A.		Eastern States Petroleum	limitation	2 A 2nd 138
11 July 1938	U.S.A.		Frost Ry Supply	licence	24 F Suppl. 20
3 September 1938	Germany	Kammergericht		licence	GRUR 1939, 66
30 January 1939	England	House of Lords	Vitafood	licence	AC 1939, 277
2 March 1939	England	House of Lords	Philippson v. Imperial Airways	transport	AC 1939, 332

Date	Country	Tribunal	Case-title and/or description	Subject of case	Reference
17 May 1939	France	Cassation		sale	Sirey 1939, 268
15 June 1939	U.S.A.			licence	107 F 2nd 27
12 December 1940	England	House of Lords	Cold Metal Process Co.	licence	AC 1941, 108
24 April 1940	France	Paris	Luxor	import	Sirey 42 II 29
24 June 1940	U.S.A.	Cassation	Chemical Foundation	licence	22 NY 479
4 June 1941	France	Cassation		licence	Jur. Cass. 1941, 133
11 July 1941	U.S.A.		Dysart	licence	40 F Suppl. 596
12 June 1942	Germany	Reichsgericht		licence	GRUR 1943, 35
15 June 1942	England	House of Lords	Fibrosa Spolka	unjust enrichment	AC 1943, 32
4 September 1942	U.S.A.		Monarch Brewing	sale	130 F 2nd 582
17 March 1943	U.S.A.		State of Delaware	sale	49 F Suppl. 467
27 July 1943	U.S.A.		Eno	licence	58 USPQ 681
27 July 1943	U.S.A.		Thrift Wholesale	sale	50 F Suppl. 998
4 August 1943	U.S.A.		American Type Founders	licence	137 F 2nd 729
13 March 1944	U.S.A.		Saco Lowell Shops	licence	141 F 2nd 597
26 August 1944	U.S.A.		Mechanical Ice Tray	licence	144 F 2nd 720
12 September 1944	U.S.A.		Dixon, Irmaos	letter of credit	144 F 2nd 759
20 October 1944	Switzerland	Court of Appeal, Berne		sale-embargo	ZBJV 1946 Vol. 82, 142
18 November 1944	U.S.A.		Sbicca-Del Mac	licence	145 F 2nd 389
7 March 1945	England		The "Glenroy"	documents	AC 1945, 124
5 February 1946	U.S.A.		Norwood Lumber	sale	153 F 2nd 753
13 February 1946	U.S.A.		Texas Motorcoaches	sale	154 F 2nd 91
10 April 1946	U.S.A.		Price	sale	37 SE 2nd 592
3 December 1946	Switzerland	Federal Tribunal		sale	BGE 72 II 405
9 June 1946	U.S.A.		Order of United Commercial Travelers of America	limitation	331 US 586
24 June 1947	U.S.A.				73 NY 2nd 523

Date	Country	Tribunal	Case-title and/or description	Subject of case	Reference
19 February 1948	England		Groupement National d'Achat des Tourteaux	sale	LLR 1962 Vol. 2, 192
29 July 1948	U.S.A.		Atlas Trading Corp.	sale	169 F 2nd 240
15 March 1949	Switzerland	Federal Tribunal	Suchard	limitation, licence	BGE 75 II 57
20 October 1949	England	House of Lords	Zivnostenska Bank	limitation	AE 1949 Vol. 2, 621
31 January 1950	France	Cassation			JCP 1950, 5541
28 February 1950	Switzerland	Federal Tribunal		foreign exchange law	BGE 76 II 33
21 June 1950	France	Cassation	Messageries Maritimes	gold clause	Dalloz 1951, 749
23 June 1950	England		Du Pont	licence	RPC Vol. 67, 144
18 December 1950	France		Pau	sale	JCP 1952, 6684
22 March 1951	Switzerland	Federal Tribunal		sale	BGE 77 II 83
22 May 1951	England		Kohnke		AE 1951 Vol. 2, 179
15 June 1951	Germany	Bundesgerichtshof	Kalisyndikat	licence	NJW 1951, 836
9 July 1951	U.S.A.		Fairbanks, Morse & Co.	sale	190 F 2nd 817
28 August 1951	U.S.A.	Lord Asquith	Abu-Dhabi	award	ICLQ April 1952, 247 = Int. Law R. 1951, 145
12 October 1951	England		Bank Melli Iran	sale	LLR 1951 Vol. 2, 367
31 January 1952	England		Yello	sale	LLR 1952 Vol. 1. 183
12 February 1952	Switzerland	Federal Tribunal		sale	BGE 78 II 74
20 February 1952	Austria	Oberst-Gerichtshof		sale	SZ XXV No. 46
22 May 1952	England		Platicmoda	sale	LLR 1952 Vol. 1, 527
21 July 1952	England		Brauer & Co.	sale	AE 1952 Vol. 2, 497
31 July 1952	England		Terrell	licence	RPC Vol. 69, 234
3 October 1952	Germany	Oberlandesgericht, Hamburg	"Le Rouge Baiser"	licence	GRUR 1953, 177
8 October 1952	Germany	Landgericht, Bremen		limitation	IPRspr. 1952/53 No. 28
16 October 1952	England		British Nylon Spinners	licence	RPC Vol. 69, 288

Date	Country	Tribunal	Case-title and/or description	Subject of case	Reference
26 January 1953	U.S.A.		Bennett	sale	119 NY Suppl. 2nd 530
11 February 1953	Germany	Bundesgerichtshof		insurance	NJW 1953, 542
3 March 1953	France	Paris		licence	Annales 1953, 1
1 April 1953	England		Compagnie de Commerce	sale	LLR 1953 Vol. 1, 532
15 April 1953	Germany	Oberlandesgericht, Munich		limitation	IPRspr. 1952/3 No. 34
28 April 1953	U.S.A.		Charles	sale	111 F Suppl. 794
12 May 1953	England			sale	2 QB 1953, 329
30 June 1953	France	Trib. civ. de la Seine	J. d' Almeida Araujo LDA	licence	Gaz. Pal. 1953, Sommaire 15
4 July 1953	Switzerland	Federal Tribunal	Intra-Handels A.G.	sale	BGE 79 II 165
20 July 1953	France	Paris		licence	Dalloz 1953, 703
14 August 1953		Prague Chamber of Commerce	Koospol	award	Journal 1956, 453
31 August 1953	Switzerland	Federal Tribunal	Patchett	sale	BGE 79 II 295
22 October 1953	England			licence	RPC Vol. 70, 269
28 October 1953	France	Cassation	Soc. Générale de Surveillance	award	Bulletin 1953, 230
3 November 1953	France	Cassation		award	Dalloz 1954, 1
2 February 1954	Switzerland	Federal Tribunal		award	BGE 80 II 61
1 March 1954		Prague Chamber of Commerce	Centrotex	award	Journal du droit International 1956, 469
15 March 1954	Germany	Patent Office	IBM	award	GRUR 1954, 266
9 April 1954	England		Kianta	sale	LLR 1954 Vol. 1, 247
3 May 1954	Italy	Cassation		contract	Il Foro 1954 I 734
17 May 1954	England		Hookway	sale	LLR 1954 Vol. 1, 491
9 July 1954	England		British Nylon Spinners	licence	RPC Vol. 71, 327
27 July 1954	England		Kwei Tek Chao	sale	2 QB 1954, 459
10 September 1954	Germany	Landgericht, Regensburg		limitation	IPRspr. 1954/5 No. 120

Date	Country	Tribunal	Case-title and/or description	Subject of case	Reference
2 November 1954		Prague Chamber of Commerce	Tangiers v. Motokov	award	Journal du droit International 1956, 458
2 November 1954	Germany	Patent Office		licence	GRUR 1954, 58
18 November 1954	Germany	Landgericht, Munich		licence	GRUR 1956, 413
20 November 1954	England			sale	LLR 1955 Vol. 2, 526
24 November 1954	France	Cassation	Moralice	sale	ICP 1955 II No. 8565
26 November 1954	England		J. Milhem & Sons	sale	LLR 1955 Vol. 2, 559
26 November 1954	Germany	Bundesgerichtshof	"Spectacle-lenses"	licence	GRUR 1955, 338
5 January 1955	U.S.A.		U.S.A. v. Henderson	sale	126 F Suppl. 626
17 January 1955	Germany	Patent Office		licence	GRUR 1955, 294= IPRspr. 1954/5 No. 149
26 January 1955	France	Cassation	Chaffrais	licence	Annales 1956, 1
27 January 1955	France	Paris		sale	Revue 1955, 330
8 February 1955	U.S.A.		Eastern Airlines ("Potomac Case")		221 F 2nd 80
21 February 1955	Germany	Patent Office	Etablissements Chainbaux	licence	GRUR 1955, 297
1 March 1955	England			sale	LLR 1955 Vol. 1, 303
1 March 1955	England		E. Reynolds	sale	LLR 1955 Vol. 1, 259
31 March 1955	Germany	Oberlandesgericht, Munich		sale	BB 1955, 748
17 May 1955	England		Entores Ltd	telex, sale	2 QB 1955, 327
10 June 1955	England		Martin Baker Aircraft	licence	RPC Vol. 72, 236
10 June 1955			Cassin	award	Rev. Crit. 1956, 278
16 June 1955	England		Tool Metal Manufacturing	licence	RPC Vol. 72, 209
18 June 1955	France	Trib. civ. Seine	Usines Calox	licence	Annales 1956, 6
8 July 1955	U.S.A.		Aron		128 NE 2nd 284
21 October 1955	England		N.V. Handel	sale	LLR 1955 Vol. 2, 317
31 October 1955	France	Paris	Banolas	licence	Annales 1957, 427

Date		Country	Tribunal	Case-title and/or description	Subject of case	Reference
16 November	1955	France	Cassation		sale	Bulletin 1955, 276
16 January	1956	France	Cassation		licence	Annales 1958, 168
28 February	1956	England		S.C.C.M.O.Ltd	sale	LLR 1956 Vol. 1, 290
6 March	1956			Ambatielos	award	H.M. Stationary Office, London 1956
18 April	1956	Germany	Amtsgericht, Hattingen		limitation	IPRspr. 1956/7 No. 128
23 April	1956	France	Seine	Henri Malsert	licence	Annales 1961, 260
22 June	1956	France	Cassation		contract	Bulletin 1956/4, 433
2 July	1956		Ripert/Panchaud	Veles-Prilep Railway	award	Journal 1959, 1074
17 December	1956	U.S.A.		Global Commerce Corp.	sale	239 F 2nd 716
29 January	1957	England	House of Lords	Board of Trade	sale	AC 1957, 602
1 February	1957	U.S.A.		Wynne v. Allen	licence	112 USPQ 405
26 February	1957	France	Colmar		sale	Revue 1957, 309
19 March	1957	Germany	Bundesgerichtshof		sale	MDR 1958, 916
27 March	1957	France	Colmar		sale	Revue 1957, 301
27 March	1957	England		Carlos Federspiel	sale	LLR 1957 Vol. 1, 240
4 April	1957	U.S.A.		Delta Tank Manufacturing	sale	150 F Suppl. 525
19 June	1957	France	Strasbourg		sale	Rev. Crit. 1959, 95
12 July	1957	U.S.A.		Aktiebolaget Bofors	licence	114 USPQ 243
16 July	1957	France	Cassation	Charvet	licence	Annales 1959, 219
21 October	1957	England	House of Lords	Regazzoni	import	3 AE 1957, 286
6 November	1957	France	Casation	Exhenry	licence	Annales 1958, 169
12 November	1957	France	Cassation		sale	Bulletin 1957, 344
25 November	1957	England	House of Lords	National Bank of Greece Fomento	limitation	AC 1958, 509
4 December	1957	England	House of Lords	(Coal and Steel)	licence	RPC 1958, 8
10 December	1957	England	European Court			Europ. Ct. Vol. 3, 200
10 December	1957	England		Hamzeh Malass	letter of credit	2 WLR 1958, 100

259

Date		Country	Tribunal	Case-title and/or description	Subject of case	Reference
10 January	1958	Germany	Bundesgerichtshof	("Canned Meat")		IPRspr. 1958/9 No. 143 = LM 3 *ad* §480 BGB
22 January	1958	France	Cassation		sale	Bulletin 1958,34
14 February	1958	Germany	Bundesgerichtshof		sale	NJW 1958, 750 = LM, EGBGB Art. 27 No. 2
12 March	1958	U.S.A.		Hyde Corporation	licence	117 USPQ 44
18 March	1958	Germany	Landgericht, Düsseldorf (not valid)		licence	GRUR Ausl. 1958, 430
27 March	1958	U.S.A.		Violet Virginia Kohagen Boris	licence	253 F 2nd 526
4 June	1958	U.S.A.	Vereinigung des Wollhandels e. V., Bremen		licence	117 USPQ 466
10 June	1958	U.S.A.		Hyde Corporation	award	AWD BB 1959, 60
19 June	1958		Foreign Trade Arbitration Commission, Moscow	"Israel Oil Case" (Jordan Investments)	award	AJIL Vol. 53 (1959), 800
25 June	1958	England	House of Lords	London Transport	licence	AC 1959, 247
11 July	1958	England		Advance Industries		RPC 1958, 392
23 August	1958	U.S.A.	Sauser-Hall	Aramco	award	Rev. Crit. 1963, 272
5 September	1958	England		Walter M. Krantz	licence	165 F Suppl. 776
17 October	1958	England		McDougall	sale	1 WLR 1958, 1126
29 October	1958	Germany	Oberlandesgericht, Hamburg			AWD BB 1958, 249
2 December	1958	England		Rapalli	sale	LLR 1958 Vol. 2, 469
8 December	1958	England		United Railways		CD 1960, 52
29 January	1959	Germany	Oberlandesgericht, Munich	"Le Mans"	licence	GRUR Ausl. 1960, 75

Date	Country	Tribunal	Case-title and/or description	Subject of case	Reference
8 April 1959	England		Matthews	contract	2 QB 1959, 57
1 May 1959	U.S.A.		Shanahan	sale	266 F 2nd 400
22 May 1959	Germany	Bundesgerichtshof		licence	GRUR 1960, 44
22 June 1959	U.S.A.		Henry J. Kaiser	licence	122 USPQ 225
29 June 1959	Germany	Bundesgerichtshof			NJW 1959, 1964
13 July 1959	Germany	Bundesgerichtshof			NJW 1959, 1873
13 July 1959	U.S.A.		De Long	licence	176 F Suppl. 104 (127)
21 August 1959	Germany	Oberlandesgericht, Bremen			Arch. VR 9 (1961 /2), 318
1 October 1959	Germany	Landgericht, Munich		limitation	NJW 1959, 2312
10 November 1959	France	Paris		licence	Annales 1960, 58
16 November 1959	U.S.A.	Warner-Lambert		licence	123 USPQ 431 = 178 F. Suppl. 665
17 December 1959	Germany	Bundesgerichtshof		foreign exchange law	BGHZ 31, 368 = NJW 1960, 1101
28 March 1960	France	Cassation	Forest	limitation	Rev. Crit. 1960, 202
5 April 1960	France	Cassation		licence	Dalloz 1960, 717
12 April 1960		International Court of Justice	Right of Passage		I.C.J. Reports 1960
5 May 1960	England	House of Lords	United Railway		2 WLR 1960, 969
9 May 1960	U.S.A.		Henningsen		32 NY 358 = 161 A 2nd 69
11 May 1960	U.S.A.		William P. Rogers	licence	183 F Suppl. 573
24 May 1960	England	House of Lords	Brown	sale	LLR 1960 Vol. 1, 289
9 June 1960	Germany	Bundesgerichtshof	("Chocolate")	limitation	NJW 1960, 1721
14 June 1960	U.S.A.		Invengineering	licence	126 USPQ 4
5 July 1960	Germany	Bundesgerichtshof		licence	BB 1960, 998
4 October 1960	Switzerland	Federal Tribunal		licence	BGE 86 II 270
19 October 1960	Germany	Bundesgerichtshof		import	JZ 1961, 261

Date		Country	Tribunal	Case-title and/or description	Subject of case	Reference
21 October	1960	Germany	Bundesgerichtshof	("Borax")	import	NJW 1961, 822 = BGHZ 34, 169
24 November	1960	Germany	Bundesgerichtshof		sale	NJW 1961, 412
9 December	1960	U.S.A.		Pennsylvania Company Archbolds	transport	166 A 2nd 726
15 December	1960	England				2 WLR 1961, 170
12 January	1961	U.S.A.		Kilberg v. Northeast Airlines	transport	172 NE 2nd 527
13 January	1961	England		Mash	sale	1 WLR 1861, 862
30 January	1961	Germany	Bundesgerichtshof		commercial representation	NJW 1961, 1061
2 February	1961	France	Trib. de grande instance d' Avesne-sur-Helpe		licence	Dalloz 1961, 652
24 February	1961	England		Bristol Repetition	licence	RPC 1961, 222
17 March	1961	Germany	Bundesgerichtshof	("Gewinderollkopf")	licence	GRUR 1961, 466
6 July	1961	Germany	Bundesgerichtshof	("Social insurance")	lien on ship	BGHZ 35, 267 =MDR 1961, 831
4 August	1961	Germany	Oberlandesgericht, Düsseldorf		licence	AWD BB 1961, 295
12 December	1961	England		Ebrahim Dawood	sale	LLR 1961 Vol. 2, 512
20 December	1961	England		Hongkong Fur Shipping Co.	sale	2 QB 1962, 26
15 January	1962	U.S.A.		Roto-Lith	sale	297 F 2nd 497
15 January	1962	France	Cassation			Bull. Cass. 1962, 24
19 January	1962	U.S.A.		American Cyanamid ("Maja")	licence	132 USPQ 302
22 February	1962	Germany	Oberlandesgericht, Frankfurt		licence	GRUR 1963, 30
19 June	1962	France	Paris	**Pulsa**	licence	Annales 1962, 168

Date		Country	Tribunal	Case-title and/or description	Subject of case	Reference
19 July	1962	Germany	Oberlandesgericht, Stuttgart		sale	MDR 1964, 412
31 October	1962	England		The "Orion"		LLR 1962 Vol. 2, 257
21 November	1962	Germany	Oberlandesgericht, Hamburg	(The "Havanna")	insurance	Versicherungsrecht 1963, 449 (453)
8 January	1963	U.S.A.	Opinion of the Comptroller-General		licence	136 USPQ 321
29 January	1963	France	Paris	Audibert	licence	Annales 1963, 361
19 February	1963	England		Fomento	licence	RPC 1963, 163
1 March	1963	France	Paris	Devos	licence	Annales 1963, 28
15 March	1963	France	Cavin	Sapphire International	award	ICLQ 1964, 1011
16 March	1963	France	Paris	Consorts Outhier	licence	Annales 1963, 385
20 March	1963	Germany	Bundesgerichtshof		sale	BGHZ 39, 173 = NJW 1963, 1200
9 May	1963	U.S.A.		Babcock	transport	12 NY 2nd 473 = 191 NE 2nd 240
6 June	1963	U.S.A.		Thys Company	licence	138 USPQ 411
20 June	1963	U.S.A.		Great Lakes Carbon	licence	138 USPQ 613
25 September	1963	Switzerland	Court of Appeal, Berne		limitation	ZBJV 1965, 101 = AWD BB 1965, 258
24 December	1963	U.S.A.		Heyman	licence	140 USPQ 403
8 April	1964	France	Paris	Gasse	licence	JCP 1964, 13876
27 April	1964	France	Cassation		contract	Clunet 1964, 819
4 May	1964	France	Cassation			Gaz. Pal. 1964-2, 233 = Clunet 1965, 126
15 May	1964	U.S.A.		Official Airlines Schedule	licence	141 USPQ 546
2 June	1964	England		Cheetham		LLR 1964 Vol. 2, 17
5 October	1964	U.S.A.		Sperry Rand	sale	337 F 2nd 364
26 November	1964	Germany	Bundesgerichtshof			NJW 1965, 489

Date	Country	Tribunal	Case-title and/or description	Subject of case	Reference
1 December 1964	Germany	Bundesgerichtshof	("Strawberry pulp")	licence	NJW 1965, 759
9 December 1964	Germany	Bundesgerichtshof	S.A.Dognin	import	NJW 1965, 847
17 December 1964	France	Cassation		licence	Annales 1965, 172
21 December 1964	England		National Broach	licence	RPC 1965, 61
18 February 1965	Germany	Bundesgerichtshof	("Polish refugees")		NJW 1965, 1127
11 May 1965	England		Fluflon	licence	RPC 1965, 562
2 June 1965	Germany	Oberlandesgericht, Hamburg		sale	Rabels Z 1968, 535
10 June 1965	U.S.A.		Tramontana	transport	Am. Bar. Asso. Jour. 51 (1965), 879
14 June 1965	Germany	Bundesgerichtshof		licence	AWD BB 1965, 275
15 June 1965	England		National Broach	licence	RPC 1965, 516
24 June 1965	England		Rosenthal & Sons	sale	1 WLR 1965, 1117
5 August 1965		Prague Chamber of Commerce	Centrotex	award	Rev. Arbitrage 1967, 25
11 August 1965	U.S.A.		Ora Lee Williams	sale	350 F 2nd 445
23 September 1965	Germany	Bundesgerichtshof		licence	NJW 1965, 1861
3 November 1965		Prague Chamber of Commerce		award	Rev. Arbitrage 1967, 67
4 November 1965	Germany	Max-Planck Institut, Hamburg	legal opinion	limitation	Gutachten 1965/1966, ed. Ferid/Kegel/Zweigert, Berlin/Tübingen, 1968, 18
16 November 1965	Switzerland	Federal Tribunal	("Futterseide")	sale	BGE 91 II 356
1 December 1965	England		Ginzberg	sale	LLR 1966 Vol, 1, 343
17 January 1966	Germany	Bundesgerichtshof		private international law	AWD BB 1966, 60
27 January 1966		Prague Chamber of Commerce		award	Rev. Arbitrage 1967, 29
2 February 1966	Germany	Bundesgerichtshof		sale	NJW 1966, 879 = LM No. 29 ad EGBGB

Date		Country	Tribunal	Case-title and/or description	Subject of case	Reference
4 February	1966	France	Paris		sale	Rev. Arbitrage 1966, 27
9 February	1966	France	Paris	Suisse Atlantique	sale	Rev. Crit. 1966, 264
31 March	1966	England	House of Lords	The "Aspasia"		AC 1967, 361
2 May	1966	France	Cassation	Wegematic Corporation		Gaz. Pal. 1966-2, 81
5 May	1966	U.S.A.		Elkins-Dell Manufacturing	sale	360 F 2nd 674
13 May	1966	U.S.A.				253 F Suppl. 864
13 July	1966	France	Cassation		licence	JCP 1967 No. 15131
27 July	1966	England		Phoenix Distributors	sale	LLR 1966 Vol. 2, 285
25 October	1966	Germany	Bundesgerichtshof	('Rivets')	licence	BGHZ 46,365
15 November	1966	U.S.A.		Frostifresh	sale	274 NY Suppl. 2nd 757
12 December	1966	Germany	Bundesgerichtshof		privat inter-national law	AWD BB 1967, 108
20 January	1967	U.S.A.		Natus Corporation trustee	sale	371 F 2nd 450
3 March	1967	Austria	Oberst-Gerichtshof			Z. Rechtsvergl. 1969, 143
13 June	1967	U.S.A.		Baffin Land Corporation	sale	425 P 2nd 623
26 October	1967	England		United Dominions Trust		1 WLR 1968, 74
6 December	1967	England		Boys v. Chaplin	car accident in Malta	2 AE 1968, 283
17 October	1968	Germany	Bundesgerichtshof		licence	GRUR 1969, 409=WuW/E 988
7 November	1968	Germany	Oberlandesgericht, Frankfurt		import	NJW 1969, 991
26 November	1968	Germany	Bundesgerichtshof	("Fowl pest")	damage	NJW 1969, 269
28 November	1968	England		The "President of India"	sale	2 WLR 1969, 125
12 December	1968	Germany	Bundesgerichtshof		sale	NJW 1969, 787
19 December	1968	Germany	Bundesgerichtshof		sale	NJW 1969, 975
26 February	1969	Germany	Bundesgerichtshof		sale	NJW 1969, 1116
22 October	1969	Germany	Bundesgerichtshof		sale	NJW 1970, 384
30 September	1970	Germany	Bundesgerichtshof		sale	NJW 1970, 2103

SELECT BIBLIOGRAPHY*

Aeberhard, *Rechtsnatur und Ausgestaltung der Patentlizenz im deutschen, französischen und schweizerischen Recht,* Berne 1952.

Anderson-Coulson, "The Moslem rules and contractual obligations", *New York University Law Review* 33 (1958), 917.

Batiffol, H., *Aspects philosophiques du droit international privé,* Paris 1952.

—, "La sentence Aramco et le droit international privé", *Rev. Crit.* 1964, 647.

—, "L'arbitrage et les conflits de lois", *Revue d'Arbitrage* 1957-II.

—, "Réflexions sur la coordination des systèmes nationaux", *Recueil des Cours* (120) 1967-I.

—, *Droit international privé,* 4th ed., 1967.

Beier/Deutsch/Fikentscher (editors), "Die Warenzeichenlizenz", *Festschrift für Ulmer,* Munich 1963.

Beitzke, "Betrachtungen zur Methodik im IPR", *Festschrift Smend,* 1957, 1.

Bendermacher/Geroussis, *Ermessensfreiheit und Billigkeitssprechraum des Zivilrechts,* Arbeiten zur Rechtsvergleichung, Heft 24, Frankfurt 1911, 1964.

Benjamin, "ECE general conditions of sale and standard forms of contract", JBL 113 (1961).

Berman, "Jordan Investments Ltd. *v.* Sojuznefteksport", *Rabels Zeitschrift* 1959, 404/414.

—, "The Uniform Law on International Sales," *Law and Contemporary Problems,* Duke University 1965, 354.

Bin Cheng, *The General Principles of Civilized Nations,* London 1953.

Blühdorn, R., *Recueil des Cours* 41 (1931-III) 141.

Bolla, "Testo italiano nella interpretazione delle legge svizzere", *Berner Festkommentar für den Schweizerischen Juristenverein,* 1955.

Braucher, "The law of contract in the UCC", *Rabels Zeitschrift* 31 (1967) 592.

—, "Sale of goods in the Uniform Commercial Code", *Louisiana Law Review* 1966, 192.

Broches, A., "The Convention on the Settlement of Investment Disputes", *Liber Amicorum Martin Domke,* The Hague 1967, 12.

—, "Choice-of-law problems in contracts with governments", Reese (editor), *International Contracts,* New York 1962.

von Caemmerer, E., "Haager Abkommen über den Vertragsabschluß", *Rabels Zeitschrift* 29 (1965), 101.

—, "Bankgarantien im Außenhandel", *Festschrift Otto Riese,* Karlsruhe 1964, 345.

—, "Unification of sales law: a German comment", *Ziegel/Foster* 130.

—, "Anmerkung zu BGH 18.9.1958", JZ 1959, 361.

* For fuller bibliography on licensing agreements, see p. 34, note 1.

−, "The influence of the law of international trade", Schmitthoff (editor), *The Sources of the Law of International Trade,* London 1964, 88.

−, "Measures for unifying the rules on choice of law", Honnold (editor), *Unification of the Law governing International Sales of Goods,* Paris 1966, 313 and 410.

−, "Rechtsvereinheitlichung und internationales Privatrecht", *Festschrift für Hallstein,* 1966, 64.

Carey, "Uncitral, its origins and prospects", *Am. J. Comparative law* 15 (1967), 626.

Cavers, "A critique of the choice-of-law problems", *Harvard Law Review* 47 (1933), 173.

−, *The Choice-of-Law Process,* Ann Arbor, 1965.

−, "Contemporary conflicts law in American perspective", *Recueil des Cours* 131 (1970-III), Leiden 1971.

Chavanne, "Brevets d'invention", *Rep. Dalloz de droit commercial,* Paris 1956.

Cheshire, *Private International Law,* 6th. ed., Oxford 1961.

Chloros, "The doctrine of consideration and the reform of the law of contract", ICLQ 17 (1968), 137.

Coing, H., *Staudinger BGB,* 10. aufl., Allgemeiner Teil, 1957.

−, "Probleme der Anerkennung besitzloser Mobiliarpfandrechte im Rahmen der EWG", *Zeitschrift für Rechtsvergleichung* 8 (1967), 65.

−, "Die Bedeutung der europäischen Rechtsgeschichte für die Rechtsvergleichung", Festvortrag auf der Berliner Tagung der Gesellschaft für Rechtsvergleichung, *Rabels Zeitschrift* 1968, 1.

−, *Die obersten Grundsätze des Rechts,* Heidelberg 1947.

Currie, *Selected Essays on the Conflict of Laws,* Durham N.C. 1963.

Dajant, "La vente de meubles", *Juris-Classeur, Droit international privé,* fasc. 552 F.

David/Grasmann, *Einführung in die grossen Rechtssysteme der Gegenwart,* Munich 1966.

Daw, "Some problems raised by the draft uniform law on the international sale of goods", *Am. J. Comp. Law* 1965, 226.

Demin, P., *Le Contrat de Know-How,* Brussels 1968.

Deringer, A., "International license agreements and antitrust law", *Inter. Bar Ass. 11th Conference,* The Hague 1966, 112, also GRUR *Ausland,* 1968, 179.

Dernburg, *Pandekten,* 3. Aufl. 1892.

Dicey/Morris, *The Conflict of Laws,* 8th. ed., London 1967.

Dölle, H., "Bedeutung und Funktion der 'Bräuche' im Einheitsgesetz über den Kauf beweglicher Sachen", *Festgabe Rheinstein,* 1969, I, 448.

−, "Zur Problematik mehrsprachiger Gesetze und Vertragstexte", *Rabels Zeitschrift* 26 (1961), 1. See also *Festschrift Yntema,* 1961, 277.

−, "Einheitliches Kaufrecht und IPR", *Rabels Zeitschrift* 32 (1968).

−, "Der *ordre public* im internationalen Privatrecht", *Beiträge zum bürgerlichen Recht,* ed. Ernst Wolff, Berlin and Tübingen 1950, 397.

Domke, M., "Expert testimony in proof of foreign law in American courts", *New York Law Journal,* 1957, 3.

−, "Indonesian nationalization measures before foreign courts", *Am. J. Int. Law,* 1960, 305.

−, "The Israel-Soviet oil arbitration", *Am. J. Int. Law,* 1959, 787.

−, *The Law and Practice of Commercial Arbitration,* Mundelin (Illinois) 1968.

Drobnig, U., "Rechtsvergleigung und Rechtssoziologie", *Rabels Zeitschrift* 18 (1953), 295.

−, "Eigentumsvorbehalte bei Importlieferungen nach Deutschland", *Rabels Zeitschrift* 32 (1968), 450.

Durand, "Le 'know-how'", *Juris-Classeur périodique,* 1967, No. 2078.

Ehrenzweig, A.A., "Specific principles of private transnational law", *Recueil des Cours* 124 (1968-II).

—, *A Treatise on the Conflict of Laws*, St. Paul-Minneapolis 1962.

—, "A counter-revolution in conflict-laws? From Beale to Cavers", *Harvard Law Review* 80 (1966), 377.

—, *Private International Law*, Leiden 1967.

Ehrlich, E., *Das zwingende und das nicht-zwingende Recht im BGB*, Jena 1899.

Eisemann, F., *Die Incoterms im internationalen Warenkaufrecht*, Stuttgart 1967.

Eisner, "Eigentumsvorbehalt und Security Interests im Handelsverkehr mit USA", NJW 1967, 1169.

Ellis, "Extra-territorial application of antitrust legislation", *Netherlands International Law Review* XVII, 1970, 51.

—, *Patent Licenses*, New York 1958.

Esser, J., *Grundsatz und Norm in der richterlichen Fortbildung des Privatrechts*, Tübingen 1964.

—, "Realität und Ideologie der Rechtssicherheit in positiven Systemen", *Festschrift für Theodor Rittler*, Aalen 1957, 13.

Farnsworth, "Good-faith performance and commercial reasonableness under the UCC", *University of Chicago Law Review* 30 (1963), 666.

—, "Some problems raised by the draft uniform law on the international sale of goods", Proceedings of the 1965 annual meeting of the American Foreign Law Association, *Am. J. Comp. Law*, 1965, 226.

—, "Formation of international sales contracts, three attempts at unification", *University of Pennsylvania Law Review* 110 (1962), 302.

Féblot/Mezger, "Eigentumsvorbehalt und Rücktrittsklausel bei Lieferungen nach Frankreich", *Rabels Zeitschrift* 20 (1955), 662.

Ferid, *Die allgemeinen Lieferbedingungen für den Verkauf von Anlagegütern*, Cologne 1954.

Ficker, H.G., "Die 10. Haager Konferenz", *Rabels Zeitschrift*, 1966, 606.

—, "Zur internationalen Gesetzgebung", *Festschrift Dölle*, II, Tübingen 1963, 38.

Forsthoff, E., *Recht und Sprache*, 1940 (reprint Darmstadt 1964).

Fouchard, Ph., *L'Arbitrage commercial international*, Paris 1965.

Fragistas, "Arbitrage étranger et arbitrage international en droit privé", *Revue critique*, 1960, 1.

Fridmann, "Should Commonwealth countries adopt Art. 2 UCC?" *Ziegel/Foster*, 32.

Friedmann, W., "The uses of general principles in the development of international law", *American Journal* 57 (1963), 279.

—, *Legal Theory*, 4th ed., London 1960.

Gentz, "Die Verhältnismässigkeit von Grundrechtseingriffen", NJW 68, 1600.

Giles, O.C., *Uniform Commercial Law*, Leiden 1970.

Goldschmiedt, W., "Die philosophischen Grundlagen des IPR", *Festschrift für Martin Wolff*, Tübingen 1952, 203.

Goldstajn, "The formation of the contract of sale", Honnold (editor), *Unification of the Law governing International Sales of Goods*, Paris 1966, 41.

—, "The contract of goods inspection", *Am. J. Comp. Law* 14 (1965), 382.

—, "International conventions and standard contracts", Schmitthoff (editor), *The Sources of the Law of International Trade*, London 1964, 117.

Goldmann, "Arbitrage international de droit privé", *Recueil des Cours* 109 (1963-II), 400.

Graveson, "Comparative aspects of the general principles of private international law", *Recueil des Cours* 109 (1963-II).

Graveson/Cohn, *Uniform Laws on International Sales Act 1967*, London 1968.

Grossmann-Doerth, H., *Selbstgeschaffenes Recht der Wirtschaft und staatliches Recht*, Freiburg 1933.

Gutzwiller, "Das internationale Privatrecht der durch die Friedensverträge eingesetzten Gemischten Schiedsgerichtshöfe", *Nussbaums Internationales Jahrbuch für Schiedsgerichtswesen*, Bd. III (1931), 123.

Habicht, "Arbitrages *ex aequo et bono*", *Recueil des Cours* (1934-III), 283.

Habscheid, "L'expertise arbitrale", *Liber Amicorum Martin Domke*, The Hague 1967, 103.

Hallstein, W., "Rechtsangleichung in der EWG", *Rabels Zeitschrift* 1964, 230.

Hawkland, *A Transactional Guide to the Uniform Commercial Code*, I and II, Philadelphia 1964.

van Hecke, G., "Principes et methodes du droit international privé", *Recueil des Cours* 126 (1969-I), 465.

Heini, "Eine neue Methode im übernationalen Privatrecht? " *Zeitschrift für schweizerisches Recht* 1967, 265.

Heldrich, *Die allgemeinen Rechtsgrundsätze der ausservertraglichen Schadenshaftung im Bereich der EWG*. Frankfurt 1961.

Hellner, "Unification of sales law: a scandinavian view", *Ziegel/Foster*.

—, *Aspects of Comparative Commercial Law*, Montreal 1969.

Henrich, D., *Vorvertrag, Optionsvertrag, Vorrechtsvertrag*, Berlin 1965.

von Hippel, "Internationale Entwicklungstendenzen des Schadensrechts", NJW 1969, 682.

Hirsch, E., Review of Coing, *Die juristischen Auslegungsmethoden und die Lehren der allgemeinen Hermeneutik*, Cologne/Opladen 1959, JZ 1961, 300.

Honnold, "The influence of the law of international trade", Schmitthoff (editor), *The Sources of the Law of International Trade*, London 1964, 70.

—, "American experience under the sales article of the Uniform Commercial Code", *Ziegel/Foster*, 38.

"A uniform law for international sales", *University of Pennsylvania Law Review* 107 (1959), 226.

—, "The Uniform Law for the International Sale of Goods. The Hague Convention of 1964", *Law and Contemporary Problems*, 1965, 338.

—, (ed.) *Unification of the Law governing International Sales of Goods*, Paris 1966.

Houin, "Some comparative aspects of the law relating to sale of goods", ICLQ Suppl. 9, 1964, 27.

von Hülsen, "Sinn und Methode der Rechtsvergleichung, besonders bei der Ermittlung übernationalen Zivilrechts", JZ 1967, 630.

Isay, H., *Die privaten Rechte und Interessen im Friedensvertrag*, Berlin 1923.

Jessup, Ph., *Modern Law of Nations—An Introduction*, New York 1949; German edition, Vienna 1950.

—, *Transnational law*, New Haven, 1956.

Jitta, J., *La Méthode du droit international privé*, The Hague 1890.

Joerges, C., *Zum Funktionswandel des Kollisionsrechts*, Berlin/Tübingen 1971.

Kahn, F., "Gesetzeskollisionen", *Jherings Jahrb*. Bd. 30 (1891) 1 = *Abhandlungen zum internationalen Privatrecht*, Bd. 1, Munich and Leipzig 1928, 111.

—, "Uber Inhalt und Methode des IPR", *Abhandlungen* I, 316.

Kahn, Ph., *La Vente commerciale internationale*, Paris 1961.

Kalensky, "Die Grundzüge des Gesetzes über den internationalen Handel", *Rabels Zeitschrift* 1966, 296.

Kegel, G., "Einführungsgesetz zum BGB", *Kommentar von Soergel/Siebert*, 9. Aufl., Stuttgart 1961.

—, *Die Grenze von Qualifikation und Renvoi*, Opladen 1962.

—, "Leo Raape und das internationale Privatrecht der Gegenwart", *Rabels Zeitschrift*, 1966, 7.

—, "The crisis of conflict of laws", *Recueil des Cours* 112 (1964-II), 91.

—, *Grundriss des internationalen Privatrechts*, 2nd ed., Munich 1964.

Klein, F.E., "L'arbitrage international de droit privé", *Annuaire suisse de droit international* 1963, 41.

Knapp/Kalensky, "La responsabilité des vices et du retard dans le domaine du commerce extérieur", Honnold (editor), *Unification of the Law...*, Paris 1966, 79.

Kötz, H., "Allgemeine Rechtsgrundsätze als Ersatzrecht"; *Rabels Zeitschrift* 1970, 463.

Kopelmanas, "International conventions and standard contracts", Schmitthoff (editor) *The Sources of the Law of International Trade*, London 1964, 126.

Kronstein, "Erfahrungen aus amerikanischer Rechtssprechung", *Festschrift Hallstein*, Frankfurt am Main 1966, 215.

—, *Das Recht der internationalen Kartelle*, Berlin 1967.

Lagergren, "The formation of contracts of sale", Honnold (editor), *Unification of the Law governing International Sales of Goods*, Paris 1966, 55.

—, *Delivery of Goods and Transfer of Property and the Risk in the Law of Sale*, Stockholm 1954.

Lalive, J.F., "Contracts between the State and foreign companies", ICLQ 1964, 1002.

Lalive P.A., "L'Arbitrage international privé", *Recueil des Cours* 120 (1967), 649.

Lando, "Decisions in international conflict-of-law cases", *Am. J. Comp. Law* 15 (1966/7), 230.

Langen, E., "From private international law to transnational law", *The Comparative and International Law Journal of Southern Africa* 1969, 313.

—, *Studien zum internationalen Wirtschaftsrecht*, Munich 1963.

—, *Kommentar zum Devisengesetz*, loseblattausgabe, 3. Aufl., Heidelberg 1958.

—, "Völkerrechtliche Verträge vom Standpunkt der Betroffenen", *Annales Universitatis Saraviensis* 1960, 217.

—, *Marktbeherrschung und ihr Missbrauch nach Art. 86 des EWG-Vertrages*, Baden-Baden 1959.

—, "Some thoughts about transnational commercial law", Seidl-Hohenveldern/Nagel (editors), *Beiträge aus Völkerrecht und Rechtsvergleichung*, Baden-Baden 1968.

—, "International commercial arbitration most energetically supports the development of supranational law", *Yearbook of World Peace through Law* (Washington World Conference), Minneapolis/St. Paul 1967, 315.

—, *Internationale Lizenzverträge*, 2nd ed., Weinheim 1958.

—, *Kommentar zum Aussenwirtschaftsgesetz*, Loseblattausgabe, Munich 1961.

—, *Kommentar zum Kartellgesetz*, Loseblattausgabe, 4. Auflage, Neuwied/Berlin.

—, "Vom internationalen Privatrecht zum transnationalen Handelsrecht", NJZ 1969, 358.

—, "Transnationales Handelsrecht", NJW 1969, 2229.

Lauterpacht, "The law of treaties", UN doc. A/CN.

Lent, F., *Die Gesetzeskonkurrenz im bürgerlichen Recht und Zivilprozess*, Bd. I, Leipzig 1912.

Lenz, K.H., *Das Vertrauensschutz-Prinzip*, Berlin 1968.

Lewald, W., "International-privatrechtliche Fragen vor den Gemischten Schiedsgerichtshöfen", JW 1926, 2815.

Lichtenstein, E., *Die Patentlizenz nach amerikanischem Recht*, Tübingen 1965.

270

—, "Ausland-Lizenzen", NJW 1964, 1350.

Lipstein, "Conflict of laws for international tribunals", *Transactions of the Grotius Society*, Vol. 27 (1942), 142.

Lorenz, W., "Konsensprobleme bei Distanzverträgen", AZP 59 (1960), 196.

—, "Formularpraxis und Rechtsvereinheitlichung im internationalen Kaufrecht", ZHR 126 (1964), 150.

—, "Rechtsvergleichung als Methode zur Konkretisierung der allgemeinen Grundsätze des Rechts", JZ 1962, 269.

—, *Vertragsabschluss und Parteiwille im Obligationenrecht Englands,* Heidelberg 1957.

Lüdecke/Fischer, *Lizenzverträge,* Weinheim 1957.

Lüderitz, *Auslegung von Rechtsgeschäften,* Karlsruhe 1966.

Luithlen, W., *Einheitliches Kaufrecht und autonomes Handelsrecht,* Freiburg (Switzerland) 1956.

MacDermott, *Protection from Power under English Law,* London 1957.

MacNair, "The general principles of law recognized by civilized nations", *British Year-Book of International Law* 1957.

Maier, D., "Patentmißbrauch durch Lizenzgebühren nach Ablauf der Patente", GRUR *Ausland,* 1965, 401.

Mann, F.A., *The Legal Aspects of Money,* Oxford 1953.

—, Review of Sandrock, *Zur ergänzenden Vertragsauslegung,* JZ 1968, 112.

—, "Internationale Schiedsgerichte und nationale Rechtsordnung" *Zeitschrift für das gesamte Handelsrecht* 1968, 89; English original in *International Arbitration, Liber Amicorum Martin Domke,* The Hague 1967, 157.

—, "State contracts and international arbitration", BYBIL 1967, 1.

—, "Die international-privatrechtliche Partei-autonomie in der Rechtsprechung des Bundesgerichtshofs", JZ 1962, 6.

—, "State contracts and state responsibility", AJIL 54 (1960) 572.

Markert, "Die Schadenshaftung für fehlerhafte Produkte in den USA", AWD BB 1965, 69.

Mathély/Plaisant, "Brevets d'invention – La licence des brevets", *Juris-Classeur commercial,* fasc. XXIV, Paris 1957.

Melchior, *Die Grundlagen des internationalen Privatrechts,* Berlin/Leipzig 1932.

Mentschikoff, S., "The Uniform Commercial Code", *Rabels Zeitschrift* 30 (1966), 403.

Mertens, *Eigentumsvorbehalt und sonstige Sicherungsmittel des Verkäufers im ausländischen Recht,* 1964.

—, "Ausländisches Kartellrecht im deutschen IPR", *Rabels Zeitschrift* 1967, 385.

Mezger, E., Review of W. Goldschmiedt, *Sistema y Filosofia, Rev. crit.* 37 (1948) 382.

Michido, "Possible sources for preparation of standard contracts", Honnold (editor), *Unification of the Law governing International Sales of Goods,* Paris 1966, 255.

Müller, D. (ed.), *Die Anwendung ausländischen Rechts im internationalen Privatrecht,* Max-Planck-Institut für ausländisches und internationales Privatrecht, Berlin/Tübingen 1968.

Möhring, "Die Bedeutung der *rule of reason* im Kartellrecht", WuW 1955, 7.

Müller-Erzbach, "Die Interessen- und Marktlage beim Kauf", *Festschrift Heinrich Lehmann,* Berlin 1937.

Nadelmann, K.H., "Uniform legislation versus international conventions", *Am. Journal of Comp. Law* 16 (1938), 28.

—, "Some problems raised by the Draft Uniform Law on the International Sale of Goods", Proceedings of the 1965 annual meeting of the American Foreign Law Association, *Am. J. Comp. Law,* 1965, 226.

Neuhaus, P.H., *Die Grundbegriffe des internationalen Privatrechts,* Berlin/Tübingen 1962.

Nussbaum, A., *Money in the Law*, Brooklyn 1950.
—, *Deutsches Internationales Privatrecht*, Tübingen 1932.
—, "Public policy and the political crisis in the conflict of laws", *Yale Law Journal* 49 (1940), 1027.
—, "Conflict theories of contracts: cases versus restatement", *Yale Law Review* 1942, 893.
Peters, E., "Remedies for breach of contracts relating to sale of goods under the UCC", *Yale Law Review* 73 (1969), 199.
Plaisant, R., "Les inventions non brevetées", *Juris-Classeur commercial*, Annex V, fasc. III bis.
Pollzien/Bronfen, *International Licensing Agreements*, Indianapolis/New York, 1965.
Pound, "Some thoughts about comparative law", *Festschrift Rabel* I (1954), 11.
Raape, *Internationales Privatrecht*, 5. Aufl. 1961.
Rabel, E., *Rabels Zeitschrift* 17 (1952), 224.
—, "Rechtsvergleichung und internationale Rechtsprechung", *Rabels Zeitschrift* 1927, 5; *Gesetzliche Abhandlungen* II (1965), 1.
—, "Der Entwurf eines einheitlichen Kaufgesetzes", *Rabels Zeitschrift* 1935, 1.
—, "Deutsches und amerikanisches Recht", *Rabels Zeitschrift*, 1951, 340.
—, *Das Recht des Warenkaufs* I (1936), Berlin 1964; II (1957) Berlin/Tübingen.
—, *The Conflict of Laws*, Vol. 1, Ann Arbor/Chicago 1945; Vol. 2, Ann Arbor/Chicago 1947; Vol. 3 (2nd edition), Ann Arbor 1964.
Reese, W.H., "Recent developments in torts", *Columbia Journal of Transnational Law* 1969, 181.
Rheinstein, M., "Die Rechtshonorationen und der Einfluß auf Charakter und Funktion der Rechtsordnung", *Rabels Zeitschrift* 1970, 1.
Riese, O., "Die Haager Konferenz über die internationale Vereinheitlichung des Kaufrechts vom 2.-25. April 1964", *Rabels Zeitschrift* 29 (1965).
—, "Das Sprachenproblem in der Praxis des Gerichtshofes der europäischen Gemeinschaften", *Festschrift Dölle* II, Tübingen 1963, 507.
—, "Einheitliche Gerichtsbarkeit für einheitliches Recht", *Rabels Zeitschrift* 26 (1961), 604.
—, "Der Entwurf zur internationalen Vereinheitlichung des Kaufrechts", *Rabels Zeitschrift* 22 (1957), 1.
—, "Ueber die Methoden der internationalen Vereinheitlichung des Privatrechts", *Zeitschrift für schweizerisches Recht* 86 (1967), 11.
Robert, J., "De la place de la loi dans l'arbitrage", *International Arbitration, Liber Amicorum Martin Domke*, The Hague 1967, 234.
Sandrock, O., *Zur ergänzenden Vertragsauslegung*, Cologne/Opladen 1966.
von Savigny, F.C., *System des heutigen römischen Rechts*, Bd. VIII, Berlin 1849.
Scheuner, "Decisions *aequo et bono* by international courts and arbitral tribunals", *International Arbitration, Liber Amicorum Martin Domke*, The Hague 1967, 282.
Schinnerer, "Zur Neufassung der einheitlichen Richtlinien und Gebräuche für das Dokumenten-Akkreditiv", *Zeitschrift für Rechtsvergleichung*, Vienna 1966, 207.
Schlesinger, R., "Research on the general principles of law recognized by civilized nations", *Am. J.* 1957, 757.
—, *Formation of Contracts*, I and II, New York/London 1968.
Schlink, "Die international privatrechtliche Behandlung der Verjährung in den Vereinigten Staaten", *Rabels Zeitschrift* 9 (1935), 418.
Schmidt, F., "The international contract law in the context of some of its sources", *Am. J. Comp. Law* 14 (1965), 1.
Schmitthoff, C.M., "Der Einfluß außerrechtlicher Elemente auf die Prinzipiengestaltung

des englischen internationalen Privatrechts", *Zeitschrift für Rechtsvergleichung,* Vienna 1970, 81.

—, *The Sale of Goods,* 2nd edition, London 1966.

—, *The Unification of the Law of International Trade,* Göteborg 1964.

—, (ed.), *The Sources of the Law of International Trade,* London 1964.

—, "Das neue Recht des Welthandels", *Rabels Zeitschrift* 1964, 47.

—, "The unification or harmonization of law by means of standard contracts and general conditions", ICLQ 1968, 563.

—, *The Export Trade,* 5th edition, London 1969.

—, "International trade law and private international law", *Festschrift Dölle* II, Tübingen 1963, 257.

Schmidt-Salzer, "Formularmäßige Gewährleistungsregelungen", NJW 1969, 718.

—, "Geltungsgrund und Anwendungsbereich der sogenannten Unklarheiten-Regel", *Versicherungsrecht,* 1966, 910.

Schnitzer, *Handbuch des internationalen Privatrechts,* 3. Aufl., Basle 1950.

Schröder, J., *Die Anpassung von Kollisions- und Sachnormen,* Cologne 1961.

Schüle, "Die Entscheidung des internationalen Richters *ex aequo et bono*", *Tübinger rechtswissenschaftliche Abhandlungen,* Band 9, Tübingen 1963.

Schulte, H.J., *Lizenzaustauschverträge und Patentgemeinschaften im deutschen und amerikanischen Recht,* Frankfurt am Main 1971.

Schwarzenberger, G., "The fundamental principles of international law", *Recueil des Cours* 87 (1955), 372.

—, *The Frontiers of International Law,* London 1962.

—, *Foreign Investments and International Law,* London 1969.

Seidl-Hohenveldern, "General principles as applied by the Conciliation Commissions established under the peace treaty with Italy of 1947", *Am. J. Int. Law* 53 (1959), 853.

Siehr, "Ehrenzweigs *lex fori*-Theorie", *Rabels Zeitschrift* 1970, 585.

Sommers/Broches/Delaume, "Conflict avoidance in international loans and monetary agreements: the preventive law of conflicts", *Law and Contemporary Problems,* 1956.

Stauffer, "Bundesgericht und Parteiautonomie", *Festschrift Hans Lewald,* Basle 1953.

Steindorff, E., *Sachnormen im internationalen Privatrecht,* Frankfurt am Main 1958.

Steiner/Vagts, *Transnational Legal Problems,* 1969.

Story, J., *Commentaries on the Conflict of Laws,* 1834, 2nd edition, Edinburgh 1835.

Stoufflet, "Contrats commerciaux", *Juris-Classeur, droit international,* 565/109.

Strohm, *Wettbewerbsbeschränkungen in Patentlizenzverträgen nach deutschem und amerikanischem Recht,* Cologne 1971.

Stumpf, H., *Der Lizenzvertrag,* 4. Aufl., Frankfurt am Main 1968.

Szazy, "The proper law of the contract in trade between eastern Europe and the West", ICLQ 1969, 103.

Tallon, "The law applied by arbitration tribunals", Schmitthoff (editor), *The Sources of the Law of International Trade.*

Tiling, "Haftungsbefreiung, Haftungsbegrenzung und Freizeichnung im Einheitsgesetz über den Kauf beweglicher Sachen", *Rabels Zeitschrift* 1968, 258.

Treitel, "Specific performance in the sale of goods", *J. Business Law* 1966, 211.

Troller, A., *Das internationale Privat- und Zivilprozessrecht im gewerblichen Rechtsschutz und Urheberrecht,* Basle 1952.

Tunc, "Commentary on the Hague Conventions of 1 July 1964", *Diplomatic Conference on the Unification of Law governing the International Sale of Goods,* published by the Ministry of Justice of the Netherlands, The Hague 1966.

Veith/Böckstiegel, *Der Schutz von ausländischen Vermögen im Völkerrecht,* Baden-Baden 1962.

Vischer, F., *Internationales Vertragsrecht,* Berne 1962.

De Vries, "Choice of language in international contracts", W.S. Reese (editor), *International Contracts,* New York 1962.

Walker, *On Patents,* 2nd ed., New York 1964.

Weber, *Die allgemeinen Geschäftsbedingungen,* Berlin 1967.

Wengler, W., "Anknüpfung des zwingenden Schutzrechts im internationalen Recht", *Zeitschrift für die vergleichende Rechtswissenschaft* 54, (1940/1), 209.

—, "Die Funktion der richterlichen Entscheidung über internationale Rechtsverhältnisse", *Rabels Zeitschrift* 16 (1951), 1.

—, "Die Nichtanwendung Nationalsozialistischen Rechts im Lichte der Rechtsvergleichung", JR 1949, 69.

—, "Die Belegenheit von Rechten", *Festschrift der Berliner Juristenfakultät zum 41. Deutschen Juristentag 1955,* 350.

—, Review of Steinhoff, *Sachnormen im internationalen Privatrecht, Archiv für die zivilistische Praxis* 158 (1959/60), 543.

Wiethölter, "Zur Frage des internationalen *ordre public*", *Bericht der Deutschen Gesellschaft für Völkerrecht,* Heft 7, Karlsruhe 1967.

Wilberforce/Campbell/Ellis, *The Law of Restrictive Trade Practices and Monopolies* 1st ed., London 1957.

Yntema, H.E., "The comity doctrine", *Festschrift Dölle* II (1963) 65.

—, "Die historischen Grundlagen des internationalen Privatrechts", *Festschrift Rabel* I, Tübingen 1954, 537; English original, *Am. J. Com. Law* 11 (1953), 297.

Ziegel/Foster, *Aspects of Comparative Commercial Law,* Montreal 1969.

Zweigert, "Nichterfüllung auf Grund ausländischer Leistungsverbote", *Rabels Zeitschrift* 14 (1942), 283.

—, "Die dritte Schule im international Privatrecht", *Festschrift Raape,* Hamburg 1948, 37.

—, "Rechtsvergleichung", *Wörterbuch des Völkerrechts,* ed. Strupp/Schlochauer.

—, "Some comparative aspects of the law relating to sale of goods", ICLQ Suppl. 9. 1964, 3.

—, *Bericht der Deutschen Gesellschaft für Völkerrecht* 1964, 208.

—, "Zum Abschlussort schuldrechtlicher Distanzverträge", *Festschrift Rabel* I, 1953, 631.

Zweigert/Drobnig, "Einheitliches Kaufgesetz und IPR", *Rabels Zeitschrift* 29 (1965), 148.

Zweigert/Kötz, *Einführung in die vergleichende Rechtswissenschaft,* Tübingen 1969.

ABBREVIATIONS

A.	Atlantic Reporter (USA)
A. 2d.	*do*. (Second Series)
A.C.	Appeal Cases, English Law Reports
A.C.P. (A.Z.P.)	Archiv für civilistische Praxis
AJCL	American Journal of Comparative Law
AJIL	American Journal of International Law
All E.R.	All England Law Reports
Am. Rep.	American Reporter
Ann. prop. ind.	Annales de la propriété industrielle (France)
Annales, API	*do*.
Annuaire	Annuaire de l'Institut de droit international
APP	Appeal Cases, District of Columbia (USA)
AWD	Aussenwirtschaftsdienst des Betriebsberaters (Germany)
Batiffol	Le Droit international privé, 4th ed., 1967
BB	Der Betriebsberater (Germany)
BGB	Bürgerliches Gesetzbuch (Germany)
BGBl.	Bundesgesetzblatt
BGE	Swiss Federal Tribunal, decisions
BGHZ	Bundesgerichtshof, Zivilsachen (Germany)
Bing. N.C.	Bingham, New Cases, English Common Pleas
Bl.f.PMZ	Blatt für Patenten und Merkzeichen
Bl.f.Zürch.Rspr.	Blätter für Zürcherischer Rechtsprechung
BLR	Business Law Review (England)
BYBIL	British Year Book of International Law
Cass.	Court of Cassation (France)
Ch. D.	Chancery Division, English Law Reports 1876-1890
C.J.S.	Corpus Juris Secundum (USA)
Cl. & F.	Clark & Finnelly's Reports (House of Lords)
Clunet	Journal du droit international (France)

Contract Formation Rules	Uniform Law on the Formation of Contracts for the International Sale of Goods, The Hague 1964
D.	Dalloz, Recueil périodique (France)
DJZ	Deutsche Juristen-Zeitung
Duke B.J.	Duke University Bar Association Journal
EGBGB	Einführungsgesetz zum BGB (Germany)
F. (2d.); Fed.	Federal Reporter (Second Series) (USA)
Fed. Cases	Federal Cases (USA)
Fed. Supp.	Federal Supplement (USA)
Folke Schmidt	(see Bibliography)
Foro Ital.	Il Foro Italiano
Gaz.Pal.	Gazette du Palais (France)
GRUR	Gewerbliche Rechtsschutz und Urheberrecht (Germany)
GRUR Ausl.	GRUR Auslands- und internationaler Teil
Hague Rules	= Hague Sales Rules and Contract Formation Rules, q.v. *supra*
Hague Sales Rules	Uniform Law on the International Sale of Goods, The Hague 1964
HGB	Handelsgesetzbuch (Germany)
HL	House of Lords
Honnold (ed.), *Unification*	(see Bibliography)
HRR	Höchstrichterliche Rechtsprechung (Germany)
ICLQ	International Comparative Law Quarterly (England)
IPRspr.	Die deutsche Rechtsprechung im Gebiete des internationalen Privatrechts
J.C.P.	Juris-Classeur périodique (France)
JR	Juristische Rundschau (Germany)
JW	Juristische Wochenschrift (Germany)
JZ	Juristen-Zeitung (Germany)
K.B.	King's Bench, English Law Reports
Kegel	(see Bibliography: *Grundriss*)

La.	Louisiana Reports
La. L.R.	Louisiana Law Review
Law and Cont. Prob.	Law and Contemporary Problems, School of Law, Duke University
LJ	Law Journal Reports (England)
LLR	Lloyds List Law Reports
LTR	Law Times Reports
LZ	Leipziger Zeitschrift für deutsches Recht
Mass.	Massachusetts Reports
MAT	Mixed Arbitral Tribunals
MDR	Monatschrift für deutsches Recht
MLR	Modern Law Review (England)
NE	North-Eastern Reporter (USA)
Neuhaus	(see Bibliography)
NJ	Nederlandsche Jurisprudentie
NJW	Neue Juristische Wochenschrift (Germany)
NW	Nort-Western Reporter (USA)
NY	New York Court of Appeals, Reports
NY Supp.	New York Supplement, National Reporter System
OLGE	Oberlandesgericht-Entscheidungen
P.	Probate Division, English Law Reports
Pa	Pennsylvania Reports
Pac. (2d.)	Pacific Reporter (2nd Series)
Pasicrisie	Pasicrisie belge, Recueil général
Patent Reports	= R.P.C. (see below)
P.C.A.	Permanent Court of Arbitration
P.C.I.J.	Permanent Court of International Justice
PQ	United States Patent Quarterly
Proceedings	1965 Annual Meeting of the American Foreign Law Association, AJCL 1965
Q.B.	Queen's Bench, English Law Reports
Rabel II; III, 2nd ed.	Conflict of Laws II; III, 2nd ed.
RabelsZ	Rabels Zeitung
RdC	Recueil des Cours de l'Académie de droit international de La Haye
Revue	Revue de droit international (France)
Revue Crit.	Revue critique de droit international (France)

RGZ	Reichsgericht, Zivilsachen
Riese 1957, 1965	(see Bibliography)
RPC	Reports of Patent, Design and Trademark Cases (England)
S.; Sirey	Sirey, Recueil général (France)
Schmitthoff (ed.), *Sources*	(see Bibliography)
S.Ct.	Supreme Court Reporter (USA)
S.E.	South-Eastern Reporter (USA)
So.	Southern Reporter (USA)
Soergel/Kegel	Einführungsgesetz zum BGB, in Kommentar zum BGB (see Kegel, in Bibliography)
S.J.Z.	Schweizerische Juristen-Zeitung
SW	South-Western Reporter (USA)
T.L.R.	Times Law Reports (England)
Tunc	Official commentary on Hague Sales Rules (Conference *Records*, 1966)
UCC	Uniform Commercial Code (USA)
UNRIAA	United Nations Reports of International Arbitral Awards
US	United States Reports
USPQ	United States Patent Quarterly
ZHR	Zeitschrift für das gesamte Handelsrecht (England)
Ziegel/Foster	(see Bibliography)
Z.int.R.	Niemeyer's Zeitschrift für internationales Recht (Germany)
Z.schw.R.	Zeitschrift für schweizerisches Recht
Zweigert/Drobnig	(see Bibliography)
Zweigert/Kötz	(see Bibliography)

SUBJECT-INDEX